CLASSICAL INVENTION
THE ARCHITECTURE OF JOHN B. MURRAY

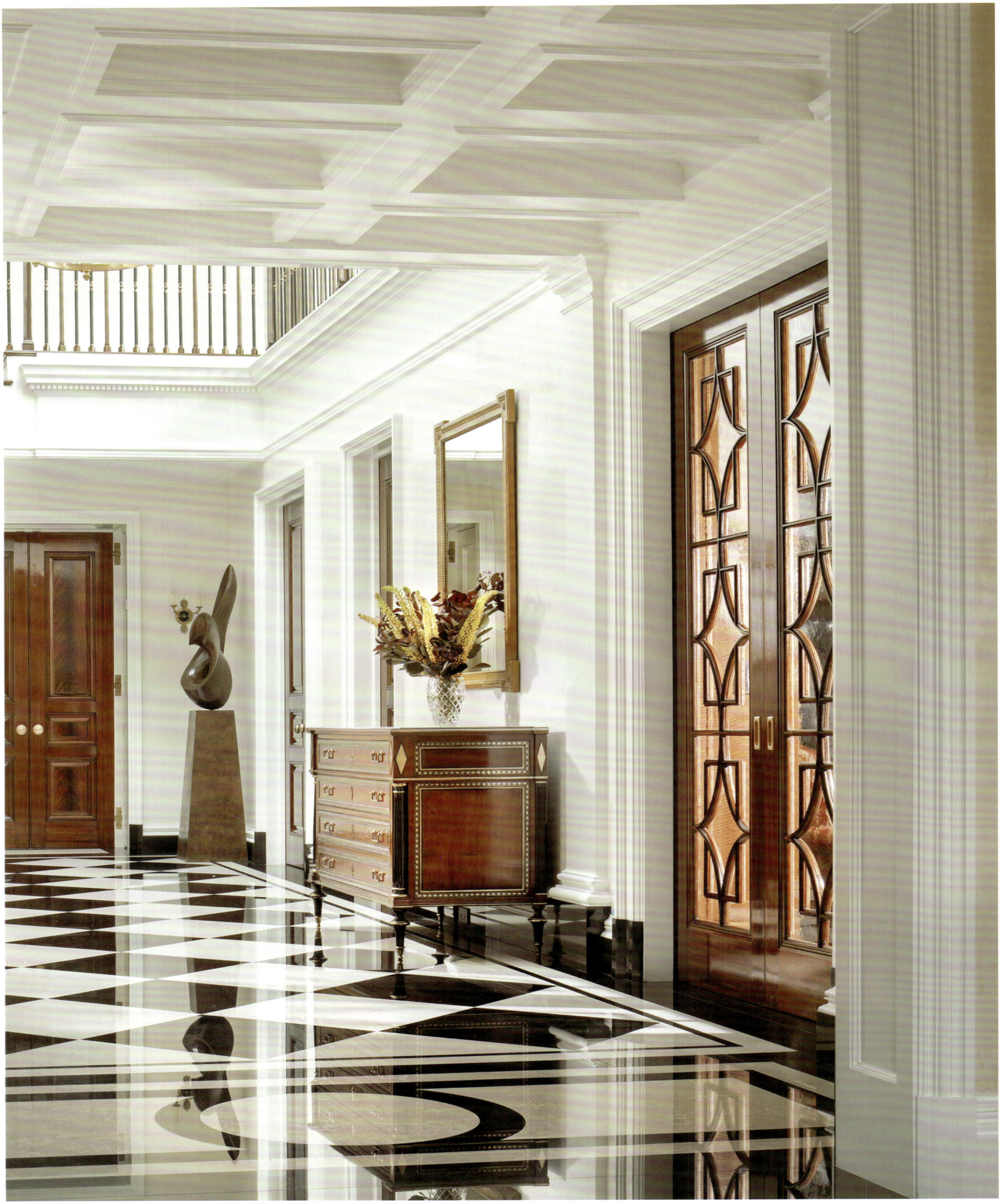

CLASSICAL INVENTION

THE ARCHITECTURE OF JOHN B. MURRAY

PRINCIPAL PHOTOGRAPHY BY DURSTON SAYLOR
DRAWINGS BY STEPHEN PIERSANTI
WRITTEN WITH JUDITH NASATIR

THE MONACELLI PRESS

To my clients, who have entrusted me with their dreams. It is forever an honor sharing in your creative process and bringing your visions to fruition. To my father, Charles K. Murray Jr., whose faith and love have time and again "raised me up" to a place of peace and strength. To my most rewarding of creations, my sons Gabriel, Luke, and Jesse Murray—hold fast to *your* dreams!

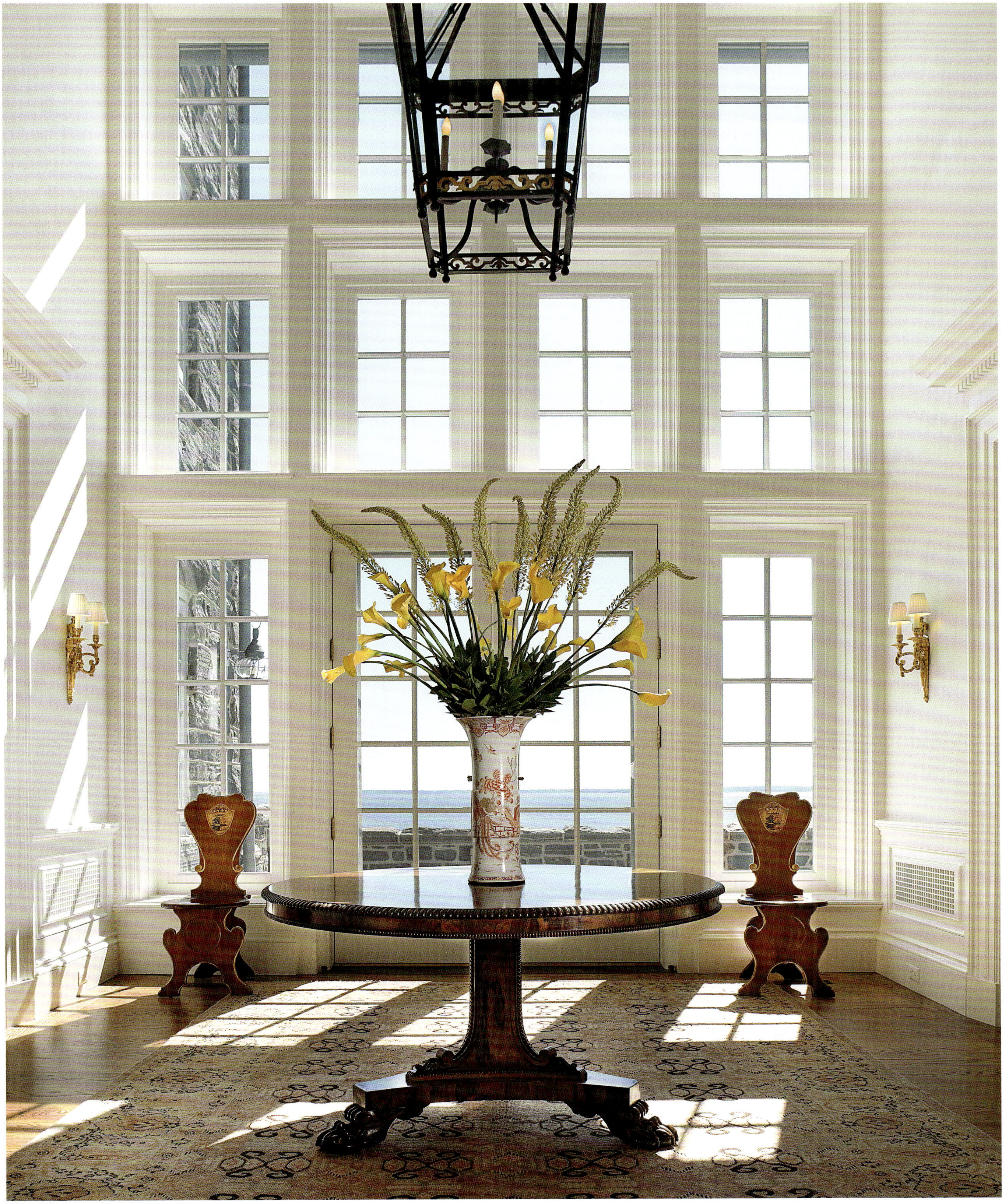

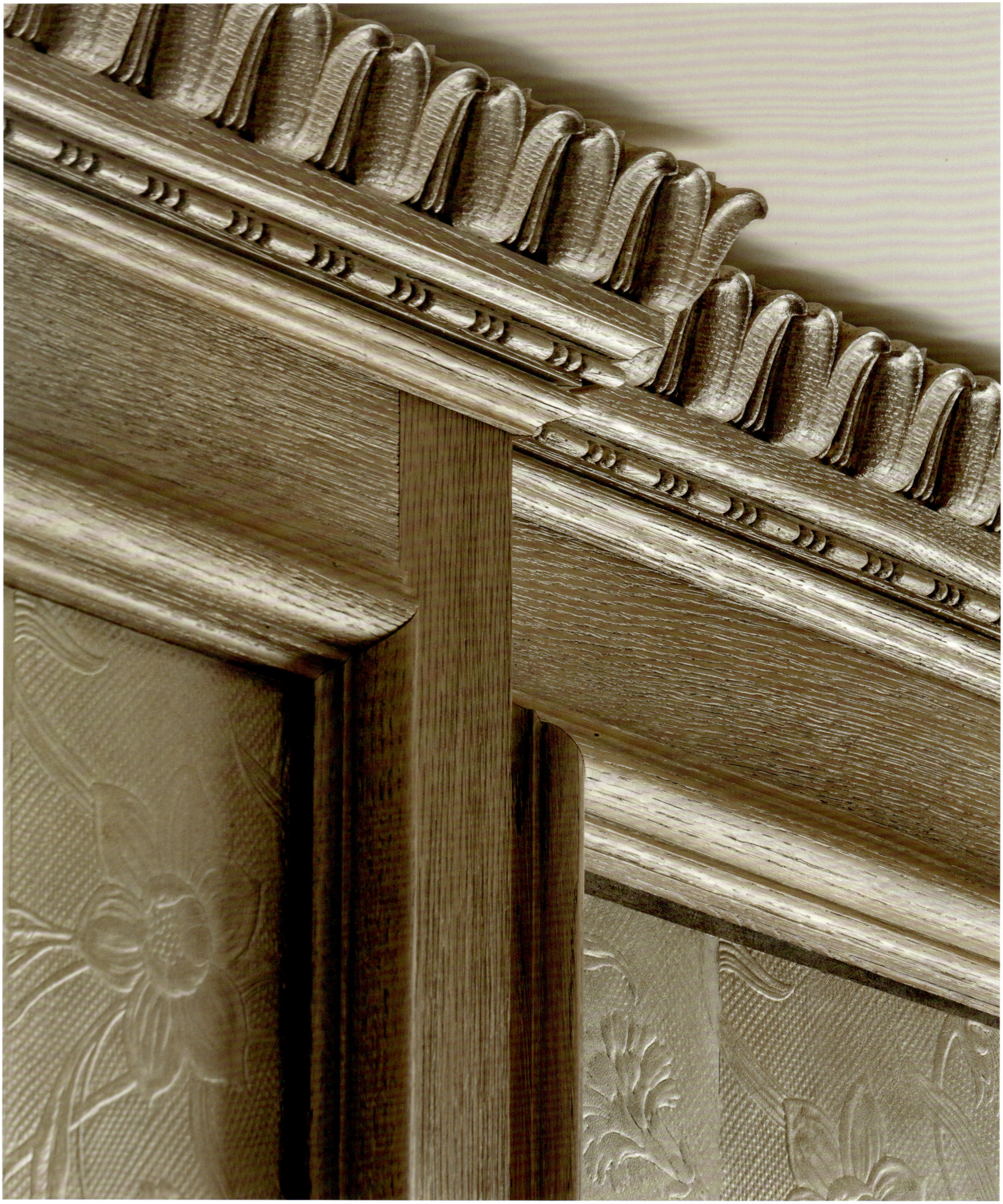

Contents

Introduction 8
Formal Logic 12
On the Peninsula 26
Skyline Haven 42
The Nature of Place 54
Approaching Perfection 72
Form and Finesse 90
Depth of Character 102
Moderne Influences 124
Restoring History 134
The Long View 146
Grace and Grandeur 166
Creating a Classic 182
A Sweet Discovery 200
A Singular Vision 218
A Change of Seasons 234
Acknowledgments 254

INTRODUCTION

In matters of design, I am both a classicist and a modernist. Like generations of architects before me—and I hope generations of architects to come—I have found the language of classical design to be a limitless source of invention as well as a true touchstone of quality. Architects of every era turn to history. We steep ourselves in the accumulated knowledge and understanding of previous practitioners. Yet we live in the now, so the architecture we make today must support a lifestyle for today and tomorrow. To me, that means we have to look at our built history with a fresh eye, using it to create classically inspired spaces that are appropriate for our times.

The legacy of beautiful design—symmetry, structural expression, the grounding of history—was everywhere for a boy growing up in the Philadelphia area. My family was also influential in this regard: Jane Clark Murray, my grandmother, had known Henry Hornbostel, the esteemed Pittsburgh architect; she also loved taking us to Colonial Williamsburg. I'm certain that our family travels and discussions influenced my understanding of the importance of architectural history and of what makes an aesthetically pleasing living space. But architecture as a profession? Much as I'd always loved creating and constructing everything from blocks to tree houses and forts, I intended to follow in the footsteps of my doctor grandfather.

Uninspired by my pre-med studies, however, I decided to take a few design courses, which initially sparked my interest in furniture design. Then my mother, Nancy Murray, recommended a summer program at Carnegie Mellon University designed to expose young people to the study of architecture. That exposure was so clarifying for me that I continued at Carnegie Mellon, where I earned my professional degree with university honors.

In the late 1970s, history and historicism were very much in the air, architecturally speaking. The backlash against the International Style and post-war modernism was underway. Michael Graves, once a militant modernist, was shifting aesthetic gears and using the past to go forward. Robert A. M. Stern had started incorporating historical references. Robert Venturi, Denise Scott Brown, and Steven Izenour had shaken up the prevailing architectural orthodoxy with *Learning from Las Vegas*. Charles Moore was assuming the mantle of the pied piper of post-modernism. And thanks to an exhibition of Beaux-Arts drawings at the Museum of Modern Art in 1975, the École des Beaux-Arts, with its inspiring compositional approach, was back in the cultural conversation once again.

When I moved to New York in 1979 in search of my first apprenticeship, the architecture world was just beginning to emerge from a deep recession—and New York City from the brink of bankruptcy. I was unaware of just how tough the times were until, bright-eyed and excited, I started the job hunt. A few days into my search, already older and wiser, I landed a position in the design department of Haines Lundberg Waehler, a large corporate firm that got its start in 1885 as Eidlitz & McKenzie. Later known as Voorhees, Gmelin and Walker, this firm in the 1920s designed the Western Union building, the Irving Trust Headquarters at One Wall Street, and the visionary Barclay-Vesey Building, which today stands in the shadow of One World Trade Center.

My first assignment involved the transformation of the Rhodes School at 11 West 54th Street—two houses in the Georgian style, designed by McKim, Mead & White in 1896 for the James Goodwin family—into headquarters for the U.S. Trust Company of New York. Before any actual design could take place, it was imperative to document which historical elements of the Goodwin house were important and how they might be integrated into the bank. Part of that process involved drawing all the moldings. When you do that, you become familiar with the distinctive nature of shape-making—and everything that shape-making means to architecture. I already had an initial understanding of the relationship between drawing and architectural intent. It came while I was working one college summer for the Historic American Engineering Record in Thibodaux, Louisiana. That effort, which was part of the Heritage Documentation Program, a division of the Department of Interiors, involved recording what was left of the buildings on a decrepit sugar plantation before they disappeared into time.

After two and a half years at Haines Lundberg Waehler, I knew that I wanted to do residential architecture. I also knew I wanted eventually to run my own firm. Those realizations led me to the next phase of my apprenticeship, at Voorsanger & Mills. While at this boutique firm, which was very fashion-forward in architectural terms, I worked with Edward Mills on an extraordinary residential project in Bel Air, California. Our purview on this commission encompassed not only the redesign of the house, but also—almost like Frank Lloyd Wright—the design of all its components. We conceived and oversaw the fabrication of the dining room chairs, coffee tables, master bed, balustrade, sofas, silverware—all in the cutting-edge style of the times.

Three years later, I put out my shingle. Busy though I was with small residential commissions, the long view appeared more precarious than I would have liked. When I received an invitation to show my portfolio to Harold Simmons, Albert Hadley's associate at Parish-Hadley, I was curious. And the more I learned about Parish-Hadley and its projects, the more intrigued I became, especially because my time at Voorsanger & Mills had taught me that I wasn't interested in the tabula rasa approach of contemporary design, with its constant search for the next new thing.

The architecture studio at Parish-Hadley developed traditional residential architecture, and the fact that they weren't reinventing the wheel with every project appealed to me enormously. The firm stressed all the components of high-quality construction: How do you course out a brick wall? How does an entablature work? What does a beautifully counter-weighted window look like? It emphasized that good design alone isn't good enough. That to be beautiful, architecture has to function—interior and exterior both. And so I began to understand this concept of good practice, and the attention to detail that it requires: buildings go up through collective knowledge, they hold up because they're assembled properly. At the same time, I really began to see that classical design is a language open to endless manipulation, transformation, and renewal. The vocabulary is there. The models are there. The invention comes from looking and interpreting it anew, and the greatest beauty lies in restraint.

When Parish-Hadley shuttered the doors of its architecture department in 1987, Mark Ferguson and I launched Ferguson & Murray Architects, an independent practice focusing on residential architecture in the classical tradition. With Parish-Hadley's endorsement and 3,500 square feet of space on Lafayette Street, we were off and running. A decade later, we split the practice and I realized my longtime dream: John B. Murray Architect, LLC, opened its doors on November 11, 1997, in a full-floor office on West 25th Street. In 2007, I moved the firm to our current space on 37th Street just west of Fifth Avenue.

Architects have always worked out design problems and communicated their intent through various types of drawings, even as the implements and technology for producing those drawings have changed. Since the late 1980s, the profession has relied on computer-aided drafting to develop construction documentation, but at my firm we continue to do the schematic design work and the traditional analytique work by hand.

A Beaux-Arts style of drawing, the analytique is a very clear, concise method of presenting the design concept for a building or a principal room. Ours show, in one drawing, the concept of the plan as well as the elevations, which pinwheel around the plan. The drawing generally includes snippets of architectural detail: the mantel, the overdoor, the corner book cabinet, the door detail. And along the perimeter, typically, are the profiles of all the moldings. The depth of information conveyed by the analytique helps our clients to feel secure that the design matches their vision. The refinement is clear because the analytique itself is unforgiving: it shows the parts, and their relationship to each other and to the whole. It reveals where there are issues and it also shows when a design is really pulled together, with all the components correctly related. And given our emphasis on both exterior and interior design, the analytique shows the variety of thematic and design motifs that run through the project as a whole.

Whatever technique or technology the architect uses, drawing is an architect's method of getting to the built world. Here we prefer not to leave anything to the imagination or to chance. When we start a design, we're working on a small scale and building up—that's when the analytique proves particularly useful. Our final documentation is full size, with every shape, piece, and component fully delineated. There's no shortcut to that process. And that's just the beginning.

I believe the art of architecture lies in that refined eye, in understanding and elucidating the form of each component and refining all the nuances. The approach to perfection succeeds or fails in that back and forth, that working out of problems on paper. If everyone does his or her part, there's no need to rectify anything on the construction site. Everything will be executed to perfection, exactly the way we intended it to be. Achieving that requires that the architect be a constant presence. Despite the most detailed drawings, questions do arise. And architects must be there to work out solutions. But by going through all the steps in their proper order, it's possible to realize architecture that comes within a hair's breadth of the ideal.

Architecture is a complicated profession, with many moving parts. Architects need to have more than a passing acquaintance with many different areas of expertise. We inevitably run into challenging situations. And that's where the will of the artist comes in: it's important to be dogged. I've learned never to give up. There's a proper way of putting architecture together that gives it that staying power, and history shows that the refinement and sophistication of classicism is forever modern.

John B. Murray

Formal Logic

When architects are called upon to transform two unrelated components into a unified, elegant whole—as they often are—the most pressing question is always "how?" The answer differs from project to project and client to client, but for me the underlying approach remains constant: find a clear, forceful internal logic, and build from there. Sometimes that logic suggests itself right away. Here, it didn't. Discerning a way to combine two adjacent Fifth Avenue apartments into one three-bedroom pied-à-terre proved a major undertaking. A sensible, functional, comfortable solution began to emerge once the clients and I decided to keep an existing entry in place because of the view toward Fifth Avenue. The resulting plan may be a little idiosyncratic in the arrangement of rooms. But with its strong axial orientation, it establishes clear public and private zones, creates a formal sense of progression, organizes the circulation, maximizes the flow of daylight, and most important, suits its occupants' needs.

The clients had a binder full of images collected over the years that made their love of classical design elements apparent. This cleared a path for us to emphasize extreme refinement in the hierarchical articulation of space and the selection and expression of its architectural details. A Greek key pattern, for instance, circumnavigates the base of the foyer dome; the foyer's marble floor design reflects the geometry overhead. Cullman & Kravis, the interior designers, also reiterated the Greek key in elements of the decor.

Straight ahead from the main rotunda is a gallery space with stone and marble architrave moldings, a patterned stone floor, an articulated ceiling with banding work, and a plaster cornice with acanthus leaf ornamentation. A vaulted hall processes through another rotunda opening toward two guest

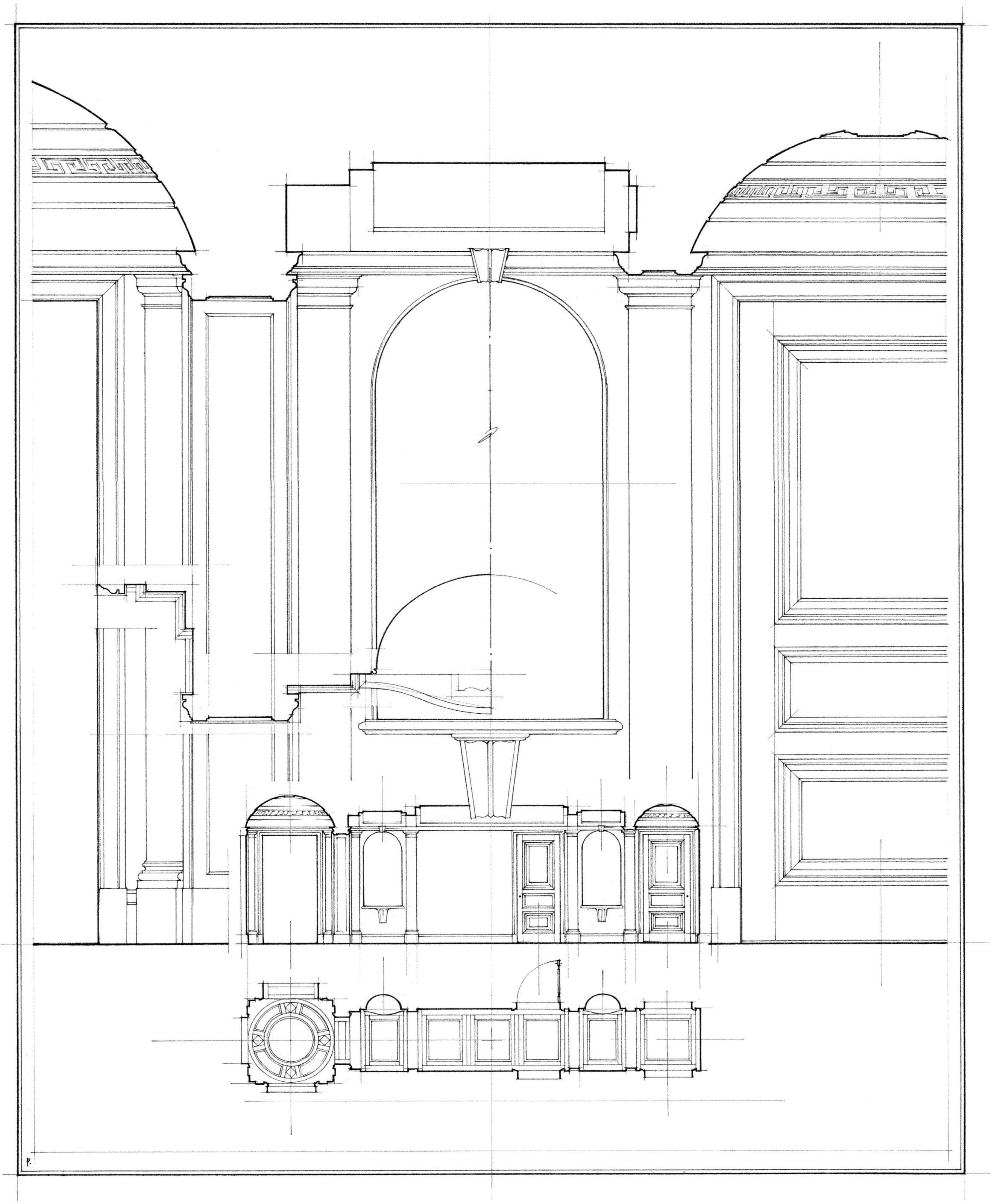

rooms (one, quite compact, is finished in bleached mahogany; the other, generously proportioned, offers all the comforts of home). The vault ribbing mirrors the stone pattern underfoot.

The resolution of the living room—formerly two separate spaces—presented a number of challenges. By shaping the corners and broadening the column zone, we were able to establish the architectural rhythm and create an art wall. A plaster cornice with a highly articulated acanthus leaf pattern, paneled walls, and a spectacular plaster fireplace mantel with flanking Ionic capitals atop pilasters with pearl banding heightened the room's classical sensibility. The fireplace surround, a custom bronze component with an incised Greek key, added another layer of detail, as did the intricate parquet de Versailles floor.

Positioning the master bedroom off the living room—behind Harmon-hinged doors—is unusual, but it made sense here: the living room can become their sitting room, making the apartment feel much more expansive. A windowed alcove off the bedroom houses a little desk flanked by integrated

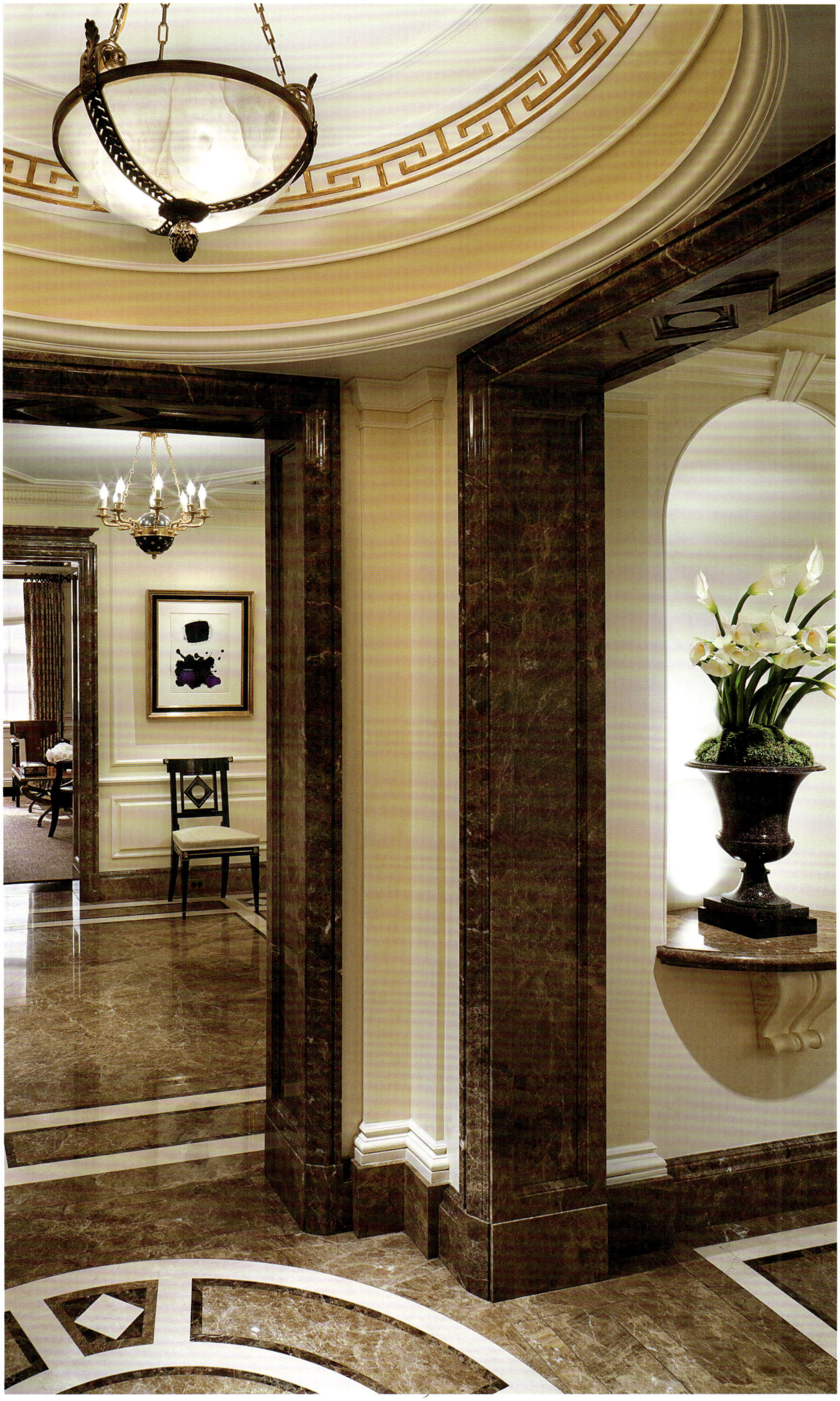

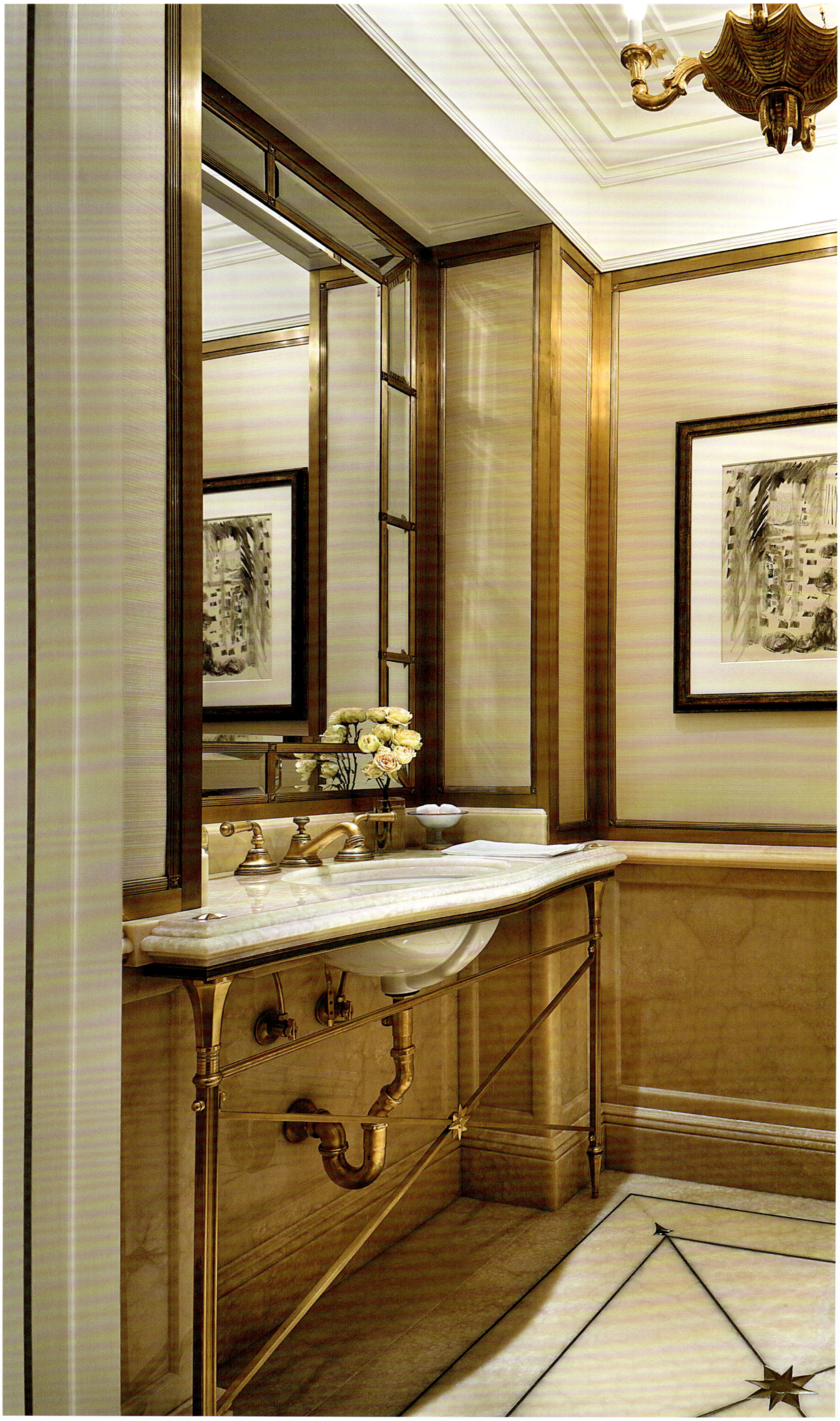

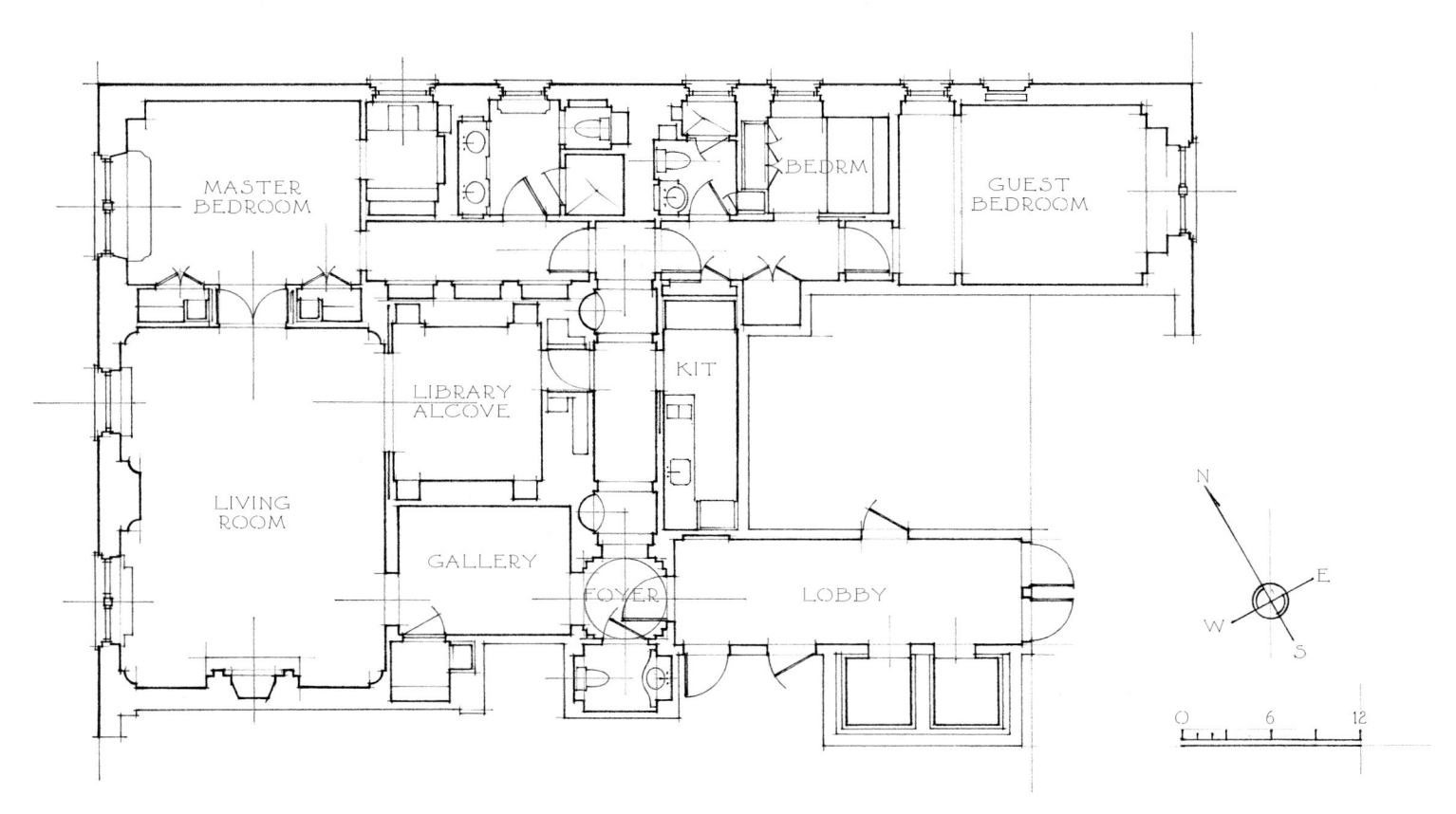

shelves, an art wall, and a back counter and shelves. Since this is not a full-time living space, we scaled back the capacity of the his-and-her closets and opted not to have a full-size dressing area. The plaster cove features an inset diaper pattern of crossed circles and finials; based on a baroque classic, it adds a flourish overhead. The master bathroom is an essay in fine detail: onyx components, plaster panels, and decorative mosaics create a very luxurious effect.

We also converted one of the old kitchens into a library alcove off the living room. There the plaster ceiling features banding and corner articulation. With walls finished in painted wood paneling, inset leather ornamented with bronze stud work, and built-in shelves with integrated lighting, it feels like a cozy reading room.

The powder room off the entry hall shares a materials palette with the master bath. Polished plaster panels, an onyx wainscot, and inset bronze banding and ornamental details make for an intricate jewel box of a space that slips neatly into the plan for the reconfigured whole—and that continues the classical themes and pattern language established so clearly and consistently from the moment of entry.

PREVIOUS SPREAD, FAR LEFT: The vaulted hallway has a patterned marble floor. PREVIOUS SPREAD, LEFT: Detailing the gallery are applied paneling, stone baseboards, and stone architrave moldings. PREVIOUS SPREAD, RIGHT: The foyer's domed ceiling incorporates a Greek key. OPPOSITE: The powder room's onyx floor has bronze insets. Bronze stiles and rails above the onyx wainscot frame the beveled mirrors and polished plaster walls.

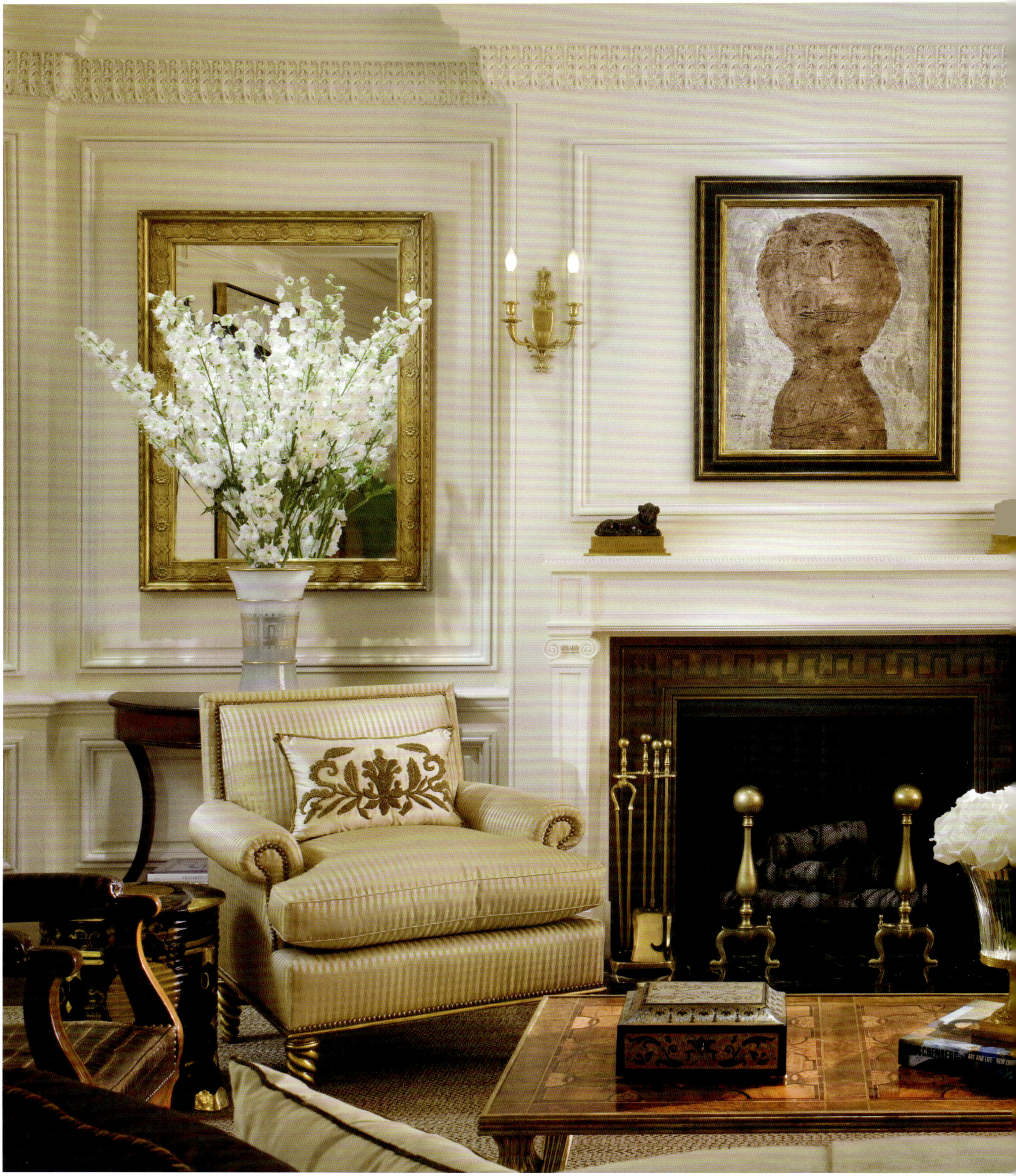

The living room paneling incorporates unique curved corner segments that give the room a graceful outline and help to conceal various structural components. The stylized plaster molding with the acanthus leaf motif that circumnavigates the top of the wall beneath the plaster cornice was custom designed for the room.

The living room adjoins the master bedroom via Harmon-hinged doors. OVERLEAF, LEFT, CLOCKWISE FROM TOP: In the master bedroom, a custom plaster cornice with a small repeated geometric motif enlivens the ceiling plane; the master bath combines onyx panels with antique gold-finished hardware and fittings; an alcove study adjoins the master bedroom. OVERLEAF, RIGHT: A small guest bedroom is lined in bleached mahogany.

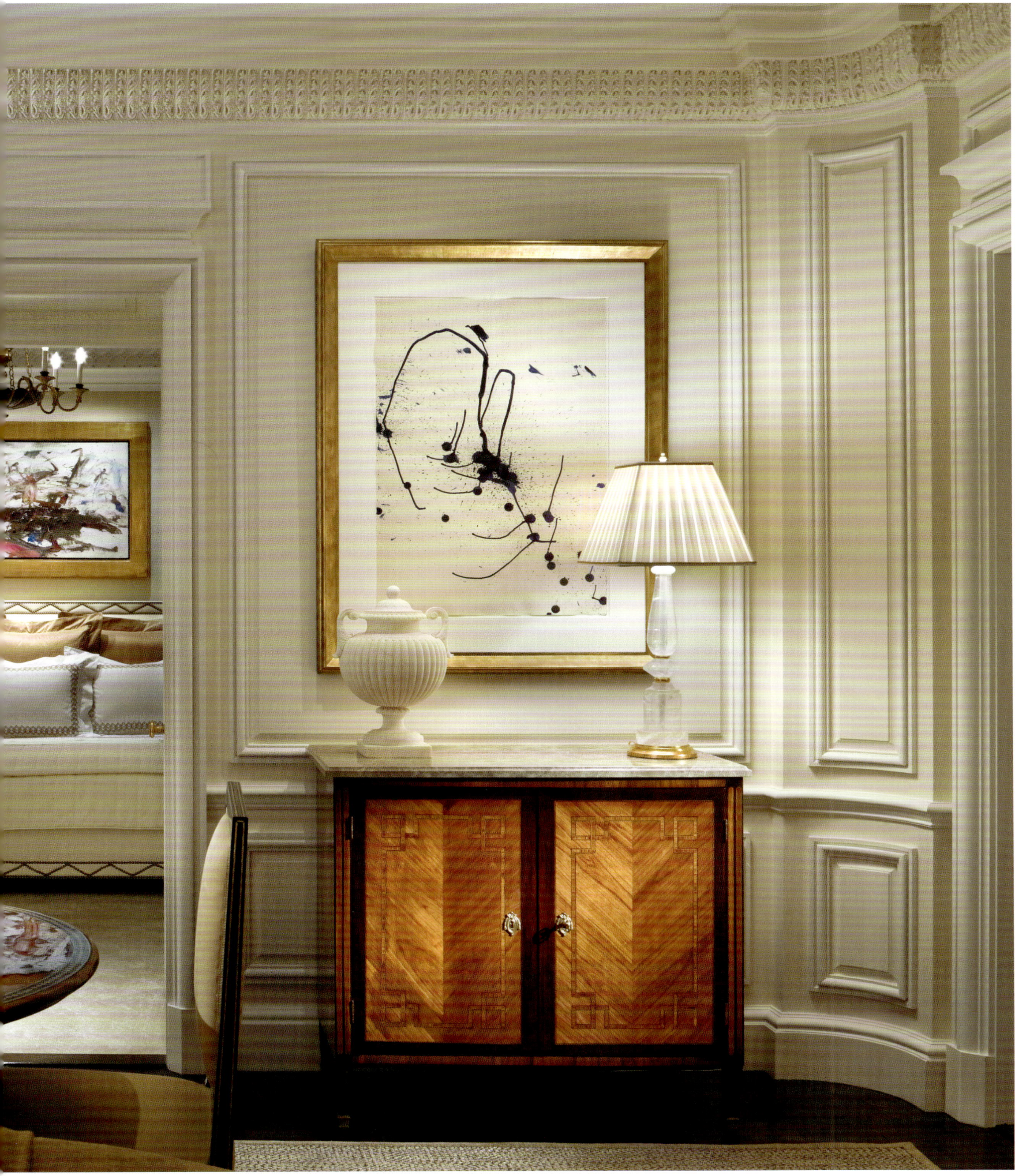

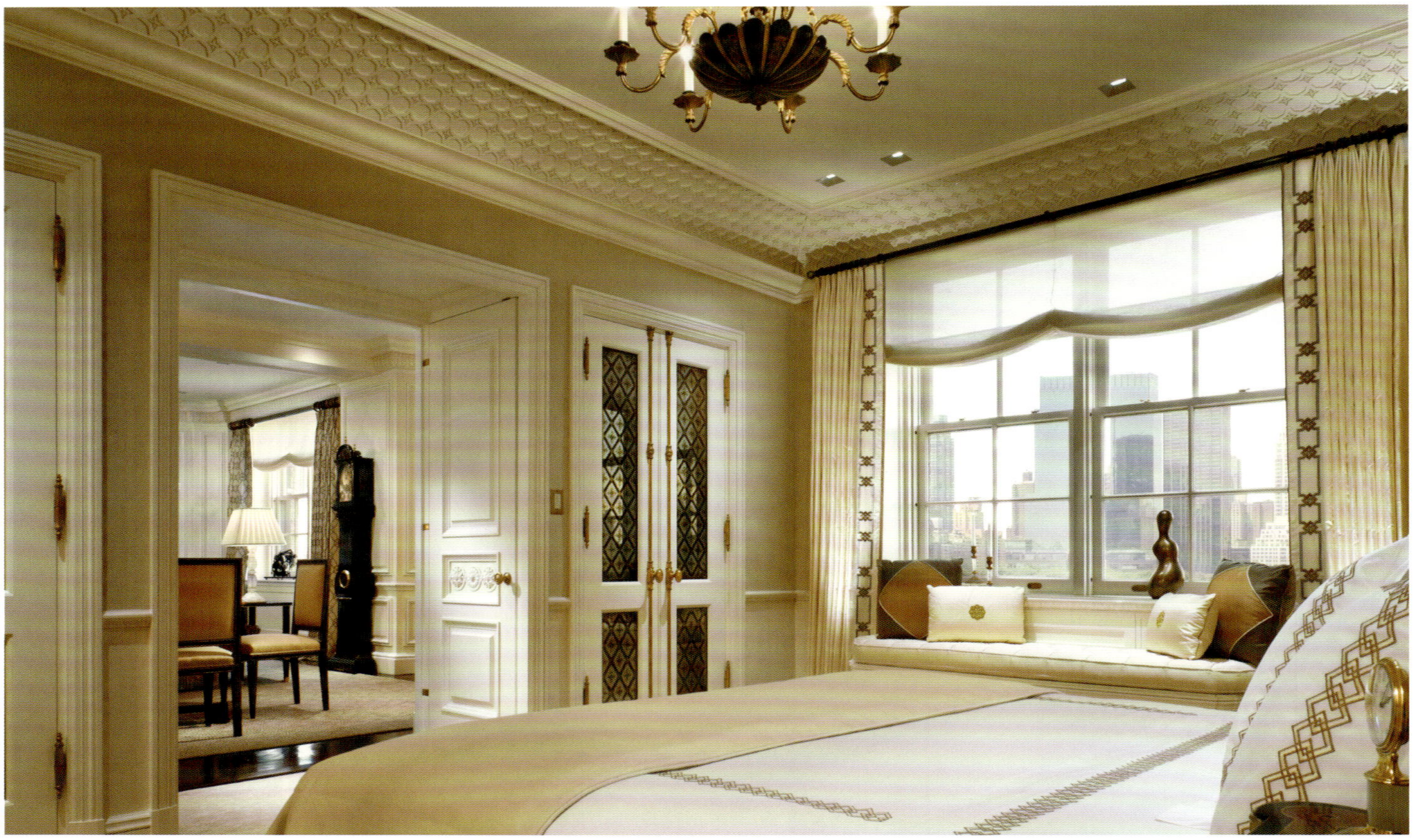

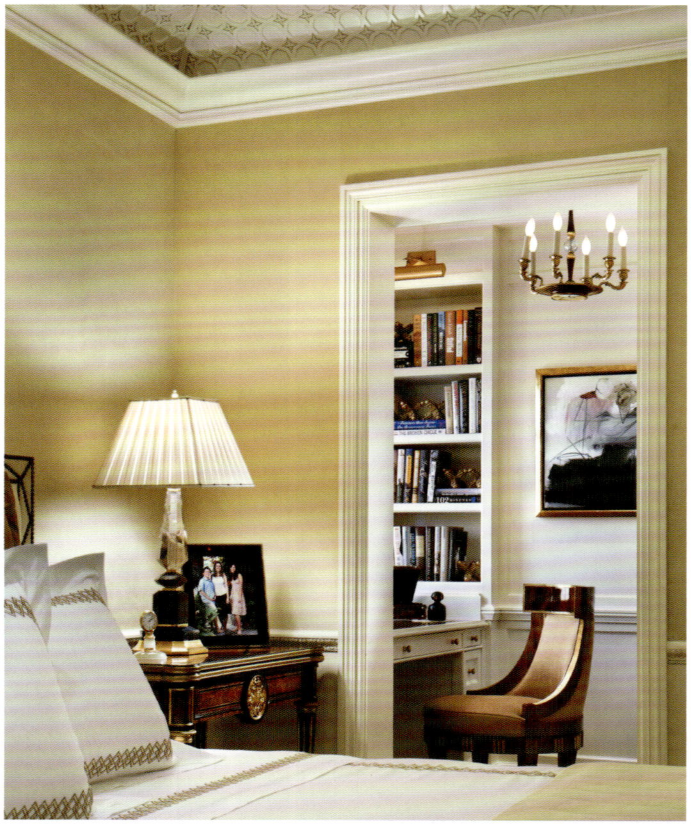

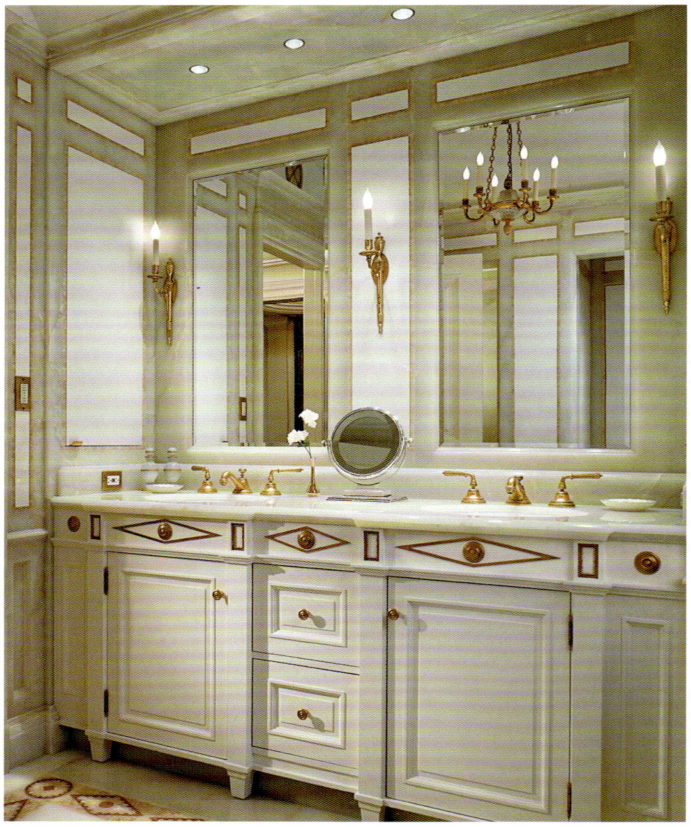

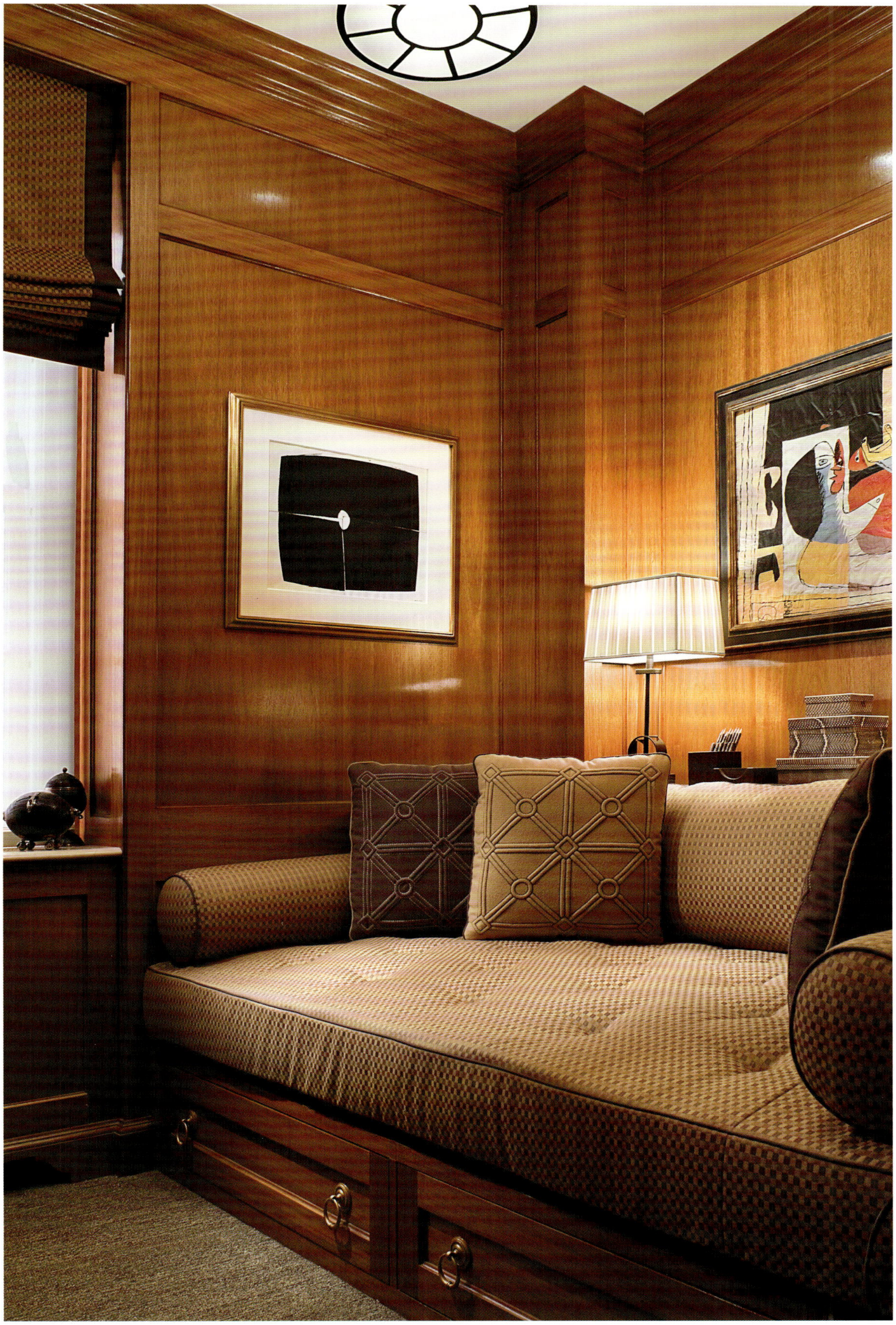

Housed in what was once a kitchen, the library opens to the living room via a pair of large pocket doors. The walls are paneled in painted wood with leather insets ornamented with bronze stud work. The articulated ceiling incorporates a unique banding motif, plus corner details that enhance the form of the ceiling cove.

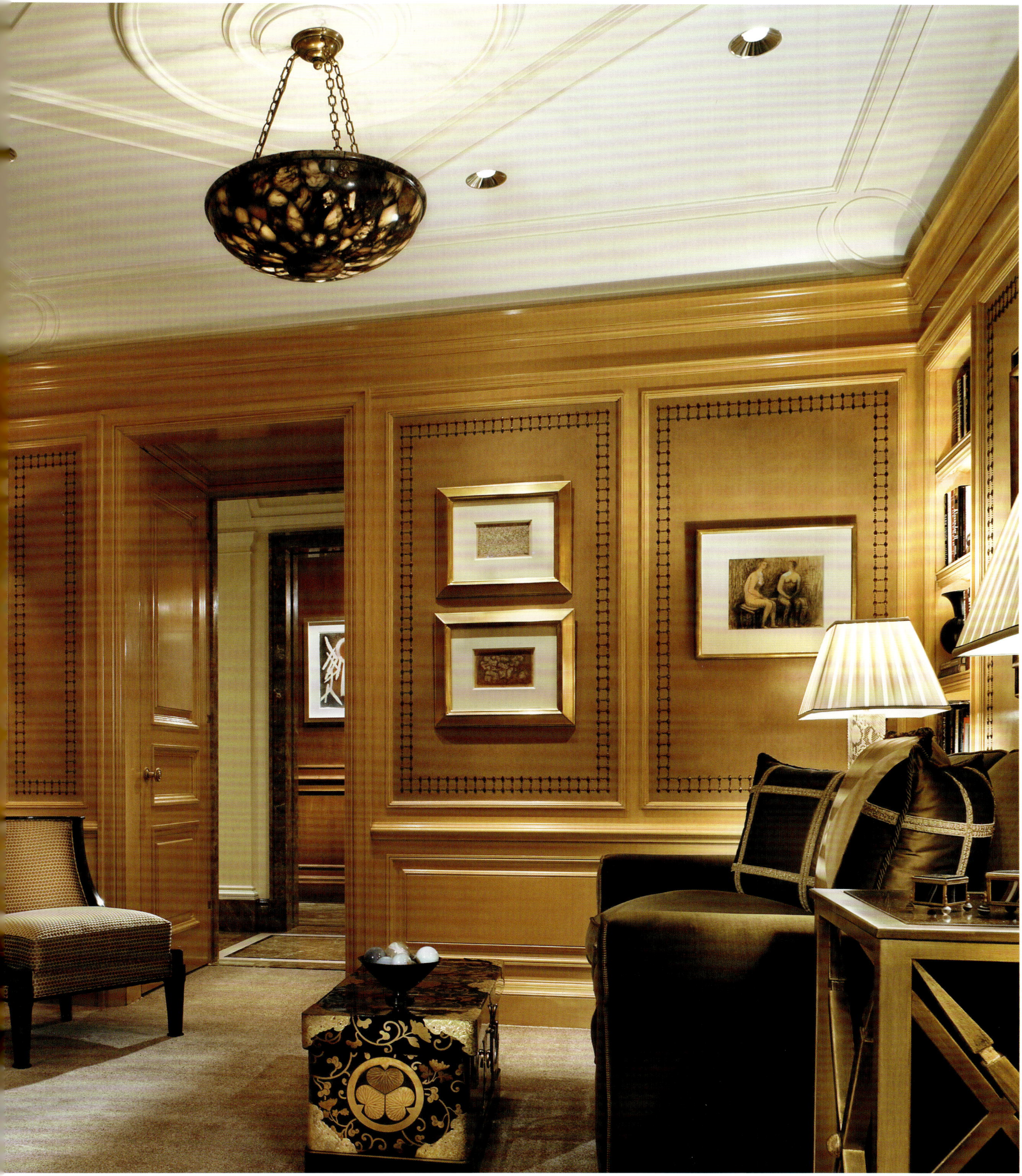

On the Peninsula

Every house has its own best form. What that may be varies with the times, the place, and the client, but it's the architect's job—and joy—to bring a house as close as possible to its perfect self within the existing set of conditions. This exceptional 11,850-square-foot Tudor-style residence embodies that challenge—in spades.

Built in 1885 and expanded in the 1920s, the four-story stone house stands alone on a rocky peninsula that juts into Long Island Sound. When my clients acquired it, it had an interior of double-height rooms with a breezy California beach house flavor and no architectural details. They wanted to restore it to its original, more formal character, and update it at the same time.

The first task was to develop a practical floor plan that worked for this modern family of five. That involved creating a new stair, finessing the circulation through the public rooms, establishing new floor and ceiling plates of many rooms that were formerly double height, and adding layers of architectural detail. Perhaps more critical, it resulted in the reshaping of the ungainly family areas and establishing a secondary entrance.

Transforming the existing double-height kitchen into a kitchen with a breakfast area that flowed into a family room started the process. The insertion of a four-story secondary stair hall and an elevator took it further. The seamless incorporation of a two-car garage addition, exercise room, wine storage, laundry with staff lounge, and cabana for the pool area completed the reconfiguring of the ground level.

On the second floor, in space created over the original kitchen, we placed a media room and game room with windows that frame carefully composed views of the Sound. We also installed a library, sitting room, master bedroom, his and her dressing areas, and master bath. We consolidated the third floor within the existing envelope by taking space from the double-height master bedroom; there we housed the three children's bedrooms and baths, plus a guest bedroom en suite.

27

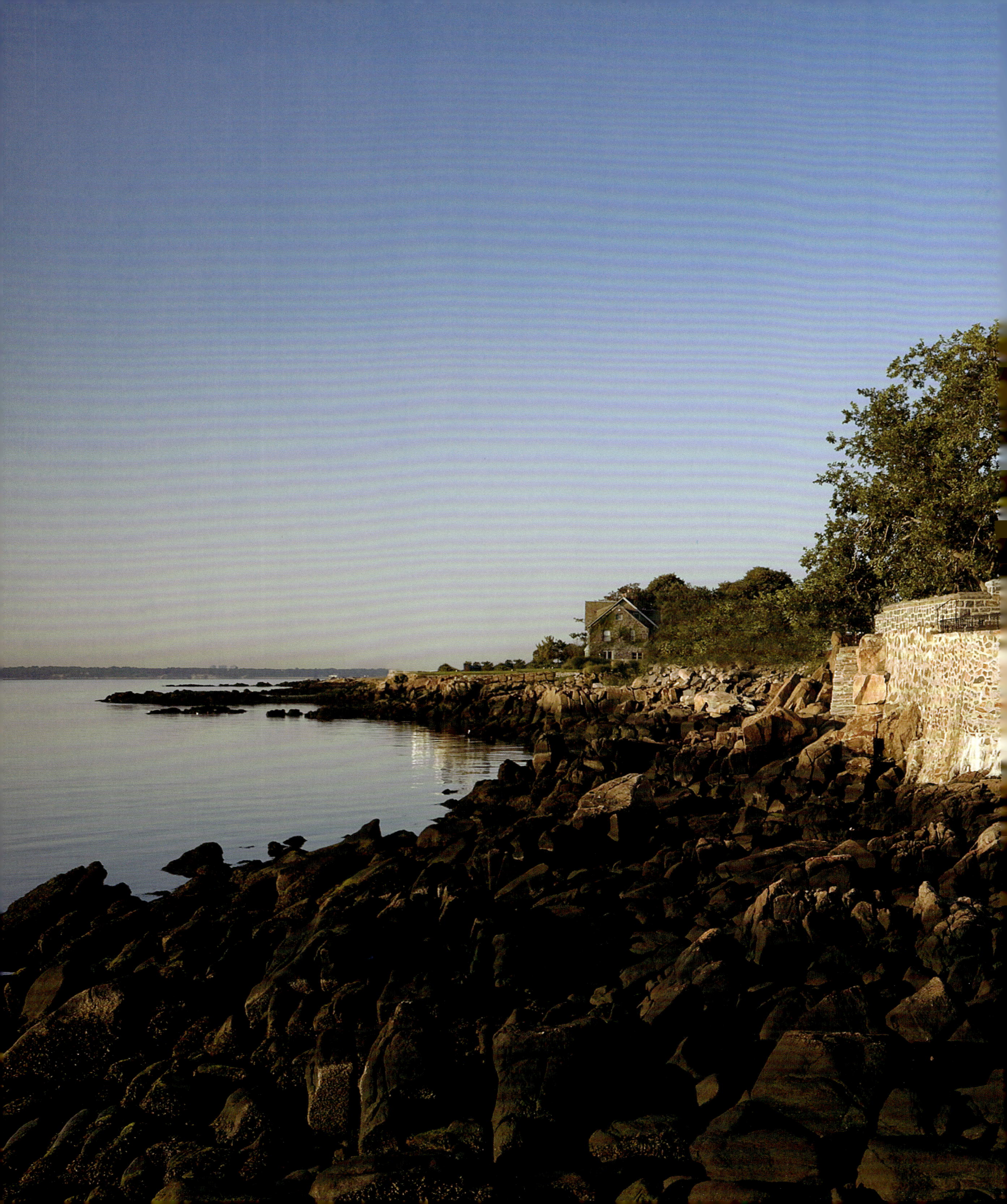

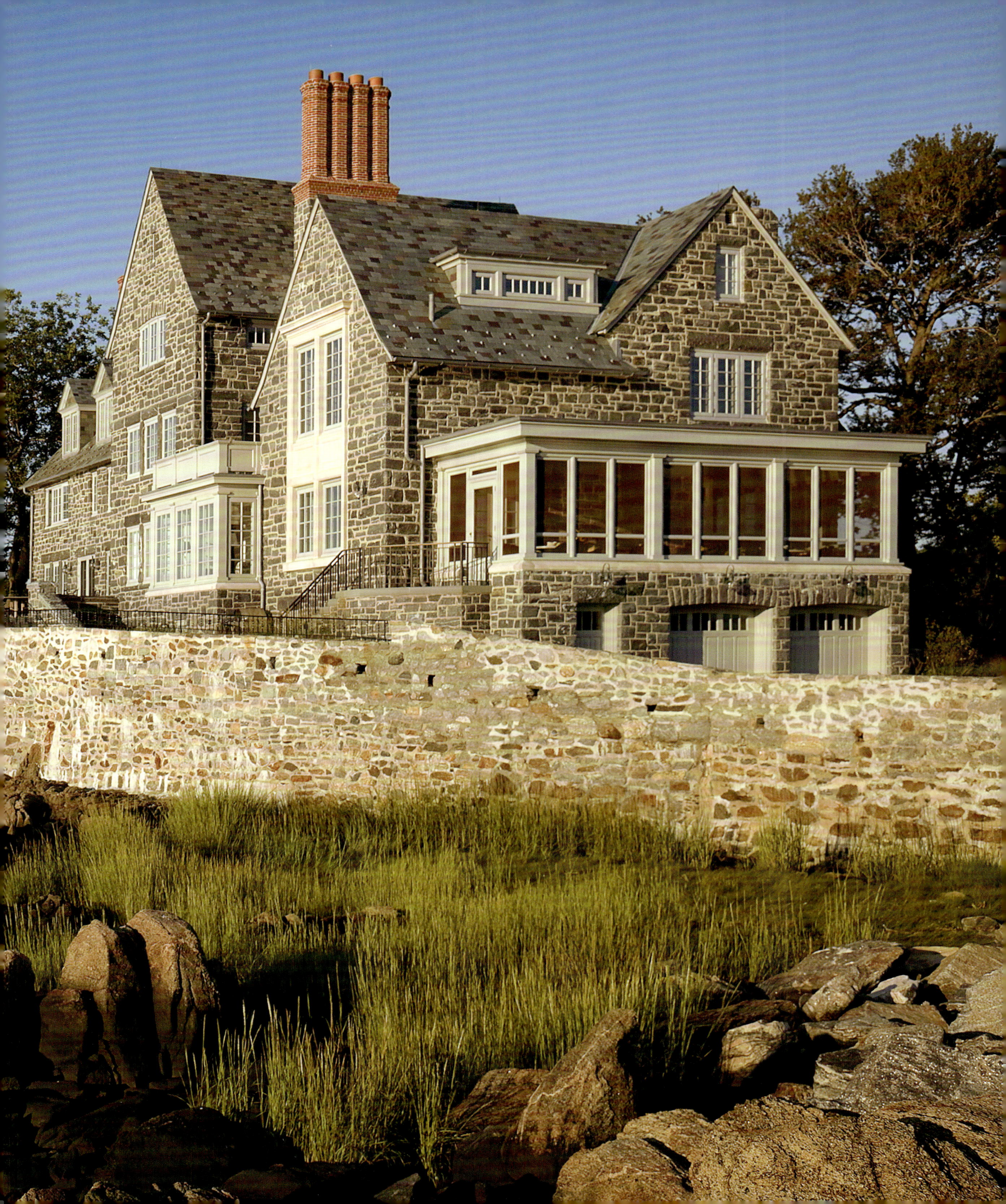

A complete reinvention of the entry gallery, main stair, and the passageways into the vast living room and formal dining room refined the organization and flow through the house's public rooms. We introduced structure to redefine the rooms in a more expected fashion, and layered in detailing with finishes full of character: new wood and stone flooring, millwork, cabinetry, custom plaster cornices, coffered ceilings, and new windows and doors. We also threaded state-of-the-art mechanical and electrical systems through the house.

The work on the exterior was equally extensive. We restored the stone walls and chimneys; added new dormers to the roofline; and installed new slate roofing. All the stonework was power-washed, pointed, and caulked—a massive undertaking.

We also replaced the original front entry, a porte-cochère that extended to the driveway, with an inviting portico made of Indiana limestone and matching granite. Other upgrades included: replacing existing windows; creating new masonry openings; fabricating new exterior woodwork in solid, gray-stained mahogany; installing exterior metalwork of lead-coated copper; and adding all new stonework for the garage and porch addition. Because of the waterside location and the potential exposure to heavy weather, we conceived and implemented safeguards to stem any possible damage.

Our work also extended to the design of the elliptical pool and adjoining pergola area. With interiors by Bunny Williams and landscaping by Eric Groft of Oehme van Sweden, the house and grounds now look and feel the way this family always intended. The restoration of the flagpole structure on the promontory—the property's once and future signature—was a wonderful final touch.

PREVIOUS SPREAD: The principal elevation faces Long Island Sound. LEFT: At the main entrance, steps and a portico replace the original porte-cochère. OPPOSITE TOP: The porch ceiling is paneled in mahogany boarding finished with marine-grade paint; the screens are bronze. OPPOSITE: By the pergola, an elliptical pool has a bluestone coping.

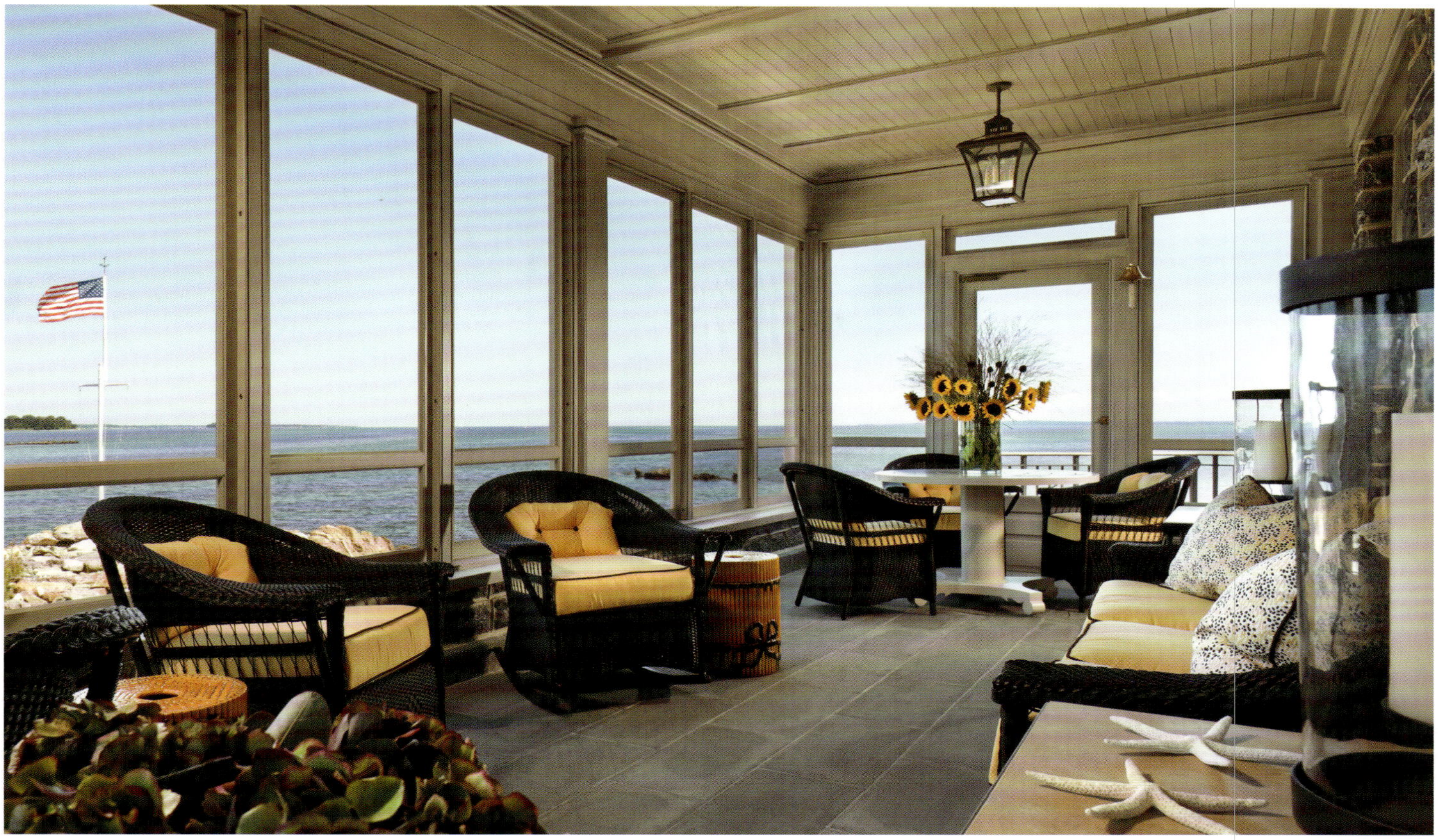

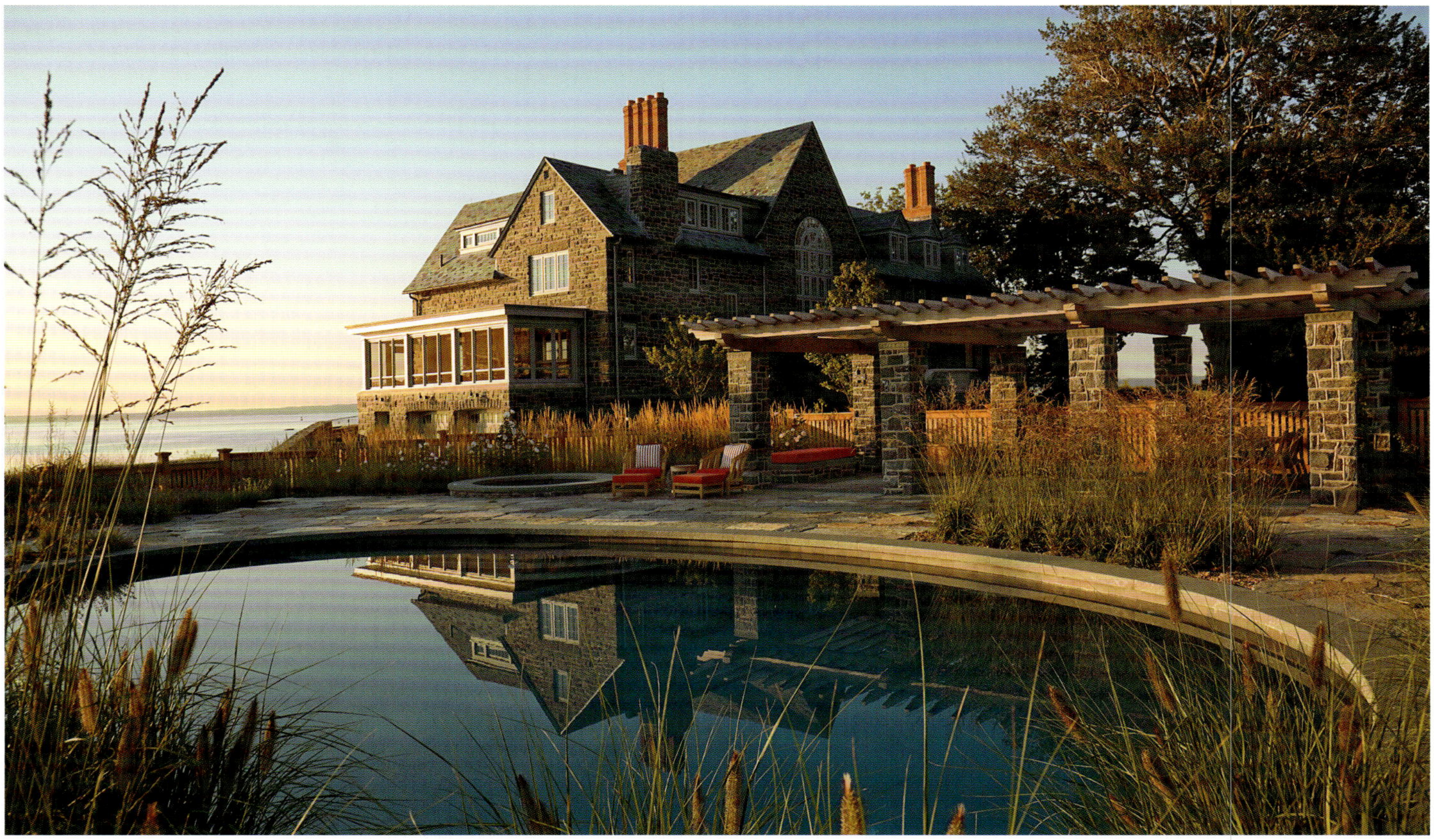

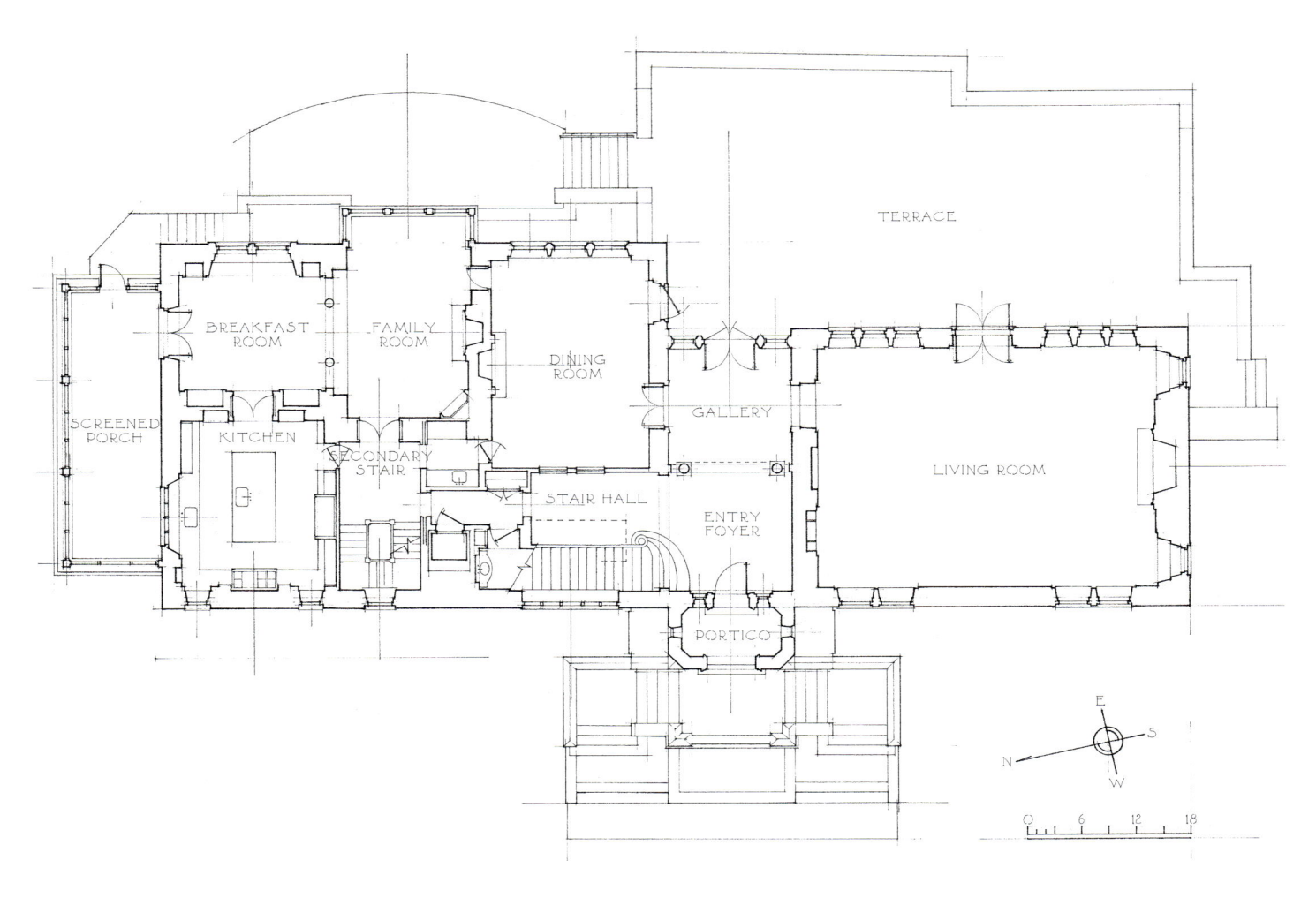

LEFT: The double-height gallery opens on the right to the living room, and on the left to the dining room and stone terrace at the back. The new central stair, OPPOSITE, is the primary circulation path from the first floor to the third floor. With the newly installed windows, it creates a suitably grand entry.

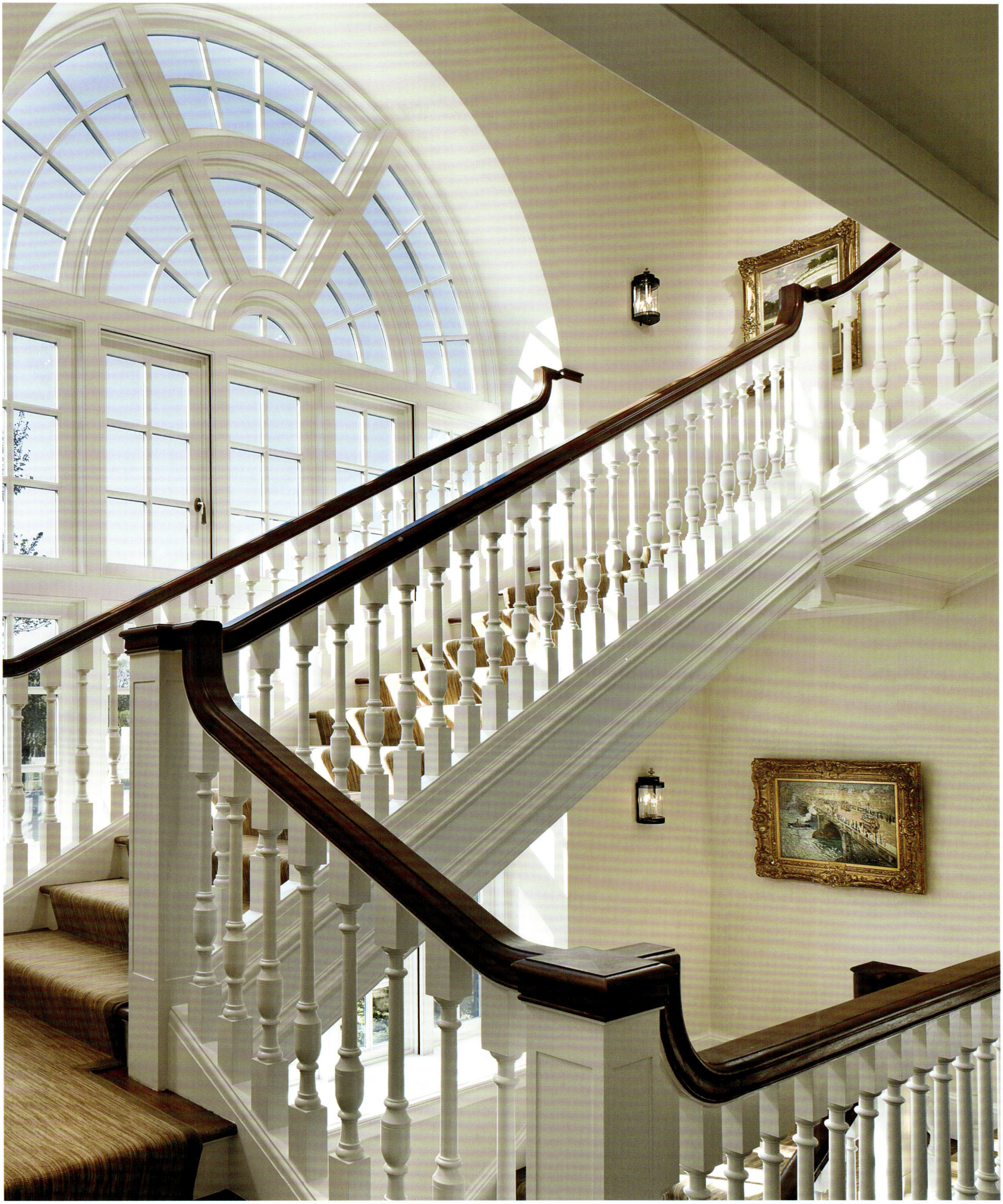

From paneled walls to plaster ceiling, surface articulation helps organize the vast area of the living room into three distinct zones. The French doors open onto the stone terrace. OVERLEAF, CLOCKWISE FROM UPPER LEFT: The breakfast room is the only interior room that opens directly to the screened porch; a corner of the family room; the kitchen casement windows open onto the porch.

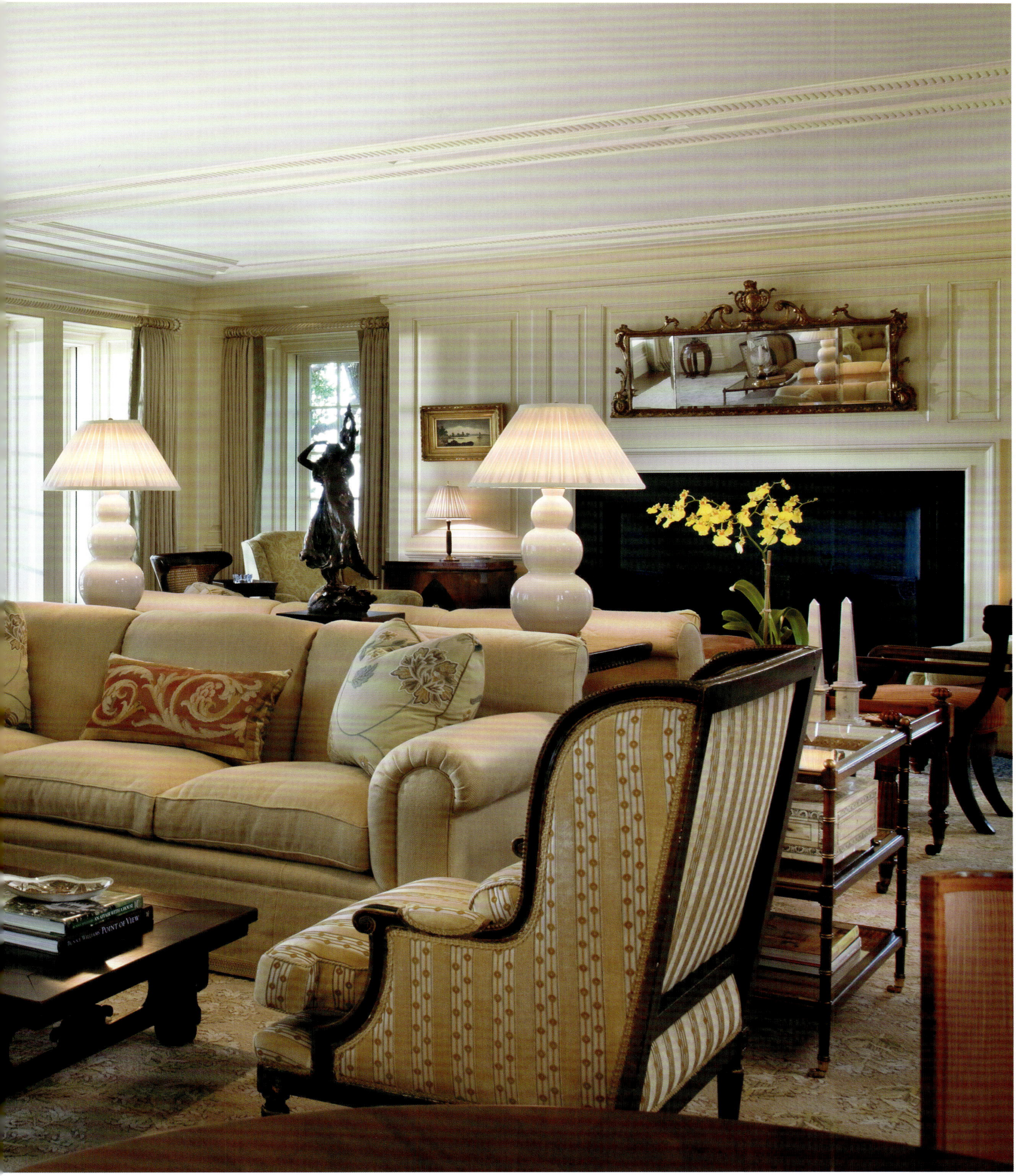
POINT OF VIEW

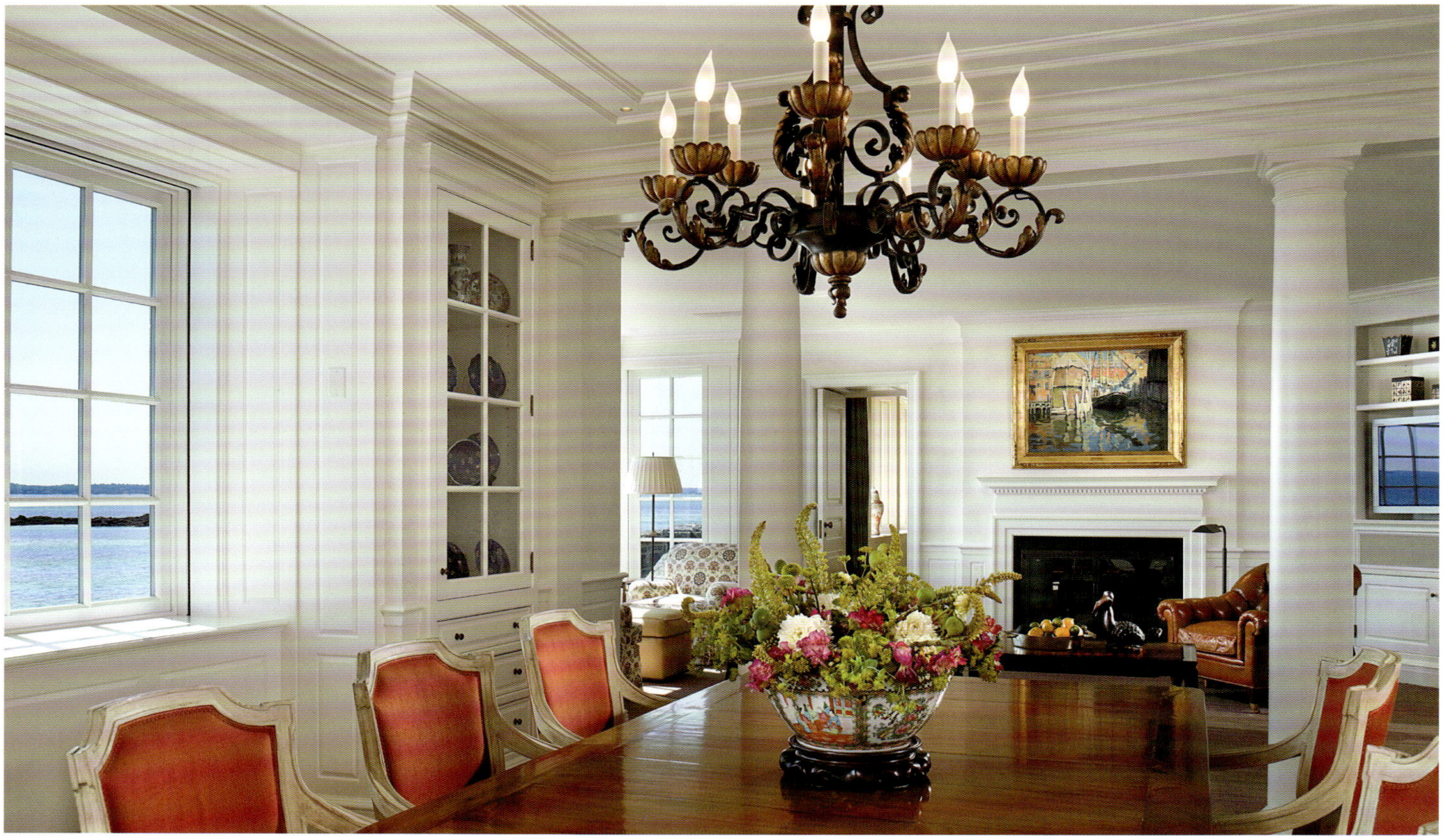

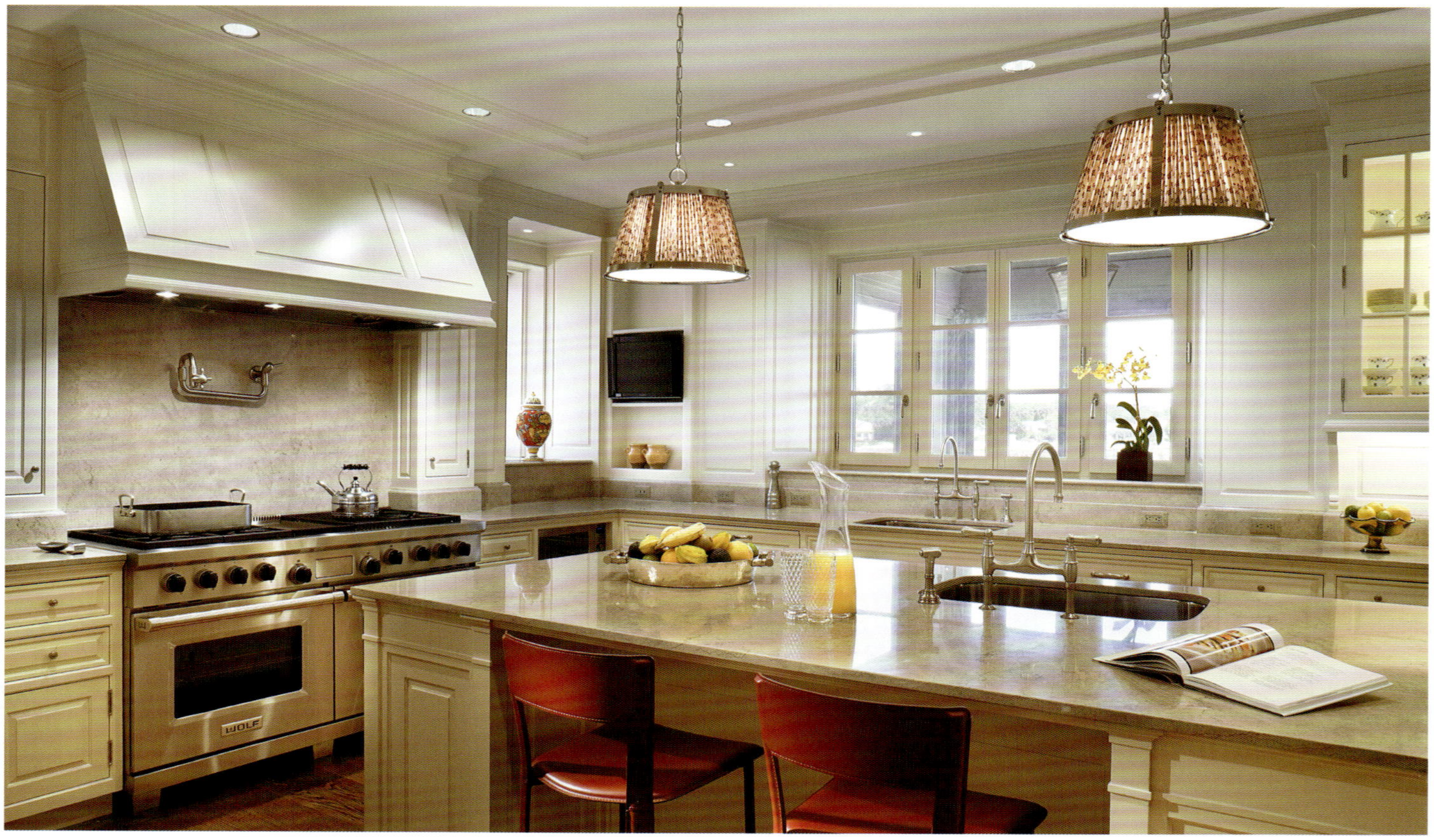

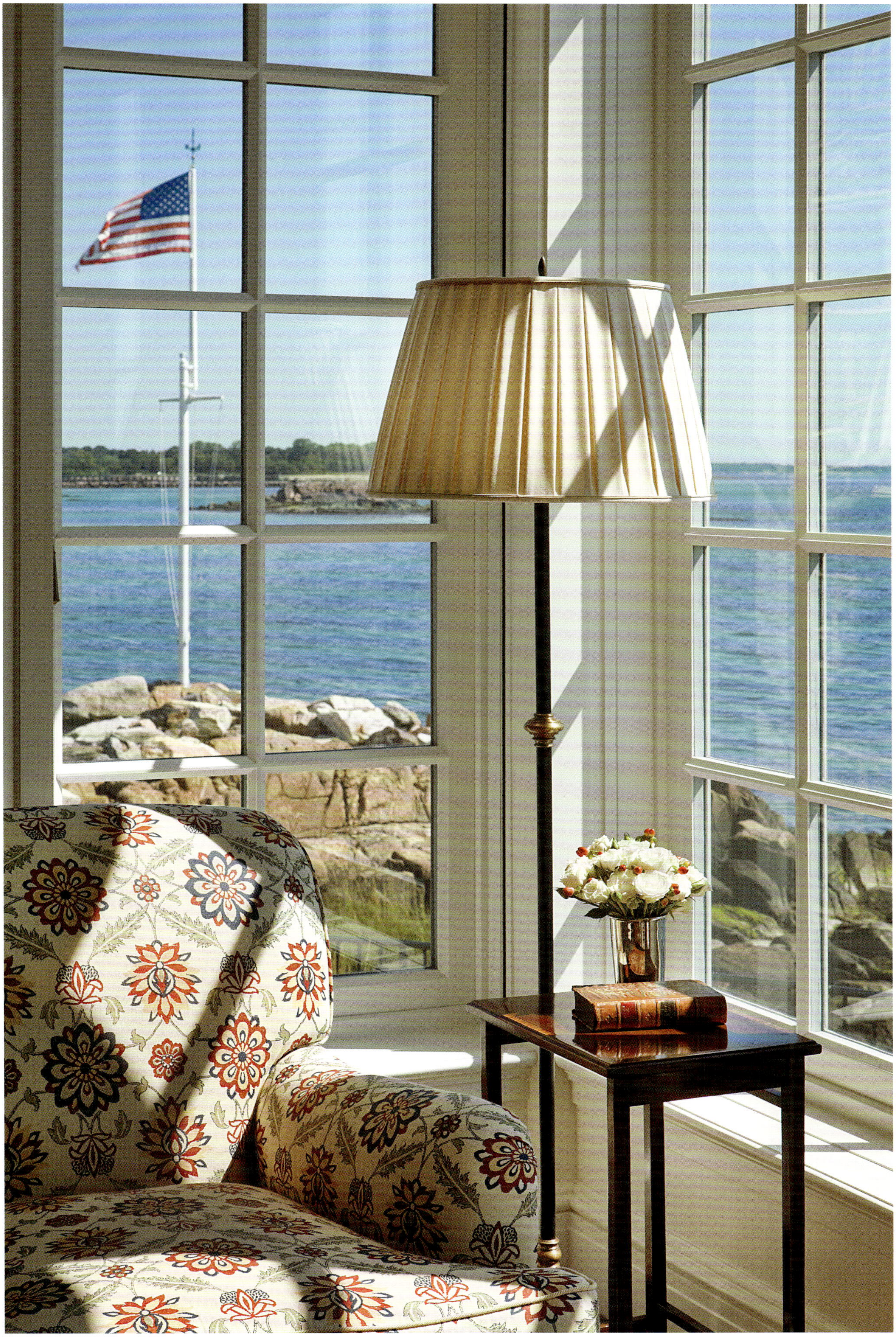

The media room, atop the kitchen and the breakfast room, is acoustically isolated from the rest of the house. The removal of staff bedrooms in the attic created the space to accommodate the media room's vaulted, double-height ceiling. Through the pocket doors is the game room, which has a wood-paneled ceiling. All the wood elements are rift-cut white oak with a cerused finish.

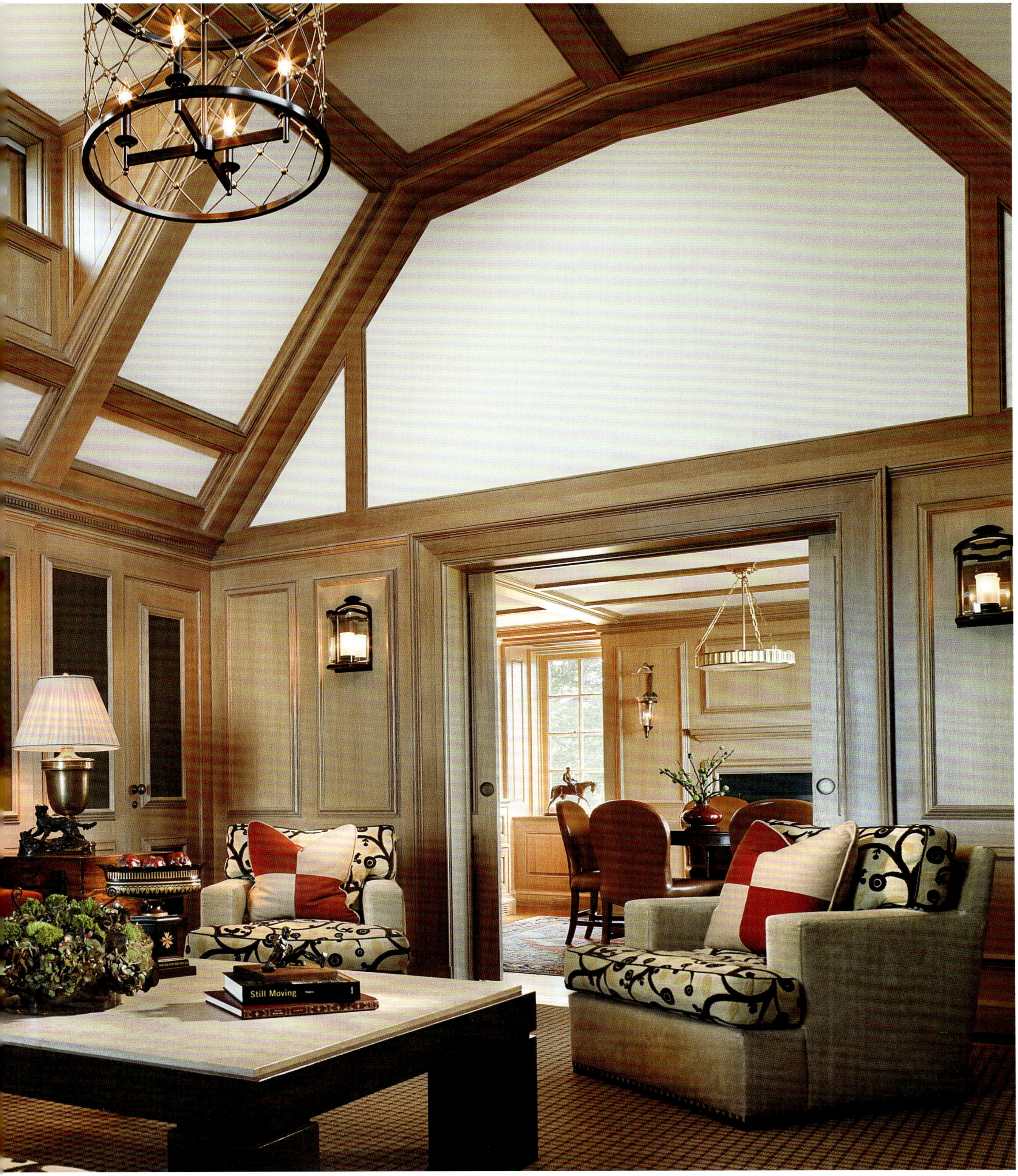
Still Moving

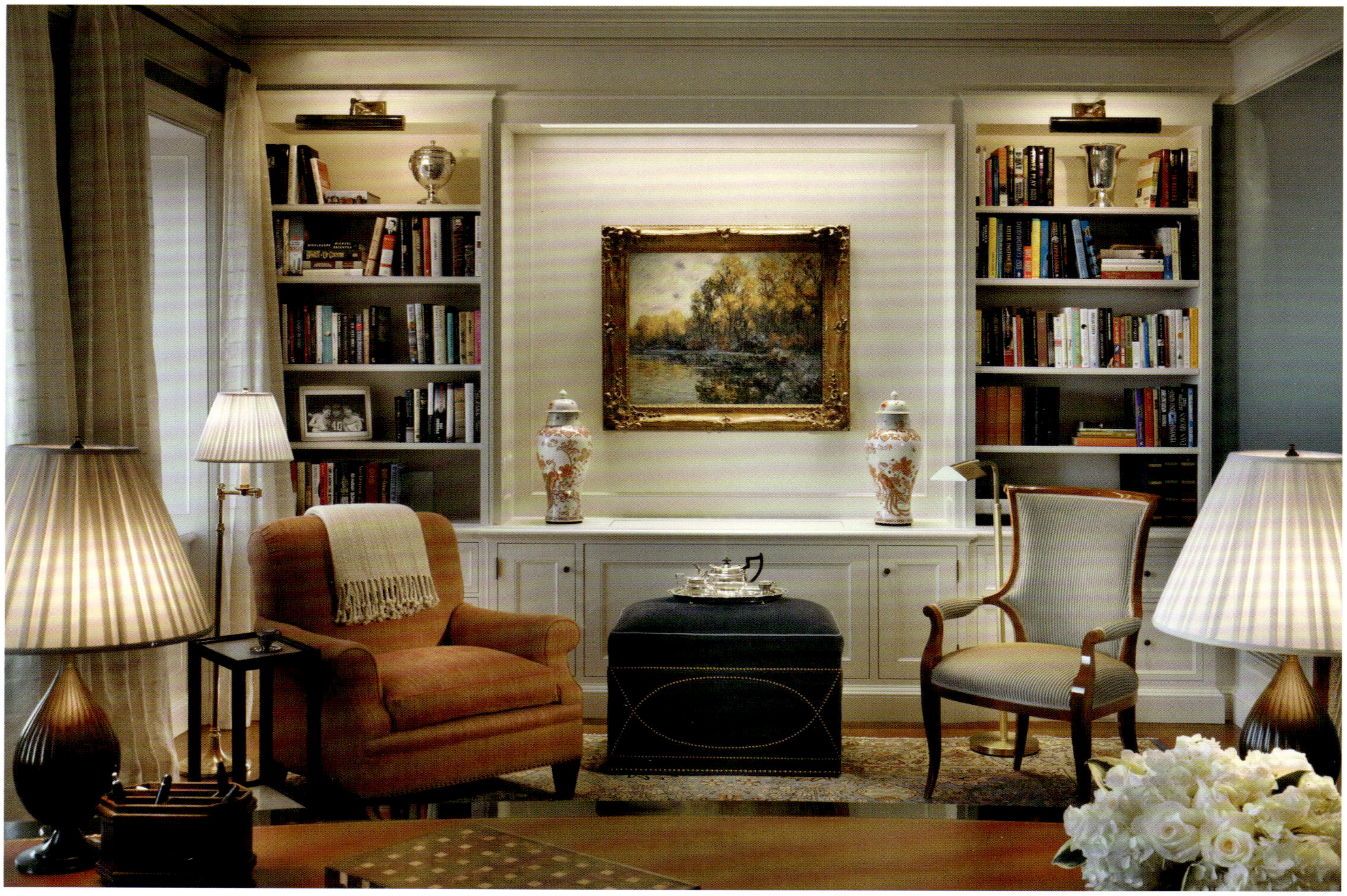

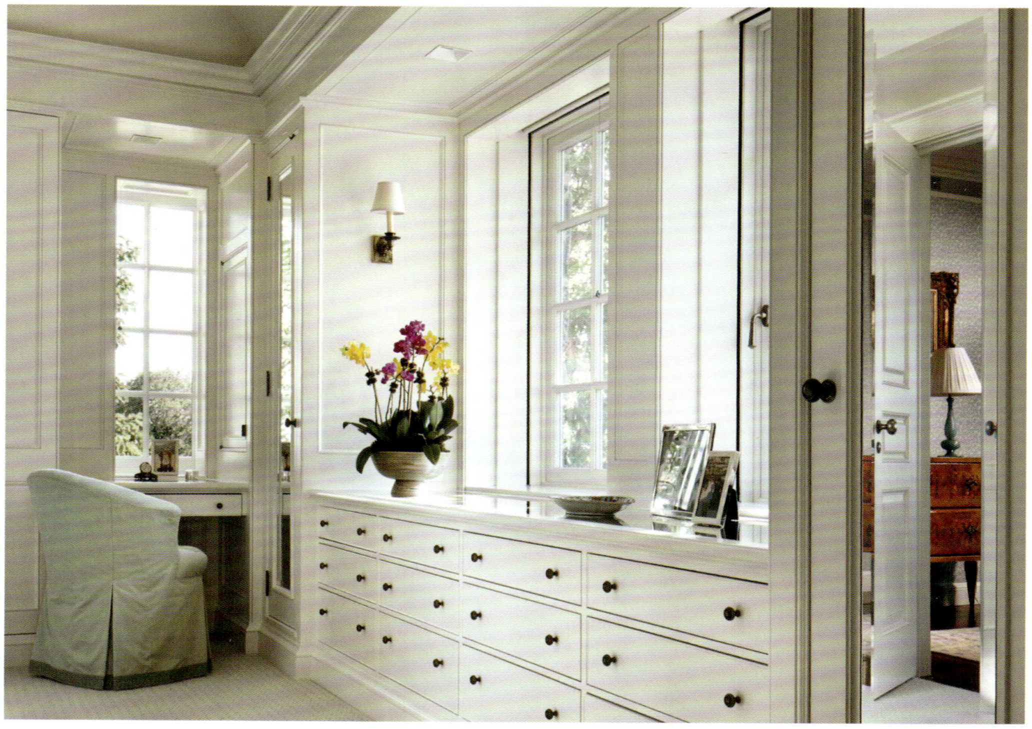

OPPOSITE, TOP: The master sitting room also serves as her study. OPPOSITE: Her light-filled dressing room is adjacent to the master bedroom. ABOVE: Like so many of this house's rooms, the master bedroom has uninterrupted water views. RIGHT, FAR RIGHT: In the master bath, articulated stone piers support the tub. The custom mosaic marble floor has an organic pattern. Vanities flank a built-in bench.

Skyline Haven

New Yorkers know that the built fabric of the city changes almost at the speed of light. We are also aware that the city has a treasury of great private residential spaces that still retain significant vestiges of their almost century-old forms. The opportunity to see and to work on those interiors is just one reason it's such a privilege to practice residential architecture in New York. This 5,800-square-foot Upper East Side residence is a fine example of that. Constructed in the 1920s, the apartment has always been a duplex with a terrace that rings its upper level. And it has always stunned visitors with its signature feature: a double-height entry gallery, topped by a skylight. When these clients purchased it, however, it was in need of a comprehensive renovation. In conjunction with the interior design firm Cullman & Kravis, we gave it a complete overhaul.

The new floor plan is consistent with its predecessor in many respects, placing public areas on the lower level and sequestering private living areas upstairs. The general type and number of rooms, and their adjacencies, are almost a given: off the downstairs entry are the living room, library, powder room, dining room, kitchen, and staff areas. Our innovations included a private bathroom off the library.

The entry foyer is a one-story space set off by an imposing, French-polished mahogany door. Overhead is a coffered plaster ceiling. Finessing a grid pattern to align perfectly with the library, entry, door, and window was something of a logistical challenge, given the existing placement of certain structural beams. Yet it's that grid that creates such a strong axial orientation upon entry. The lower ceiling contributes to the drama of walking into the gallery beyond.

Replacing the existing stone staircase with a grand wood stair was one of the larger decisions we made, and it significantly enhanced the character of the entire interior. The bronze-and-iron balustrade travels the full distance from base to top and continues around the upper gallery. A patterned stone floor in the gallery adds a foundation of drama under the skylight.

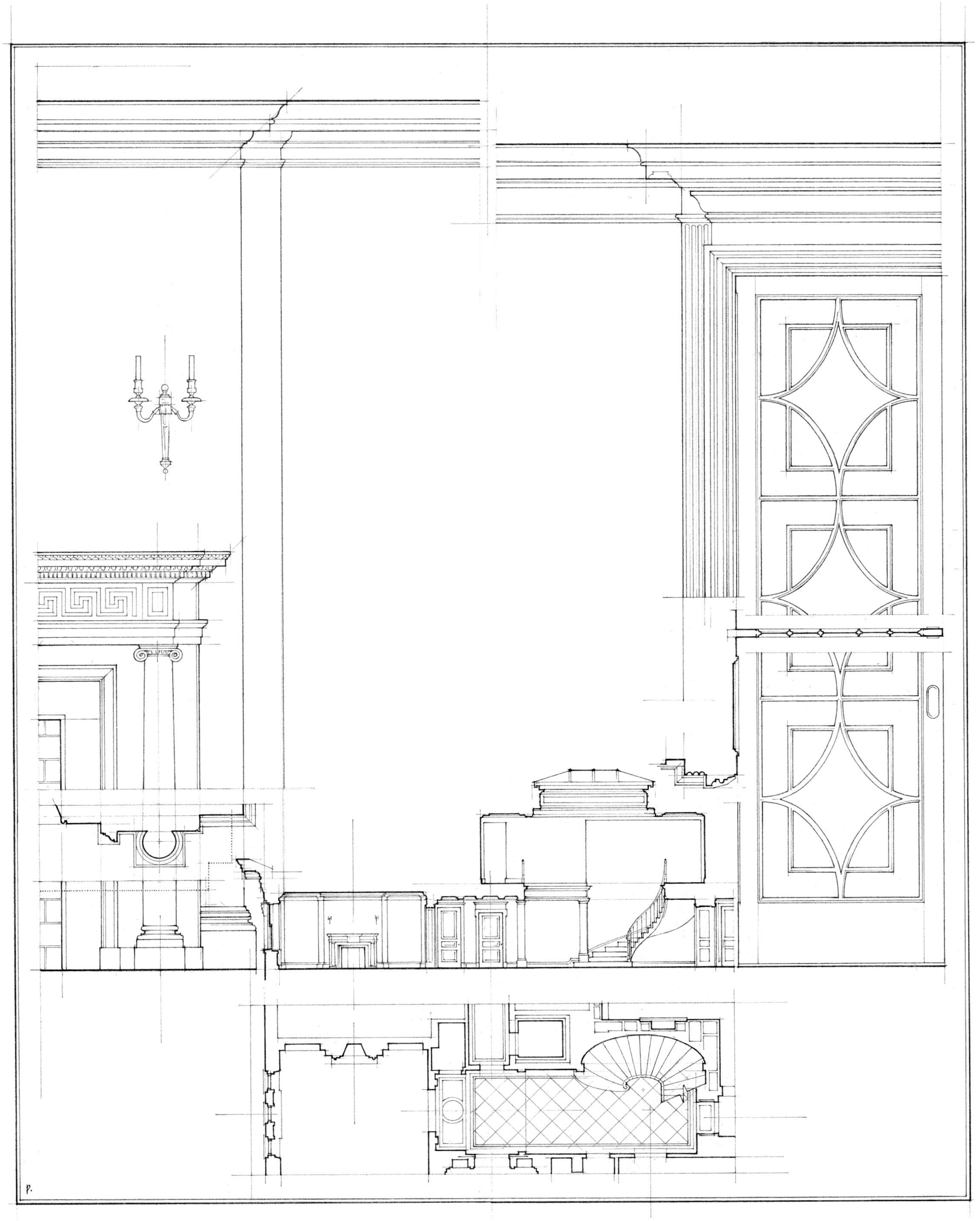
p.

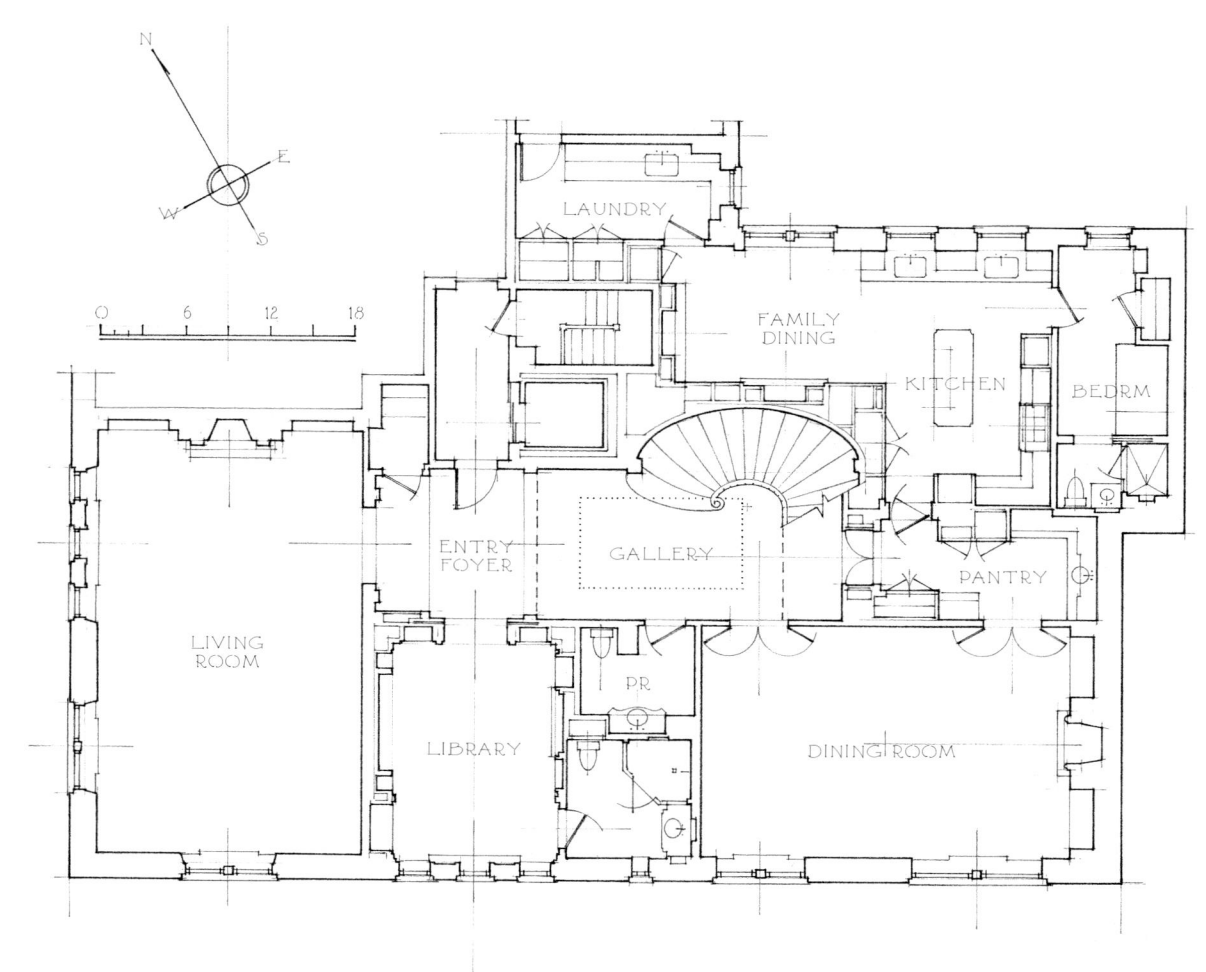

With its black and white marble floor and series of doors veneered in crotch mahogany French polished on site, the double-height gallery under a new state-of-the-art skylight creates a dramatic entry. A graceful elliptical stair and balustrade replace the original staircase.

Pocket doors—glass panels encased between patterned wood grilles—divide the library from the gallery. Even when the doors are closed, natural light flows into the room from the gallery to create an expansive feeling. Natural light from the gallery also diffuses into the dining room, which has a coffered ceiling to maximize the sense of height. The mahogany-paneled butler's pantry connects the gallery to the kitchen and dining room.

The upper floor has a master suite, three children's rooms with baths en suite, a family room that opens to the upper gallery, and a kitchenette/bar to serve the terrace with its pergola-covered dining area, outdoor gathering space, and sitting areas under awnings.

Windows are always a key element of design, and we lavish great effort on them. Here we revised the pattern of the fenestration, altered over the years, to make it consistent with the lower levels of the facade. Designed in the style of the 1928 building standard, the new windows add considerable character—and a great deal more light—to the rooms.

When an architect can effect change on an existing building facade in New York, he has—and sometimes creates—a window into history. To do so while reinventing one of the city's more storied residential spaces, that's historic—at least for me.

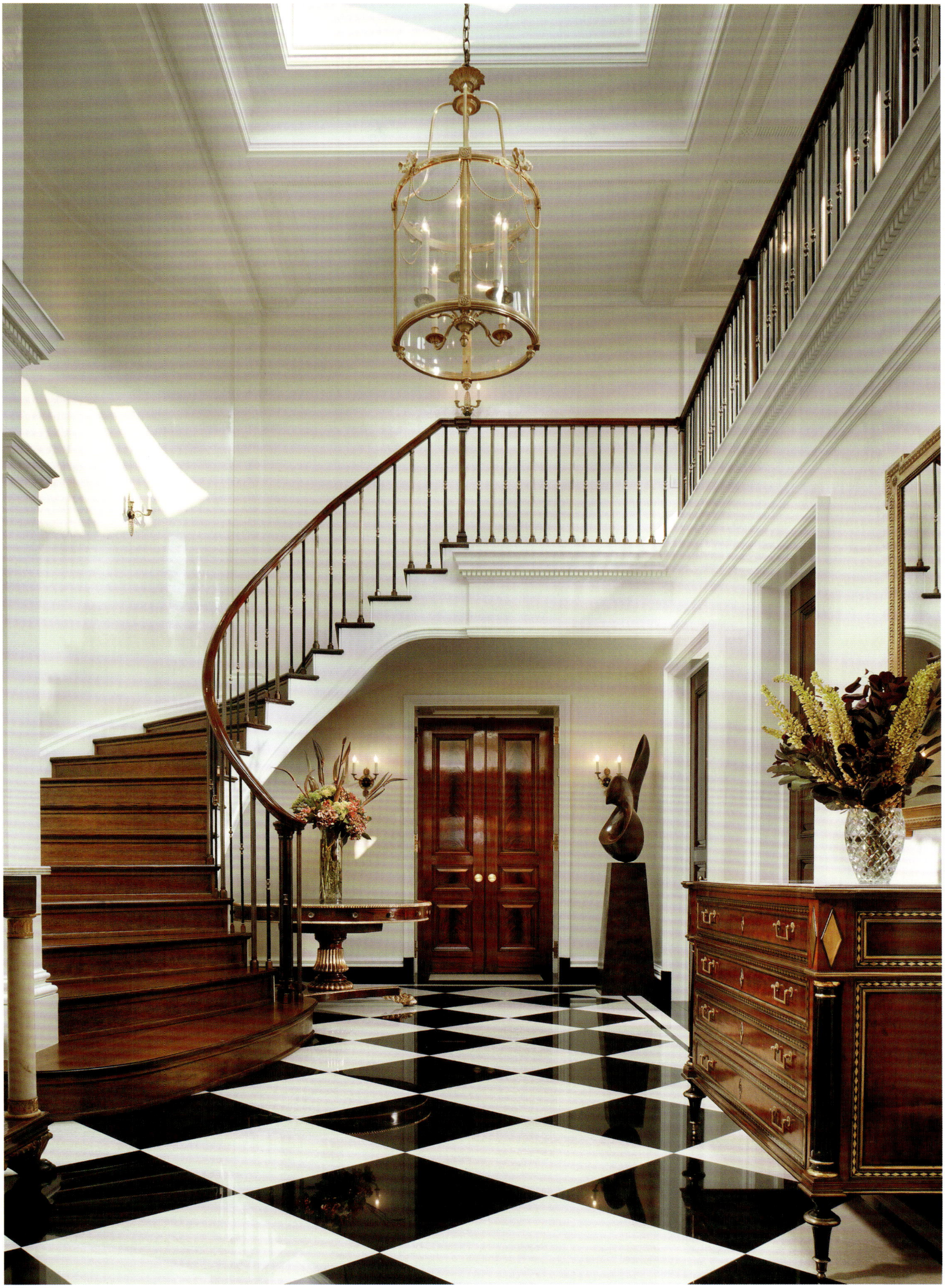

ABOVE: The stair incorporates a French-polished mahogany handrail, balustrade of cast bronze and steel, and treads of rift-cut white oak. LEFT: A plaster entablature with dentil details wraps the gallery level between the first and second floors. OPPOSITE: The upper level landing opens via French doors to a wraparound terrace.

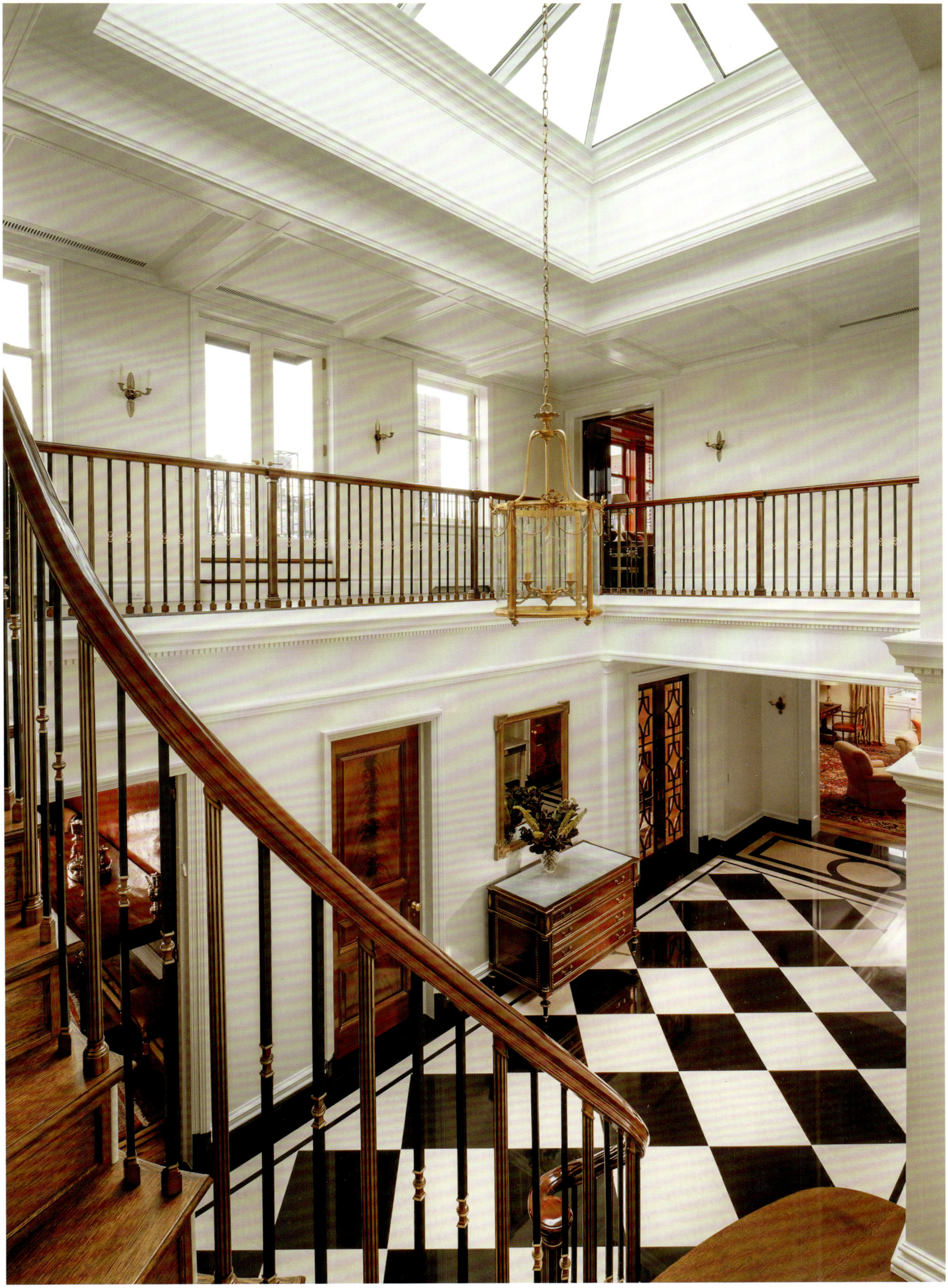

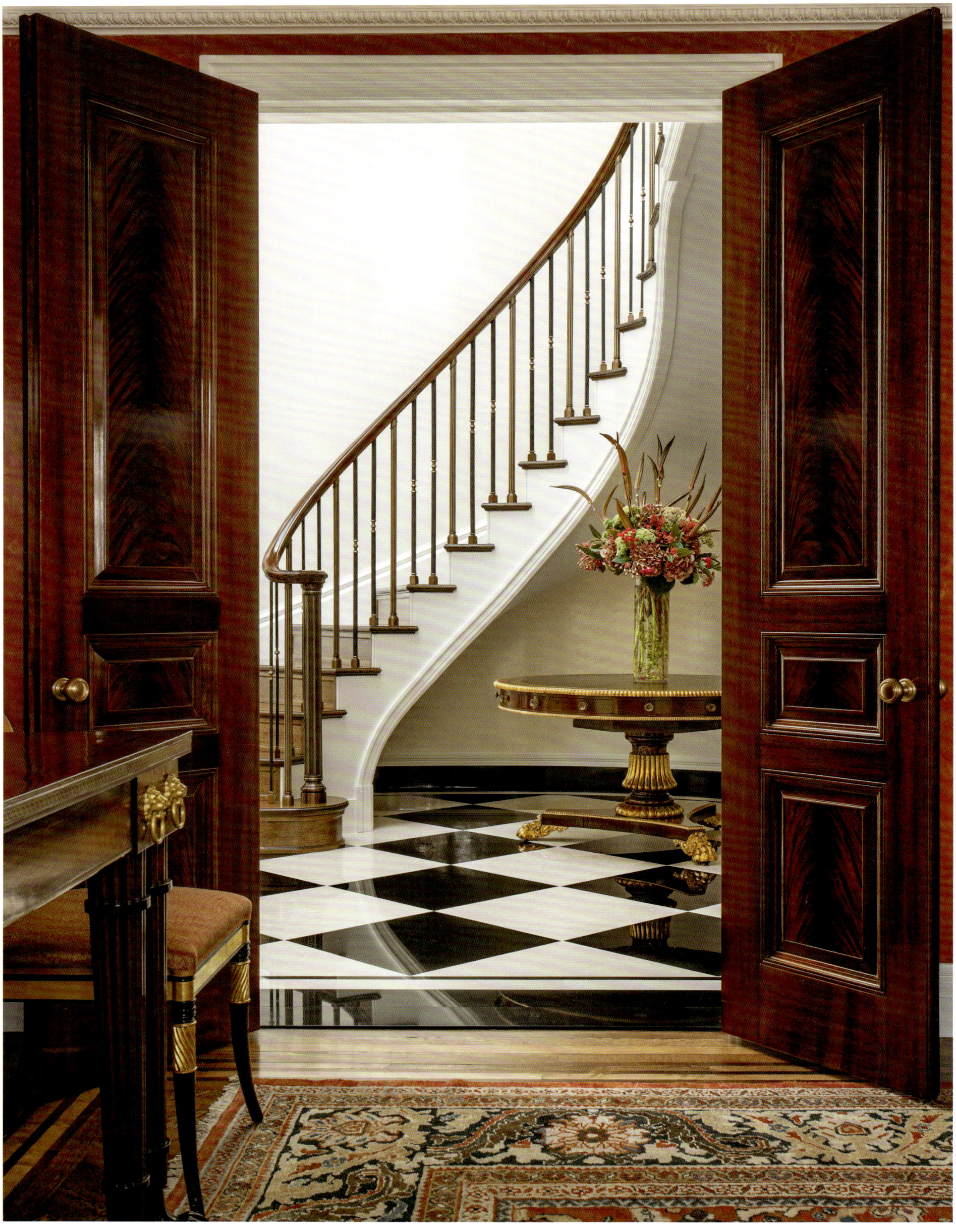

OPPOSITE: Trimmed with plaster egg-and-dart molding, the dining room is directly off the entry gallery. ABOVE: Access to the anigre-paneled library is through a pair of glass pocketing doors ornamented with wood fretwork. RIGHT: In the library, fluted pilasters and cornices differentiate the built-in cabinetry components. FAR RIGHT: His marble-lined bath is adjacent to the library.

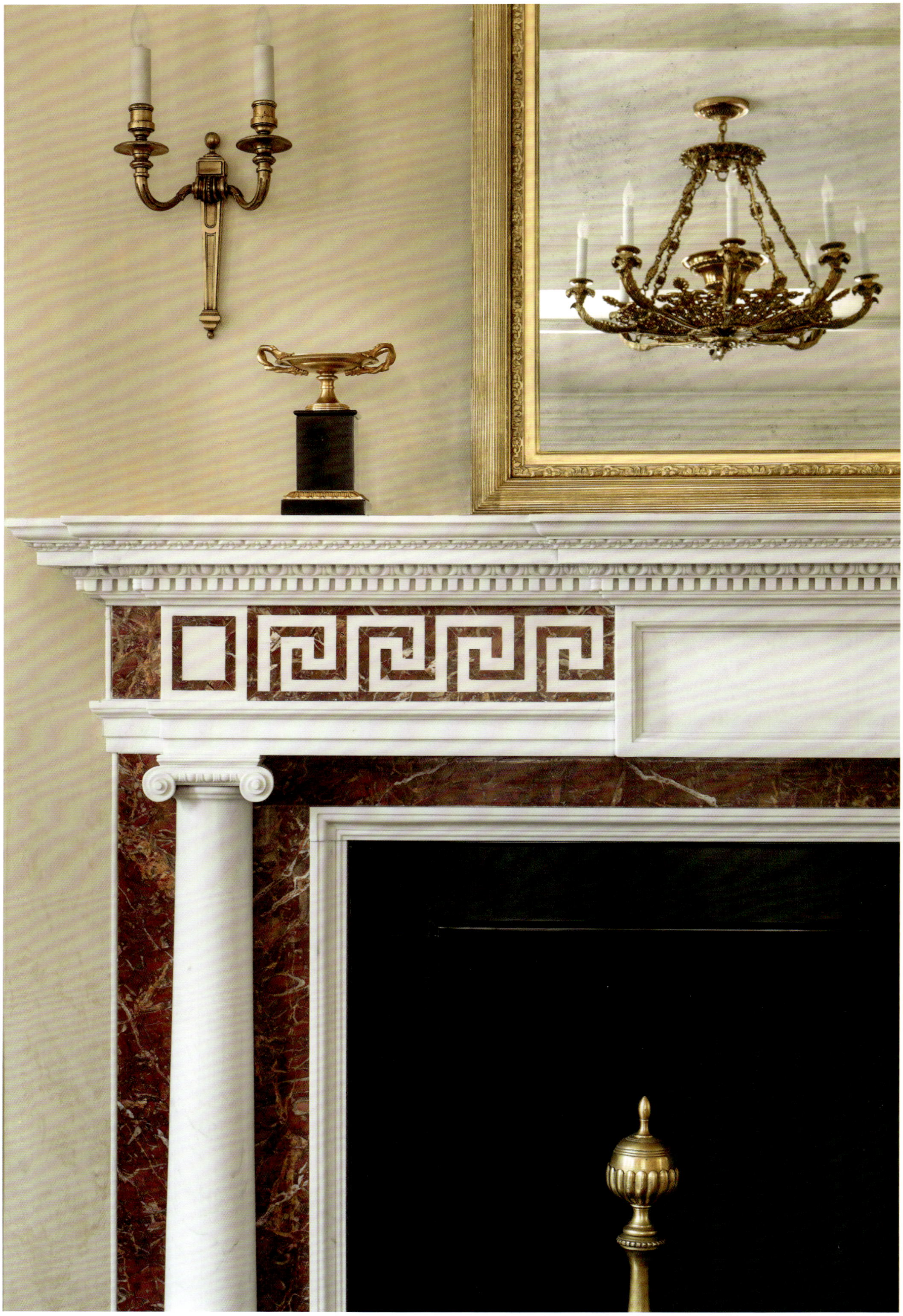

OPPOSITE: The living room mantel incorporates numerous classical components, including pilasters with Ionic capitals, a Greek key frieze, and a dentilated cornice with bead and reel detail. The firebox surround is black honed slate. ABOVE, LEFT: The Greek key motif carries through to the powder room floor; the custom vanity is finished in black lacquer. ABOVE RIGHT: A detail of the floor, with black and white marble Greek key patterned border around a field of dark Emperador marble. OVERLEAF, LEFT: The butler's pantry is lined in mahogany, French polished on site. OVERLEAF, RIGHT: In the kitchen, raised ceilings define distinct areas over the island and family dining table.

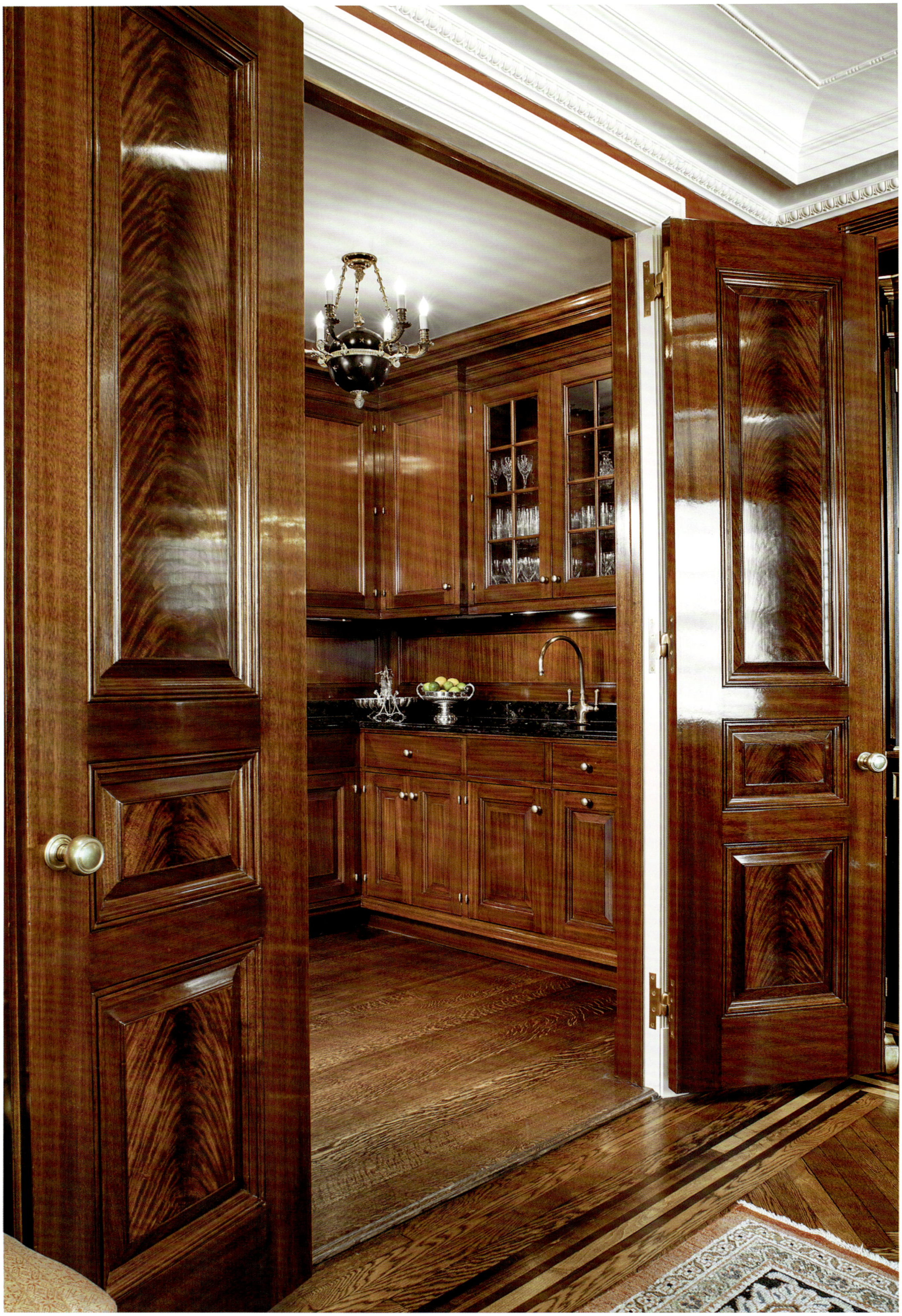

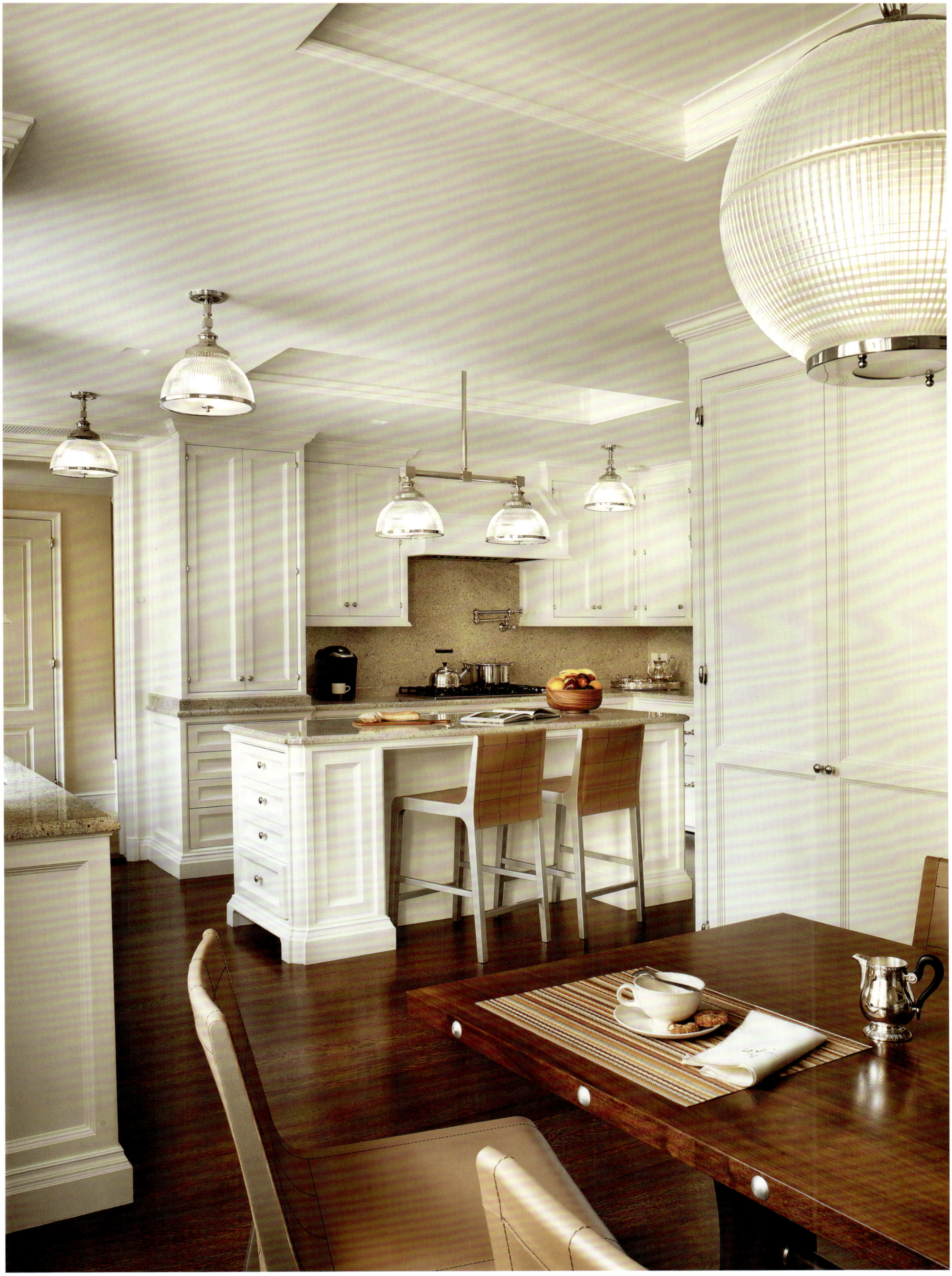

The Nature of Place

There's an ideal structural expression for every residence, and the architect's job is to define it, shape it, and bring it into being. How each of us does that depends on the particular circumstances, as well as our own aesthetic philosophies. Some of us prefer to enhance the existing essence, quirks and all. Others would rather smooth out the idiosyncrasies, aiming for symmetry and balance. Still others go for the tabula rasa approach. For this weekend house, a wonderfully eccentric accretion of a century and more that bellies up to the banks of the Hudson River, the client preferred the first. So did I. Here, that involved rebuilding the entire structure under its existing mansard roof, then cladding it in parging tinted to match the local Palisades stone.

Given the house's unique proximity to the river, we wanted to make it as extroverted as possible. That we did with new windows that open the house to the river. But we hewed to the house's rather unusual ground-floor parti, which had the porch connecting the living room and dining room, the kitchen, off-side with a corner work area, one guest bedroom adjacent to the stair hall, and a tall studio.

From the quaint, compressed entry through the new stair hall, the interior opens up into the beamed living space. The position of doors, windows, and fireplace—all are part of the design. The simplicity of the finishes is intrinsic to making the new architecture appear timeless. Painted woods, natural plaster walls, stone floors, and hand-hewn beams with plaster interstices overhead feel solid and organic, and recall the vernacular architecture of the area's early Dutch settlers. The built-in cabinetry reinforces that effect. The decor, by interior designer Sam Blount, captures the spirit of the house.

The kitchen is at the heart of this house. Framed by windows overlooking the water, it incorporates a generous work area, simple semi-overlay style cabinetry, and a breakfast table by a raised hearth. The shallow firebox brings the fire front and center. Elevating the hearth puts the fireplace right in the sightlines of those in the work area and at the table.

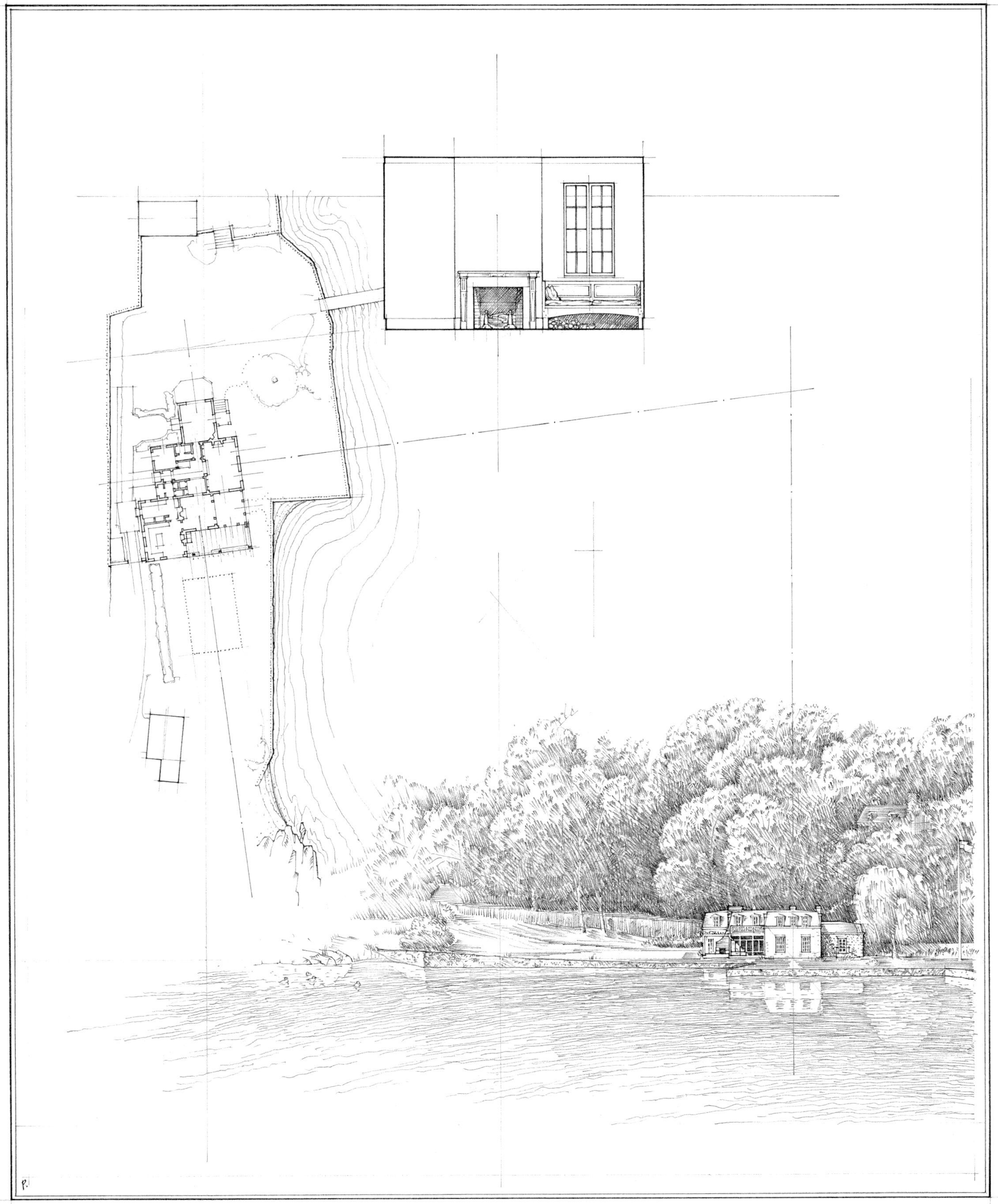

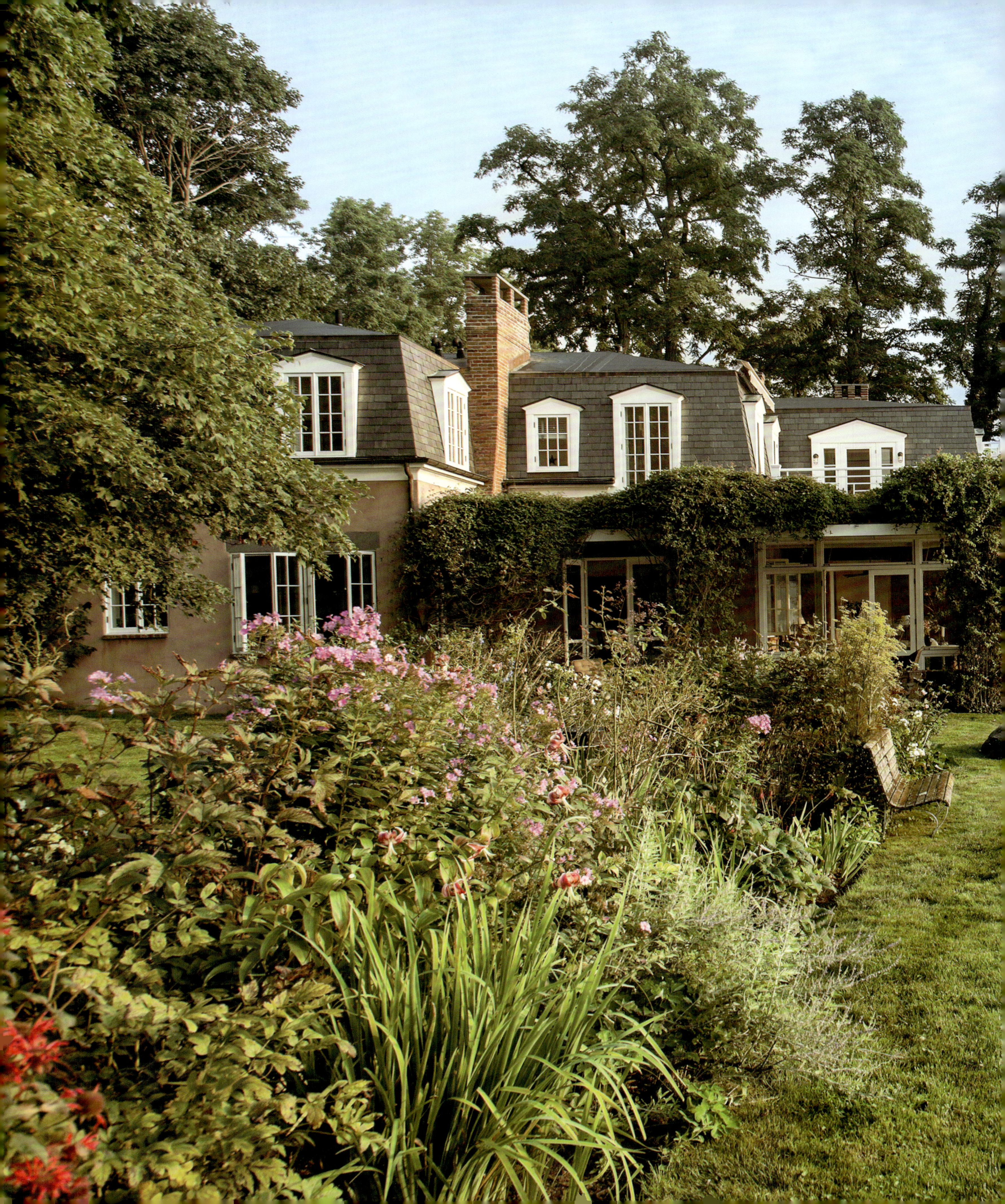

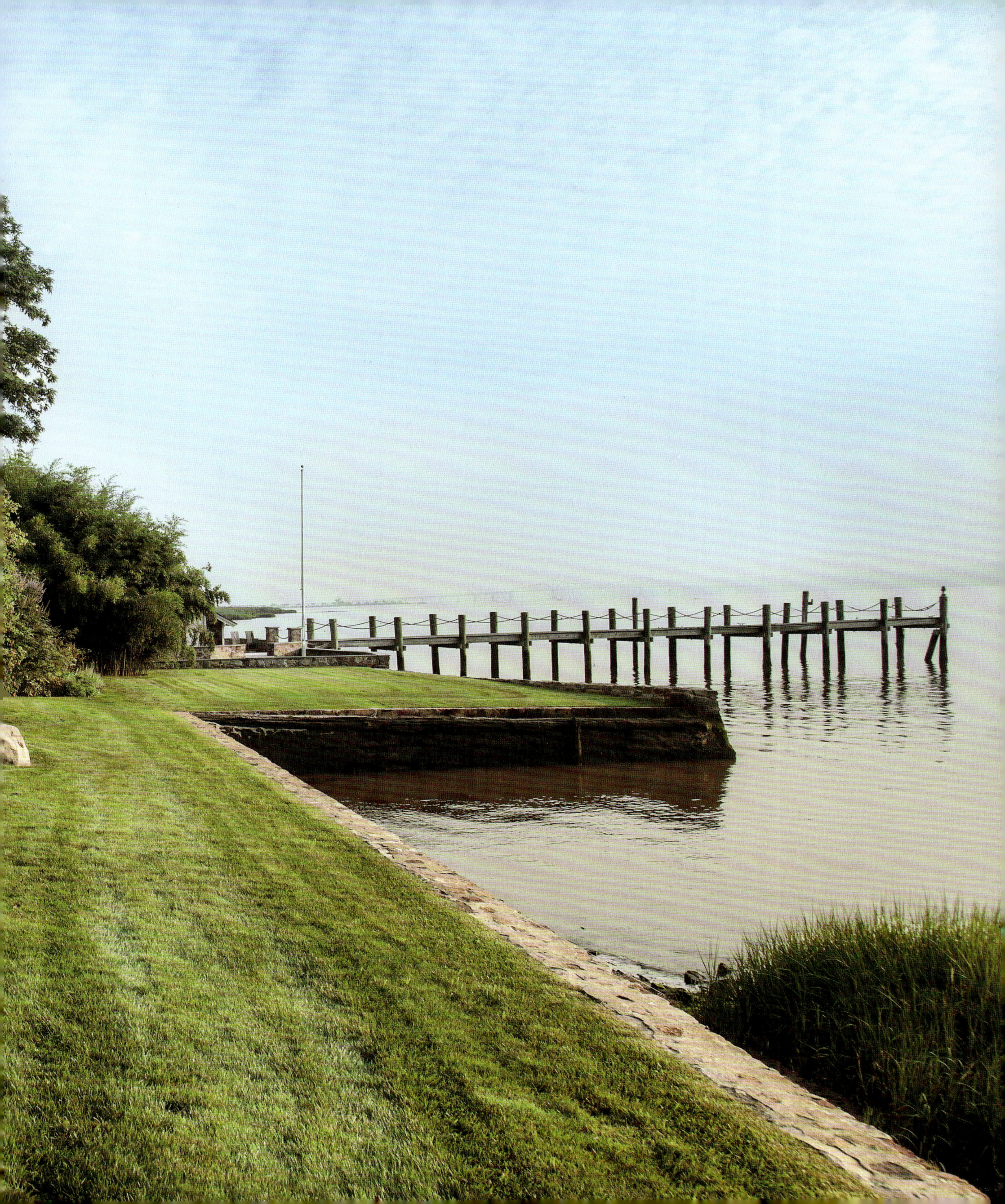

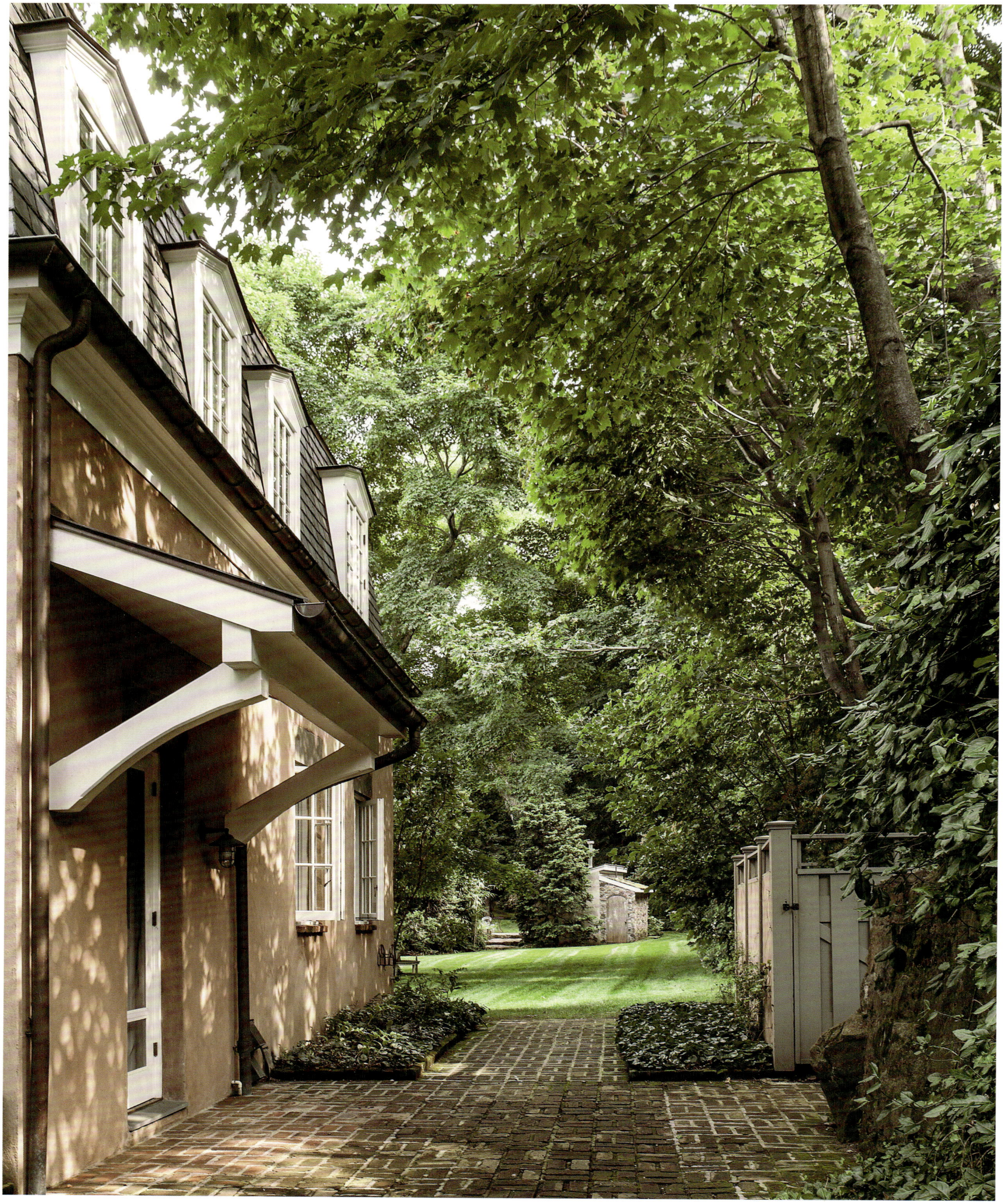

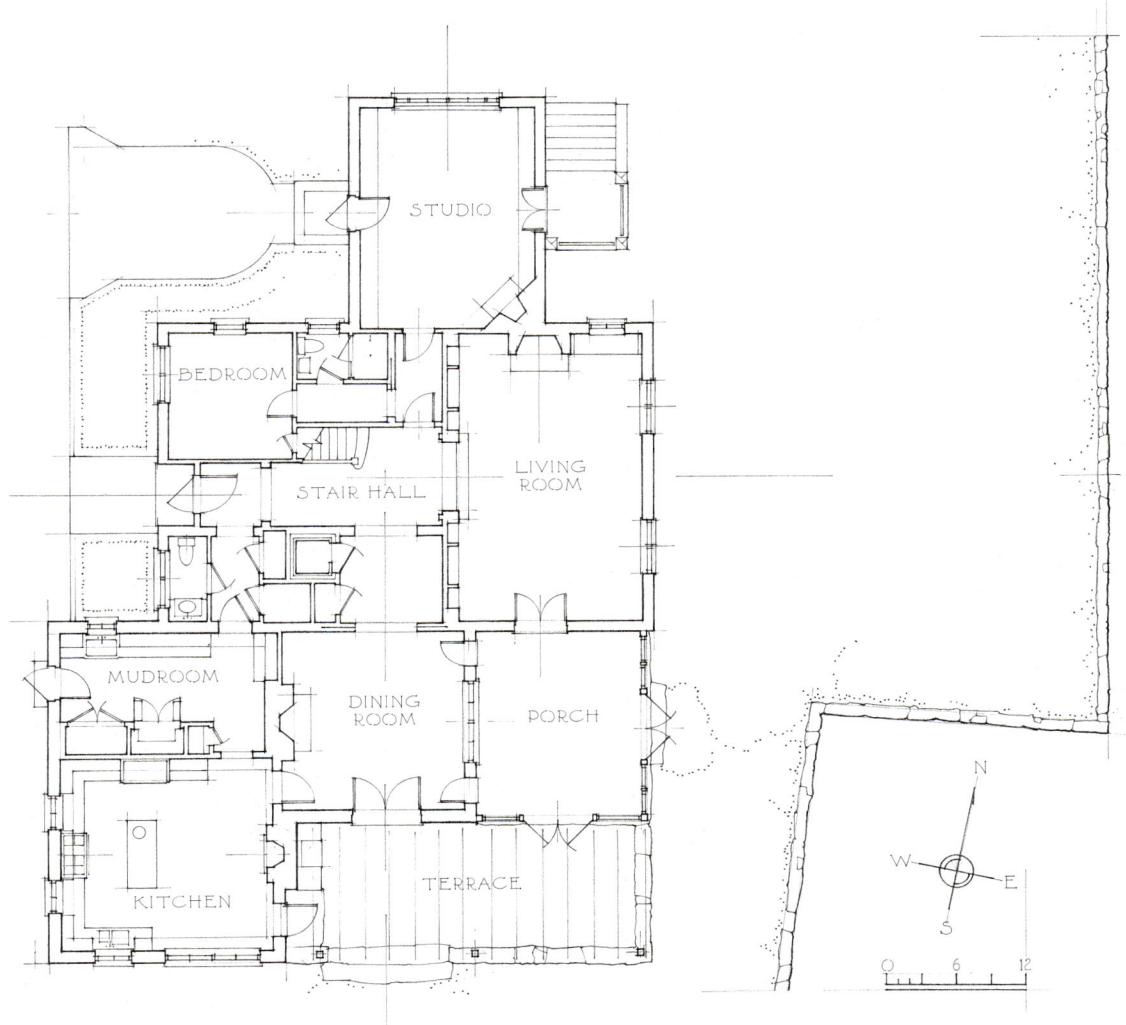

PREVIOUS SPREAD: The goal of the renovation was to maximize the house's presence along the river. OPPOSITE: Under a pent roof, the secondary entrance is via the mudroom adjacent to the kitchen. BELOW: The front door leads to the stair hall. The tinted stucco walls complement the Palisades stone used throughout. BELOW, RIGHT: The south-facing terrace under the pergola is paved in multi-hued Palisades stone.

59

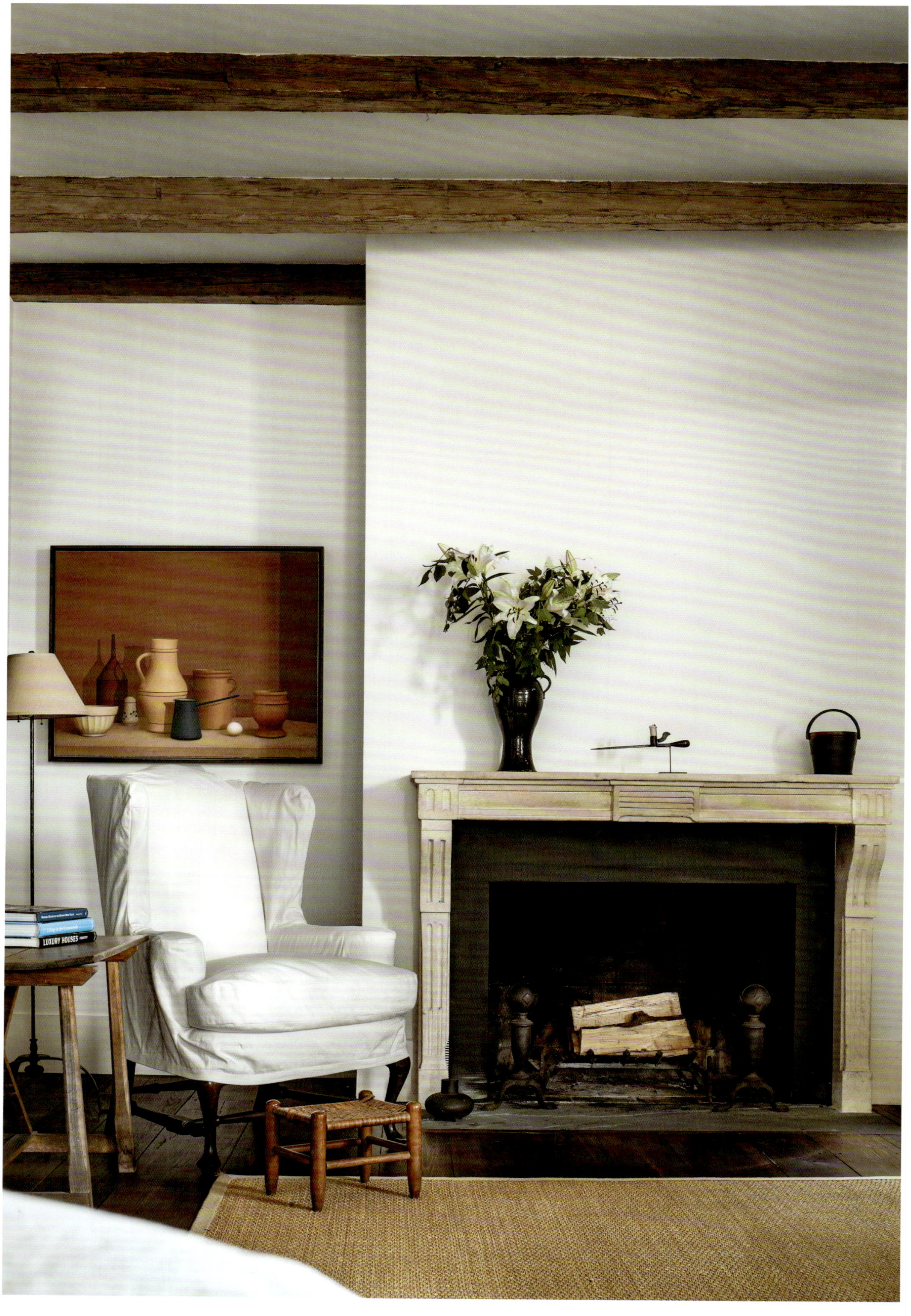
LUXURY HOUSES

Arrayed off the second floor landing are the master bedroom suite, a guest bedroom, and his study. In a first for us, the master bedroom incorporates Harmon-hinged French doors, flanked by sidelites, that open onto a new deck with magnificent river views. Finely engineered casement windows include pull-down screens. The doors from the master bath provide additional access to the deck.

The porch adjacent to the living room offers a transitional area that opens gracefully to the pergola beyond. There, wisteria now cloaks the stone terrace and creates beautifully dappled shade. The effect? A celebration of nature's glories, the wonders of place, and of history, root, branch, and all.

PREVIOUS SPREAD, LEFT: On the living room's north end is a fireplace with a honed slate firebox and antique limestone mantel. The walls are simple plaster. Hand-hewn beams articulate the ceiling. PRECEDING SPREAD, RIGHT: The stair hall steps down to the living room, where cabinetry casings align with the top of the doorway. RIGHT: The living room's east elevation faces the Hudson. Two added windows, the house's only in-swing casements, created wall space for art.

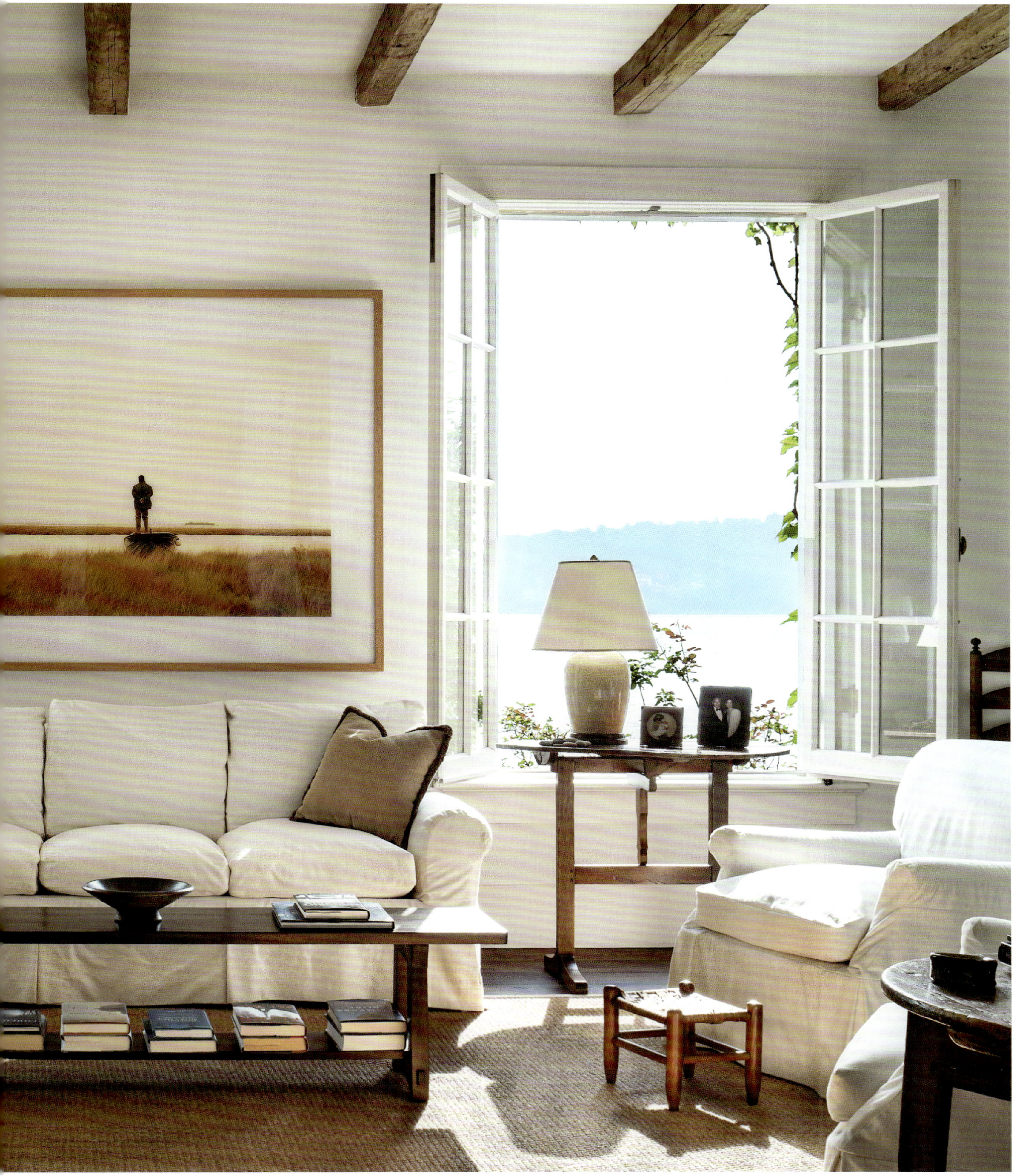

The porch is part of the effort to make the most of the riverside site. Designed for year-round use, it accommodates screens to replace glazing during the warm months. Cast-iron radiators are set into grate-covered troughs in the Palisades stone floor for radiant heat. French doors lead out to the pergola, and a pass-through window opens to the dining room.

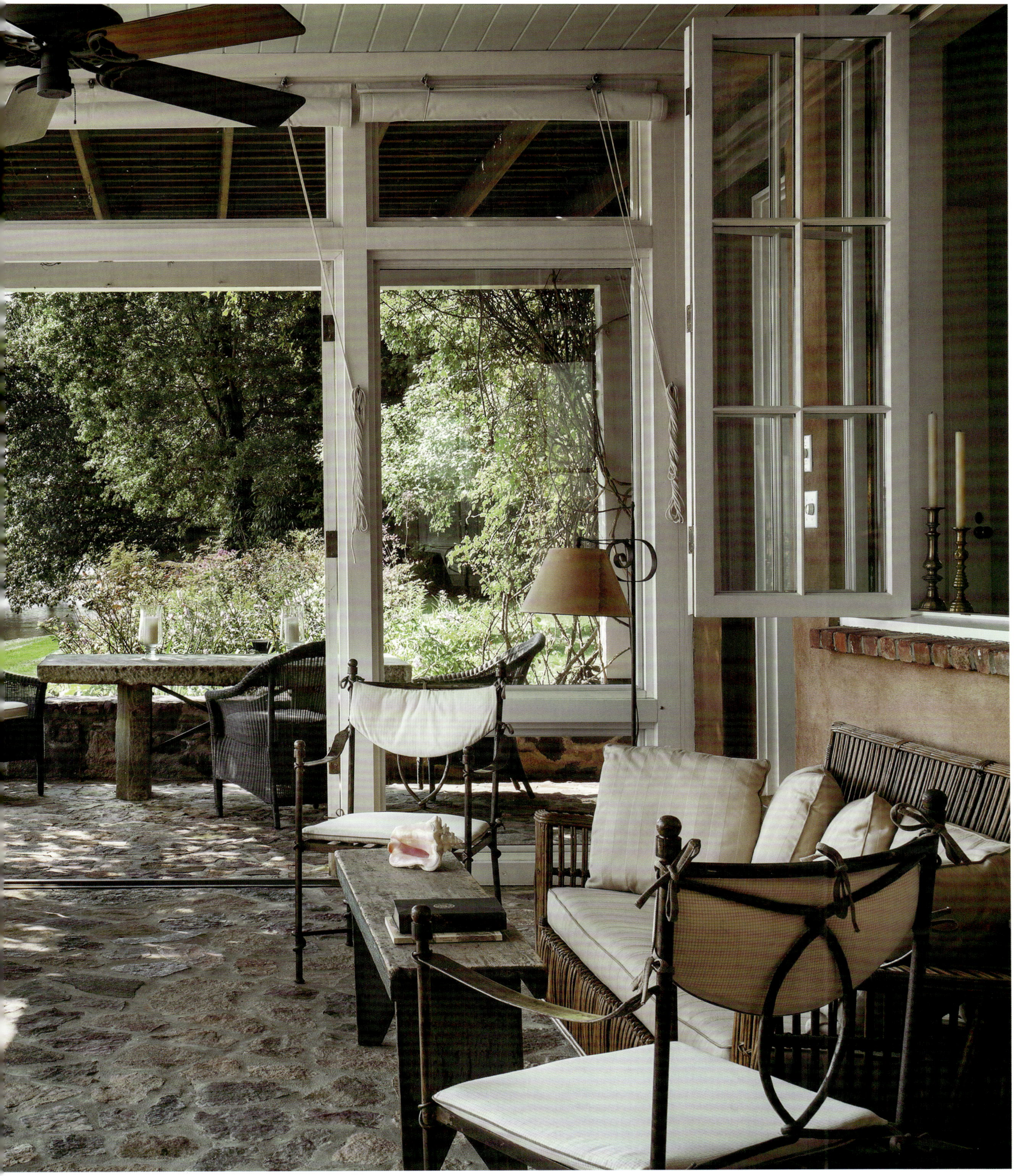

ABOVE: The kitchen ceiling features hand-hewn beams with plaster in-fill. Simple cabinetry frames out-swinging casement windows, each of which has a roll-down screen. Reclaimed wood planks line the floor. OPPOSITE: The kitchen, which opens to the dining room, houses a Rumford fireplace with a raised hearth that creates room underneath for wood storage.

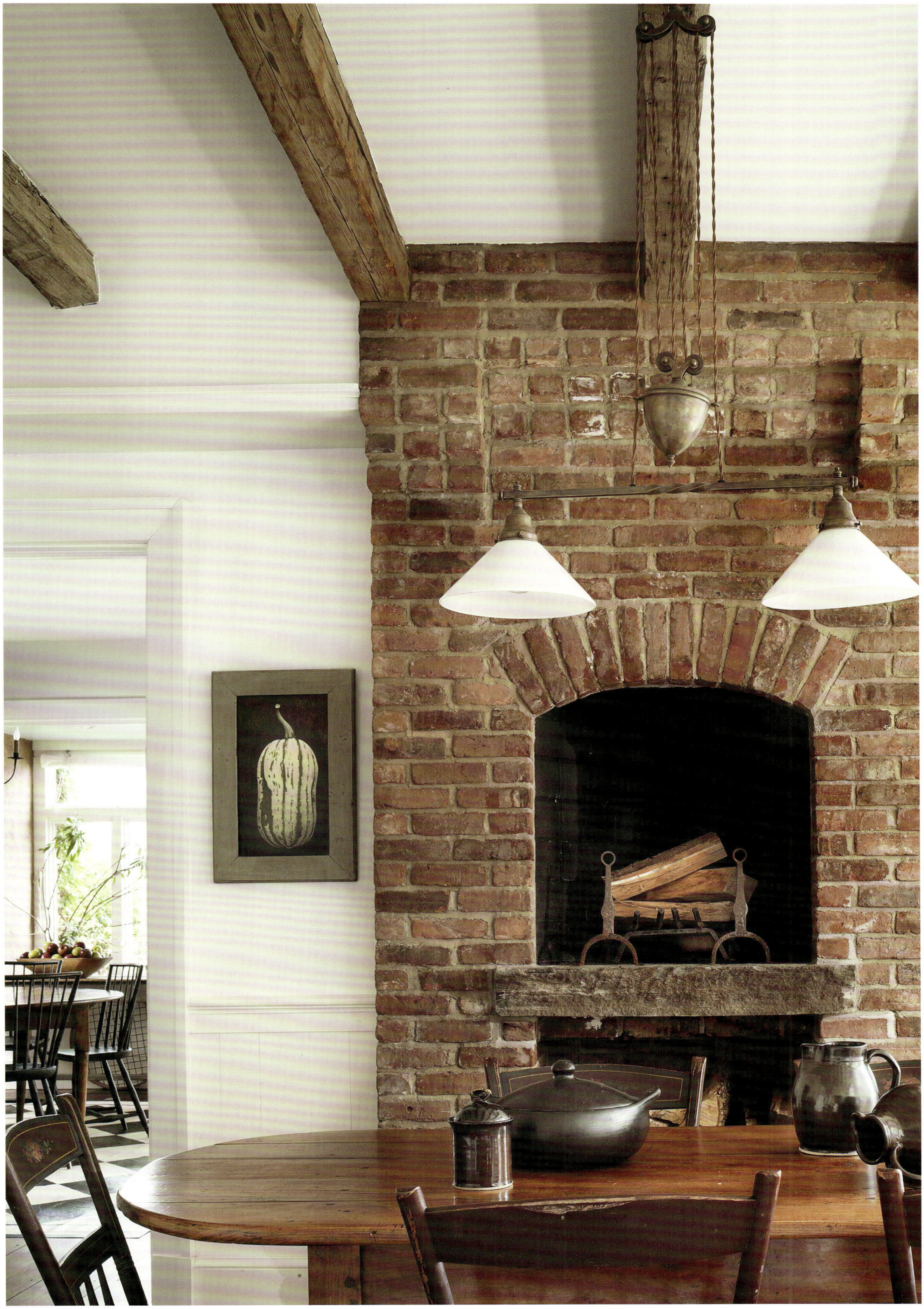

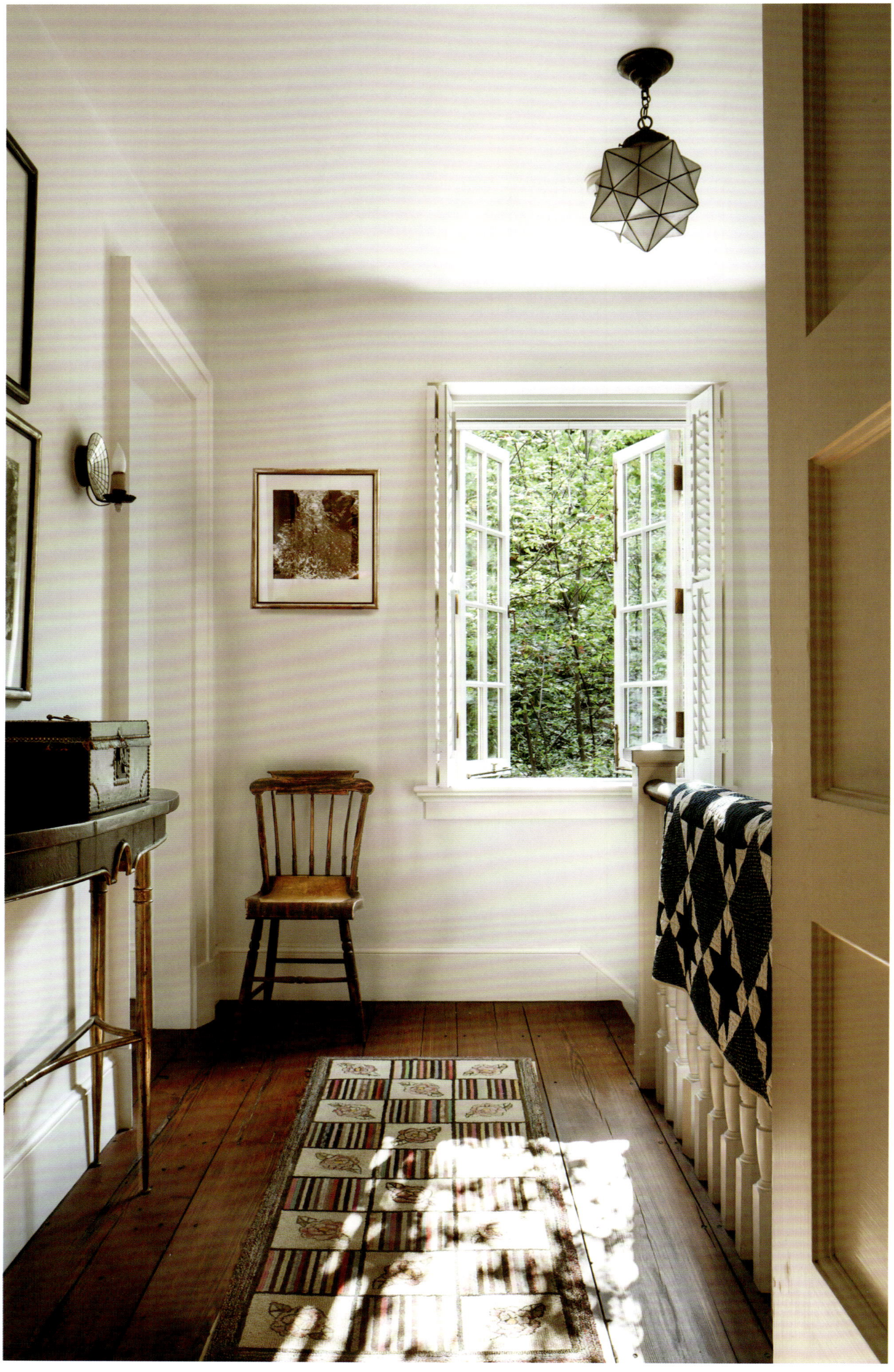

OPPOSITE: On the upstairs landing, the floors are set with cut nails.
ABOVE: The master bedroom faces the river. Three out-swinging windows with pull-down screens make the most of the view.

70

OPPOSITE, ABOVE: In the master bedroom, Harmon-hinged French doors open to the upstairs deck. The doors swing 180 degrees to pocket in perfect alignment with the sidelites. OPPOSITE, BELOW: In the master bath, a pair of single-glazed doors opens to the upstairs deck on the left and right sides of the vanity. ABOVE: The mansard roof was a given with the massing of the original house and a significant part of its charm. An Arts and Crafts pattern influenced the design of the balustrade. In addition to the French doors, the master bedroom also has a single screen door that leads to the attached deck.

Approaching Perfection

For an architect, perfection is relative. So are dream clients. But when the clients come as close as possible to the ideal, chances are the project will too. That's what happened here. Discerning and experienced, this couple—Francophiles in design sensibility and understanding of the art of craft—loves absolutely everything about the design process. The first presentation, the refining of the floor plan and architectural details, the final selection of materials—all engage them, as Llewellyn Sinkler, their decorator, and I know well from working with them on two other residences. So when they opted to move from their longtime Park Avenue home to this 4,000-square-foot, full-floor Fifth Avenue residence, they took charge of the project wholeheartedly.

The initial decision: strip the interior to the concrete and reconstruct it anew. The goal: create a refined, seamless, utterly natural twenty-first century environment within the early-twentieth-century structure. The clients wanted the apartment to function at a superior level for family living. And they wanted it to incorporate all of the latest technological amenities.

We organized the rooms and their flow to support their five-person family, refining the floor plan to ensure that private areas were out of sight and public areas open, polished, and presentational. We abjured any direct historical references in the architectural detailing, and instead reinterpreted the classical vocabulary to suit the family's needs and the proportional requirements of the room.

A coved ceiling in the entry and a vaulted hallway leading to the private family areas add interest and rhythm to the volumes. Strategically composed moldings in the gallery lightly articulate the walls. Shallow cornices that extend onto the ceiling visually enhance the wall height. Complementary, but distinctly differentiated details distinguish one room from the next yet instill a sense of flow throughout. Some ornamental selections have an almost mid-twentieth-century sensibility, to suit the eventual decor.

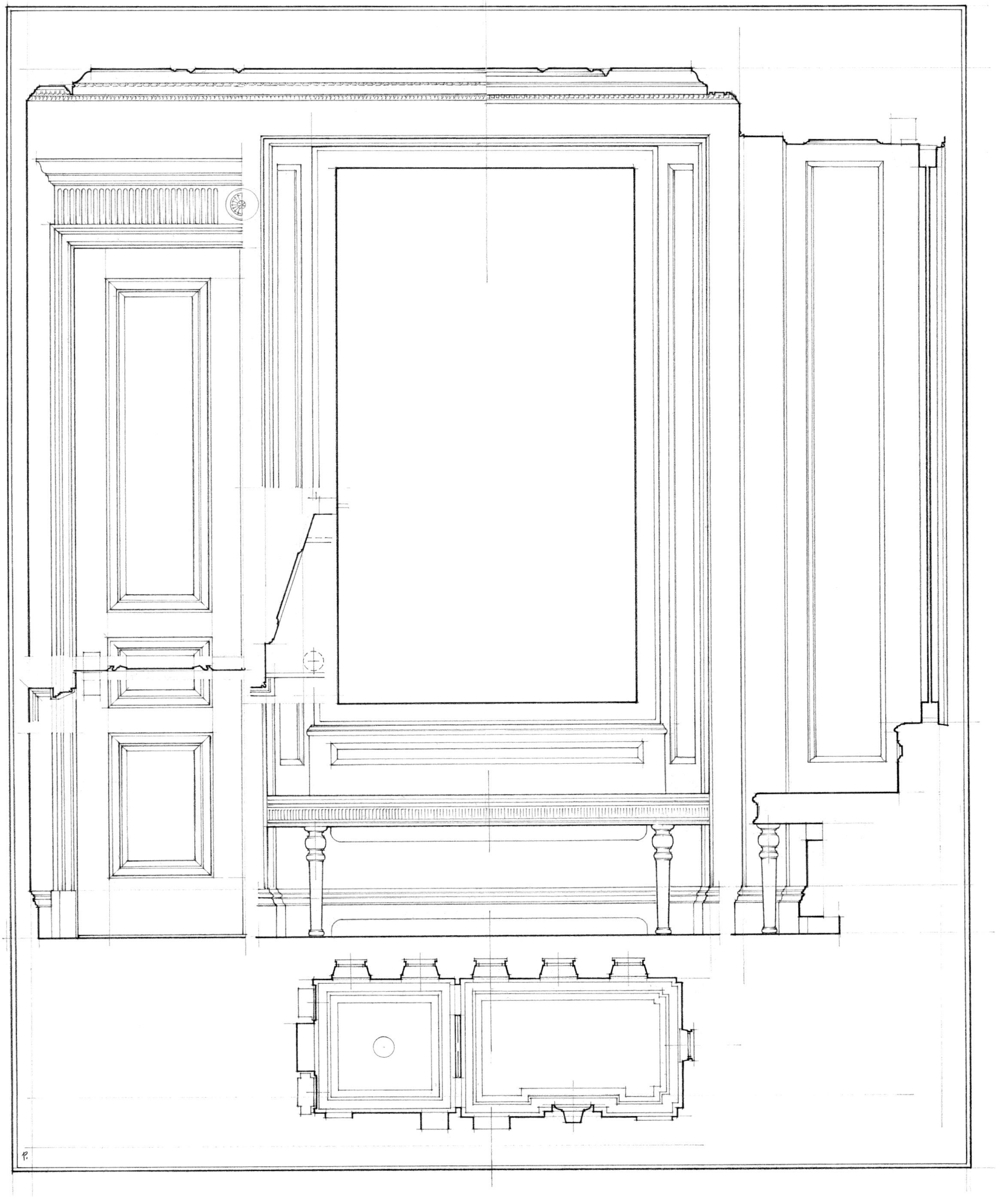
P.

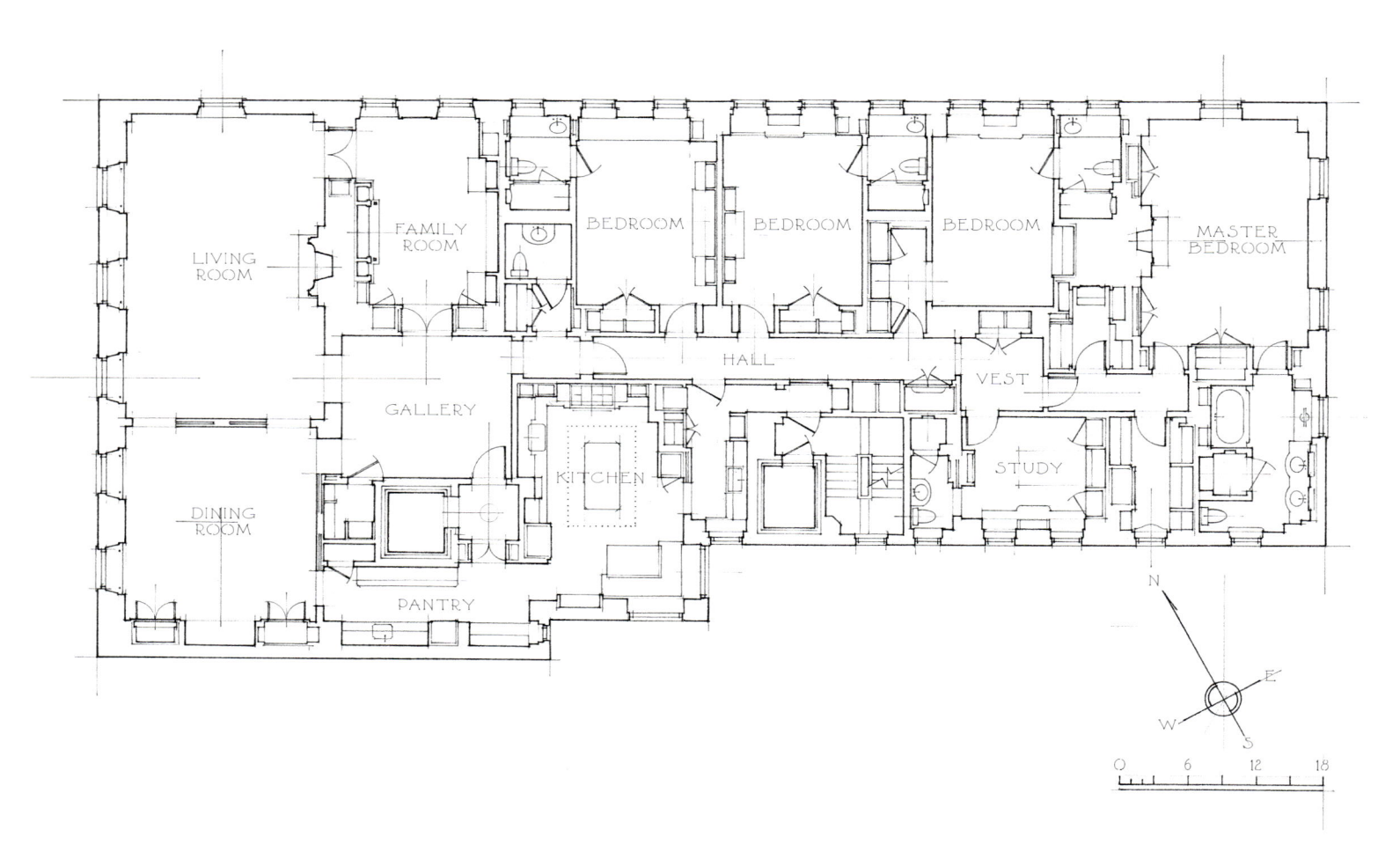

OPPOSITE: Of French-polished mahogany, the main door has a single oversized pull. The floral floor medallion, repeated in the gallery, combines onyx with bronze in a field of Botticino marble.
DETAIL AT LEFT: The gallery doors sandwich seeded restoration glass set in a steel frame with lead caning between decorative bronze grilles.

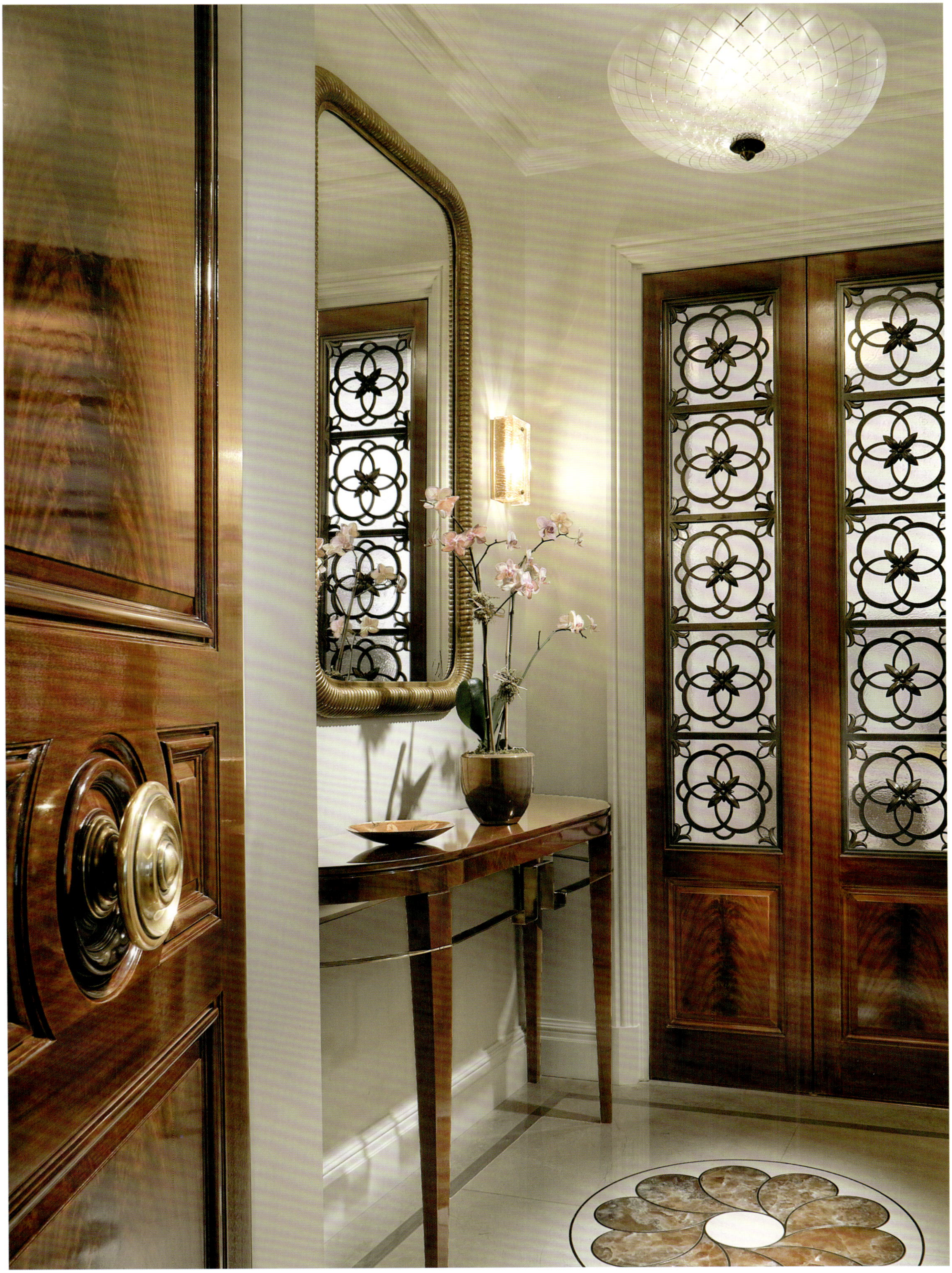

Applied panel molding subtly articulates the gallery walls. Above the cornice is a cove with integrated lighting. Articulated in two species of marble, the pattern of the gallery floor features a rectangular border framing an elliptical band that circumnavigates the perimeter; at the center is an onyx, bronze, and marble floral medallion akin to that of the entry.

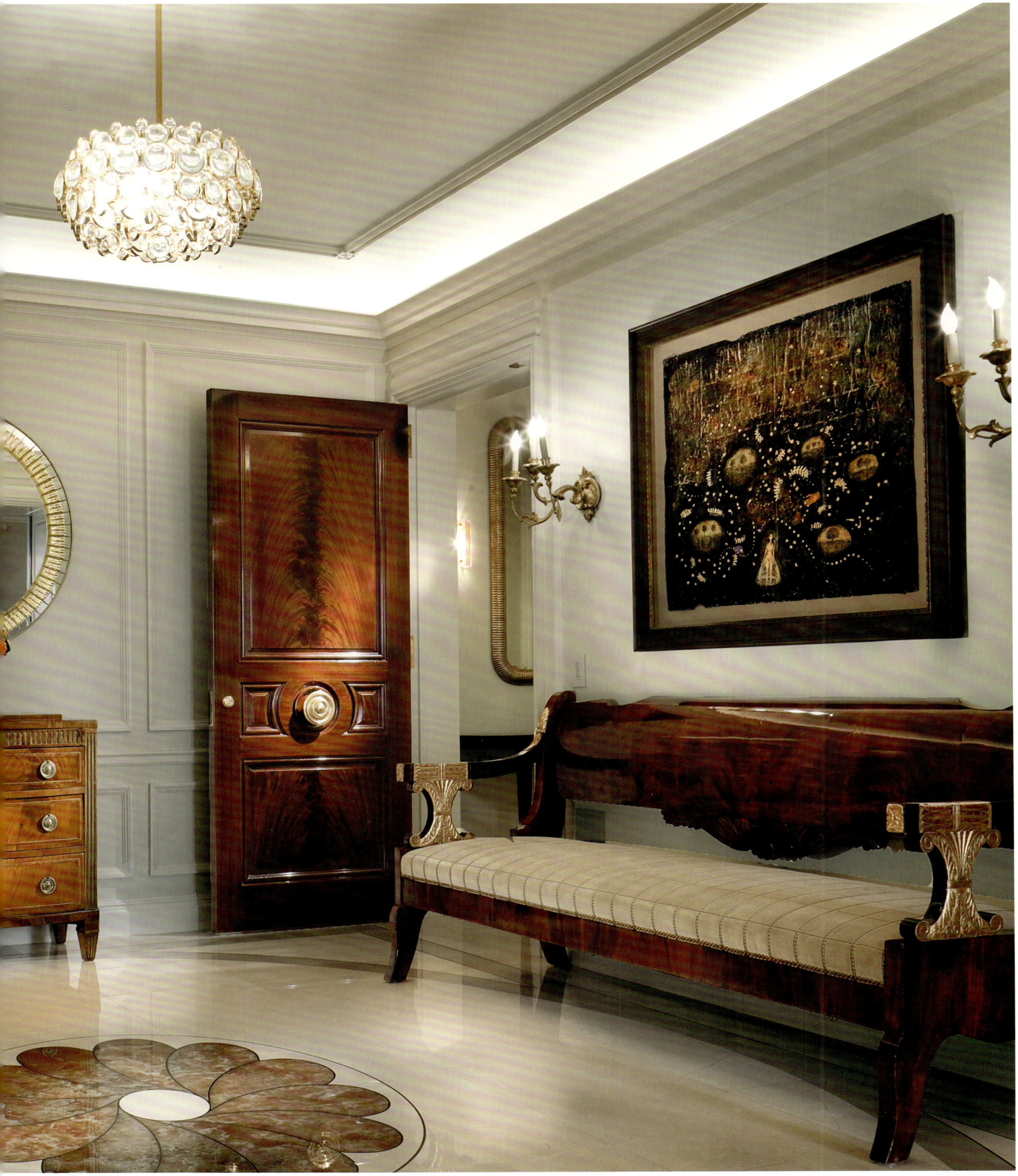

Tall doorways in the living room create an illusion of added height. Symmetrical framed doorways on the room's south face lead to the dining room. The limestone fireplace mantel is antique with a new shaped and honed black slate surround. To accentuate the height of the walls, a shallow cornice extends onto a ceiling articulated with applied plaster bands.

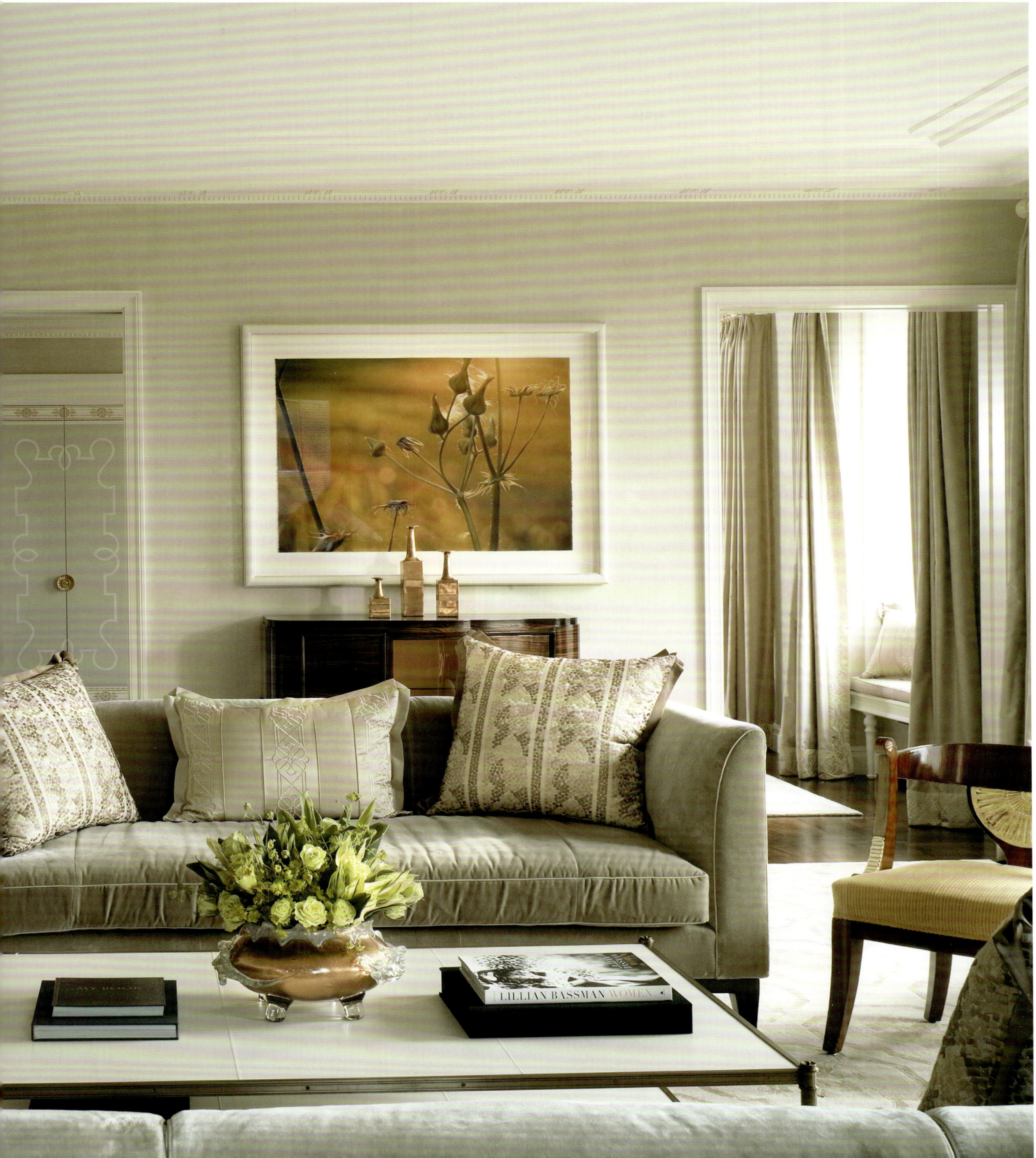
LILLIAN BASSMAN WOMEN

This apartment's golden element is the view to the west. How could we not make the most of it? The process of developing the enhanced architectural articulation for the five identical windows proved to be among the most technically demanding and one of the more satisfying aspects of this project. Each is a completely refined millwork construct, just like a cabinet. The chamfered enclosures incorporate pockets for a motorized shade, beaded outboard edges, paneling at the head and at the jamb, and stone sills above bench-like window seats that conceal the apartment's steam radiators. The repetition creates a visual force.

The unusual level of refinement also extends to the palette of materials and surfaces. The exotic woods include French-polished and crotch mahogany, anigre, avodire, and burled walnut, with eight-inch-wide planks of American black walnut for many of the floors. The pièce de résistance? Bespoke components of a kind, variety, and scale that every architect aspires to create at least once in a professional lifetime.

Custom-crafted elements begin, exceptionally, with the entry foyer doors: set into French-polished mahogany frames, the ornamental forged and repoussé metal grilles lie in front of custom antique seeded glass, and give a secondary window-like glimpse from the entry foyer to the kitchen. The foliate motifs of the grilles echo those of the entry foyer and gallery's onyx-and-bronze floor medallions, decorative flourishes inspired by the design of the husband's cufflinks. The entry door's unusual, large singular knob in burnished brass is yet another made-to-measure element. The range of extraordinary design and fabrication opportunities certainly contributes to an environment where everything truly is just so, from the floor plan to the nth detail.

LEFT: A detail of the living room's ornamental cornice as it breaks around the chimney breast reveals finials, attenuated and delicate, that recall modillion blocks. OPPOSITE: The five windows that face Central Park are identically appointed with a chamfered jamb, an integrated bench articulated like a window seat, a stone window stool, and a motorized solar shade.

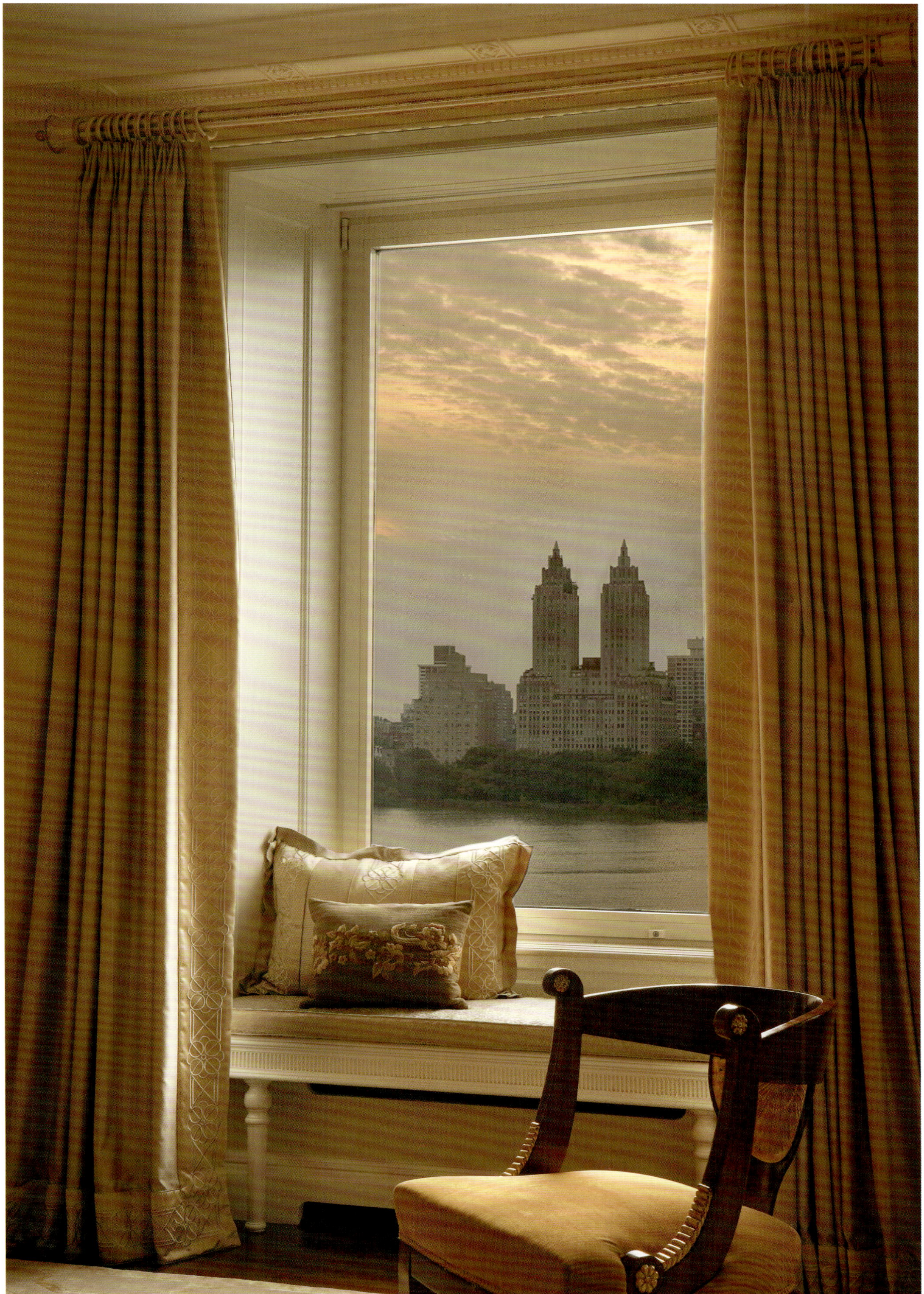

The consistent treatment of the windows along the
Fifth Avenue elevation creates a dramatic architectural
effect. Fluted friezes ornament the overdoors of
the dining room passages. The living and dining room
moldings are equally attenuated but contrasting in
scale, which subtly reinforces the identity of each room
and differentiates one from the other.

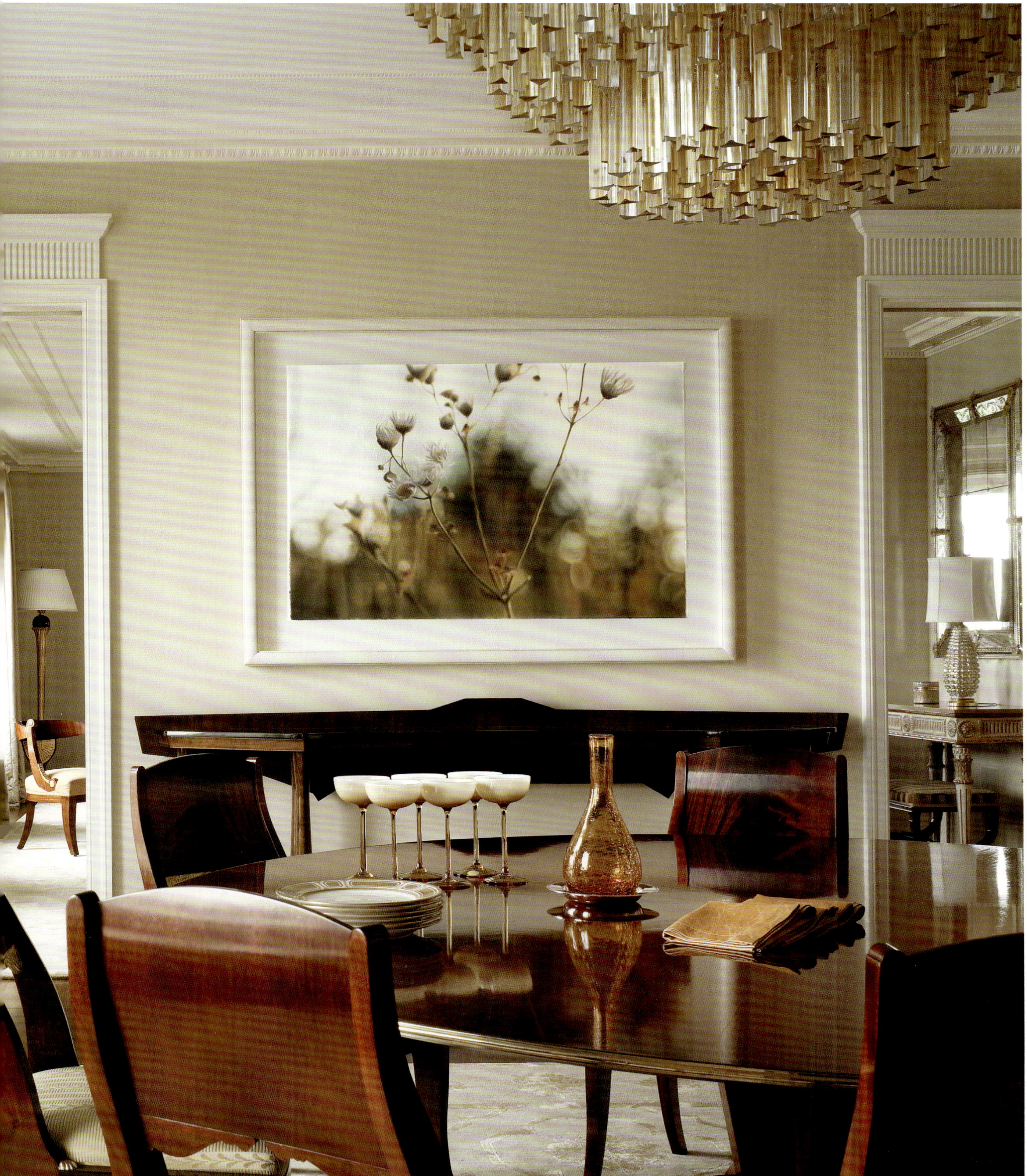

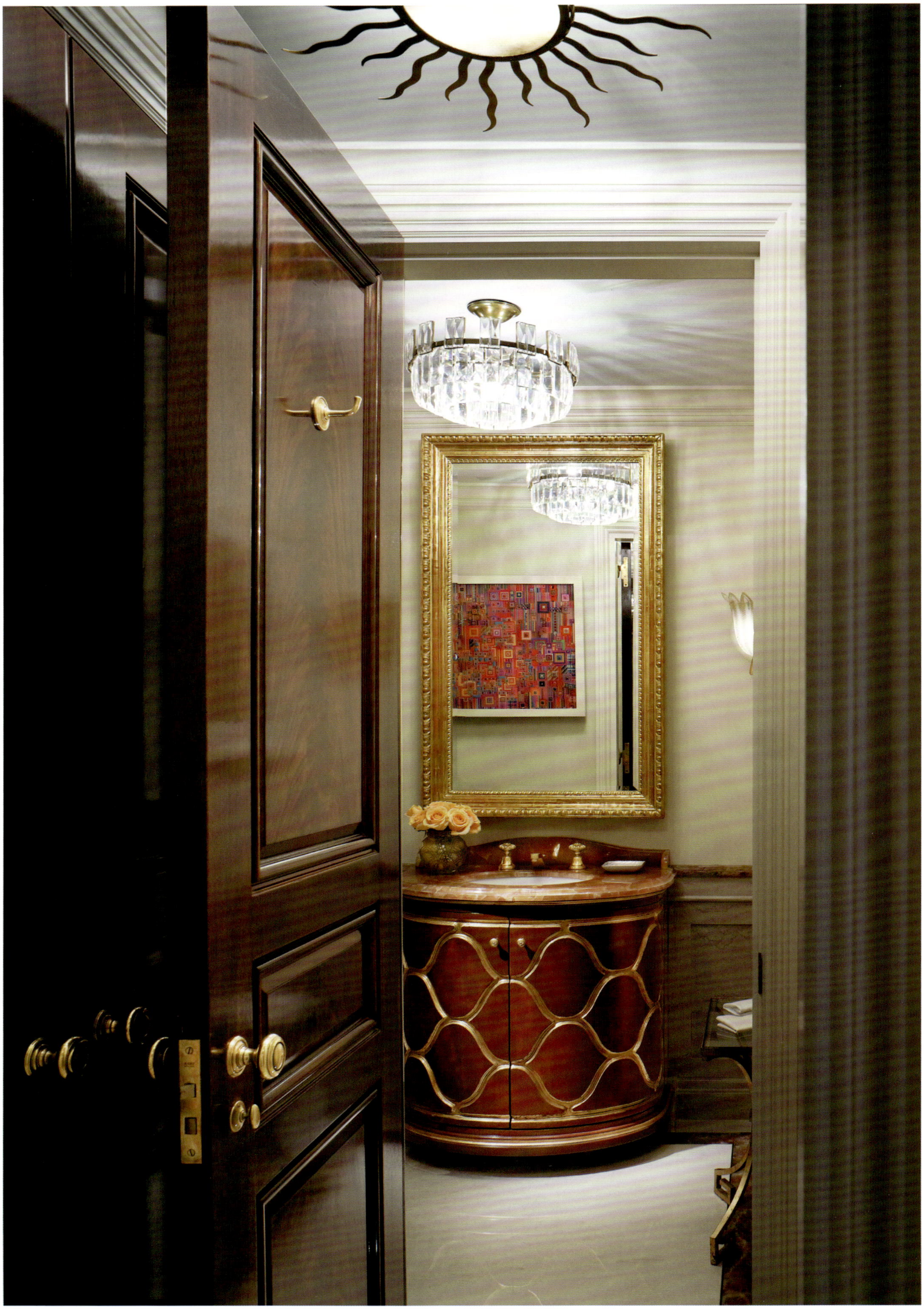

OPPOSITE: The stone floor of the gallery extends into the adjacent powder room, which also has a stone wainscot and a custom vanity with stone top. ABOVE: Through mahogany doors off the gallery is the anigre-paneled family room, where built-in anigre storage and display units support a range of uses. The hardware is finished in durable antique gold.

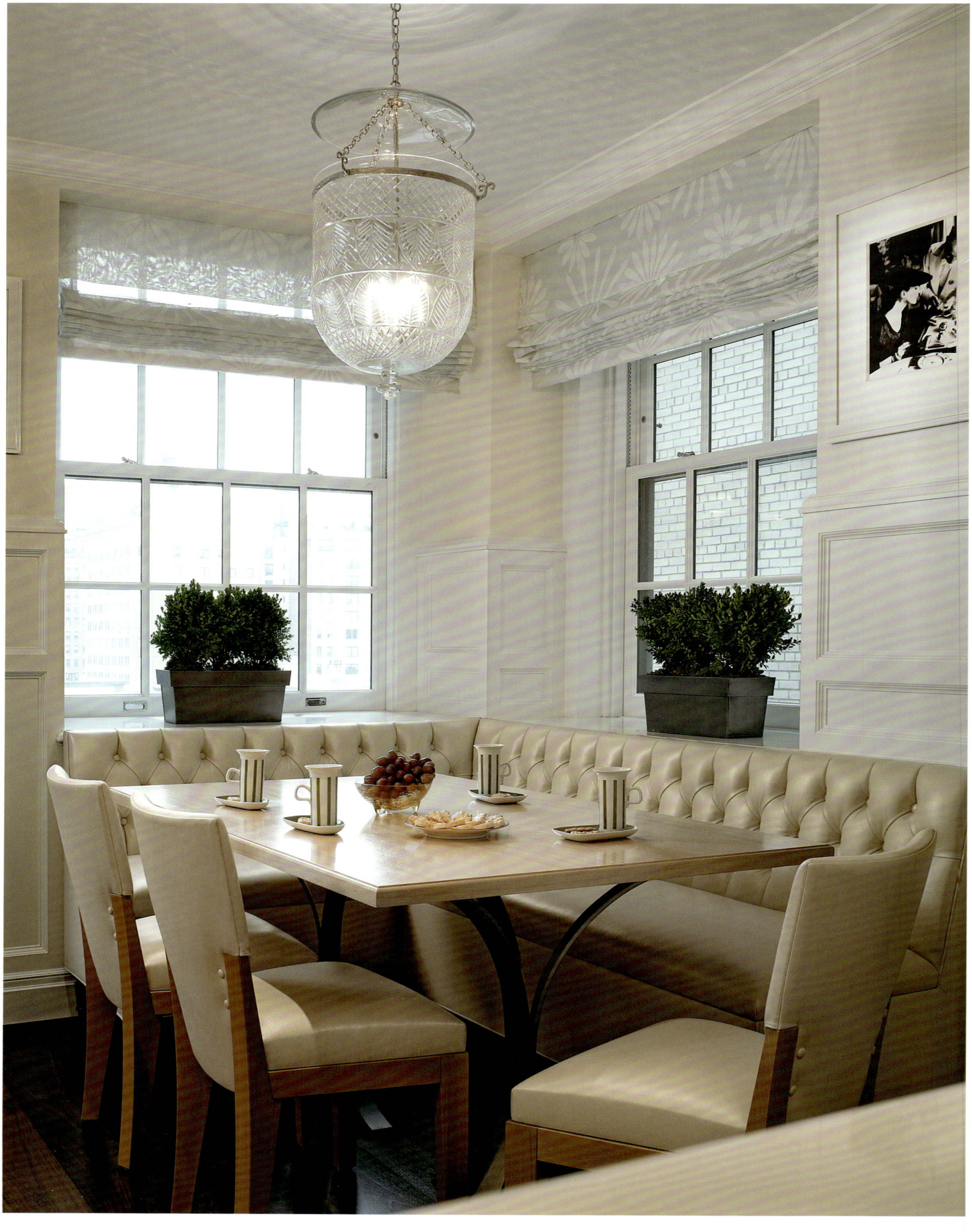

OPPOSITE: The built-in banquette area seats six. ABOVE: Lifting the ceiling over the kitchen island enhanced the custom pot rack, which has engraved plates with the initials of each family member and the numeric address of each family residence. Seeded glass doors partially obscure the contents of the kitchen cabinets. The gold-veined marble of the paneled backsplash adds dimension to the mostly white space.

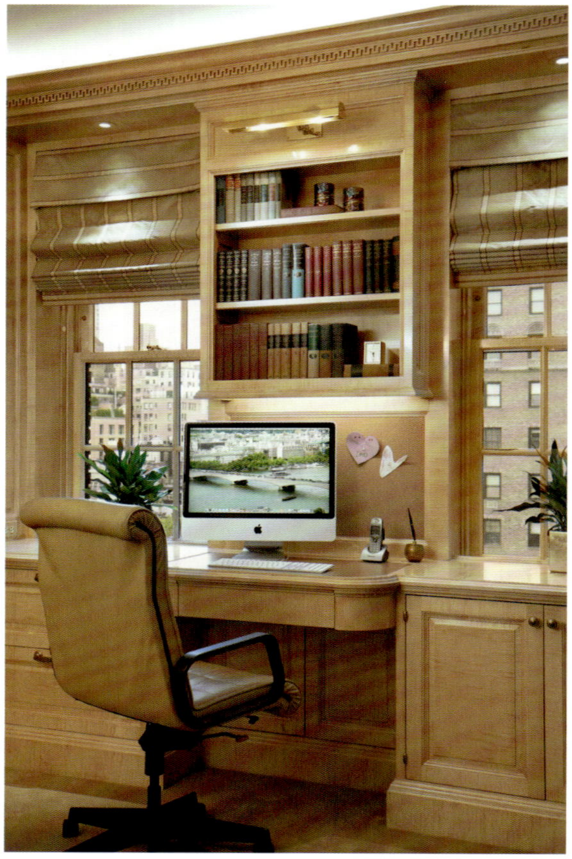
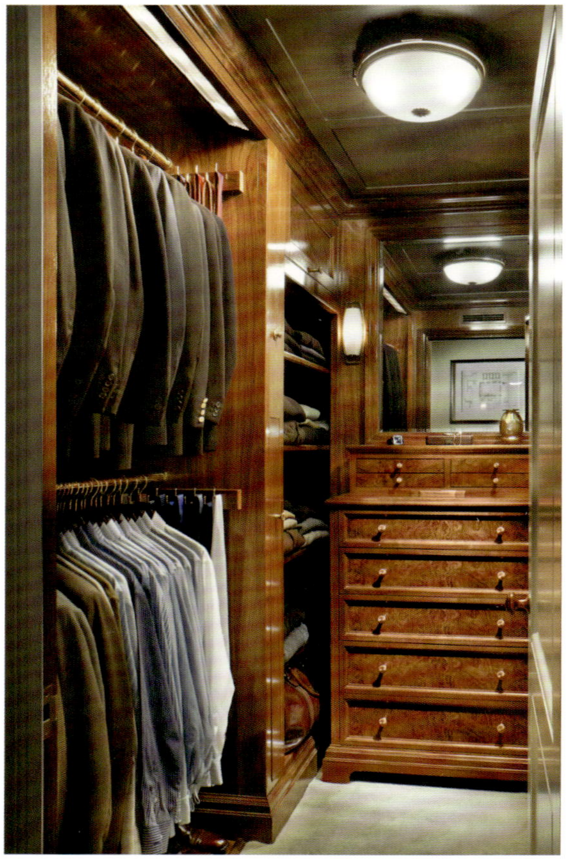
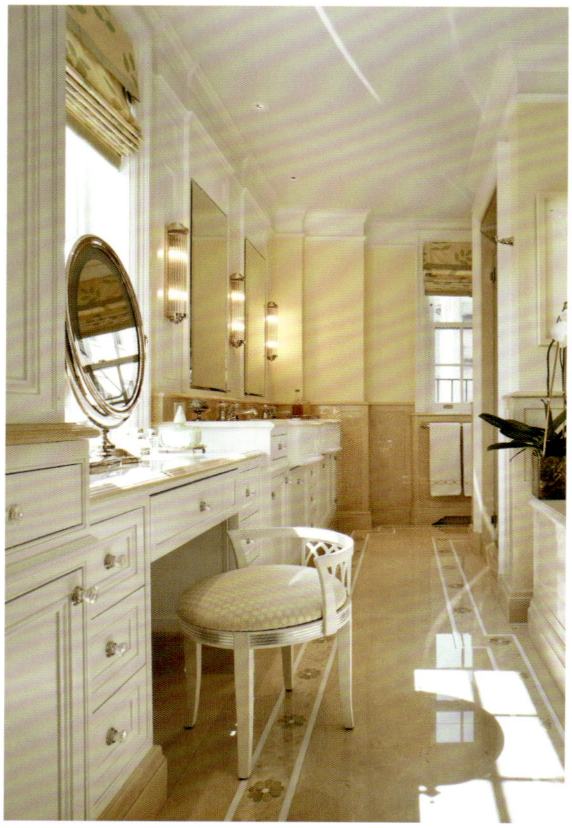
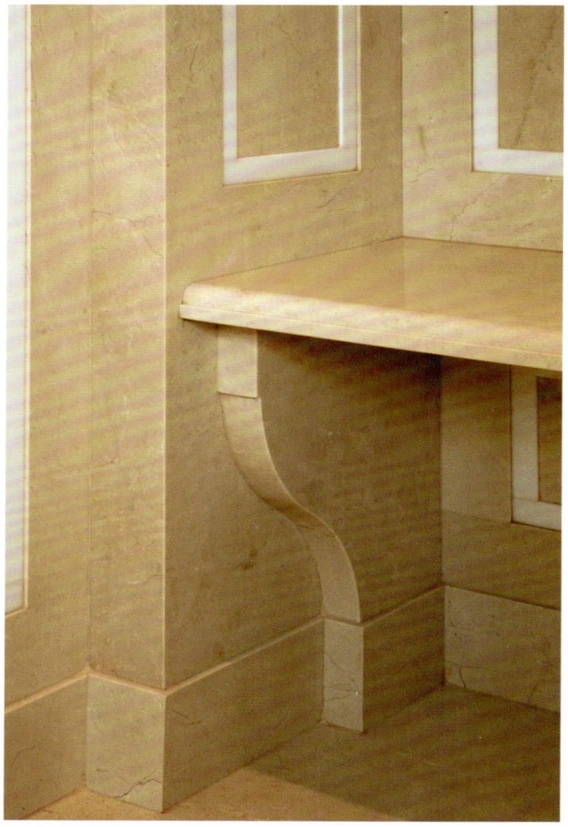

OPPOSITE, CLOCKWISE FROM TOP LEFT: His study is paneled in avodire wood; his dressing room is lined in walnut with a burl veneer; a stone bench in the steam shower is framed by stone paneled walls with contrasting stone banding; a custom mosaic band adds interest to the stone floor of the master bath, where her vanity area includes a custom makeup mirror. ABOVE: The plaster soffit in the master bedroom incorporates overhead lights that, like those on an airplane, can shift direction and focus as required.

Form and Finesse

Building a house is a labor of love, trust, and commitment for all involved. Yet despite a team's best efforts, sometimes the end result simply doesn't work the way everyone envisioned. That's the reason this New York–based family commissioned us to renovate and reconfigure their traditional nineteenth-century-style four-bedroom Connecticut weekend getaway, which was perfectly adequate but not as functionally effective as they wished for their twenty-first-century family lifestyle.

Having designed this family's first New York apartment, we knew them and their preferences. Passionate about design and experienced in the process, they diagnosed the roots of their problem in straightforward terms. They felt that the house lacked an informal dining area and any family space off of the kitchen, the heart of their family lifestyle. They also found the screened porch to be uncomfortable and difficult to maintain.

Resolving these issues while maintaining as much as possible of the existing house required considerable finesse on our part and that of their decorator, Llewellyn Sinkler. Demolishing the screened porch proved key to achieving the kind of family-centric, multi-functional area that made sense for them. We replaced the porch with a family room. Then we created an addition for casual dining with a wraparound porch, and renovated the kitchen.

The family room now includes an intimate alcove area with a game table, and shares back-to-back fireplaces with the wraparound porch. I'm a firm believer that no family room should be without plenty of natural light—the more the merrier, and from all directions if possible. Instead of a skylight, we installed a monitor, which tends to soften the light as it comes in laterally through clerestories. For fun, we used four shades of restoration glass; the monitor's drum contains faceted mirrors that reflect and highlight that polychrome effect.

The primary reason we found ourselves finessing the existing spaces and inserting new ones was the desire to create a fully unified composition. Our guiding thought was to enhance the functionality of each room and create easy circulation within the interior spaces and from the interior rooms through the

91

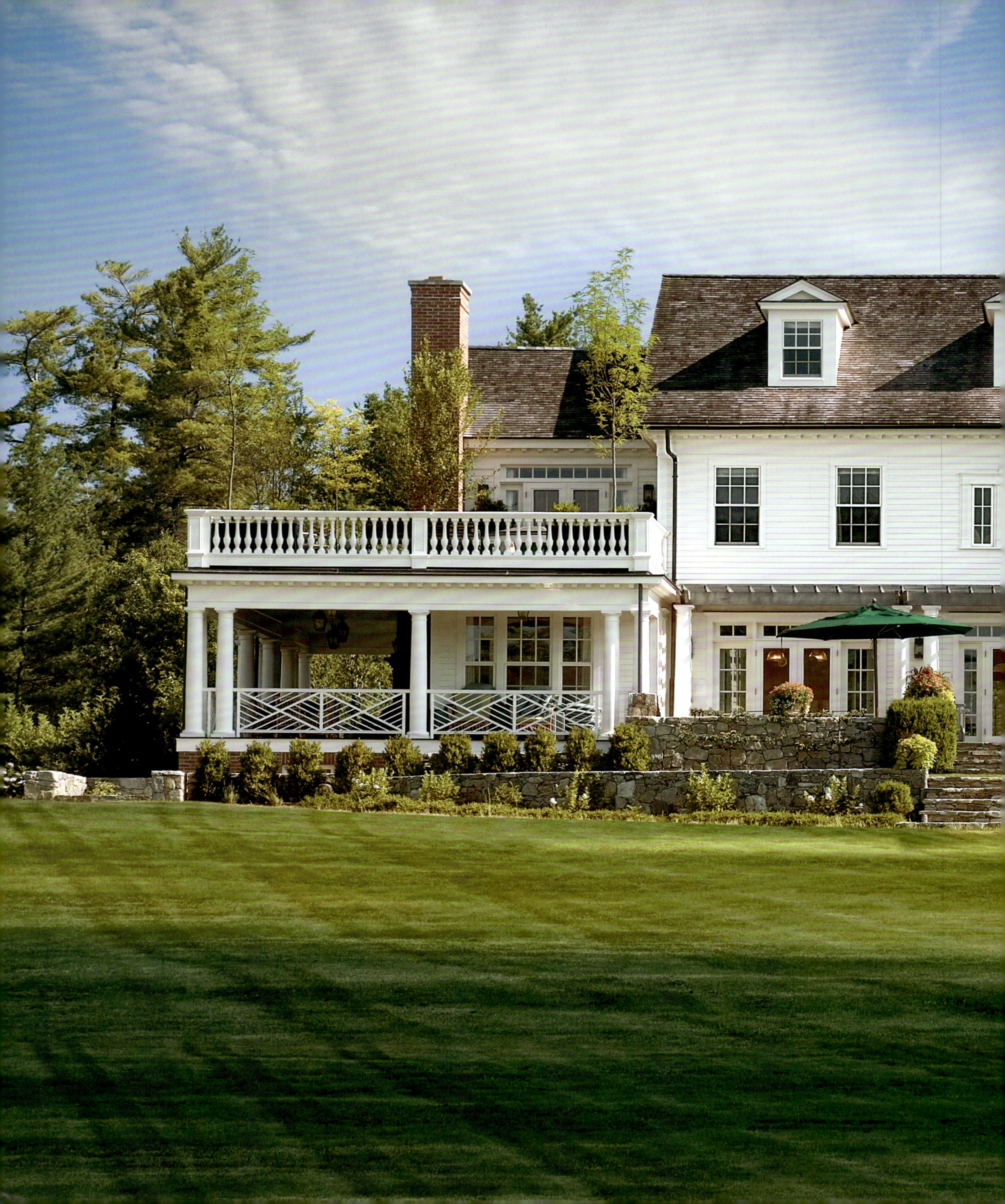

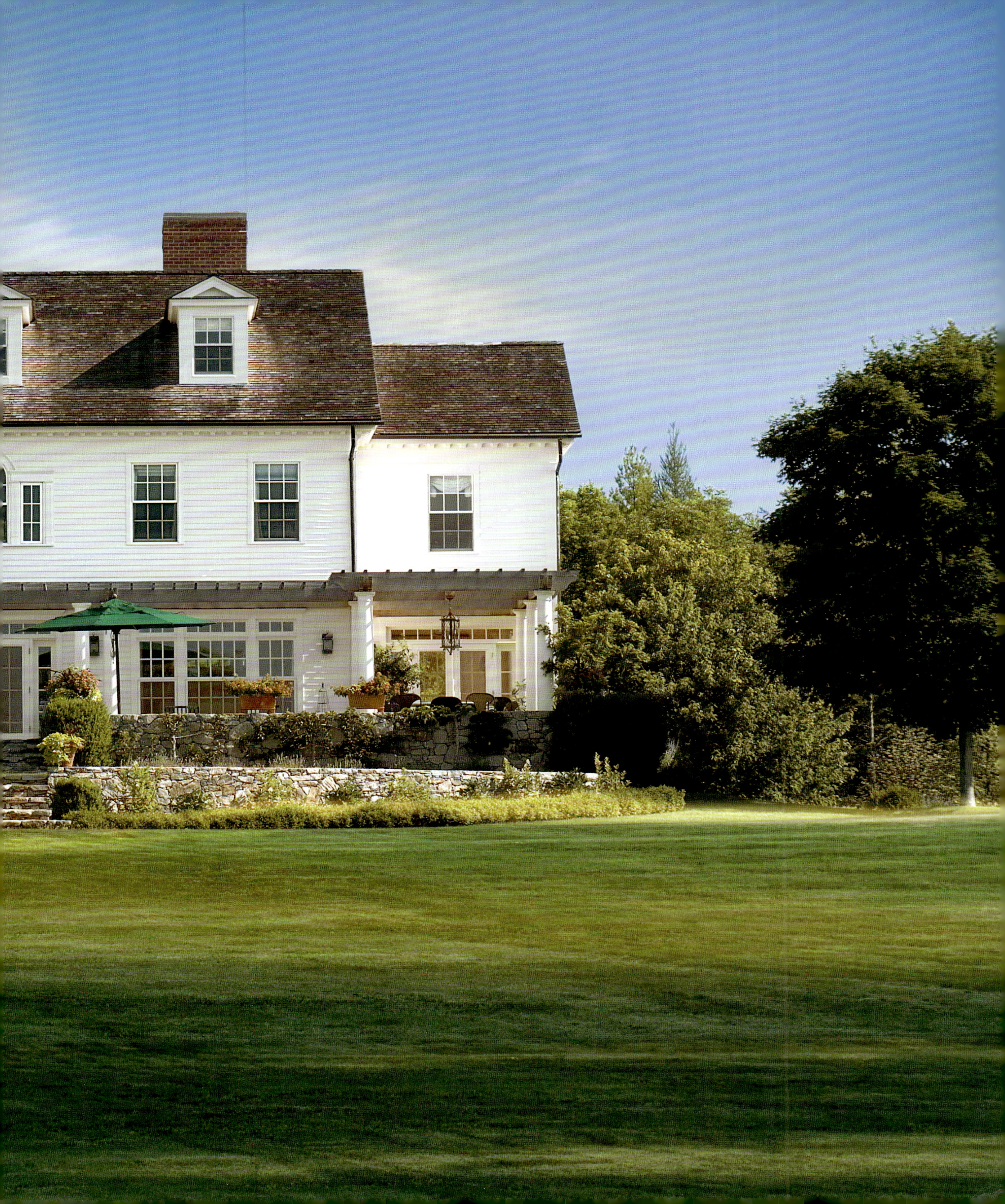

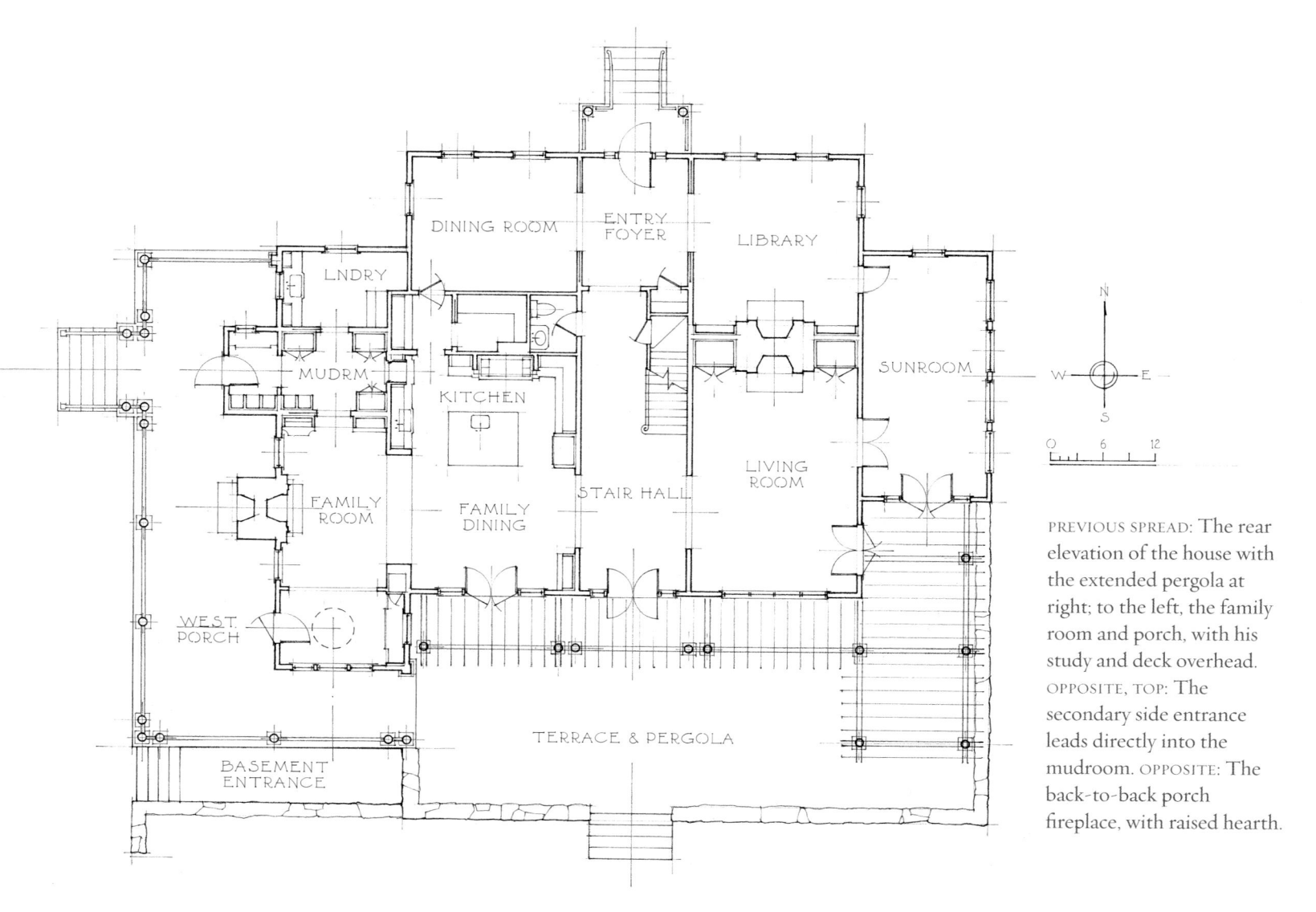

PREVIOUS SPREAD: The rear elevation of the house with the extended pergola at right; to the left, the family room and porch, with his study and deck overhead. OPPOSITE, TOP: The secondary side entrance leads directly into the mudroom. OPPOSITE: The back-to-back porch fireplace, with raised hearth.

transitional areas to the exterior rooms. With that in mind, and as the project grew to involve a new pool and pool house, our goal for the addition was that it should resolve the way the house opened itself up toward the newly active section of property. To that end, we made sure the addition included a porch and pergola that wraps two sides of the facade.

Like so many renovations, this one evolved as it proceeded. We built out the basement area completely, finishing it with a wine room, exercise room, bunkroom and sauna. The second and third floors received adjustments as well: the newly finished upstairs study afforded access to the roof of the wraparound porch, which became an important deck area for family use.

The mudroom then required a transformation. Since the original secondary entrance was somewhat awkward, we devised a new floor plan for a mudroom that fed into the laundry and family room. With that final component of reinvention, the house became what they had originally intended—and so much more.

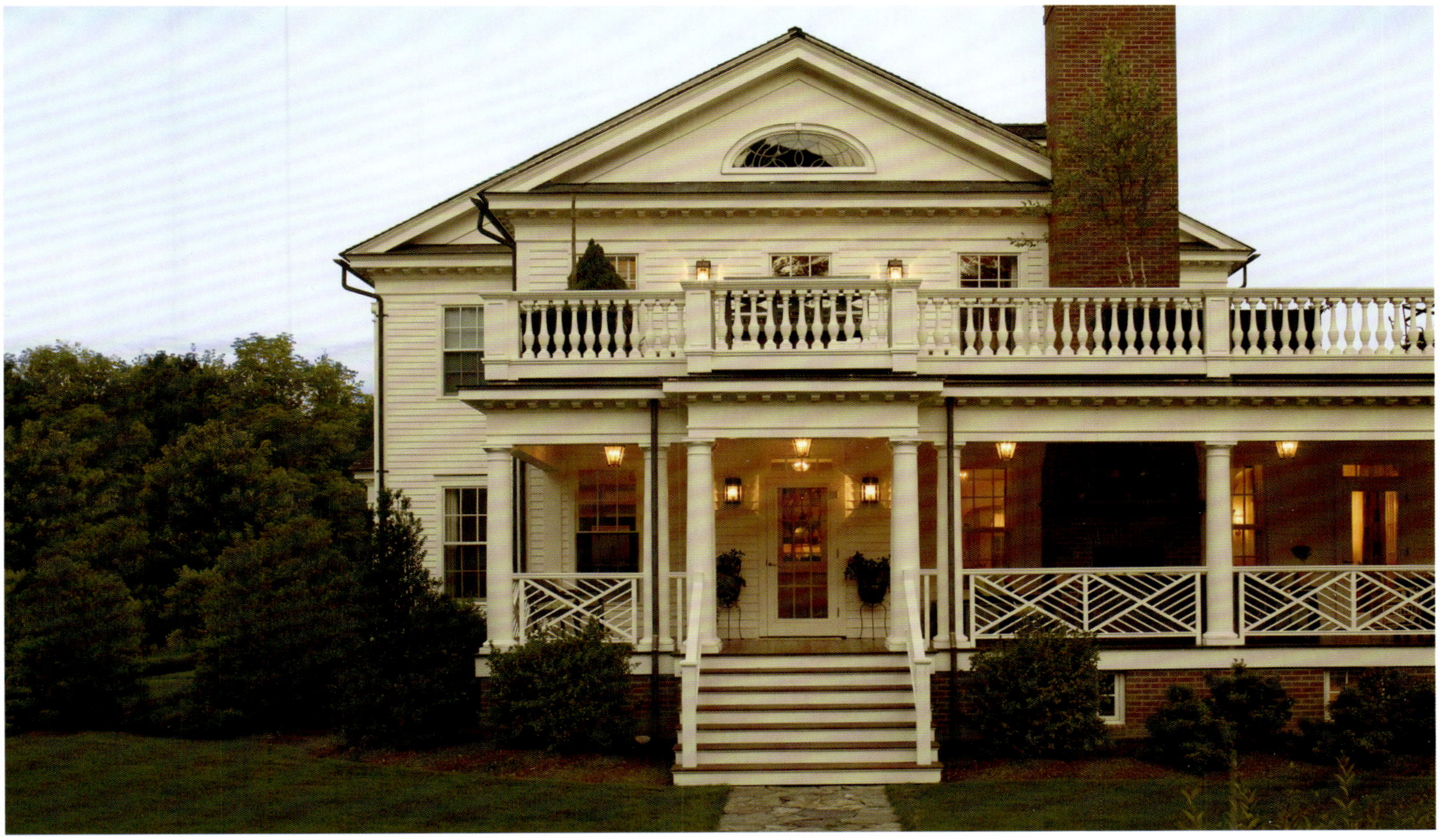

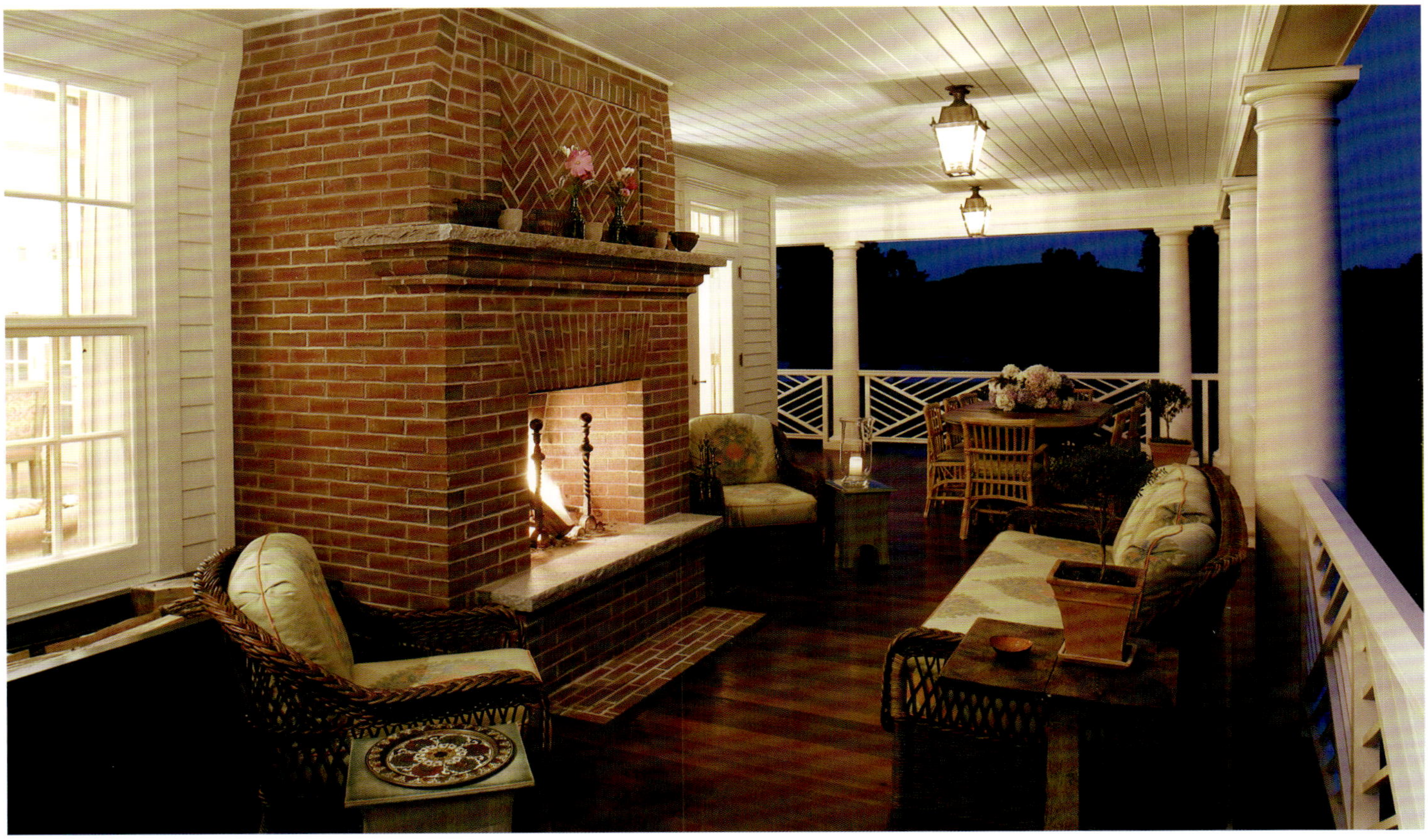

ABOVE: The flagstone-paved dining porch under the pergola faces the pond. The Tuscan columns are painted wood. OPPOSITE: The secondary entrance and mudroom, with a radiant heated floor and storage organized into cubbies for each family member. OVERLEAF: An expansive view of the crux of the solution shows the redesigned kitchen, now fully integrated with the family dining room and family room. The natural-finished wood island is topped in Pietra Cardosa stone.

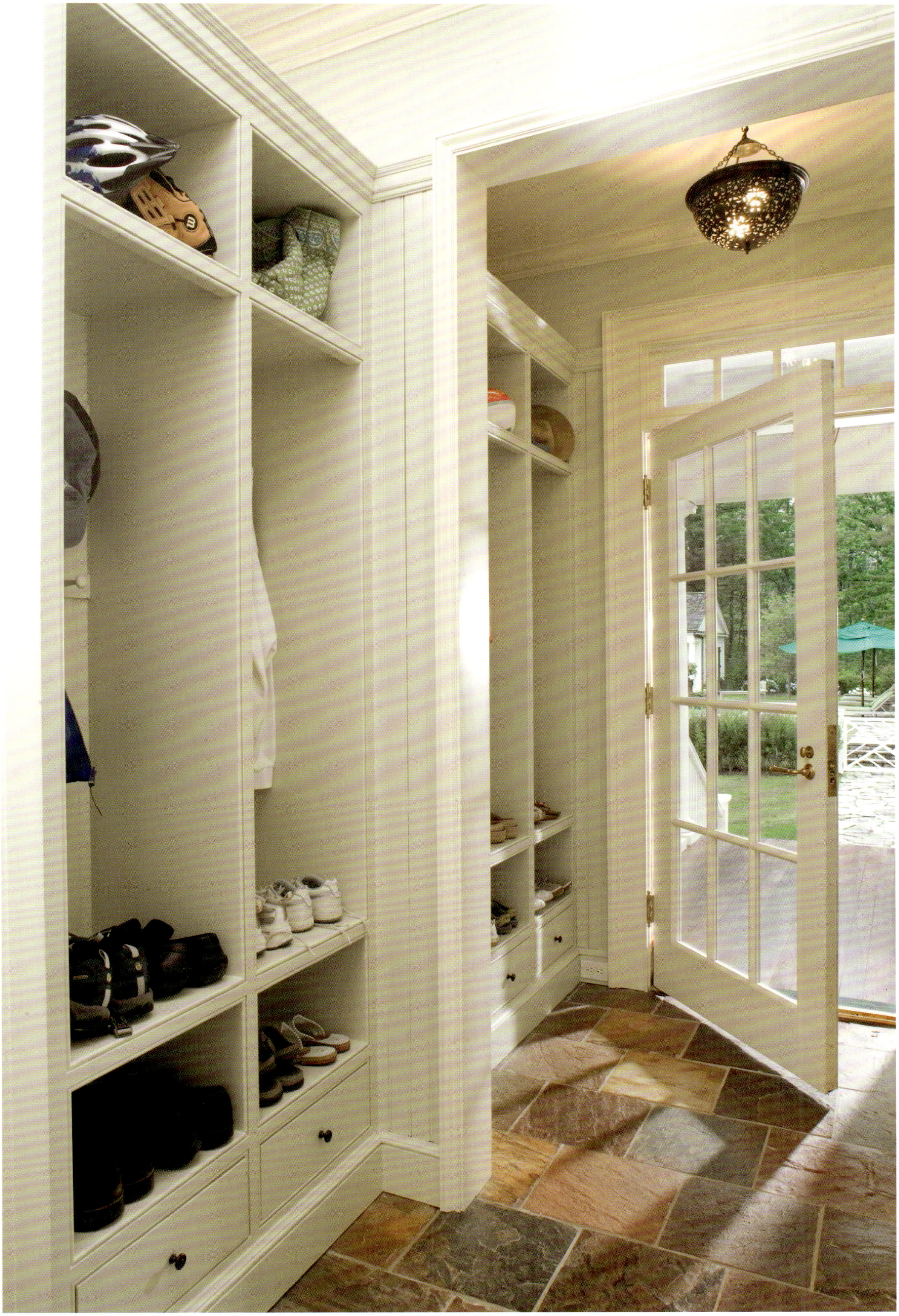

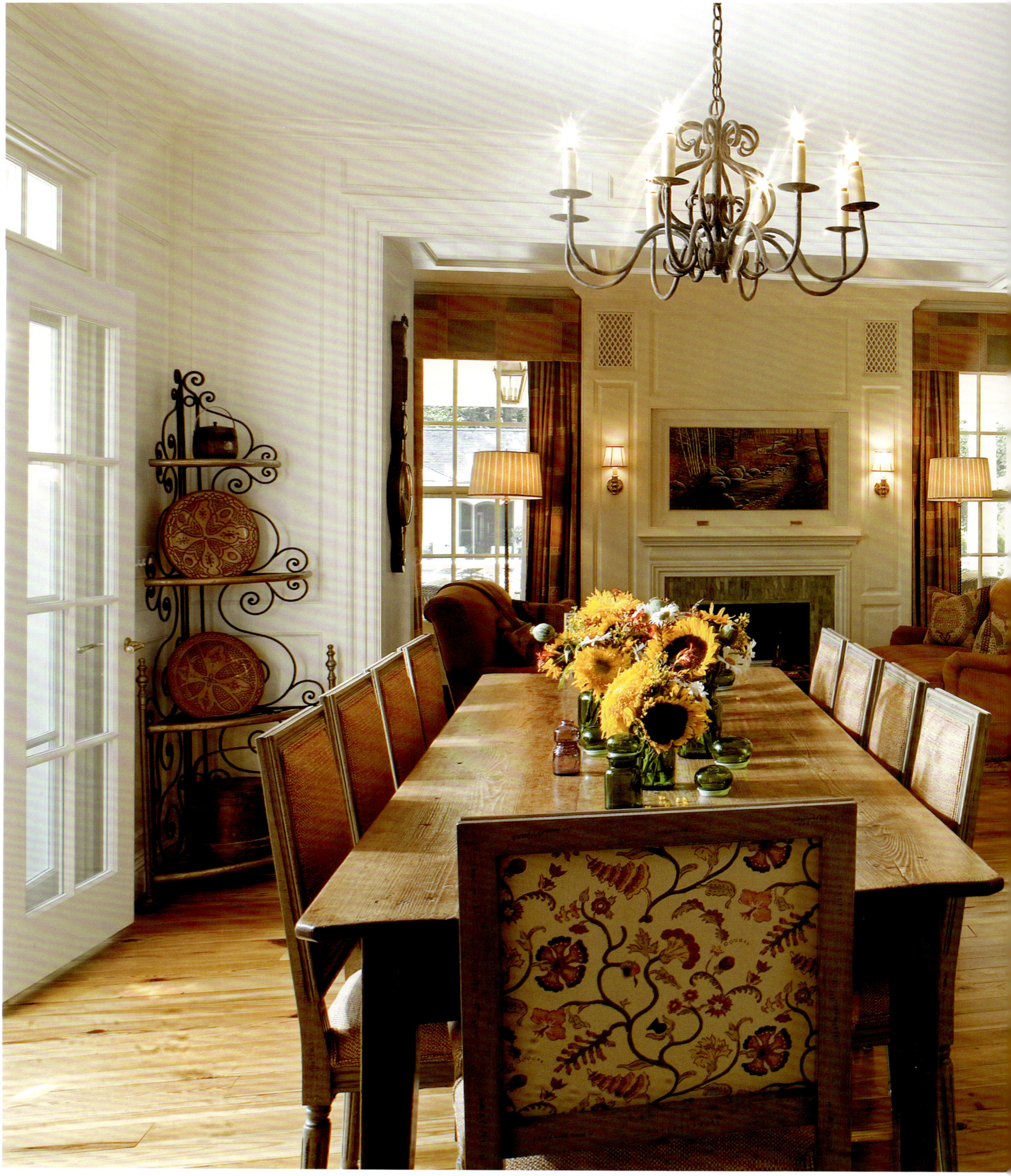

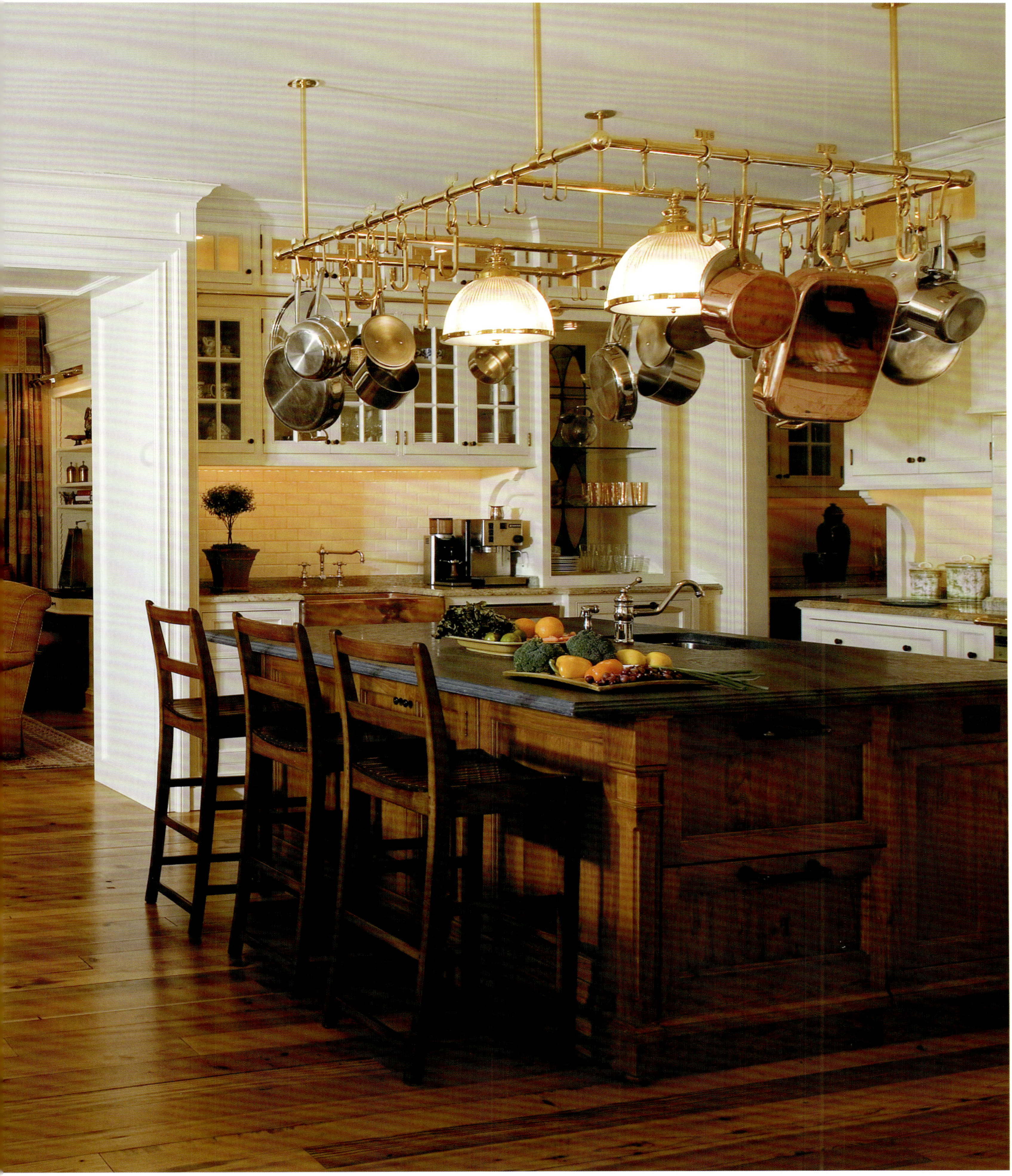

ABOVE: In the kitchen, the rolling ladder provides easy access to overhead storage. An interior stained-glass window looks into the mudroom. LEFT: In his study, French doors open to the deck, where at night the monitor glows. OPPOSITE: With insets of polychrome glass and reflective mirror, the monitor filters colored light into the family room.

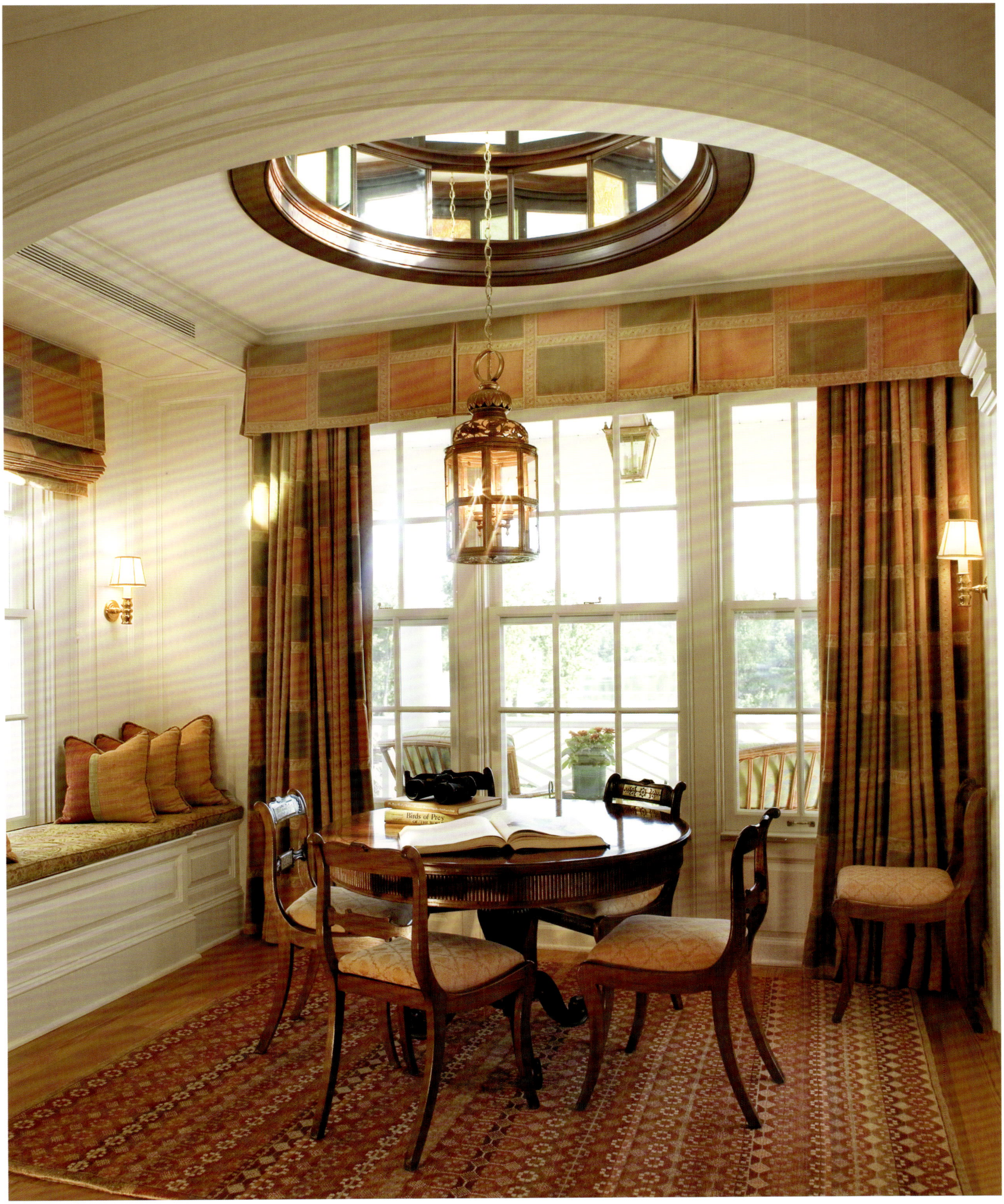
Birds of Prey

Depth of Character

Every architect cares about context. But when the client has a decided historical bent and the site a definitive architectural legacy, the architect tends to up the contextual ante—as we did for this 10,500-square-foot, Colonial-inspired vacation house on Sea Island, Georgia. One of Georgia's barrier islands, Sea Island emerged as a resort colony and golfer's paradise in the late 1920s. Much of the island's wonderful residential architecture is by Francis Abreu and dates to that era, as does its Addison Mizner–designed grand hotel, the Cloister. That history influenced the choices we made for this three-story, six-bedroom house, which sits just a stone revetment from the Atlantic Ocean.

The clients and David Guilmet of Bell-Guilmet Associates, the interior designer, envisioned a house that would be American in feel, with Colonial roots and a certain degree of formality. Working closely together, we developed a parti that—with a portico entry and rear veranda, plus a second-floor balcony wrapping the east and south perimeter—met their desires.

Achieving real depth of character is never easy, but a close structural analysis of Sea Island's remaining 1920s houses yielded useful clues for our design. The stained mahogany cornice, for instance, harks back to the older houses and is one of the defining attributes of the new exterior. Built-in box gutters ensure that the cornice is uninterrupted. The tinted parged plaster finish gives the structure, which sits on a molded-brick water-table base, a patina of age.

We all wanted the house's portico and veranda, so characteristic of Southern architecture, to feel organic and appropriate; square piers, brick paving, and wood beam-and-board ceilings foster this sense. The windows also capture the Southern vernacular, with pegged frames under window aprons and stained mahogany paneled shutters that extend from the window top to the veranda floor. Designing the metal balustrade in a way that would avoid cliché was particularly painstaking: we made mockups of the elements, then paired and repaired them with the stained mahogany paneled posts until we established a harmonious rhythm. Round columns, flanked by square-paneled columns, indicate where the veranda turns, offsets, and terminates.

103

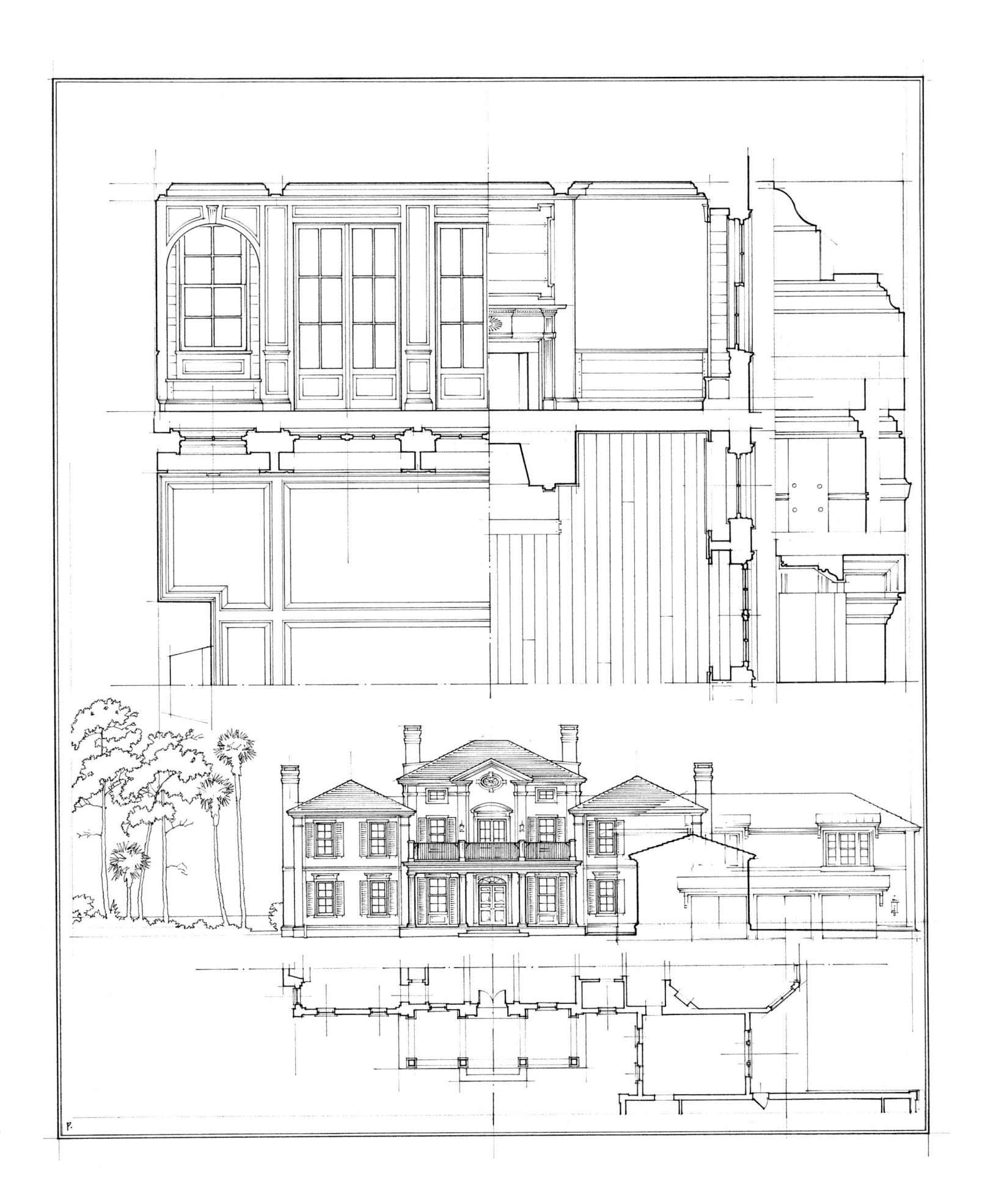

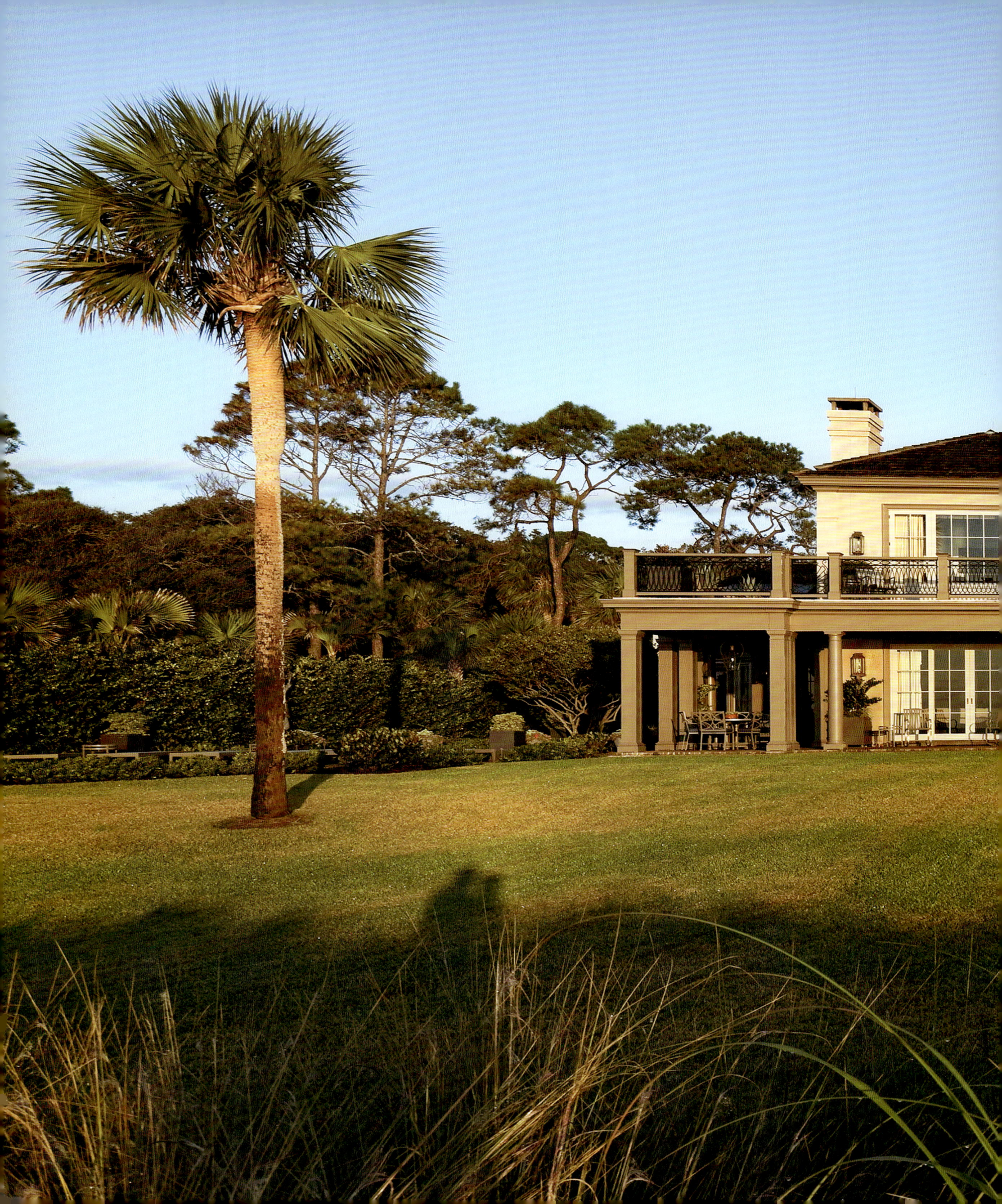

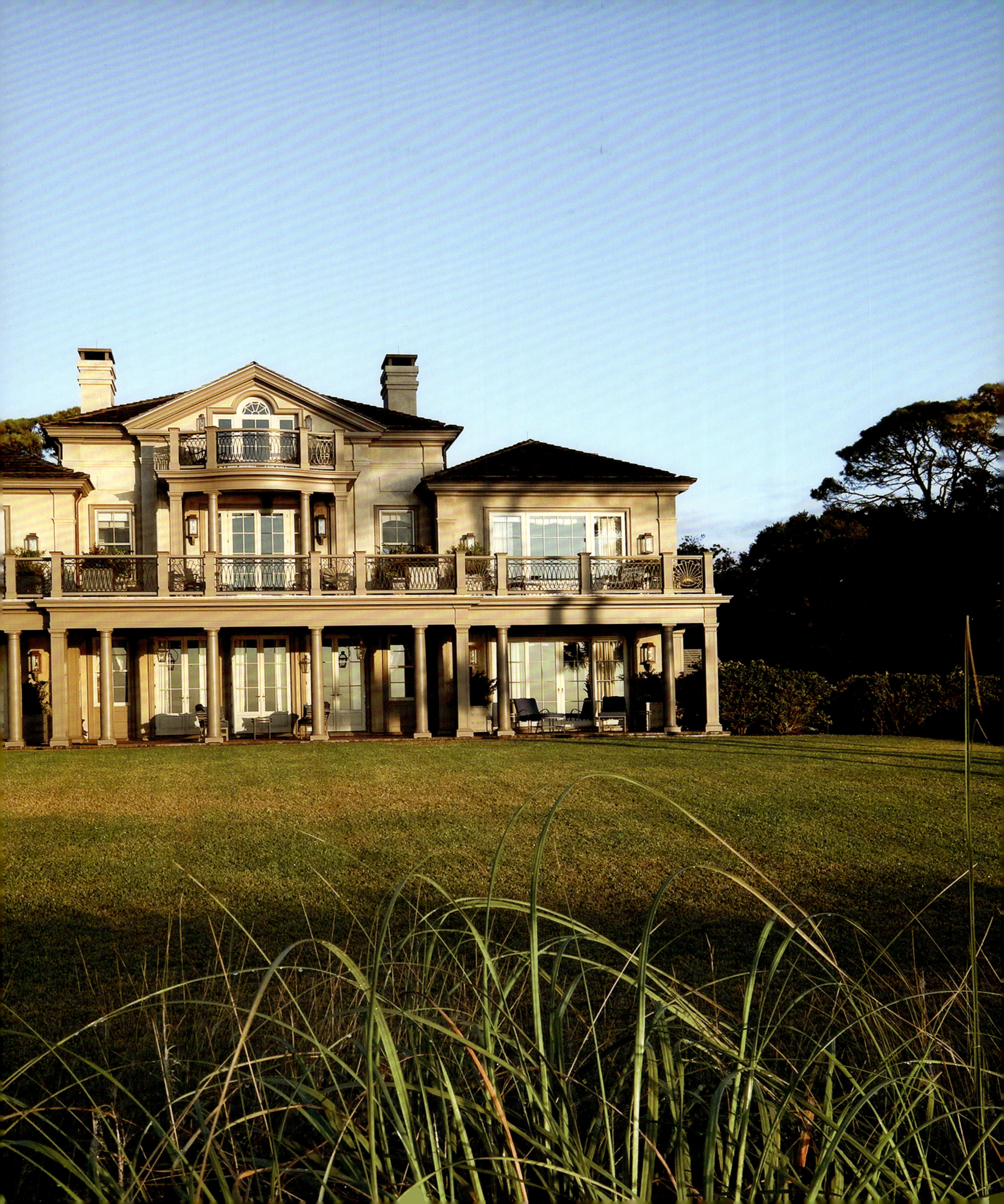

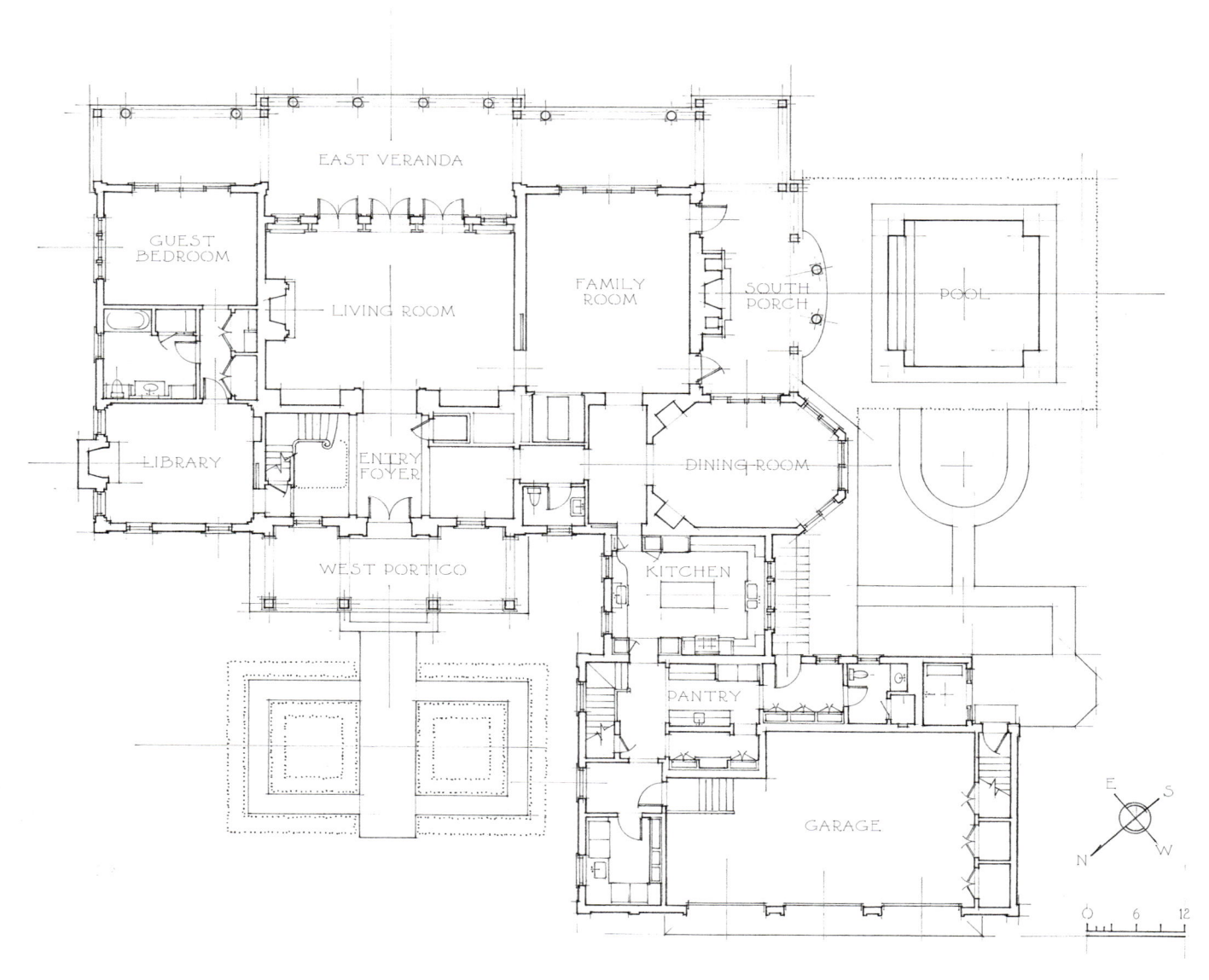

PREVIOUS SPREAD: The oceanfront elevation has a veranda and balcony wrapping the south and east sides; the central portico frames the French doors of the master bedroom and the private balcony attached to the third-floor study. LEFT: The entry portico, with balcony above, offers a view straight through to the Atlantic. OPPOSITE: The entry floor is slate inlaid with white marble.

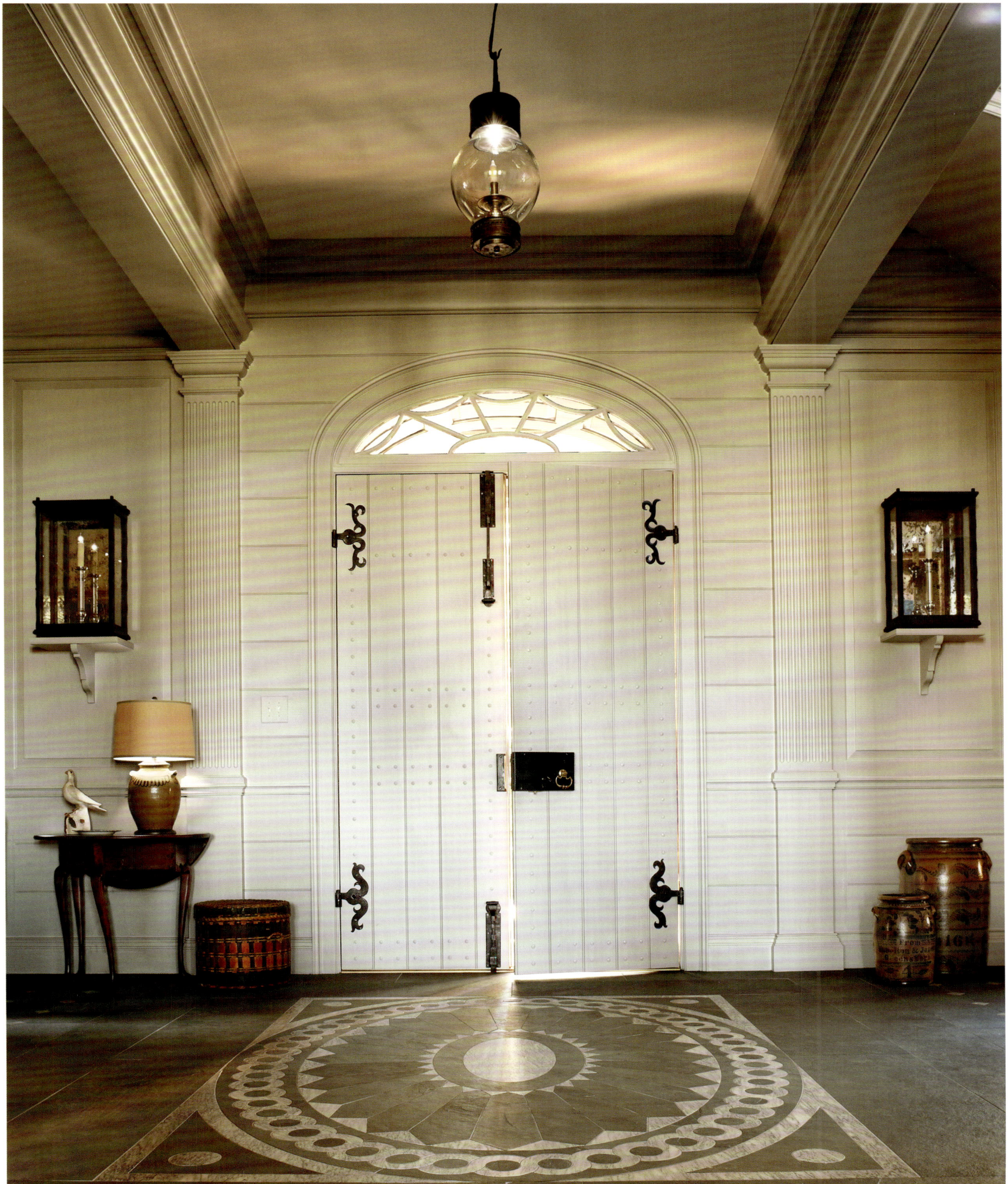

The wood-paneled entry foyer incorporates fluted pilasters and other references to the clients' preferred Colonial style, including the door hardware and nailhead trim. Both the hallway and the stairwell have raised wood paneling. The arch under the stair carriage frames the opening to the library beyond.

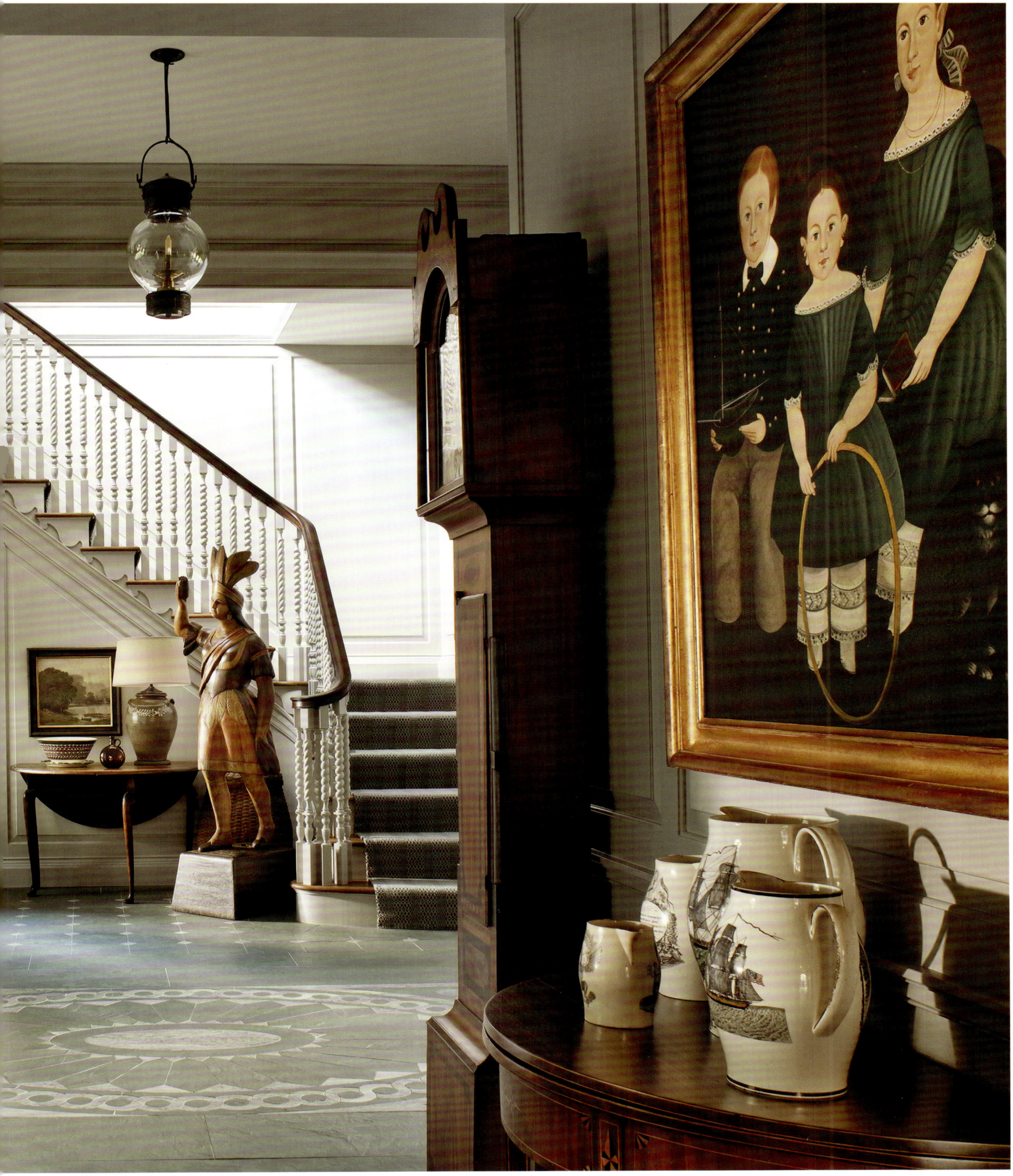

The interior design looks to both comfort and function, and capitalizes on the finest views. The ocean is visible from the portico, which leads into the slate-and-marble-floored entry stair hall. Straight ahead is the living room, which opens to the veranda. To the left is a library and guest suite; to the right, a family room with breakfast alcove, dining room, and kitchen wing.

The master bedroom occupies the central area of the second floor; also here are three guest rooms and a child's bedroom with bunk beds. A secondary stair in the kitchen wing leads to the billiard room and a TV/media room over the garage. His and her studies occupy the third floor, where an oculus in the hall opens a view through the interior core.

We considered every detail of the architectural components, from the articulated beamwork and coffers that differentiate each ceiling, the beadboard and wainscot configurations that animate the plaster walls, the dark-stained reclaimed oak flooring in each room, and the mahogany balustrade of the main stair with its distinctive rope-patterned painted pickets to each and every custom doorknob; the Georgia-based contractor and Charlottesville, Virginia–based millwork shop were integral to this effort. The house now embodies not only its historic context but also, from conception to final nuance, the clients' hopes and dreams.

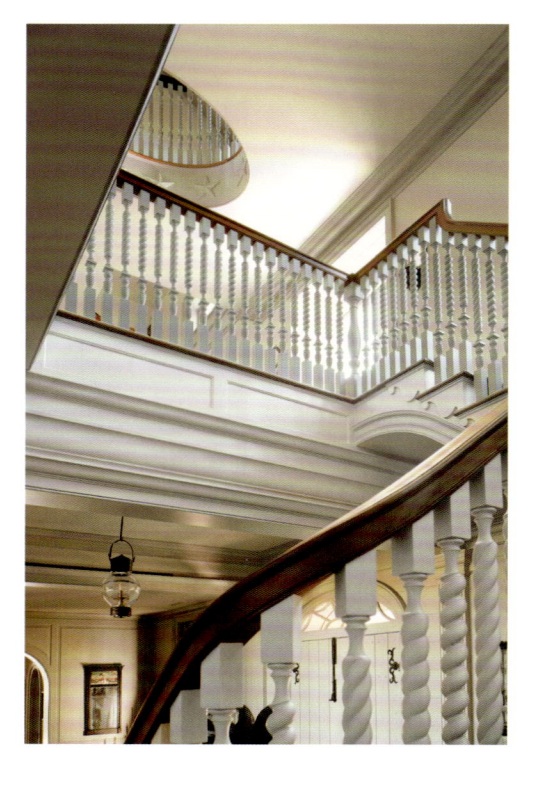

FAR LEFT, AND LEFT: The stair rises up through the core of the house; looking up from the landing towards the third floor oculus. OPPOSITE: A view down through the oculus to the second floor reveals the star embellishments on the drum opening. The rope pattern of the balusters incorporates three distinct designs arranged in alternation.

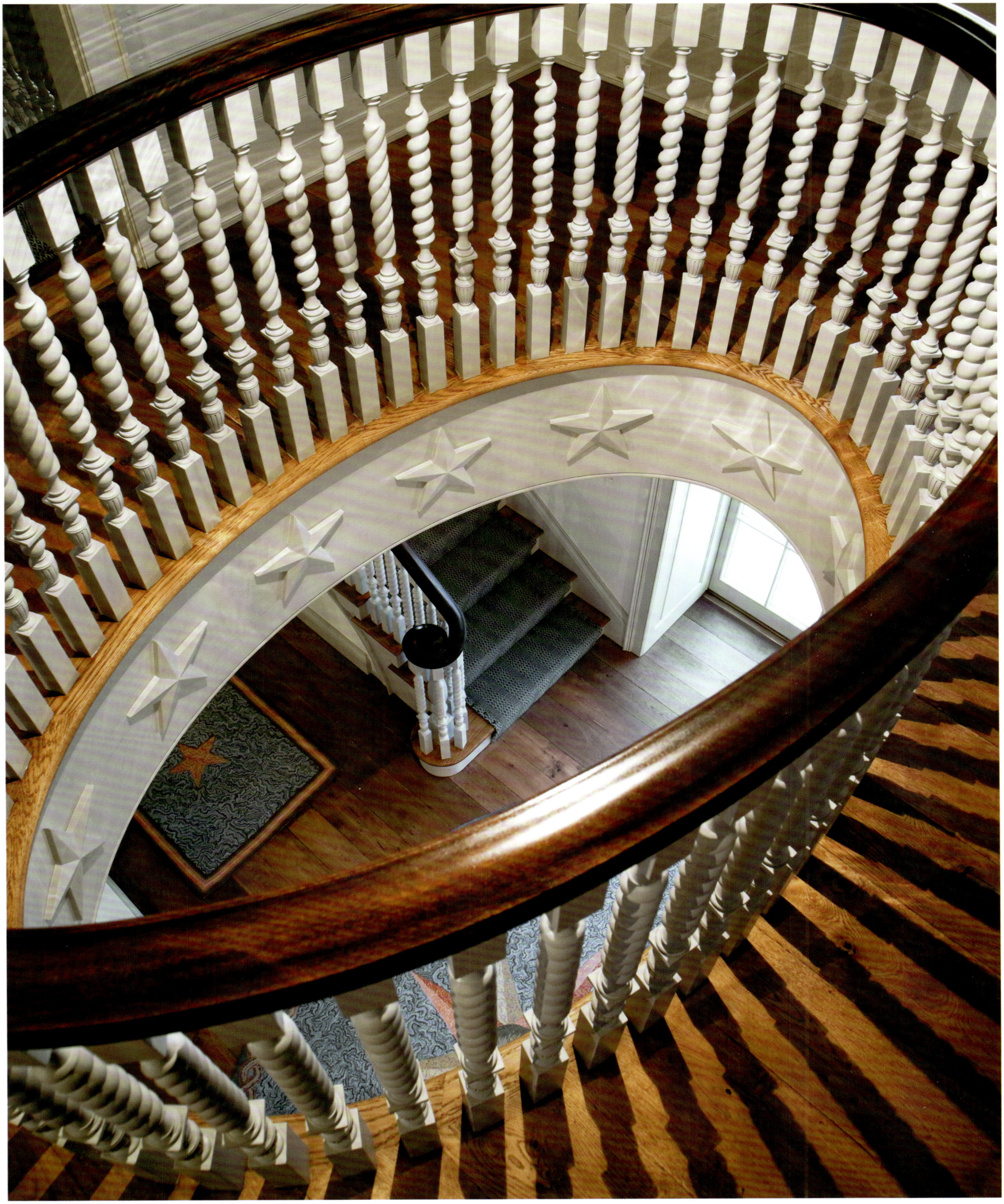

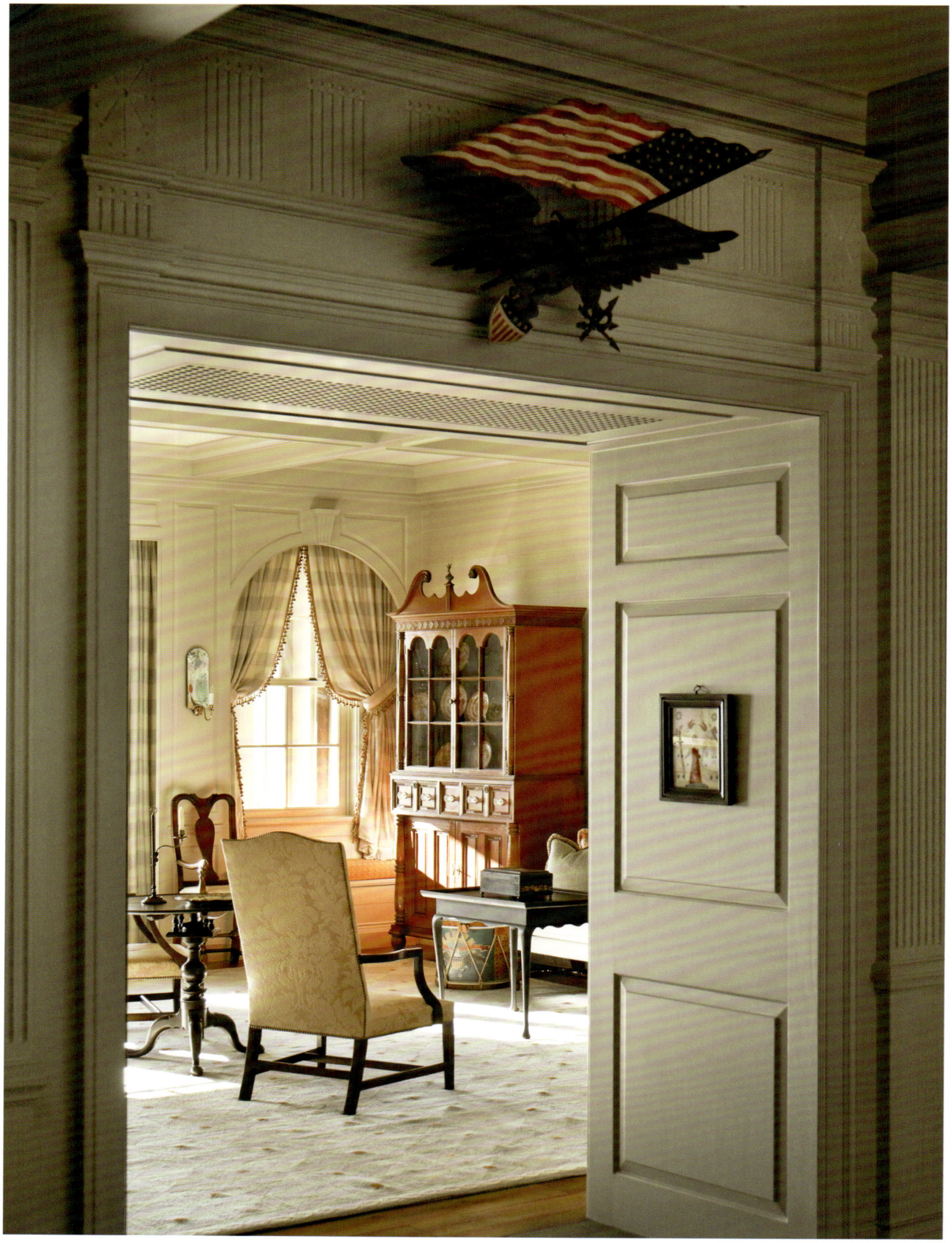

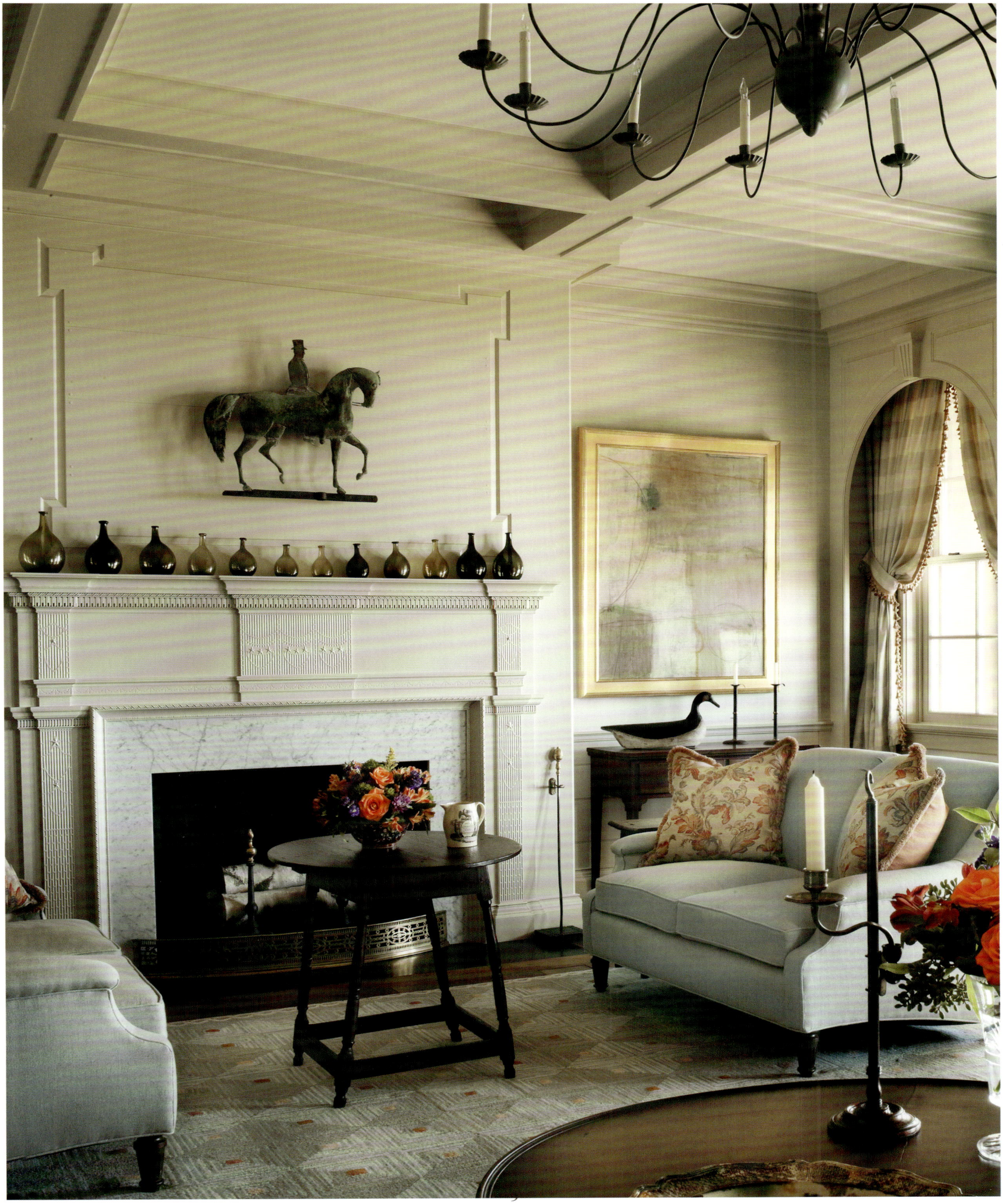

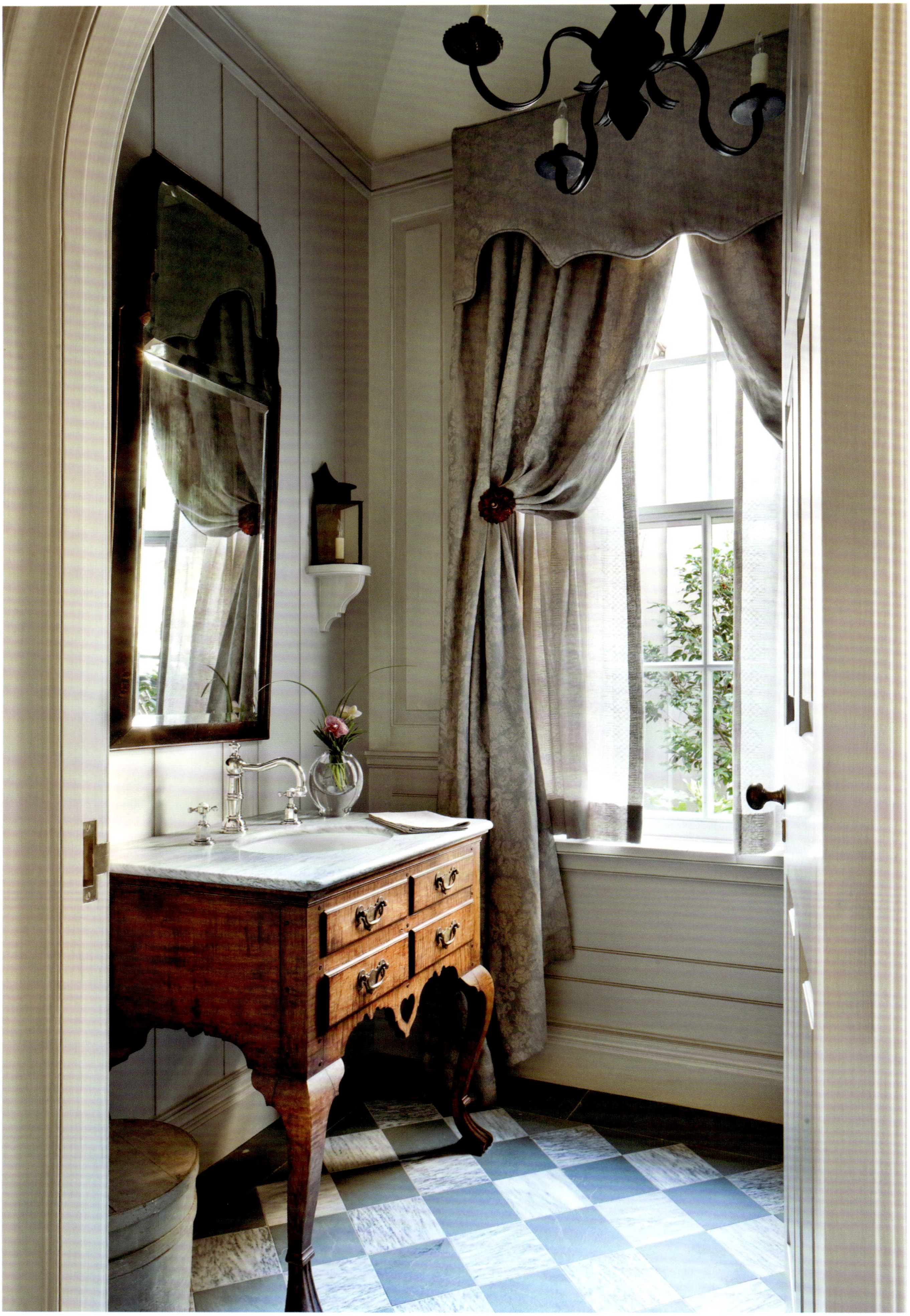

PREVIOUS SPREAD, LEFT: The paneled passage to the living room from the entry hall is flanked by fluted pilasters and capped with a stylized Doric overdoor design. PREVIOUS SPREAD, RIGHT: The living room has a coffered ceiling. The deep window seat reveals have arched panelized fascia set with a keystone. OPPOSITE: Under a coved ceiling, the powder room is entirely paneled in painted wood, with vertical bead boards on the vanity wall and raised paneling with a wainscot on the other three. ABOVE: The reclaimed yellow-heart pine paneled library has a coffered ceiling and a simple limestone mantel.

115

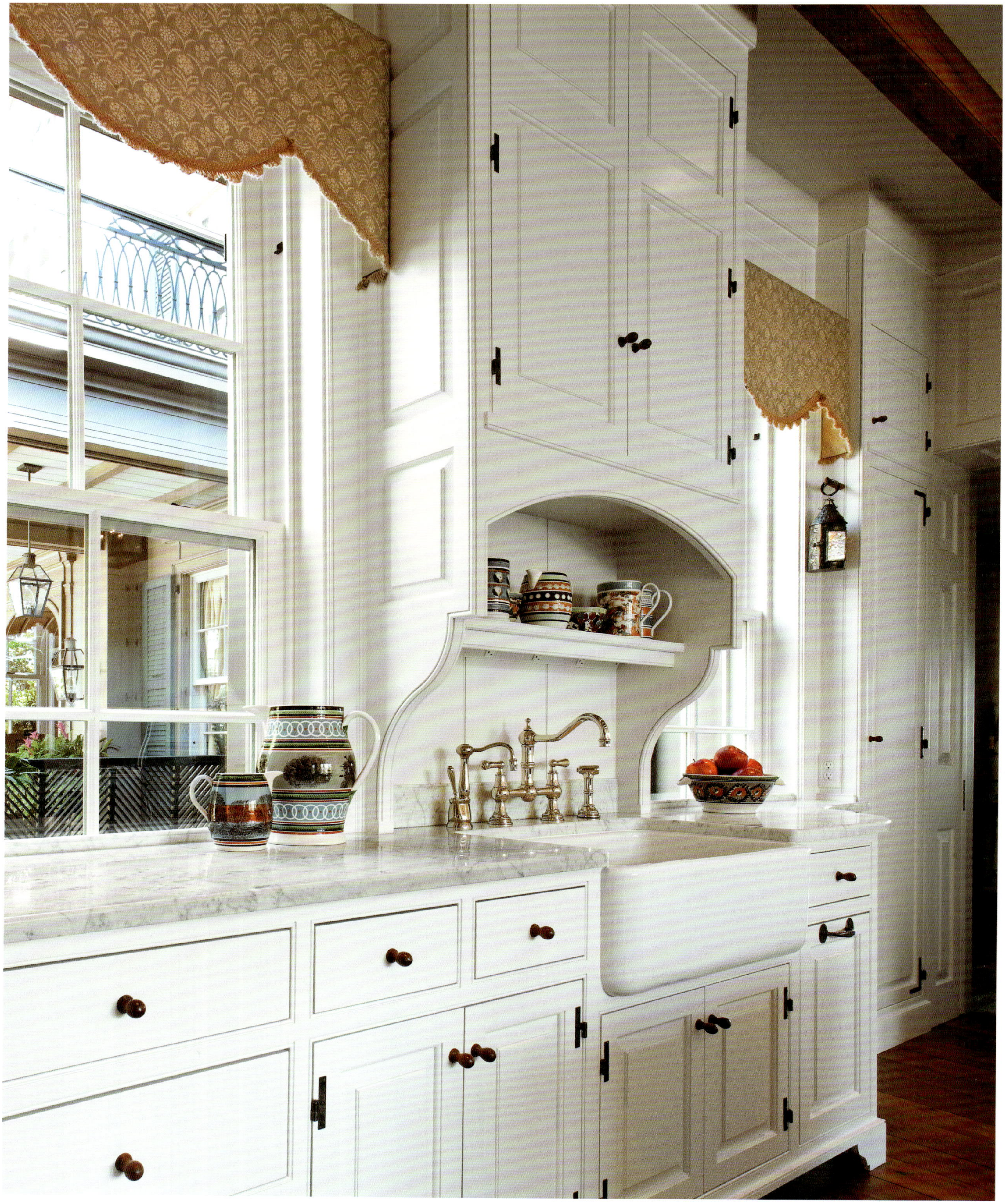

OPPOSITE AND ABOVE: In the kitchen is white-painted wood cabinetry detailed with raised panels, black iron H hinges, and walnut knobs. Countertops are white carrara marble. LEFT: In the breakfast alcove, custom benches and a custom table nestle within beaded board walls and ceiling.

CLOCKWISE FROM ABOVE: Behind an arched paneled fascia, French doors open from the master bedroom to the east balcony; a guest bedroom also opens to the east balcony; in the children's bedroom, a bunk bed with integrated spiral stairs; in her bathroom, bracketed lantern stands flank the vanity mirror.

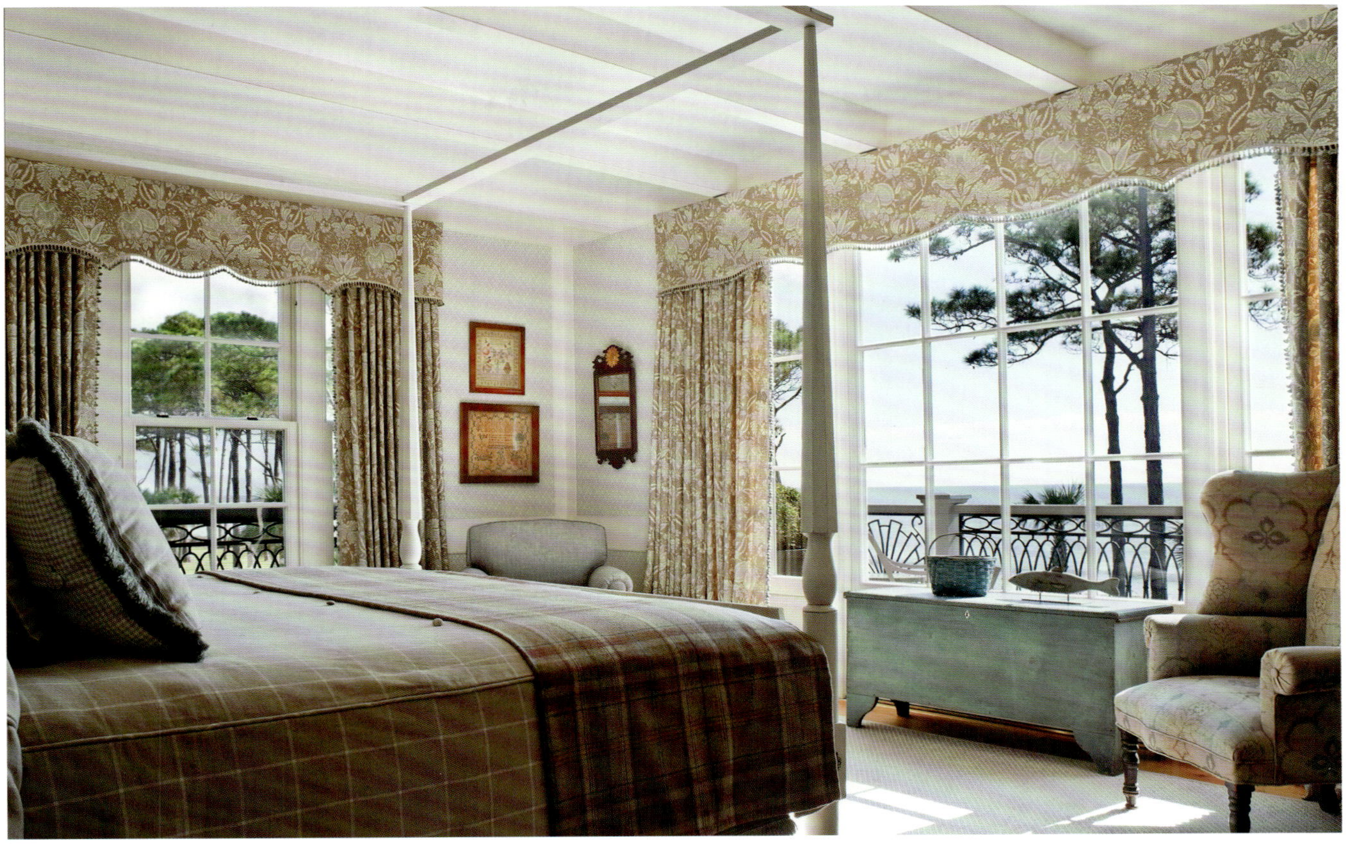

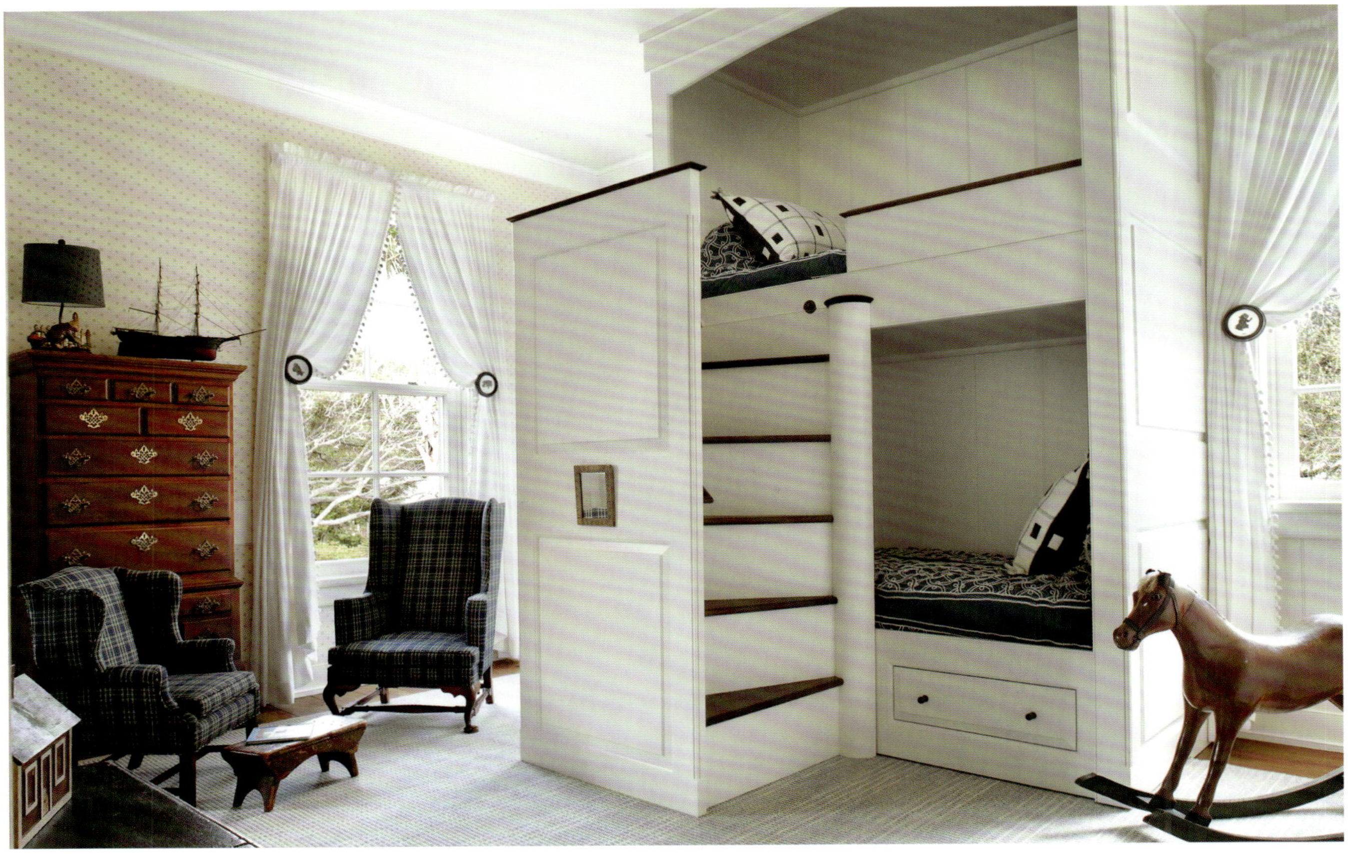

ABOVE: The east balcony overlooks the property and the ocean beyond. Running the length of the porch is a stained mahogany balustrade with a patterned metal grille. OPPOSITE, CLOCKWISE FROM TOP: The third-floor balcony opens off his study; the door from his study to the balcony is a singular opening with an integrated fan light; the wood cornice on the exterior of the house is finished with an opaque, marine-grade stain; on the east veranda, the play of round columns and square-paneled piers, all of mahogany.

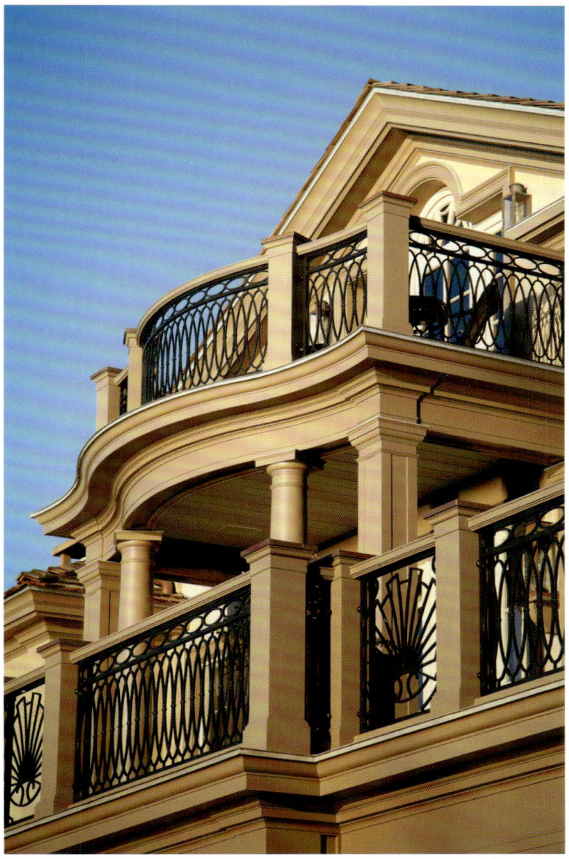

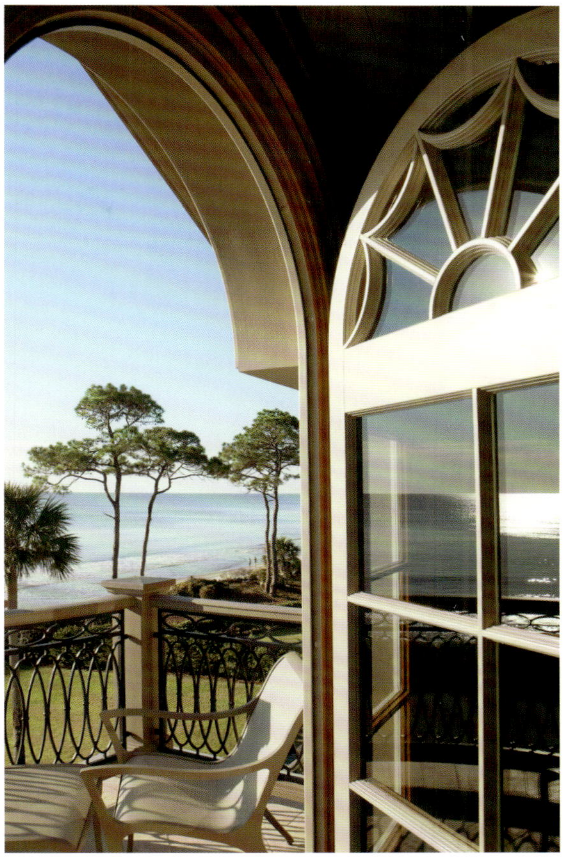

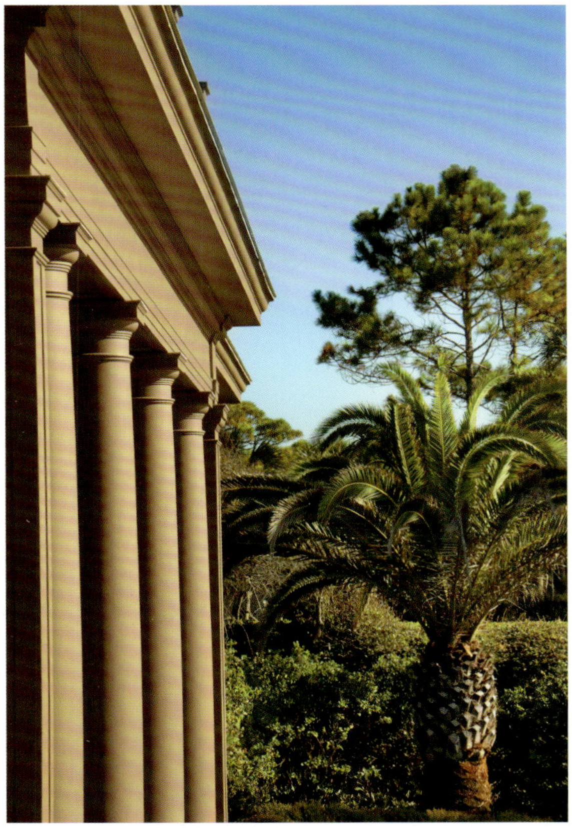

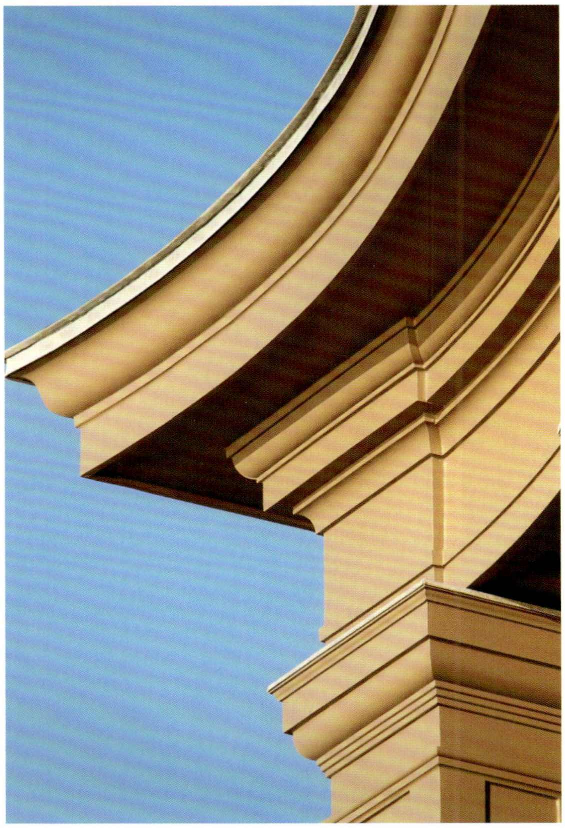

ABOVE: Directly beyond the family room, with which it shares back-to-back fireplaces, is the south dining porch, with the swimming pool one step and a short lawn away. The porch flooring is brick. The detailing, columns, and piers are mahogany finished with an opaque, marine-grade stain. The French doors on the left lead to the dining room.
OPPOSITE: Just a step up from the lawn, the east veranda has a beamed and boarded ceiling with a molded brick floor. Square-paneled piers and round Tuscan columns articulate the modulation of the balcony above.

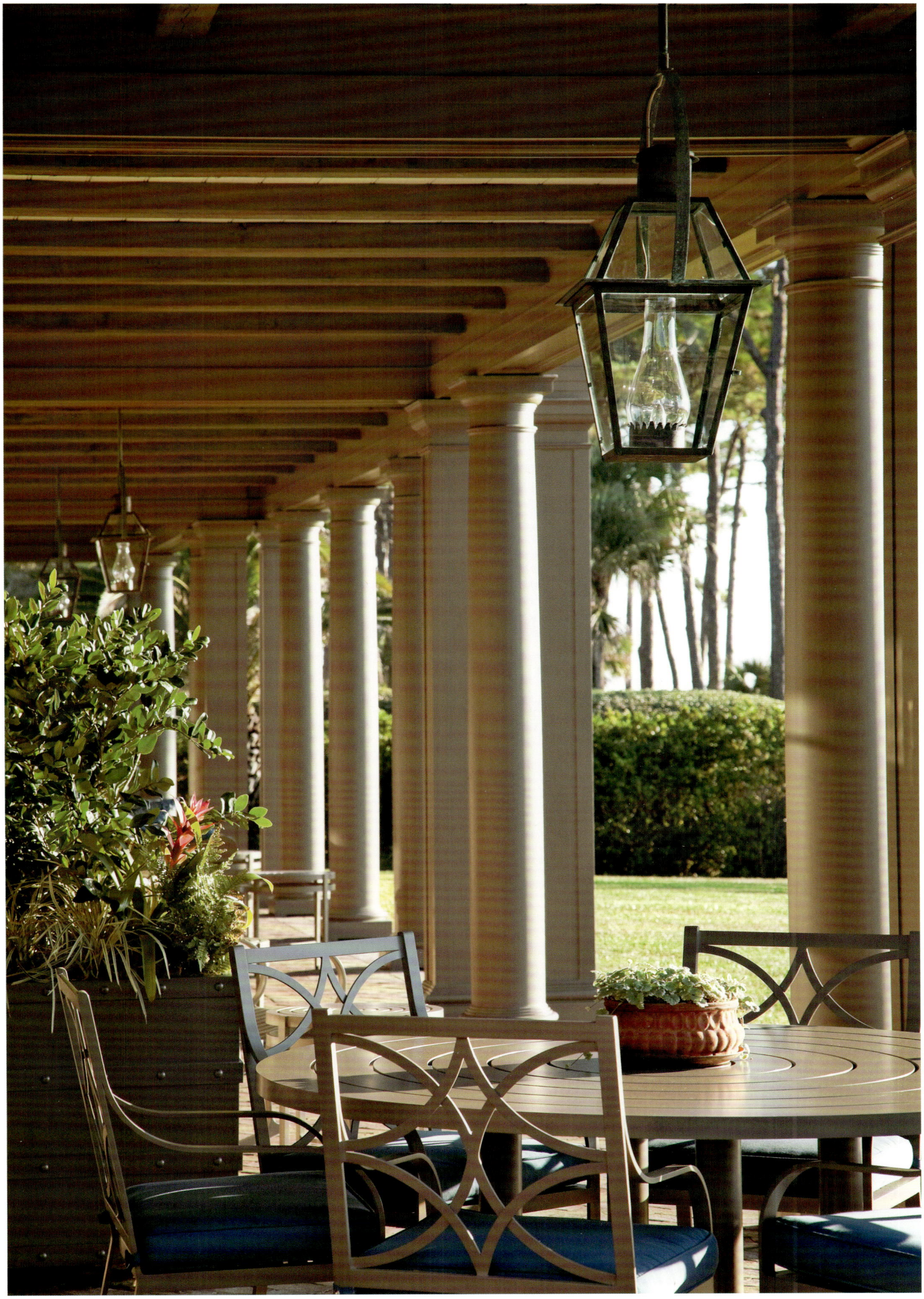

Moderne Influences

So much of the practice of residential architecture involves creating places that suit the distinct phases of family life. There's that first home, ideal for a young couple but too confining when the first child arrives. As the family begins to grow, it then leaves behind that place of fond memories for a residence that usually becomes the family homestead. And when the nest is eventually empty, a couple may decide to reconfigure that homestead to suit the arrival of grandchildren—or perhaps establish an urban pied-à-terre, which is precisely what this couple did.

After years of living in a large, beautiful apartment, these clients wanted a smaller beachhead in the very heart of Manhattan. Longtime traditionalists when it came to decor, their tastes had evolved to a mid-twentieth-century French aesthetic. As serious art and photography collectors, they also felt it imperative that their new 3,200-square-foot, two-bedroom residence would display the works they owned to best advantage—a large design brief for what was initially a plain vanilla space within one of midtown Manhattan's architectural treasures.

To create a design language that felt appropriate to their mid-twentieth-century French leanings, we looked to European art moderne for inspiration. Sophisticated, streamlined, and with understated art deco flourishes, the resulting residence—designed in close collaboration with the interior design firm Cullman & Kravis—captures more than a hint of that French 1940s spirit. It also shows off the owners' assembled works of art to perfection.

The entry foyer contains the most direct period quote: a gilded, flat-domed ceiling. With a central mosaic medallion, the floor echoes the dome above. In another period-inspired touch, metal bands outline the mosaic's stone tesserae.

The foyer leads directly into an expansive living room, with fantastic city views. His study lies behind a pair of glass pocket doors with ornamental wood fretwork, which add another layer of period-inspired detail. The functional kitchen is behind glass doors, off to one side of the foyer. A hallway with

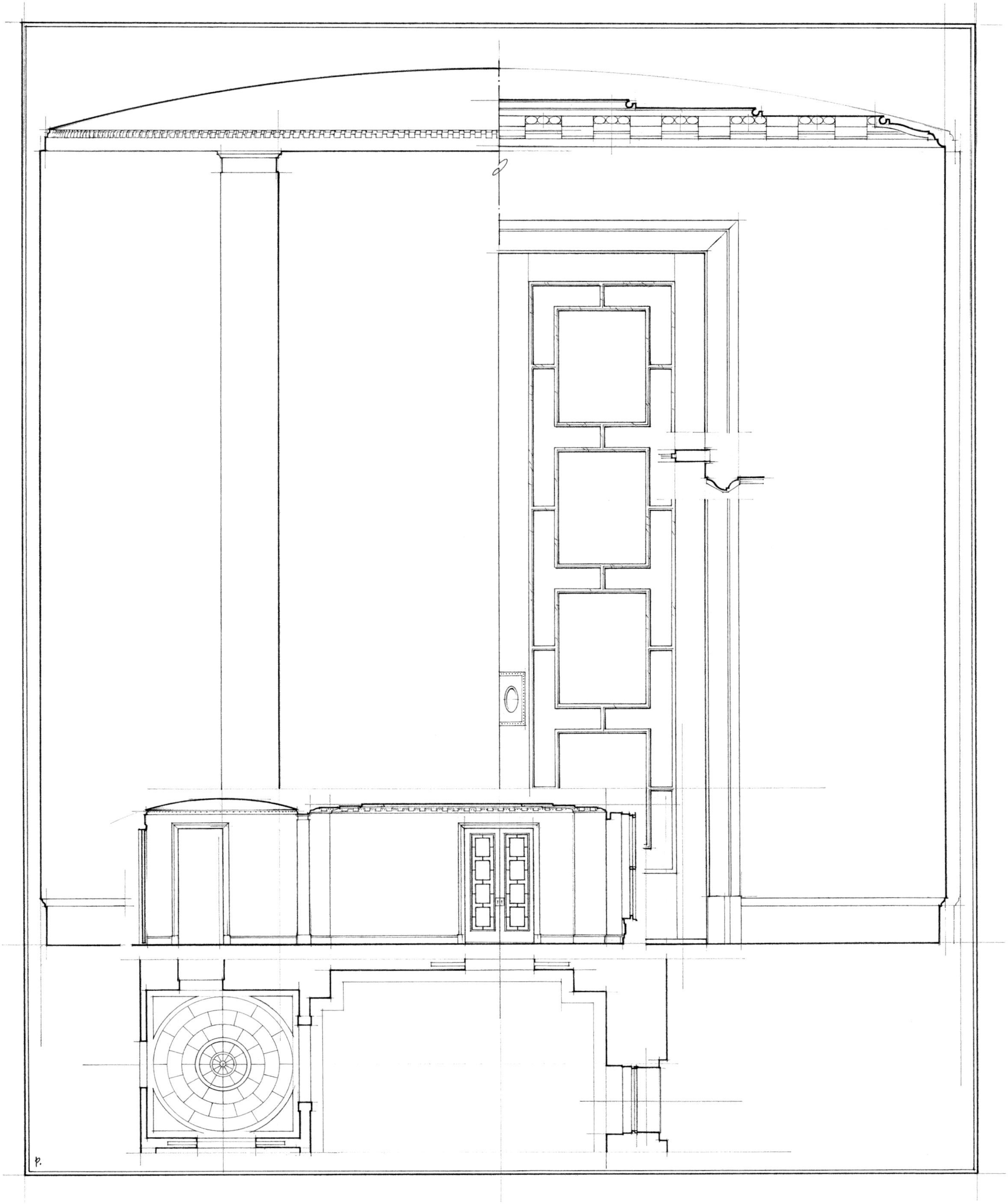
P.

LEFT: A flat dome edged with scalloped fluting tops the entry foyer; the stone floor mosaic with nickel banding directly underneath echoes the circle-in-the-square theme. OPPOSITE, CLOCKWISE FROM TOP LEFT: Framing the dome is a plaster cornice with modillion blocks and egg-shaped scalloped dentils; the living room looks through to the entry; the built-in custom cabinet has integrated lighting to display the clients' photography collection.

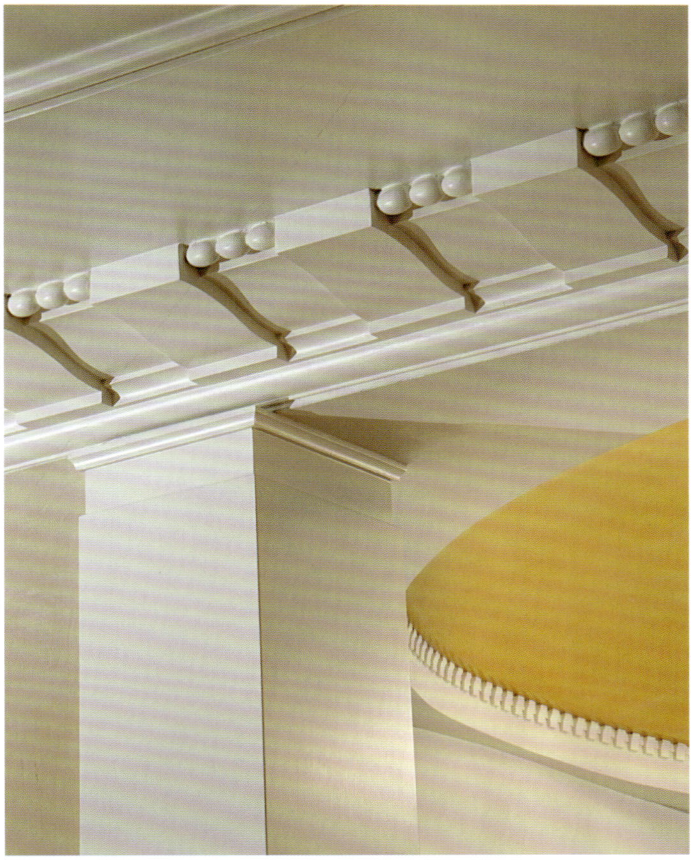

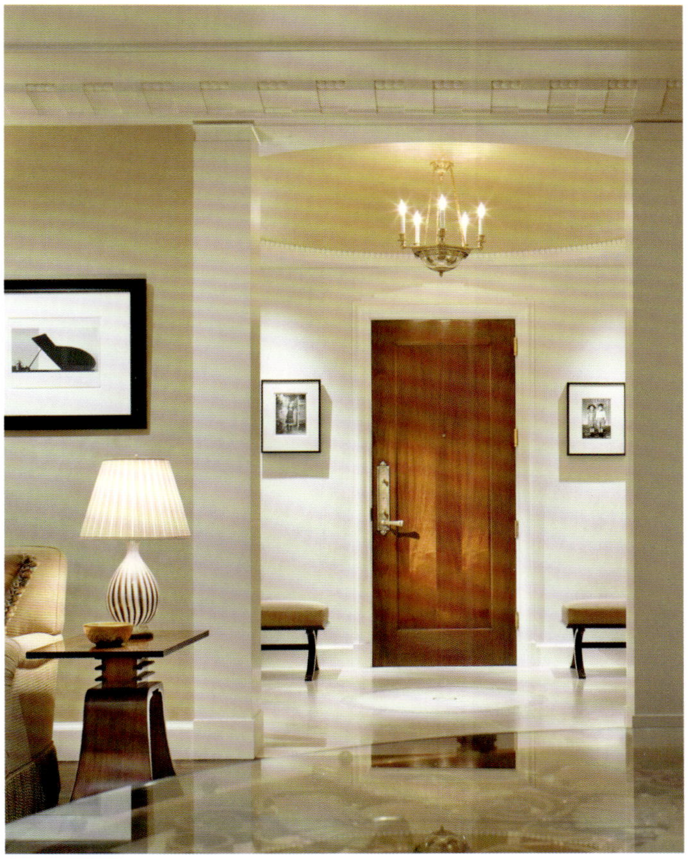

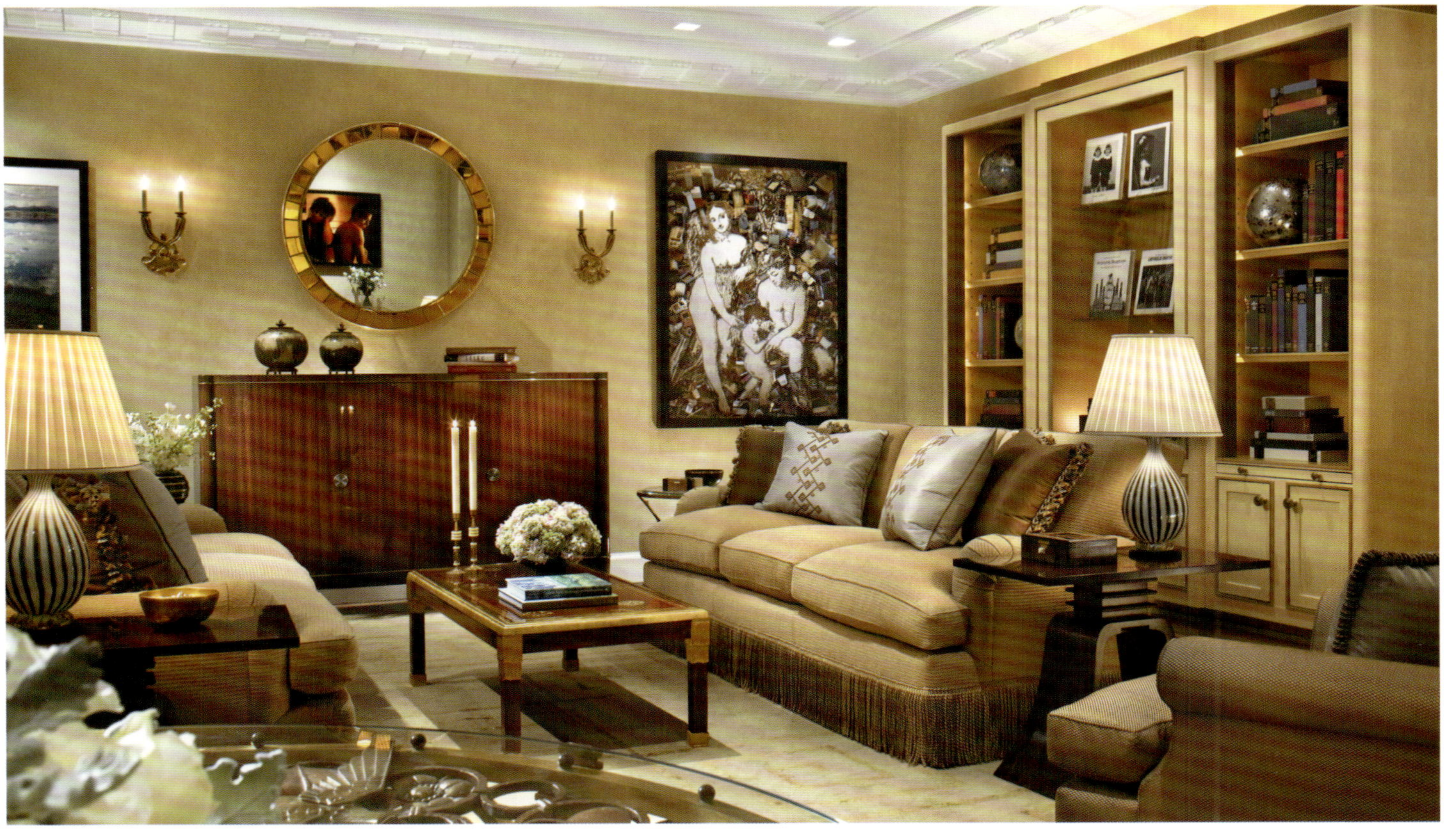

Inspired by the streamlined elements of art moderne and the clients' midcentury French furniture, the living room's cornice and banded ceiling detail help organize the placement of the recessed light fixtures. The windows offer spectacular views of Central Park and the Manhattan skyline.

128

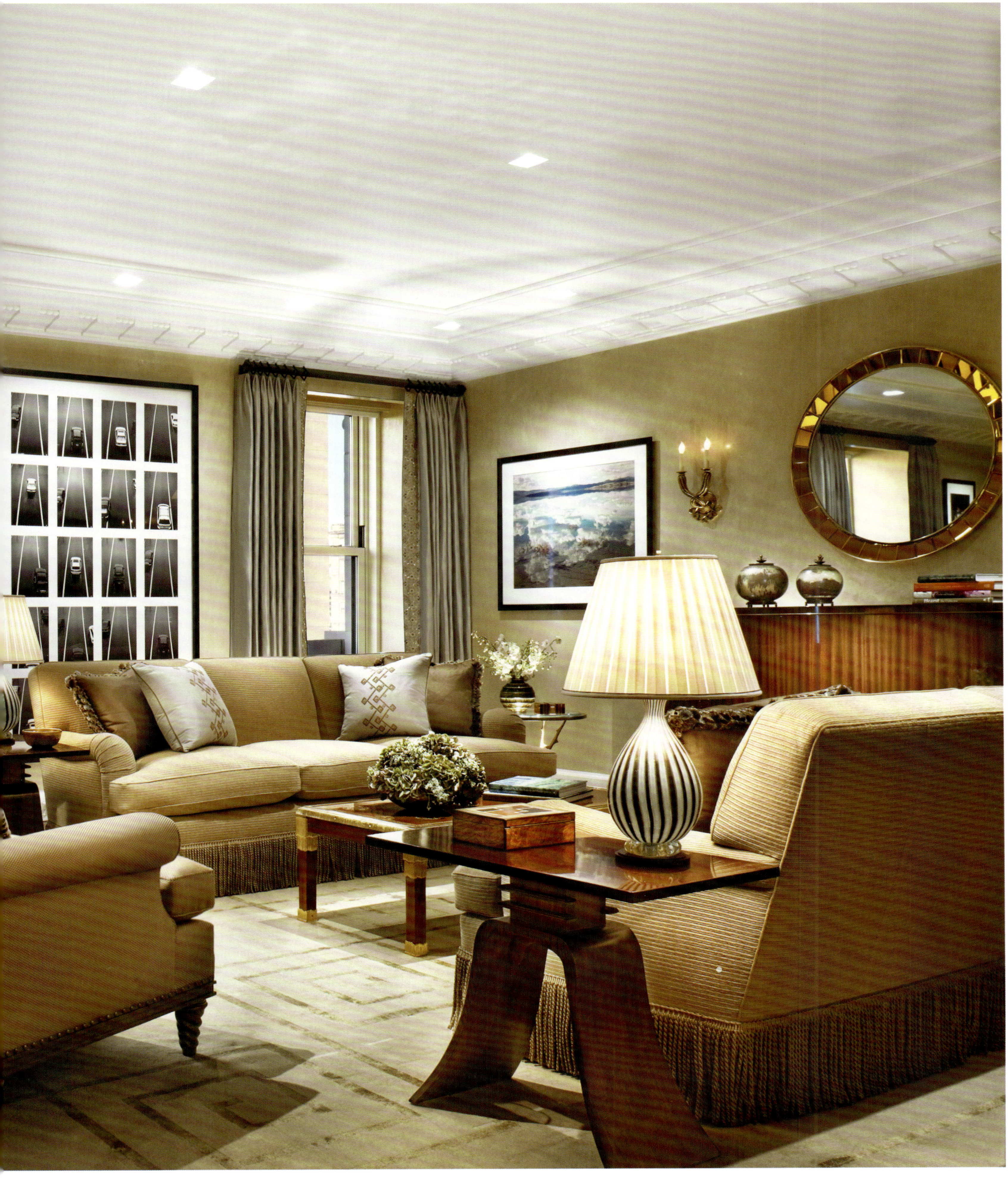

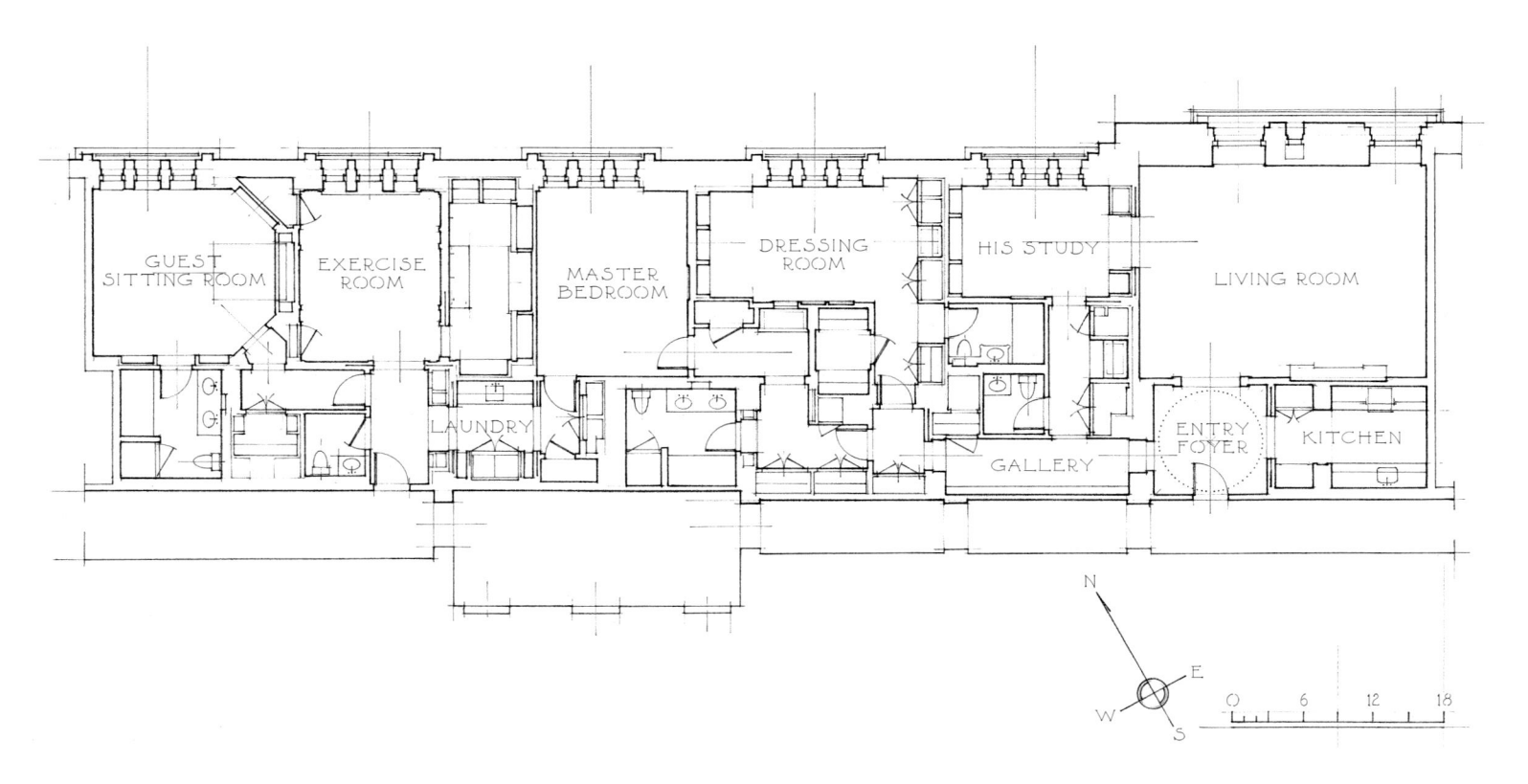

a vaulted ceiling and a gallery rail proceeds to the master bedroom, her dressing area, and a powder room. An area connected to the master bedroom includes a kitchenette/laundry, an exercise room, and a sitting room with a fold-down bed for the occasional guest.

Among the many thoughtful elements of the living room interior is a built-in illuminated cabinet that we designed as a display unit for the bound elements of the owners' photography collection. The living room cornice, rather inventive in scale and detail, incorporates a play of modillion blocks interspersed with a run of almost egg-shaped pearls. The pattern repeats itself around the entire upper perimeter of the room.

In classical design as we understand it, ornament plays a functional role as a nuanced animator of space in all dimensions. That's why ceilings are as important to us as walls and floors. Throughout this residence, we articulated the ceiling plane to add a subtle layer of visual interest. That articulation also structures the placement of overhead lighting so that the fixtures become organic elements of each room's overall architectural composition. The inextricable relationship of part to whole? It's essential to the moderne aesthetic, to the classical approach to design, and most of all, to the nature of family life.

OPPOSITE: Wood grilles sandwich the glass panels of the sliding doors that lead into his study. A wall of built-in storage incorporates lower doors with flat panels and ample shelf and display space for books and photographs. The room also incorporates a wall-mounted flat screen and windows to the city beyond.

ANDY WARHOL
ART NOW
RICHARD PRINCE
COOL RESTAURANTS
RICHARD AVEDON
TITAN
CENTURY
VANITY FAIR PORTRAITS
THE PHOTO BOOK
ECONOMICS DOES NOT LIE
Fall Fashion

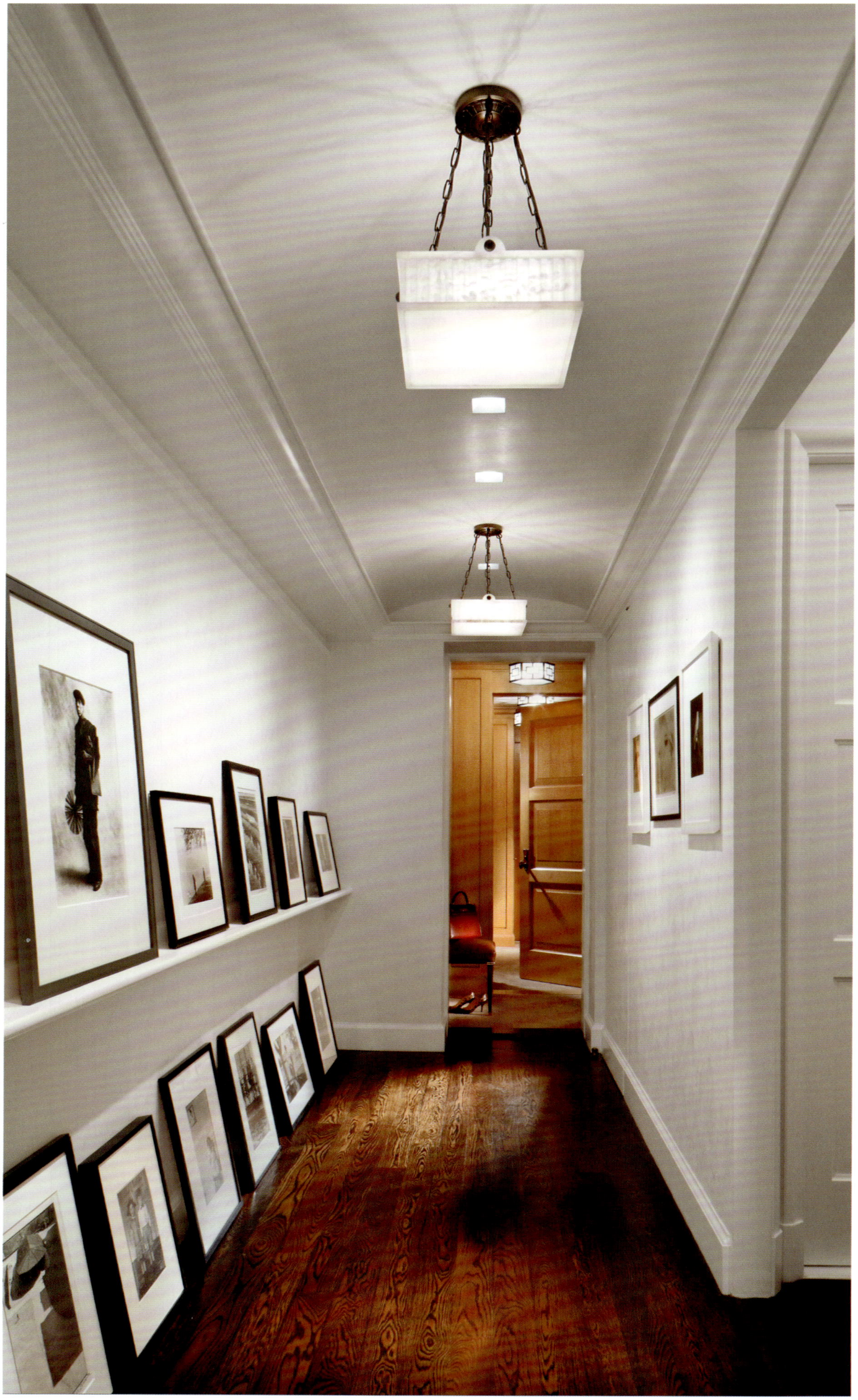

OPPOSITE: Lined with an art rail that displays the clients' rotating collection, the vaulted hallway leads to the private areas and terminates in the anigre-paneled dressing room. ABOVE: The master bedroom has double-hung windows with stunning views of the city.

Restoring History

American history begins with the land and its cultivation, which is likely why agrarian building types in all their variety—the farmhouse, the barn, the stable—form the nucleus of our polymorphic vernacular architecture. Nowhere, perhaps, is this more immediately apparent than in New England, where traces of our seventeenth- and early eighteenth-century beginnings survive to this day. They certainly do at this country residence, with four historically inspired structures. The property seems to have been a working farm of one sort or another since the Colonial era. When these clients purchased it, it was a horse farm with a main house, a small guest cottage, and two barns—all in need of major renovation. After studying the structures closely and removing materials that we thought we could salvage, we re-integrated those components into four "new" buildings—main house, guest cottage, stable barn, and guest barn—totaling 19,200 square feet.

Our goal was to create suitable, comfortable, technologically state-of-the-art buildings that look as if they had existed for centuries. To that end, we collaborated with designer David Guilmet of Bell-Guilmet Associates and landscape architect Eric Groft of Oehme van Sweden. David Guilmet was especially instrumental in helping us to develop project elements that became signature flourishes, such as the graduated rail boards, the lantern stands, and the pent roofs.

The original portion of the farmhouse dates to the early 1700s. A century later, an addition was built and given as a wedding gift. The core of that house was intact, but had evolved over the years into a Federal-style house with wings. In re-creating the main house, we opted to keep as much of the original material as possible. Underpinning and substantially reinforcing the rubble foundation walls allowed us to build on the original footprint and permitted a comfortable ceiling height within the basement, which let us activate that space for various functions.

135

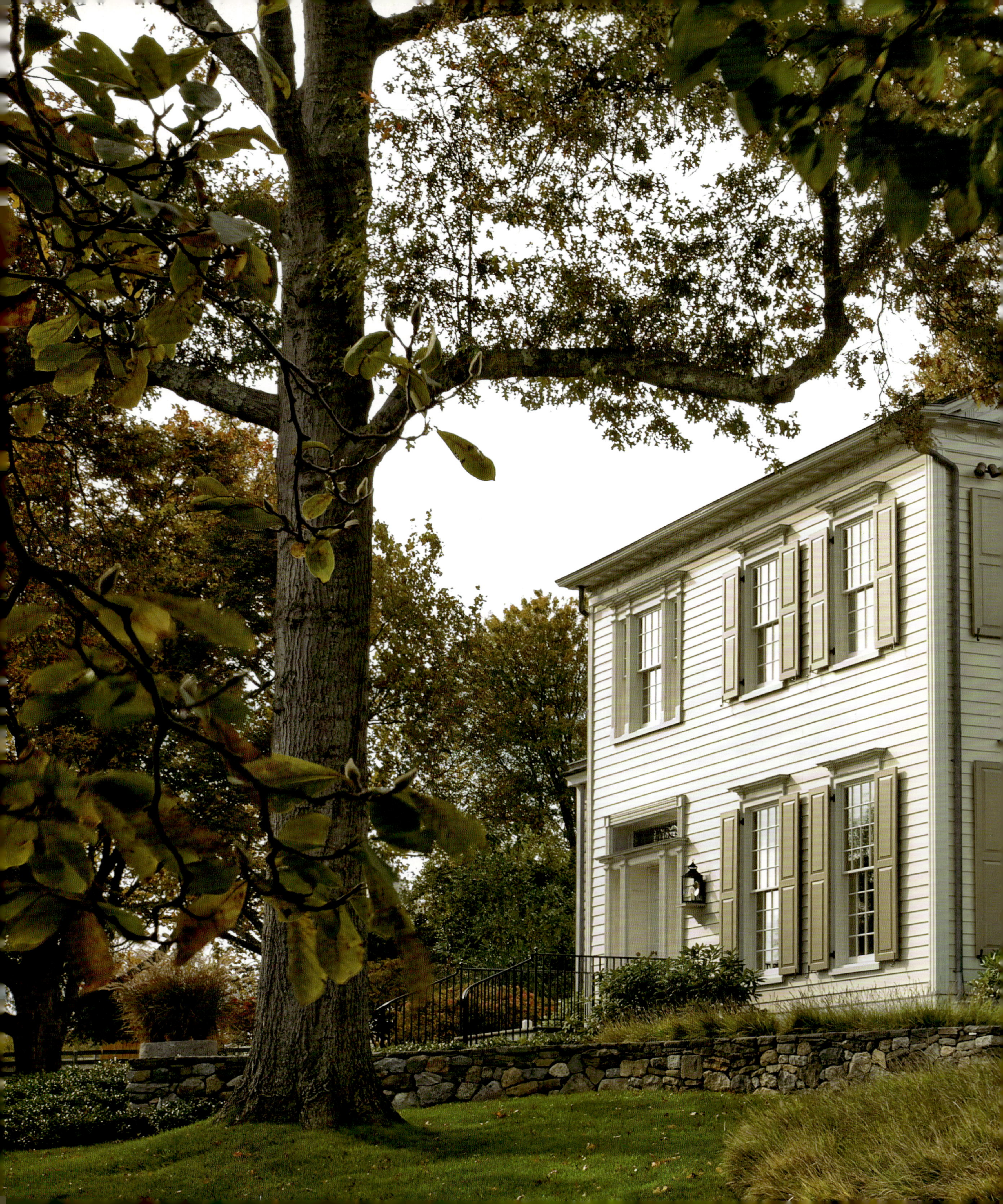

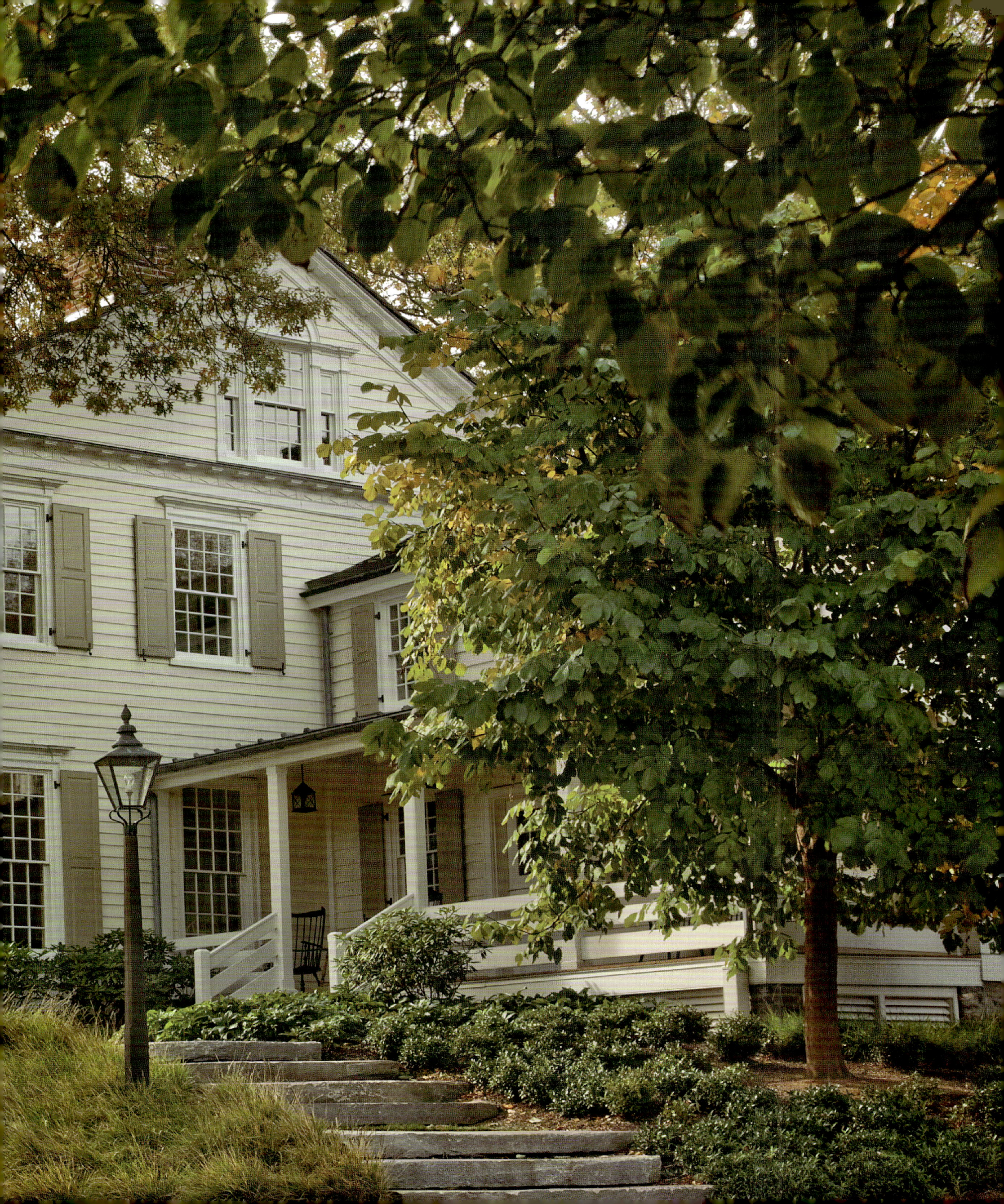

Together with Guilmet, we selected construction materials, techniques, and paint colors that clearly suggested a much older structure. Yet virtually every component of this house is new: the clapboard, the double-hung entablature windows with insulated restoration glass, the shutters, the shake roofs. We retained the original articulation of the eaves almost exactly, and completely reconstructed the front door with sidelites and transom to fit the original restored leaded glass motifs. During the long construction process, the clients occasionally stayed in the renovated 1,200-square-foot guest cottage, which we brought up to date first with a living room, eat-in kitchen, bedroom, bath, and a guest room loft with dormer windows.

Both barns were in such a state of disrepair that we decided to raze them. Two replacement structures configured in classic, unadorned barn style (and stained deep red) integrate what materials we were able to salvage. The new primary barn continues the equestrian tradition with a working stable with six stalls, a tack room, timber-framed hay loft, two-car garage, washroom, and stairs, as well as a cupola for ventilation.

At the core of the guest barn—a two-bedroom guesthouse with a kitchen and living space—is a reclaimed eighteenth-century timber barn frame, which we carefully restored and re-erected. The older component serves as a great room, with the kitchen tucked in underneath the loft space. A long hall houses the bedrooms with dedicated baths; in one of the bedrooms, the bed lies directly under the cupola. This structure also houses a one-car garage, mudroom, powder room, and coat closet. Below is the battleship of systems that bring the entire property into the twenty-first century, while allowing it to appear untouched by time.

PREVIOUS SPREAD: The east-facing front of the main house, with the Federal block on the left. A custom iron railing frames the walk to the front door. LEFT: The rear of the main house. OPPOSITE: The entry gate features graduated rails and strap hinges.

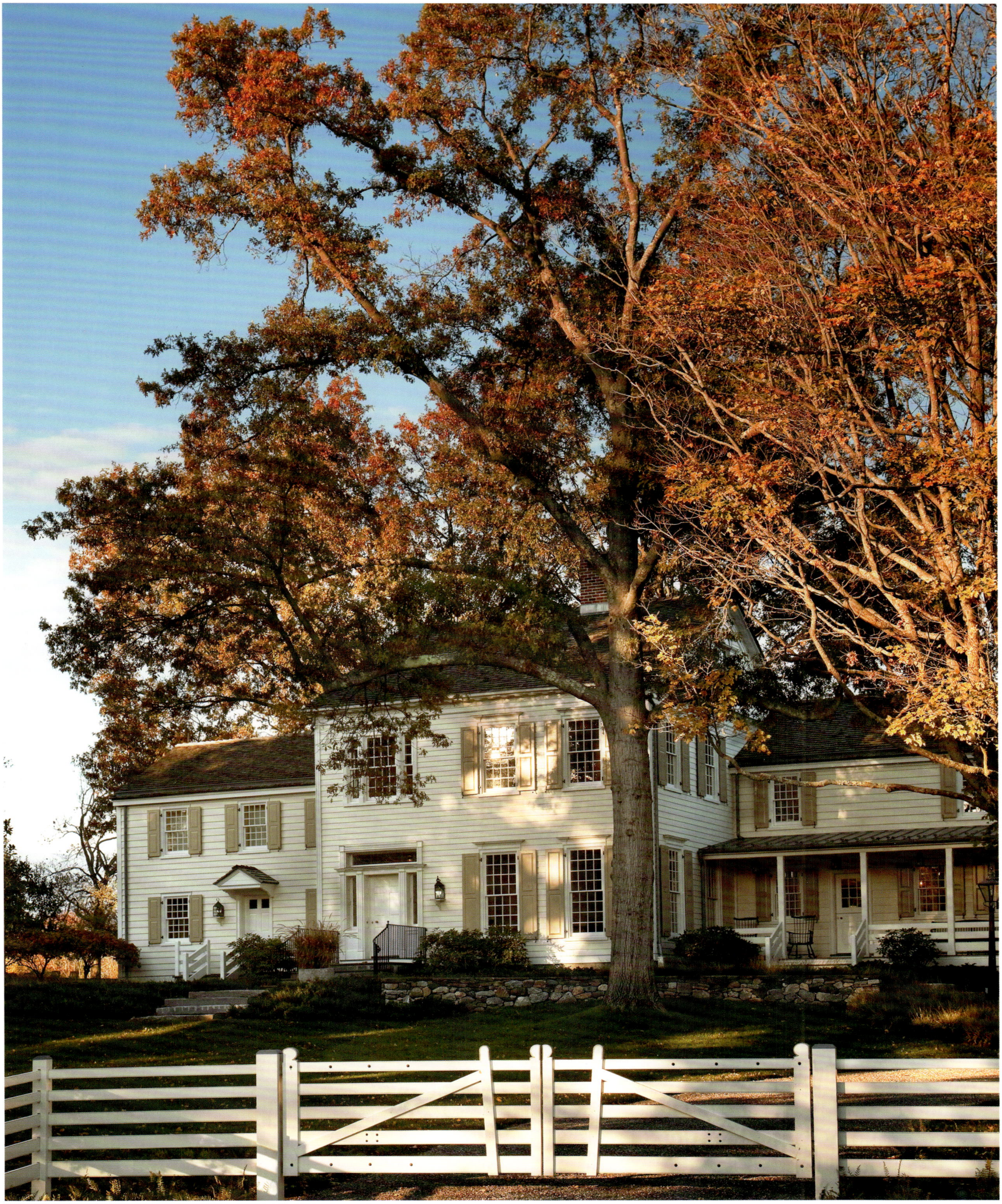

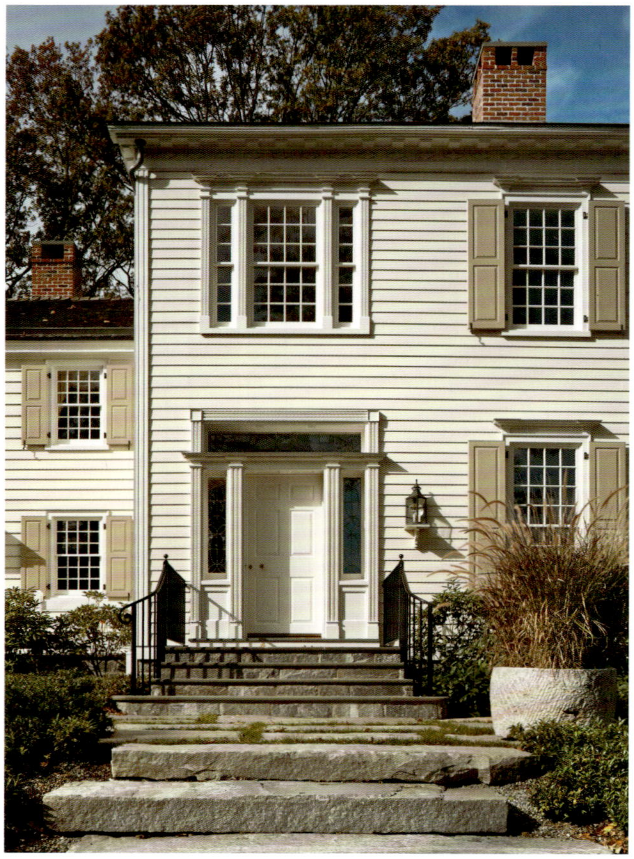
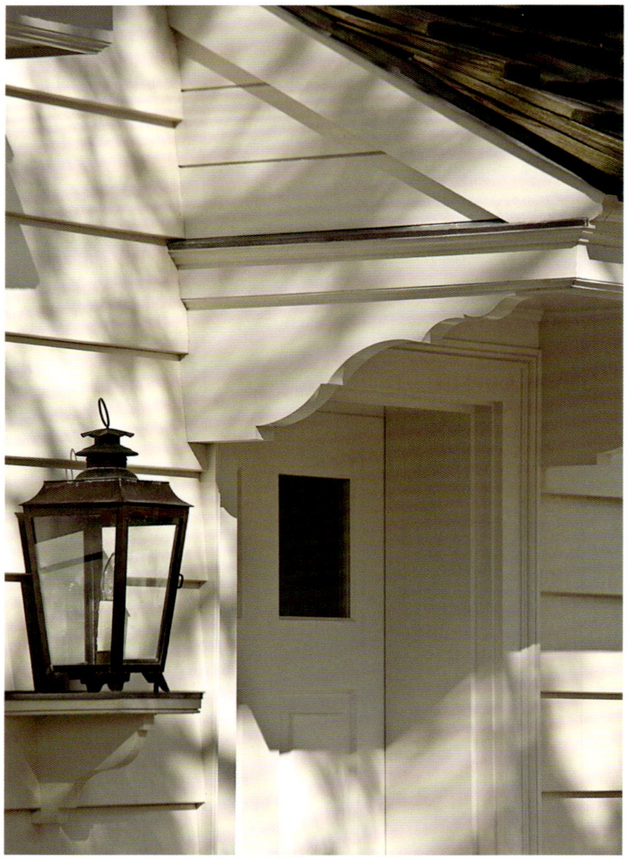
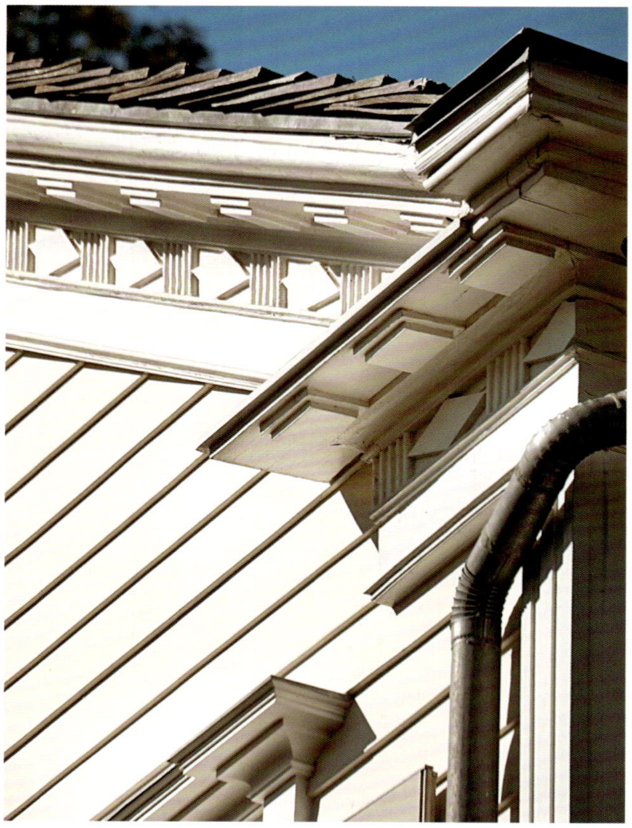
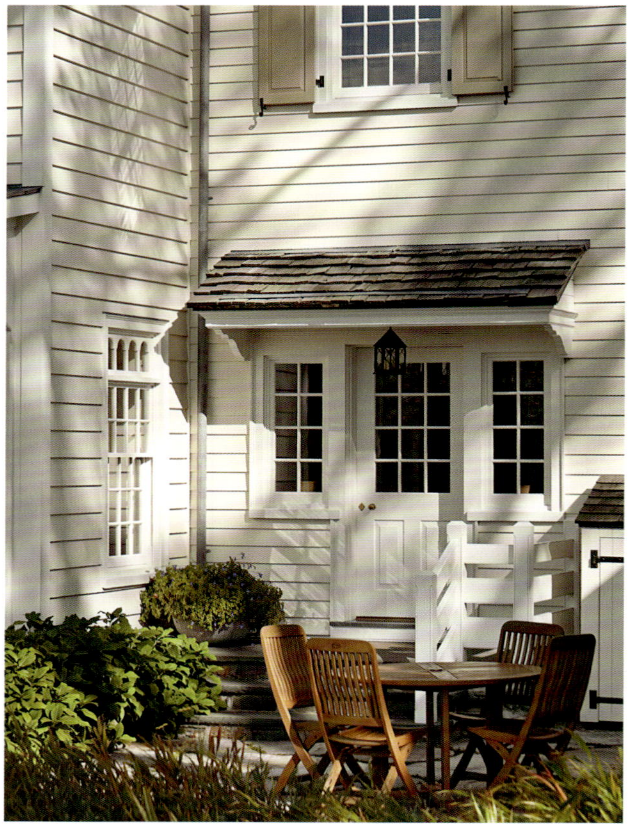

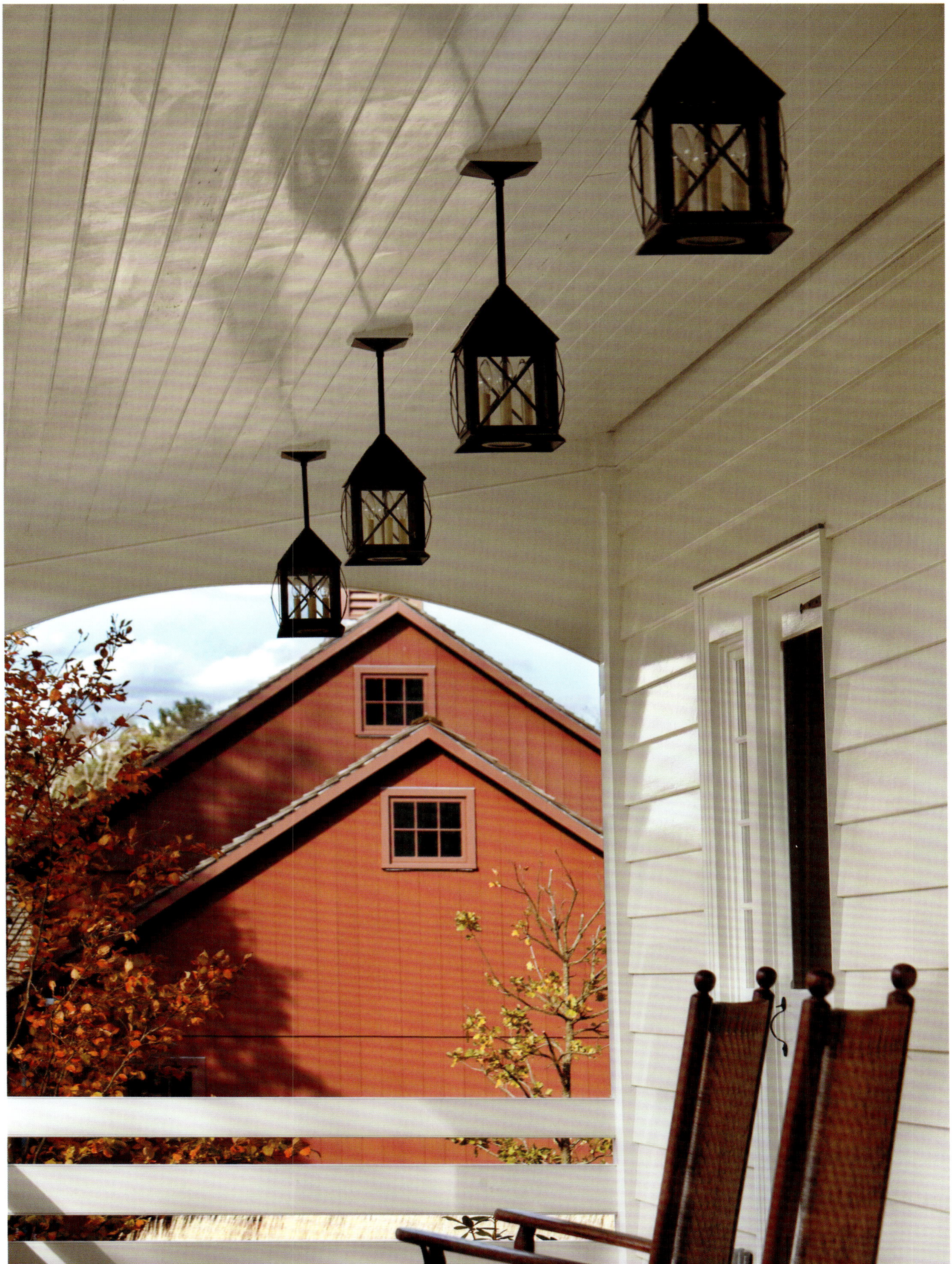

PREVIOUS SPREAD, LEFT, CLOCKWISE FROM UPPER LEFT: The primary entry replicates the original; custom exterior lantern; mudroom entrance; cornice ornament includes modillion blocks and triglyphs with diamonds. PREVIOUS SPREAD, RIGHT: The main house's west porch looks to the horse barn. RIGHT: The guest barn is on the left. In the stables, right, each stall has a Dutch door.

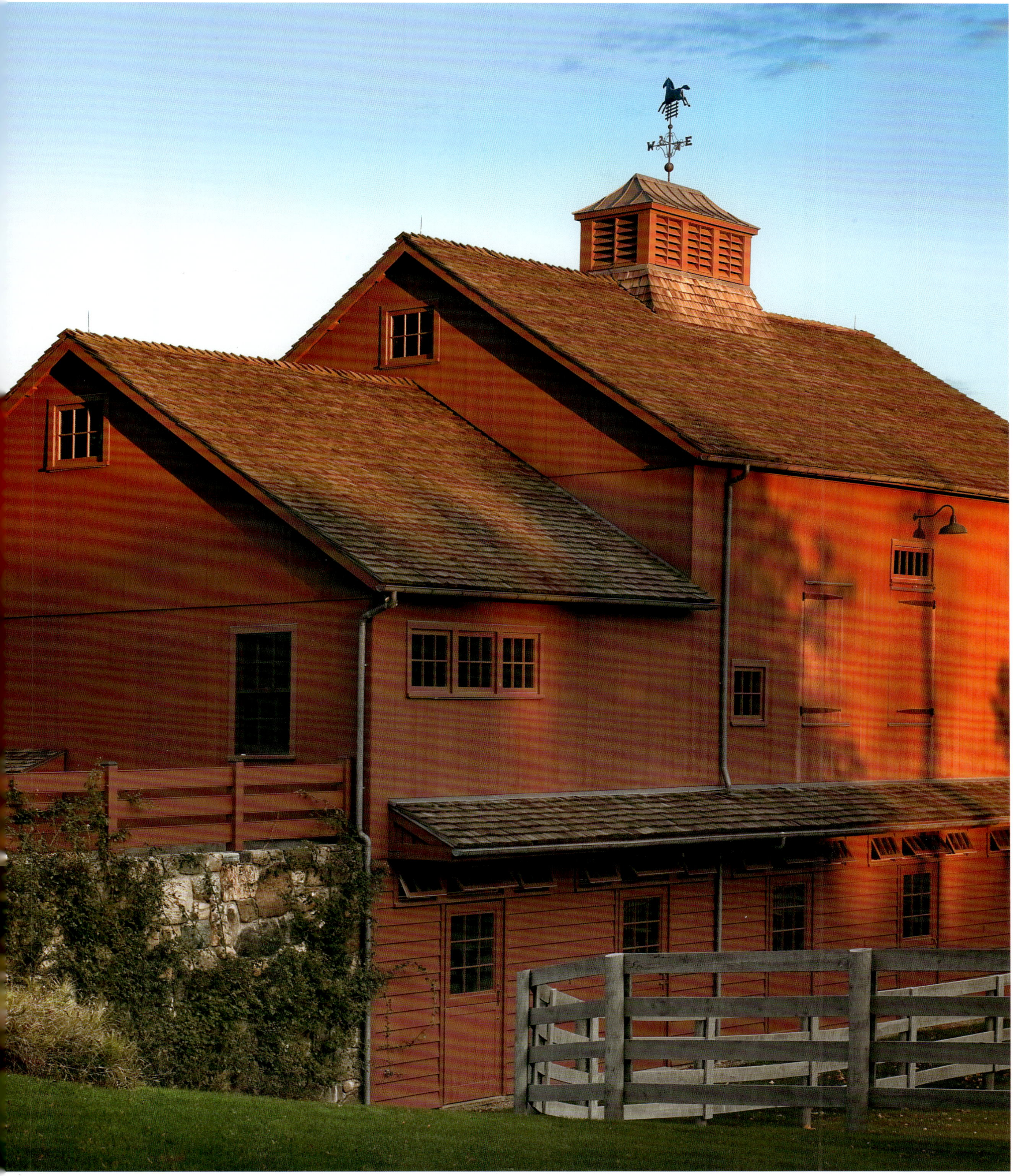
W
E

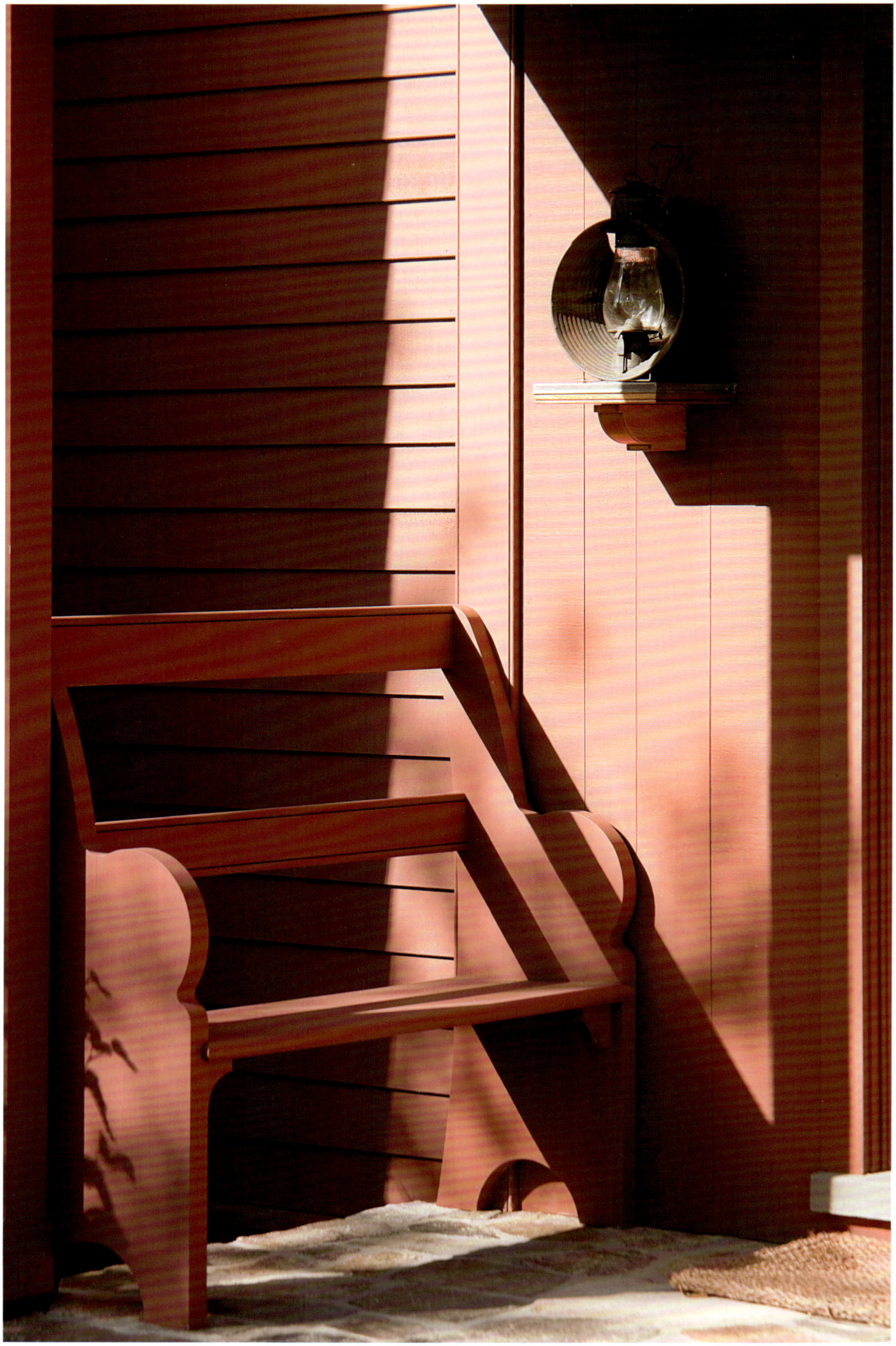

LEFT. At the threshold to the guest barn, a built-in bench adds a note of welcome, as does a lantern on a bracket by the door. Subtle architectural effects include contrasting boarding, with vertical elements framing the doorway with horizontal clapboard predominant. ABOVE: The cupola atop the guest barn sheds light into the guest room below. Sliding barn doors frame the guest barn's great room windows, which are glazed with both restoration and laminated glass.

The Long View

For architects who work in the classical tradition, history is many things—joy, discovery, and responsibility among them. All three came into play with these clients, whose unusual commission developed in four phases over the course of a decade. Keenly observant and design aware, the clients occupy a Cotswolds-style, slate-roof Tudor of stucco with limestone quoining and limestone window surrounds that dates to the late 1920s. Encompassing eleven and a half acres of elegantly wooded, Capability Brown–inspired grounds, the property lies amid a unique, park-like Connecticut enclave planned and subdivided by the Olmsted Brothers in 1925.

The first phase of the project involved reinventing a flat-roof garage into a full, two-story wing addition that is so stylistically aligned with the original structure that the combined parts feel organically at one. The process was a journey. We first needed to take the time to understand the very particular vocabulary of the house—the scale of the windows, the ratio of wall to fenestration, the pitches, and so on. As a result, we created a secondary entry from the garage framed in stucco, limestone, and rough-hewn oak. This phase of the project also included the creation of a ground-floor mudroom, a game room distinguished by a high wainscot, a billiard room paneled in English brown oak, and a wine cellar constructed with wood reclaimed from pallets used on a mushroom farm. A new stair hall leads to newly framed volumes atop the garage, housing a guest room and bath and a library lined in cerused white oak—all under intricate ceilings and a roof with multiple pitches.

Phases two and three involved significant modifications to the main house. Upgrades to the kitchen and breakfast area included lining the spaces in cerused oak, creating alcoves that lead to an outdoor dining terrace, and encompassing the cooktop in a stone hearth. Subsequent revisions to the existing upstairs floor plan addressed his office, now lined in English brown oak, a new master bedroom connected by a mirrored vestibule to his and her dressing rooms, and a master bathroom with intricate detailing.

147

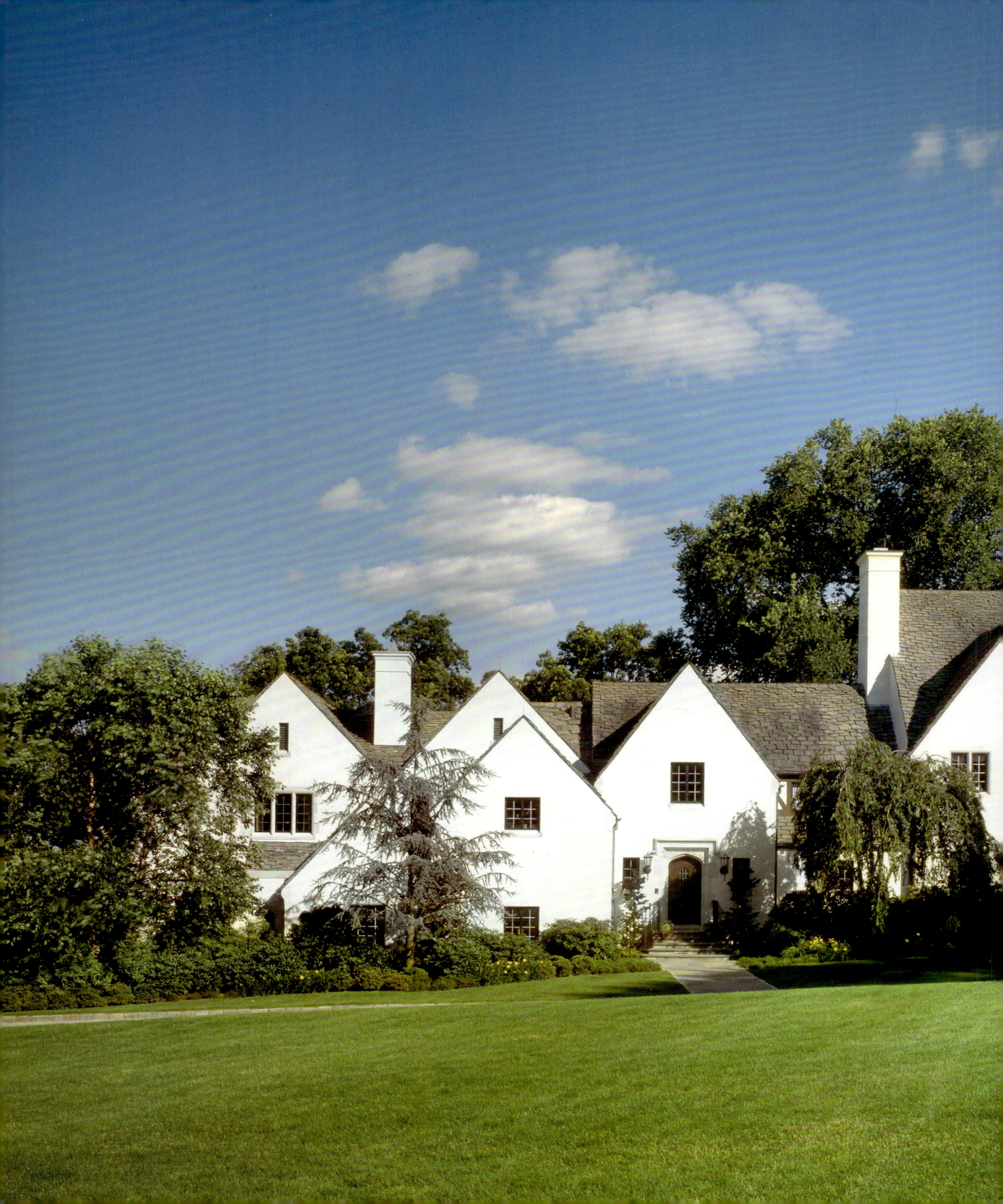

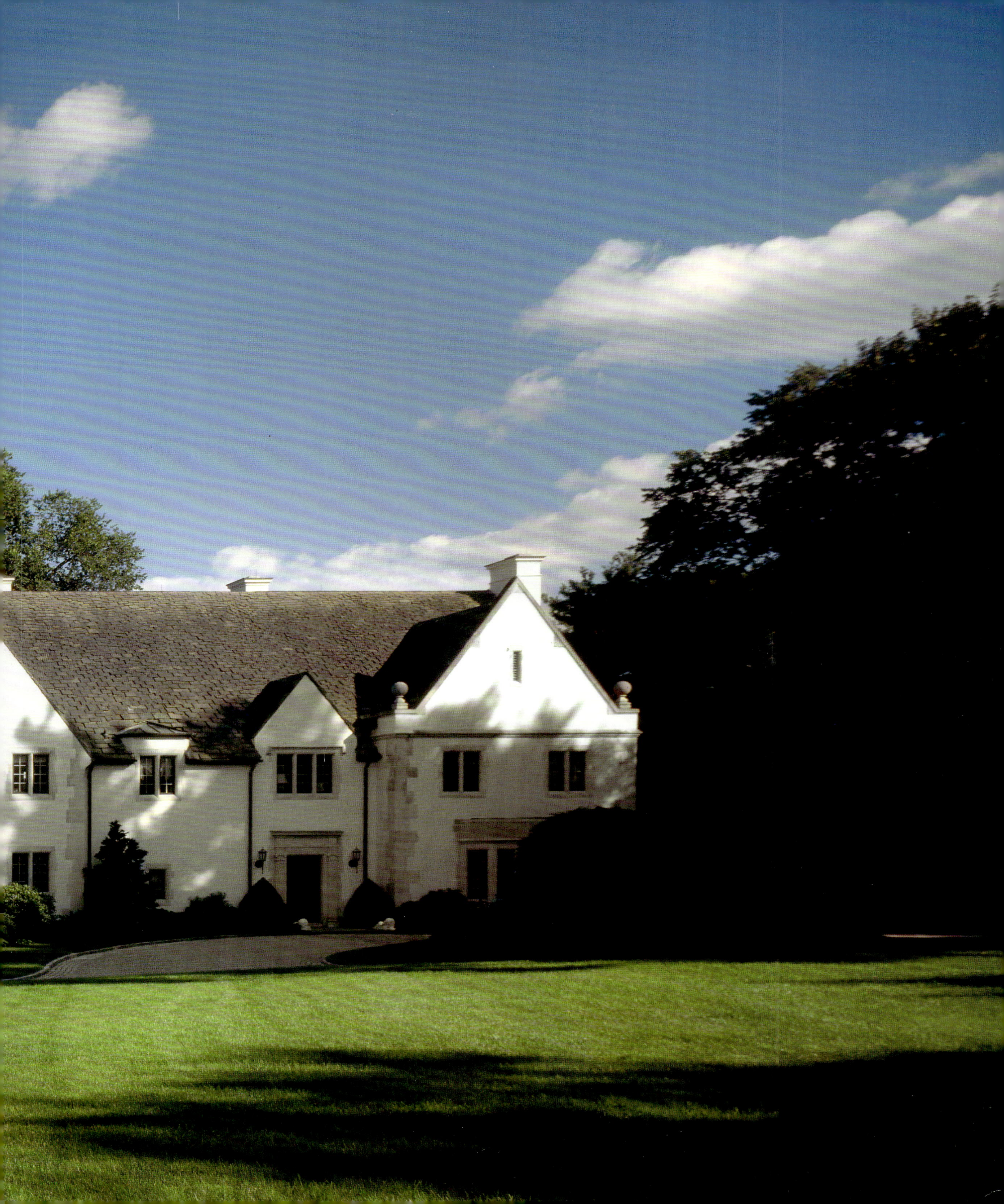

Phase four involved the construction of an 1,800-square-foot limestone and stucco pool pavilion—a chance to build something of rare refinement in quite unique circumstances. The clients had annexed the neighboring property, allowing us to integrate the additional land into the overall composition and carefully select the site for the swimming pool complex within the expanded boundaries. After deciding to site the new structure in formal address with the main house, we realized we had to reshape the topography to create a plateau for the pool house and the pool itself. We opted to orient the pool house on axis to address a massive elm tree that stands slightly to the side of the main house; the cross axis traverses a path toward a glorious copper beech, another of the property's significant trees. In the end, the two structures faced one another directly, but not in perfect alignment—a fact that makes their relationship both to one another and the landscape more interesting.

The zoning required that any newly built, stand-alone structure include all the attributes of a house. That's what we designed. With a bedroom, bathroom, central living area—which we call a tea room, and which feels quite expansive under a pendentive vault—and kitchen, the pool house can do double duty as a guesthouse when required. Two newly planted magnolia trees flank the building, which also encompasses a spectacular outdoor fireplace.

Surrounding the pavilion is a park-like setting created with the landscape designer Deborah Nevins. There, mounds of yew bushes conceal a four-foot-high stone masonry wall, which protects a bluestone-coped rectangular pool surrounded by a soft lawn. In the best tradition of a folly, the pool pavilion and the main house seem to admire each other. They're certainly right at home, just where they are.

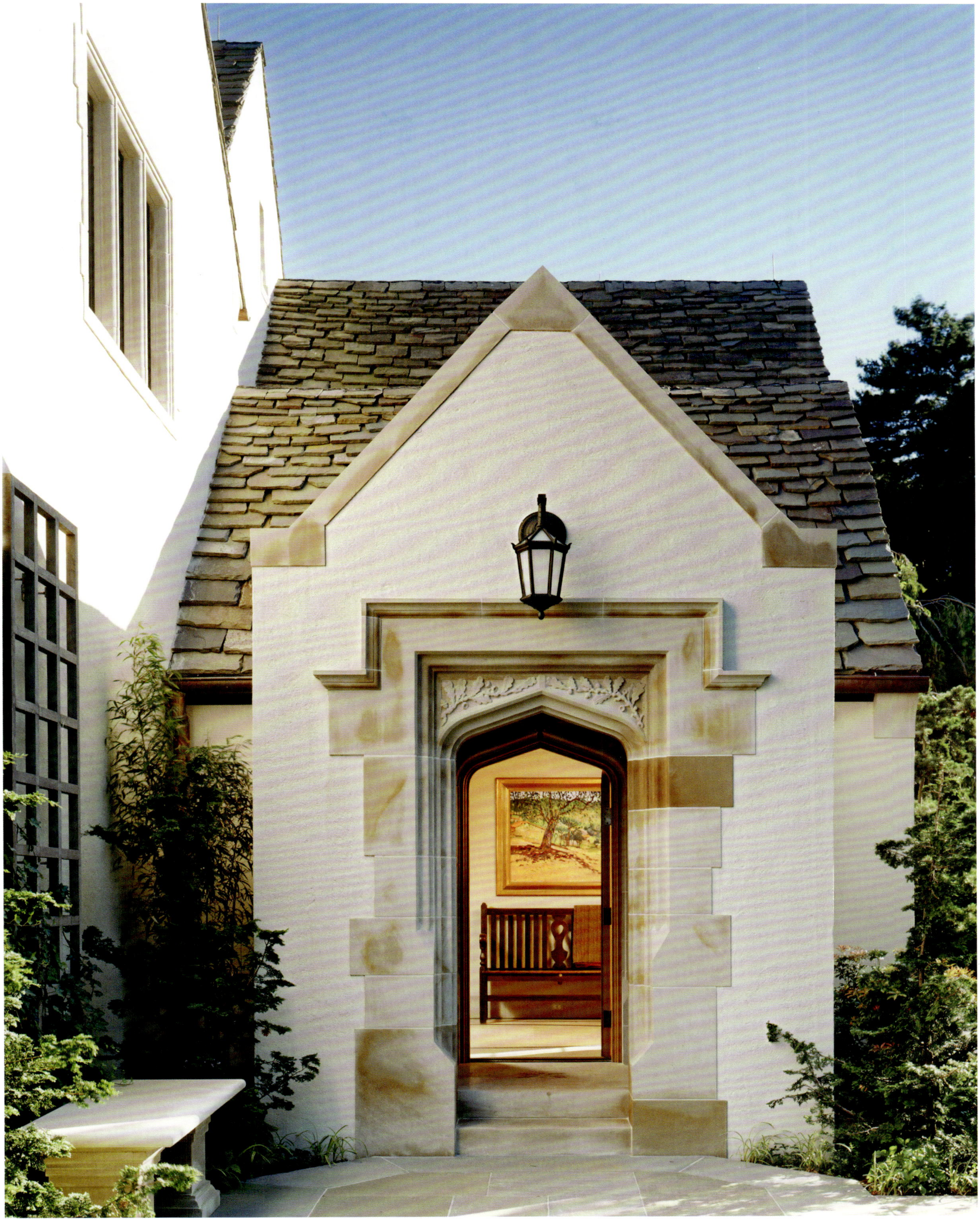

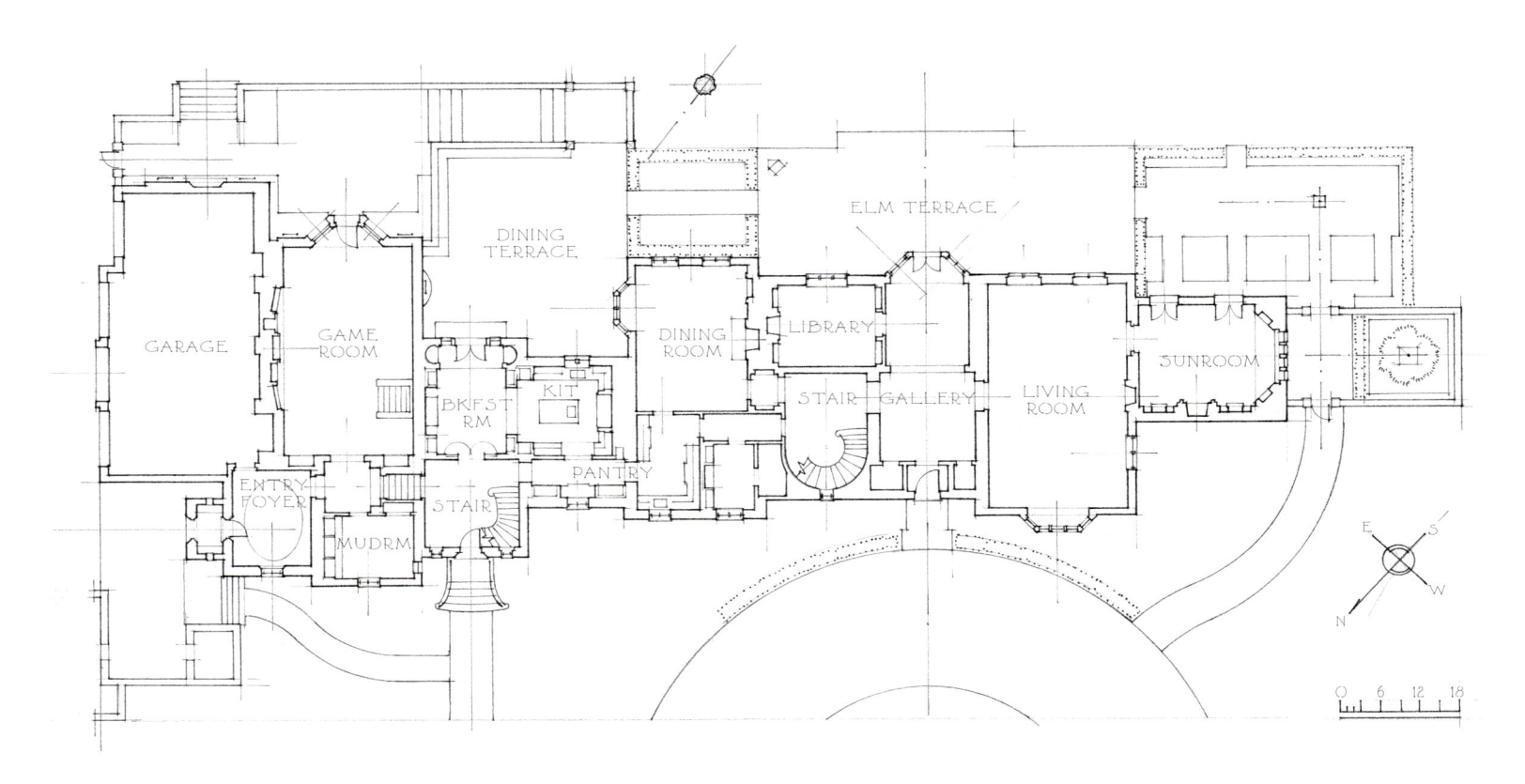

TWO SPREADS PREVIOUS: On the front elevation, matching rooflines, materials, and fenestration create an integrated whole. PREVIOUS SPREAD, FROM FAR LEFT TO RIGHT: The phase one addition, with rooms over the garage; a custom-carved stone inset of the Tree of Life; the secondary entrance, with graduated flagstone roof tiles and limestone quoining and coping. LEFT: The foyer of the addition, with a boarded, coffered distressed oak ceiling and limestone floor of custom inlaid oak leaves. OPPOSITE: The secondary stair features a teak handrail and bronze balustrade.

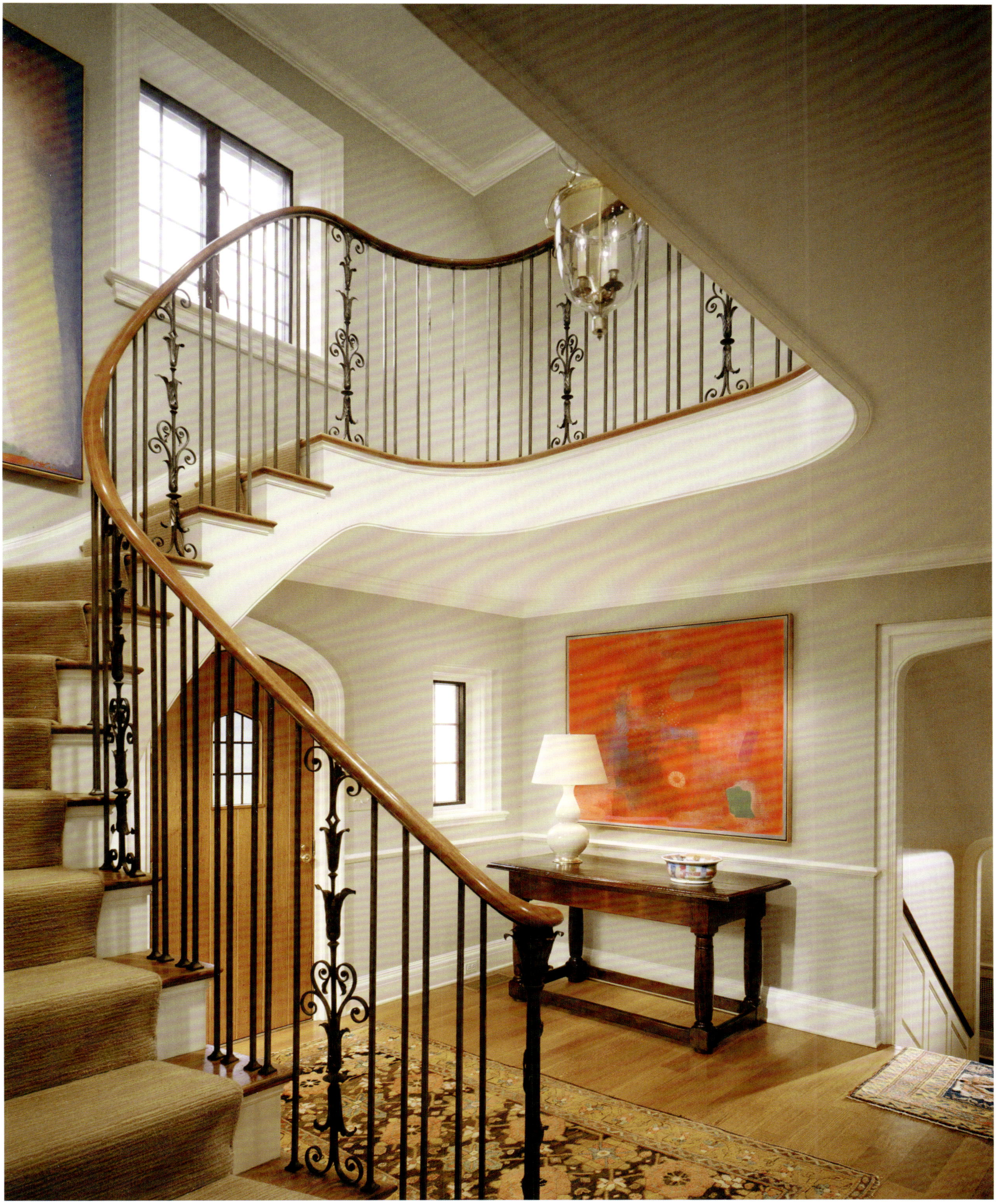

The library incorporates a cerused oak soffit with extended modillion blocks and wainscot paneling, as well as new windows that match those of the older portion of the house. The high paneled portion of the wainscot between the windows projects to reveal a concealed television cabinet.

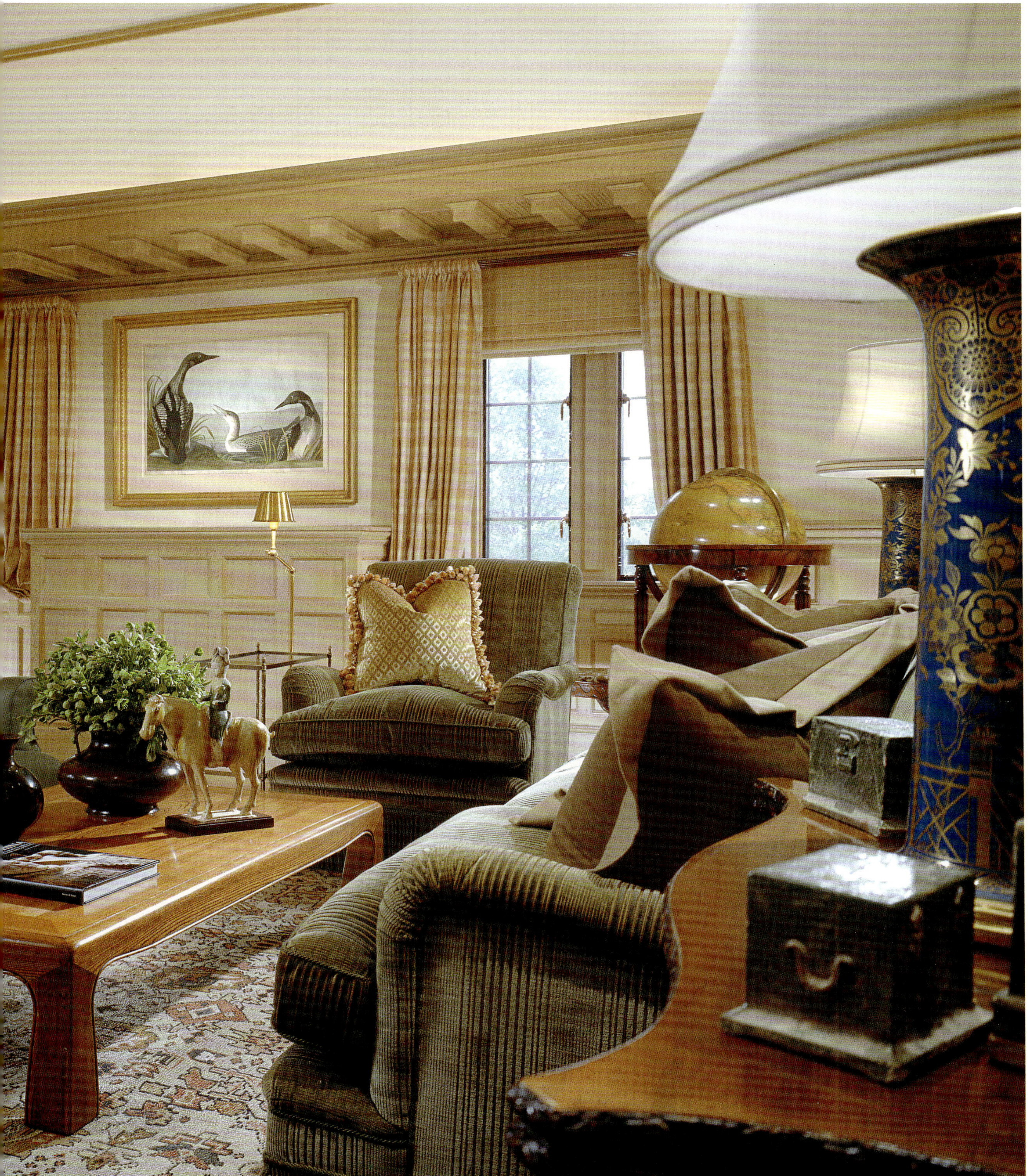

ABOVE: At the heart of the second phase is the redesigned kitchen, with cerused oak paneling, custom backsplash and hood of Giallo Elena limestone, and an integrated system of custom storage cabinets glazed with restoration glass. OPPOSITE, TOP: The billiard room is paneled in English brown oak; built into the bar is storage for the cue sticks. OPPOSITE: The game room is painted wood with a high wainscot. Sound speakers are hidden behind custom trellis grilles.

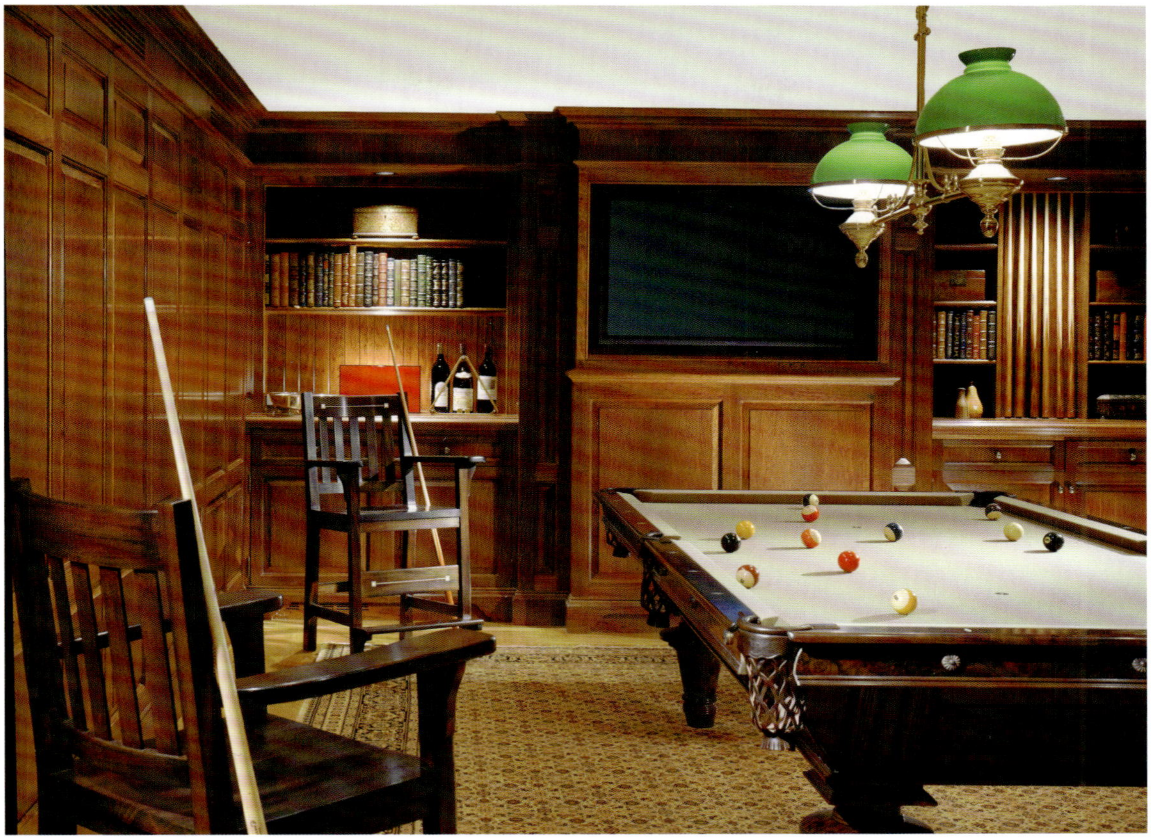

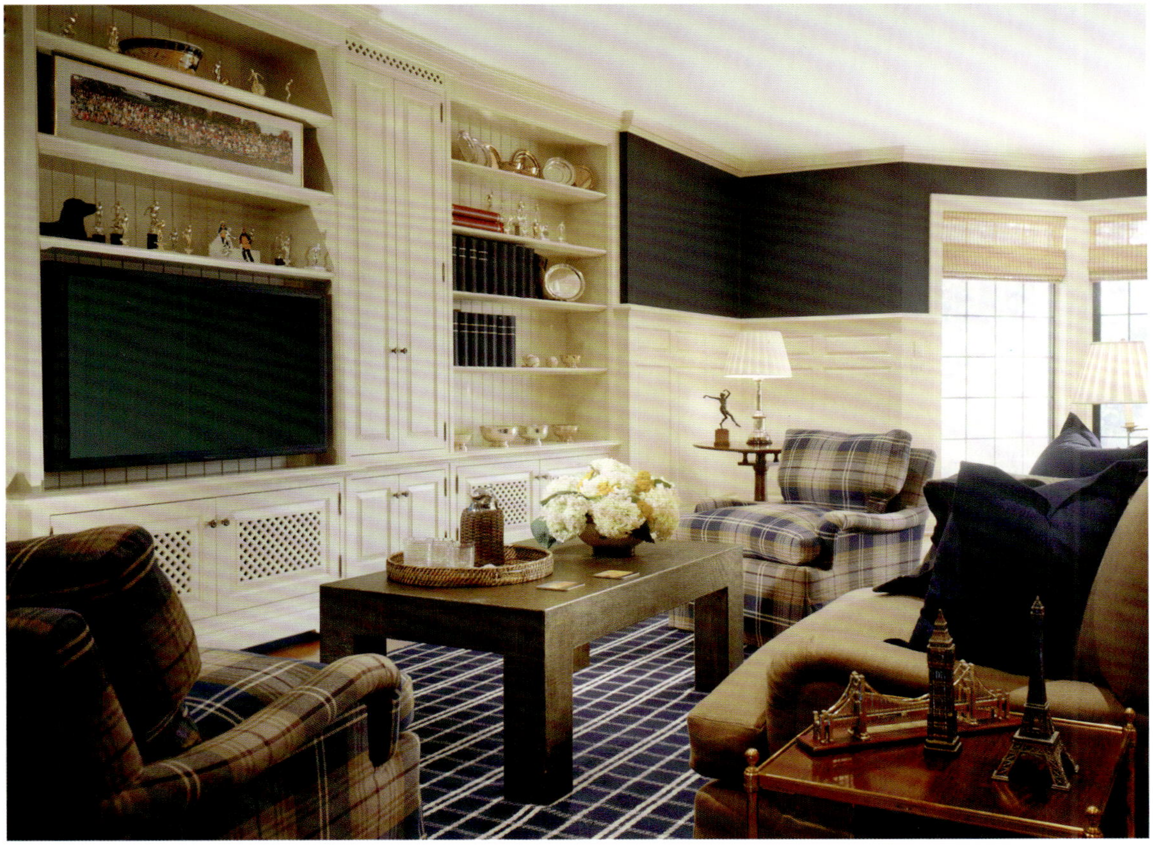

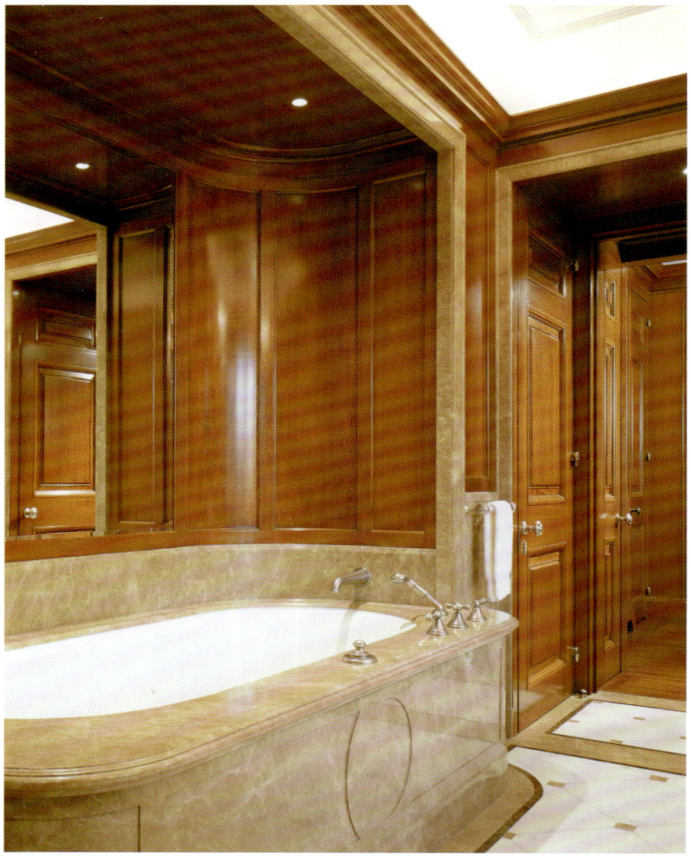

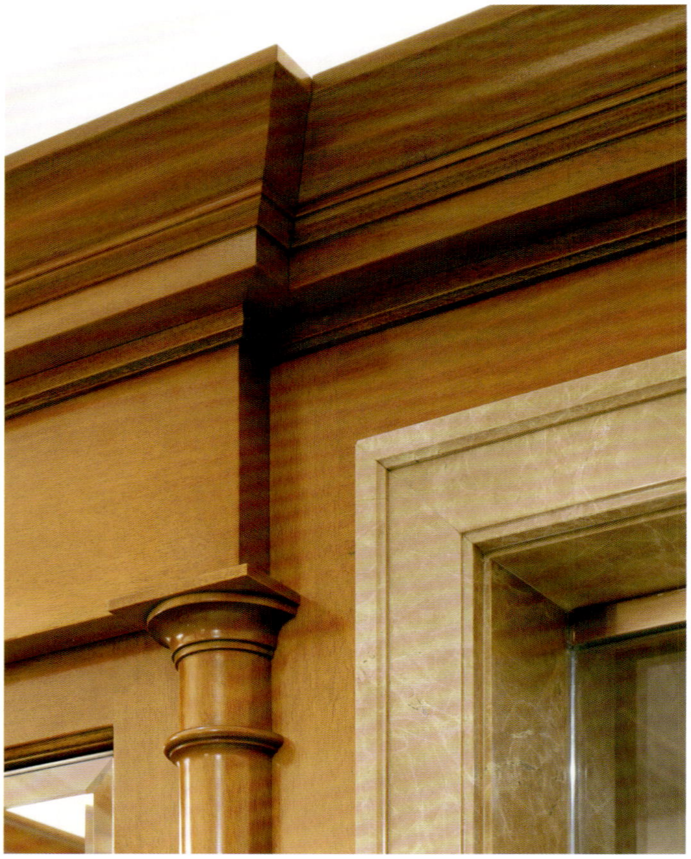

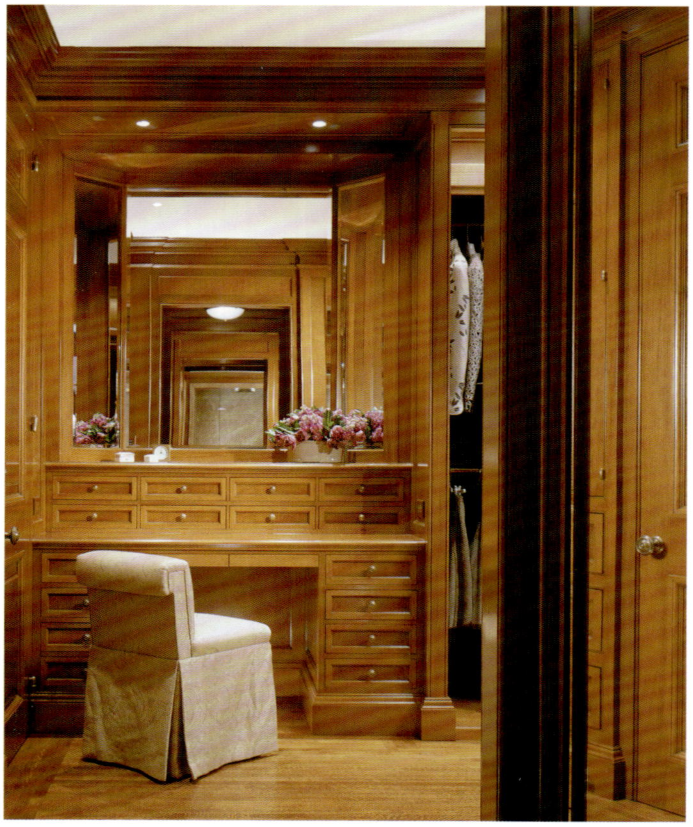

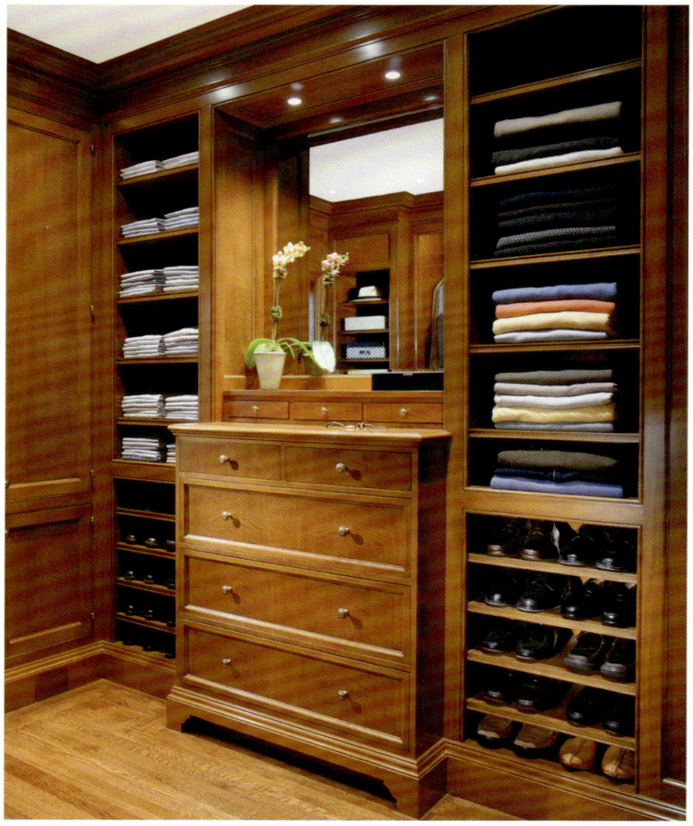

OPPOSITE, CLOCKWISE FROM UPPER LEFT: The master bath, with convex tub apron and concave paneling over the tub; a columnette at the edge of the vanity flanks the vanity mirrors; his and her adjacent anigre-lined dressing rooms. ABOVE: The curved vanity in the master bath is paneled in anigre and incorporates symmetrically placed his and her sinks and mirrors between columnette details on either side of the tripartite window. Three different marble species animate the room: light and dark Emperador and Botticino.

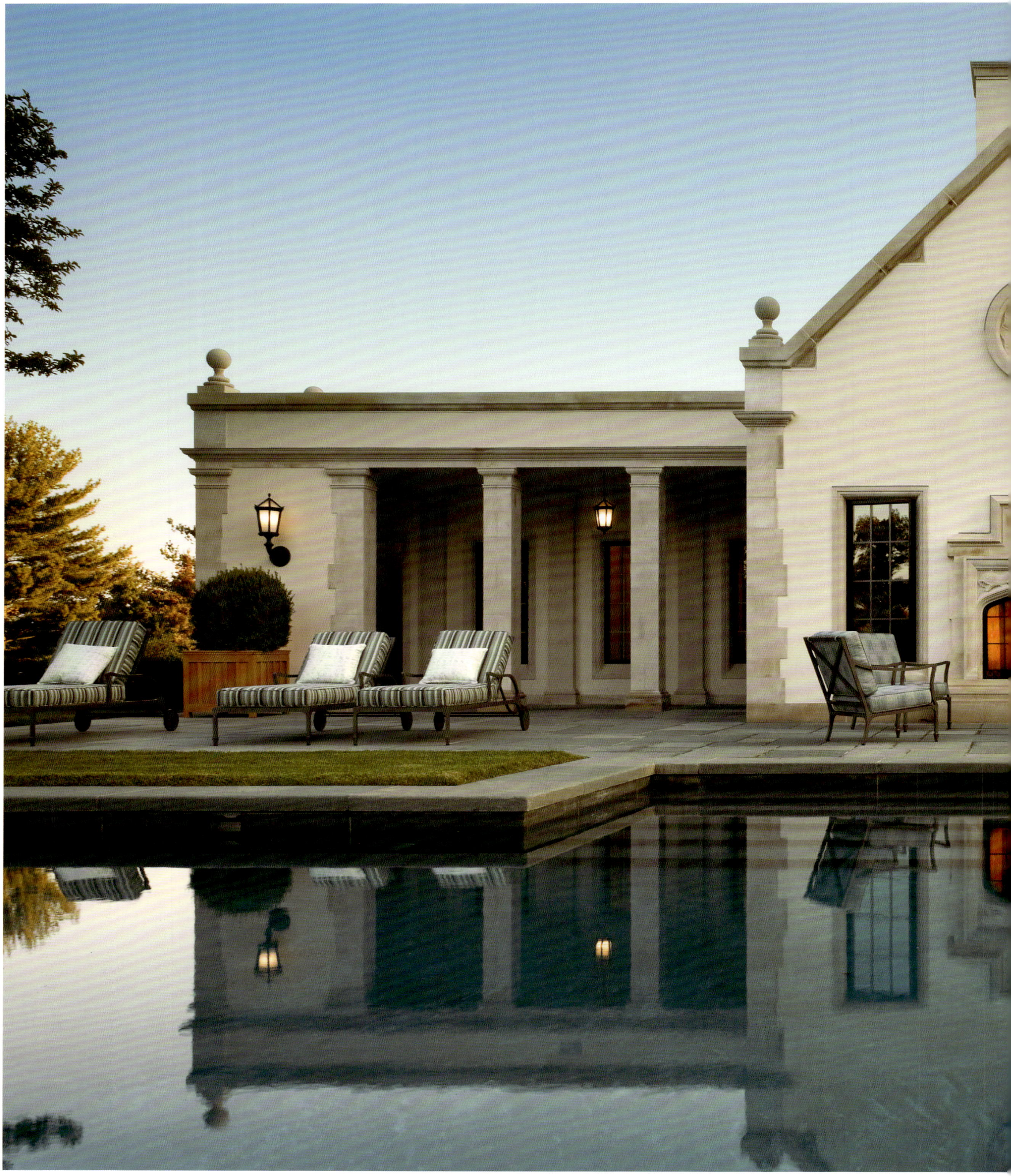

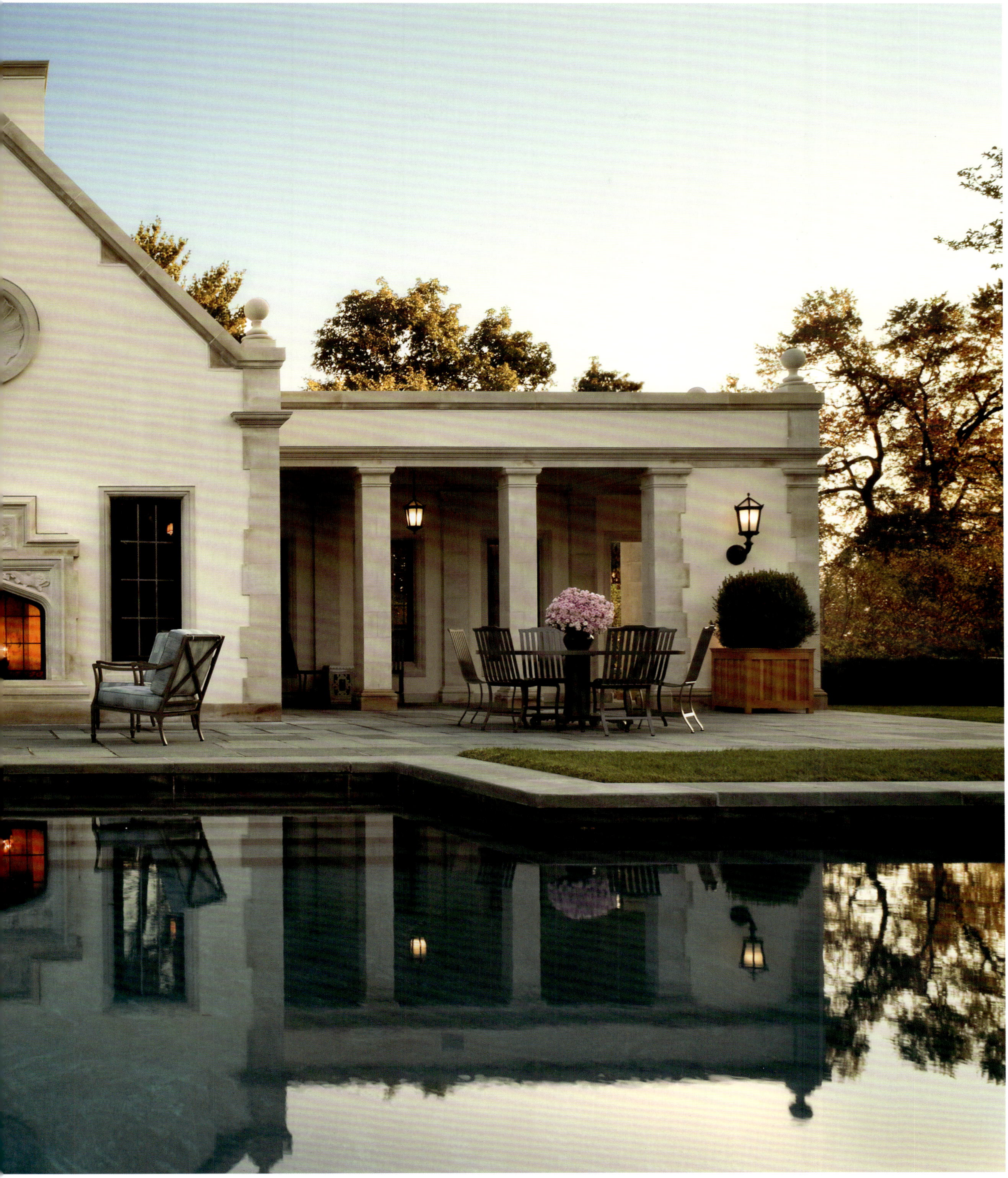

PREVIOUS SPREAD: The pool pavilion, with outdoor fireplace of carved Indiana limestone, bronze spark-arrester screen, and custom bronze lanterns. ABOVE: The grass steps lead up to the pool level, flanked by a pair of magnolia trees and a magnificent copper beech. OPPOSITE, CLOCKWISE FROM TOP: the plan of the pool pavilion and guest house; the outdoor shower topped by a pergola; the interior view of the teak-framed shower, which nestles neatly into the new structure.

163

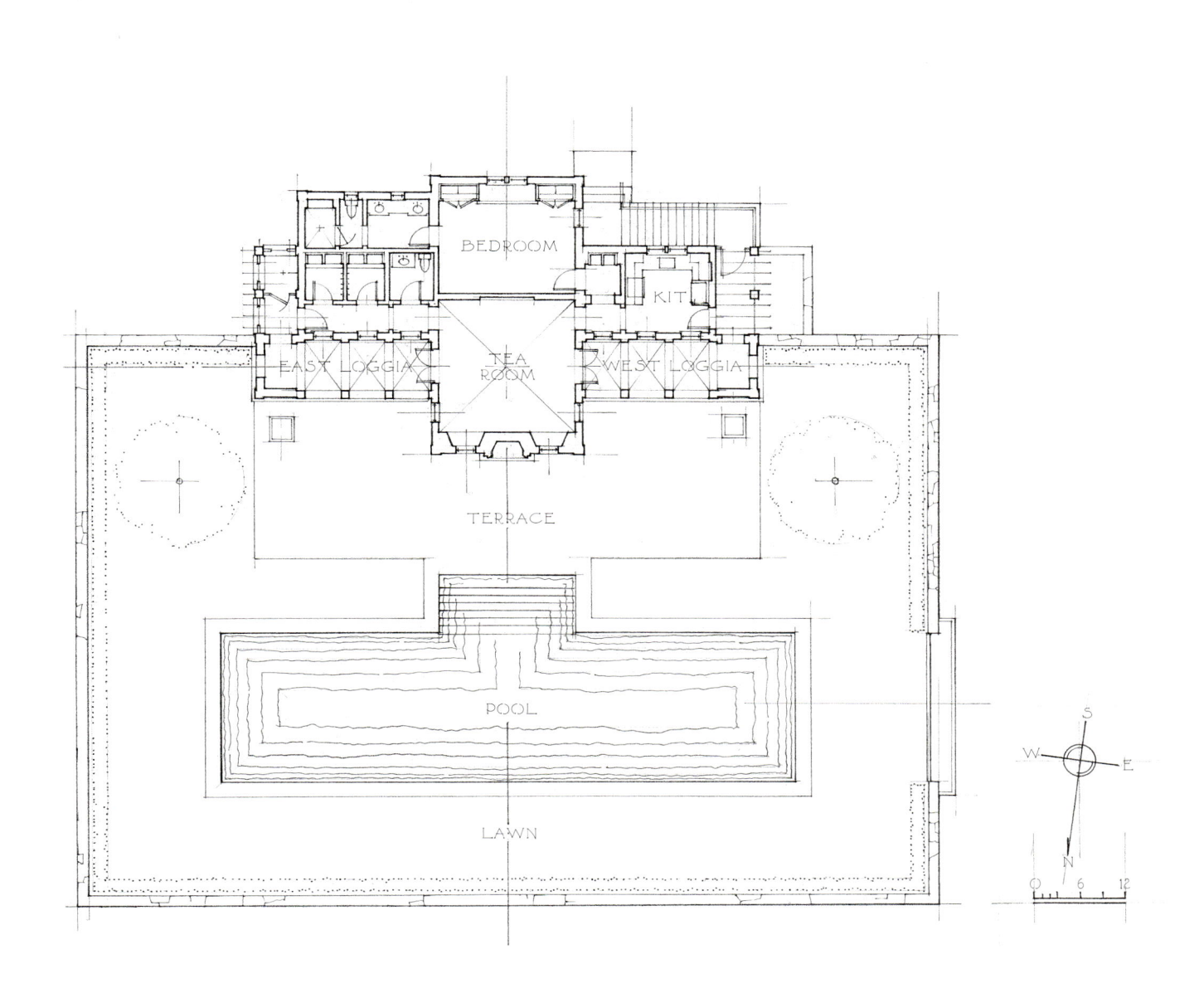

LEFT: The tea room, with arched plaster window returns, has views back to the main house. BELOW: Limestone corbels and Indiana limestone trim punctuate the tea room's pendentive vaulted ceiling. OPPOSITE: The groin-vaults in the loggia feature plaster ribs. Custom bronze pendant lanterns articulate each vault. The loggia columns are limestone; the floor is paved in bluestone.

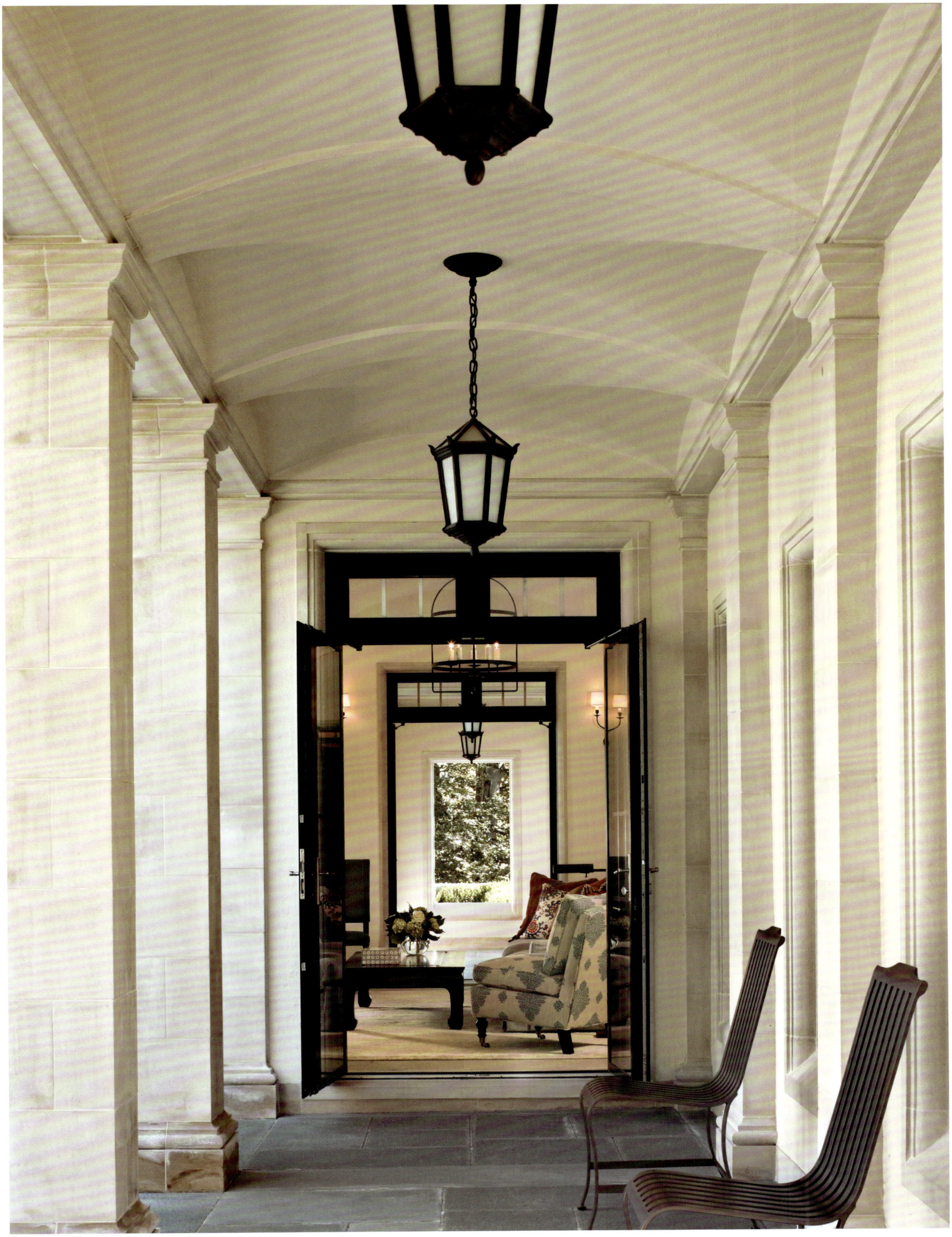

GRACE AND GRANDEUR

Design invention can be a very subtle thing, especially within the formal language of classical architecture. But for those who appreciate nuance, there are always numerous opportunities to innovate within classicism's hierarchical parameters. Take this Upper East Side apartment, a 6,000-square-foot, six-bedroom residence renovated in collaboration with interior designer Stephen Sills. The clients desired a grand, extremely gracious residence with rooms that were utterly unique in character, but framed by architectural elements clearly rooted in the historical framework so appropriate to the space and its context.

The apartment opens with a formal gallery. There, the interior's distinctiveness and axial orientation are immediately apparent, as carefully framed views provide a clear sense of interior direction. The continuity of flooring materials further underscores the paths through the residence's public and private zones.

Defined by a trabeated system of pilasters, an articulated cornice, and a patterned stone floor, the gallery leads directly to the formal dining room. That particularly glamorous space (connected to the family room via a concealed doorway) features window frames cerused with a silvery gray pigment and oak panels with the same finish surrounding gauffraged leather insets in a matching silver gray.

Dark-stained, French-polished walnut doors stand at the threshold between the dining room and living room—grandeur embodied. A cerused oak architrave molding with ornamental guilloche articulates the living room's upper reaches and the window, door, and chimney breast surrounds. A cornice set below the ceiling cove enhances the spatial definition. With wall panels cerused the same silvery gray as the dining room and window frame interiors rubbed in gold, the living room has a very distinctive allure.

The treatment of the fenestration contributes significantly to the overall effect. Tall counterweighted mahogany replacement windows throughout are true to the building's period. The curtains in the living room slip into pockets set behind the architrave molding to create a neatly tailored look and a proscenium-like effect.

Both classic wood-lined study and light-filled sanctuary, the library connects with an alcove that leads to the guest room beyond. These two rooms share a bathroom; when the pocket doors to the library are shut, the bath and guest room are en suite.

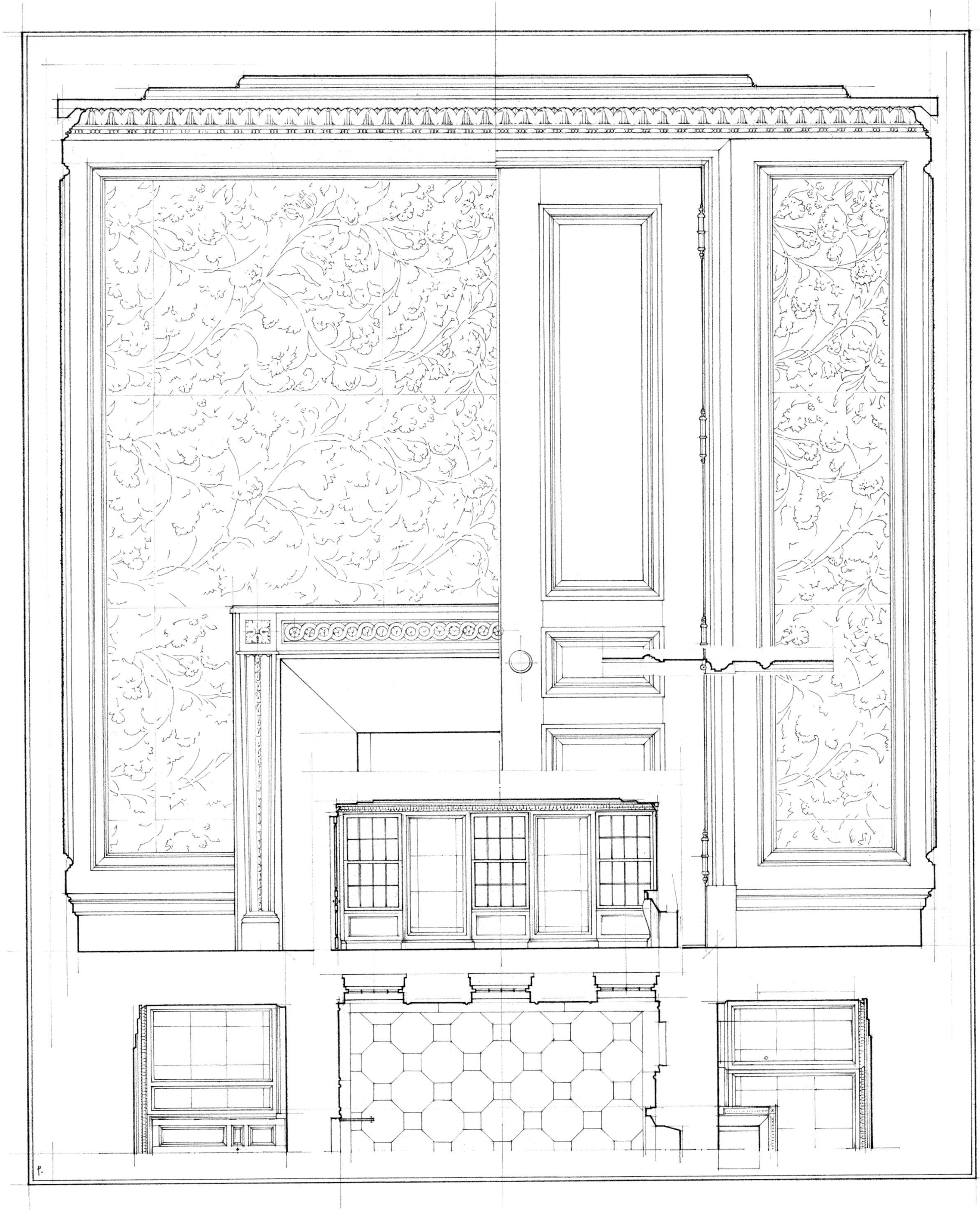

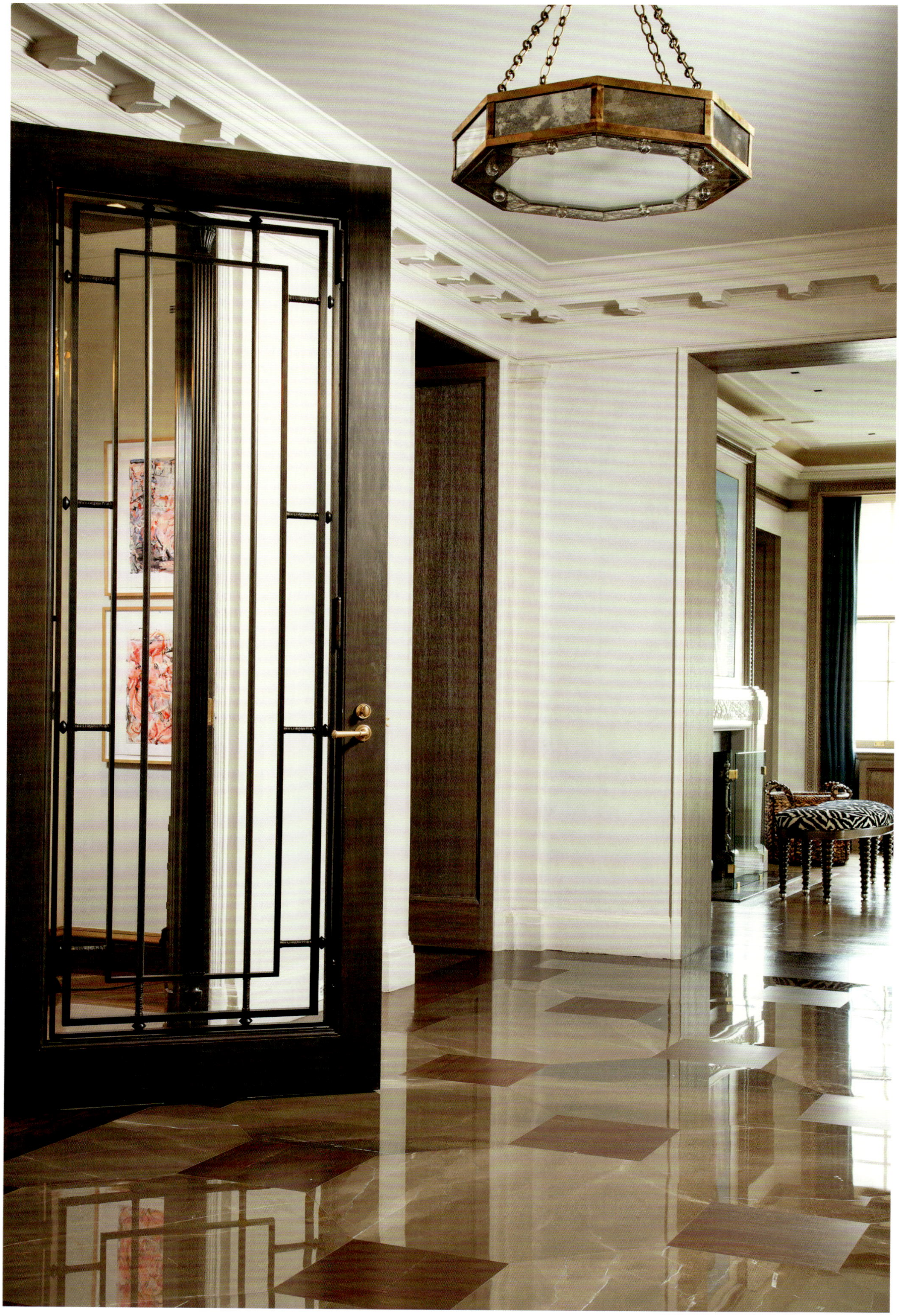

The stone floor delineates the public side of the residence, setting a path from the entry gallery through the dining room, down the west corridor to the library, and through to a vestibule leading to the powder room. At that point, a deep threshold of Harmon-hinged doors offers entrance to the family corridor. There, a guest bedroom, one child's room, and the master suite are organized in an enfilade of openings that terminates in a centralized vestibule, which then turns a corner to another hallway with two additional children's rooms.

The kitchen is quite contemporary, with a charcoal porcelain floor, stainless steel and oak cabinetry, substantial (three-inch-thick) white marble countertops, and white marble backsplashes and returns around the windows. The breakfast area beyond features a comfortable and practical organization of banquette and table; an opening to the family room reinforces the easy movement between the two spaces. Her study occupies the north half of the breakfast room, where a completely new window opens up the area with light.

This project afforded numerous opportunities for design innovation, among them the unusual wood finishes and contrasting stone floor pattern. The chief pleasure, however, goes back to the architect's classic tool of trompe l'oeil, or tricking the eye to see what the architect wants seen—in this case, expansive volumes, elegant detailing, and grandeur.

OPPOSITE: A trabeated system with pilasters defines the structure of the gallery. The floor is a combination of honed Muyu Brown and polished Gaudi marbles. RIGHT: The patinated bronze entry door grille incorporates a flat fluted columnette topped by a lotus capital. FAR RIGHT: With Harmon-hinged doors, the clearly articulated juncture of interior hallways creates a sense of arrival and balance.

The ten-foot ceilings, attenuated pilasters, articulated entablature, and very tall openings help to provide the requisite sense of grandeur. The gallery and dining room (center) share the marble floor treatment, a critical aspect of the design. All the hardware has an antique gold finish.

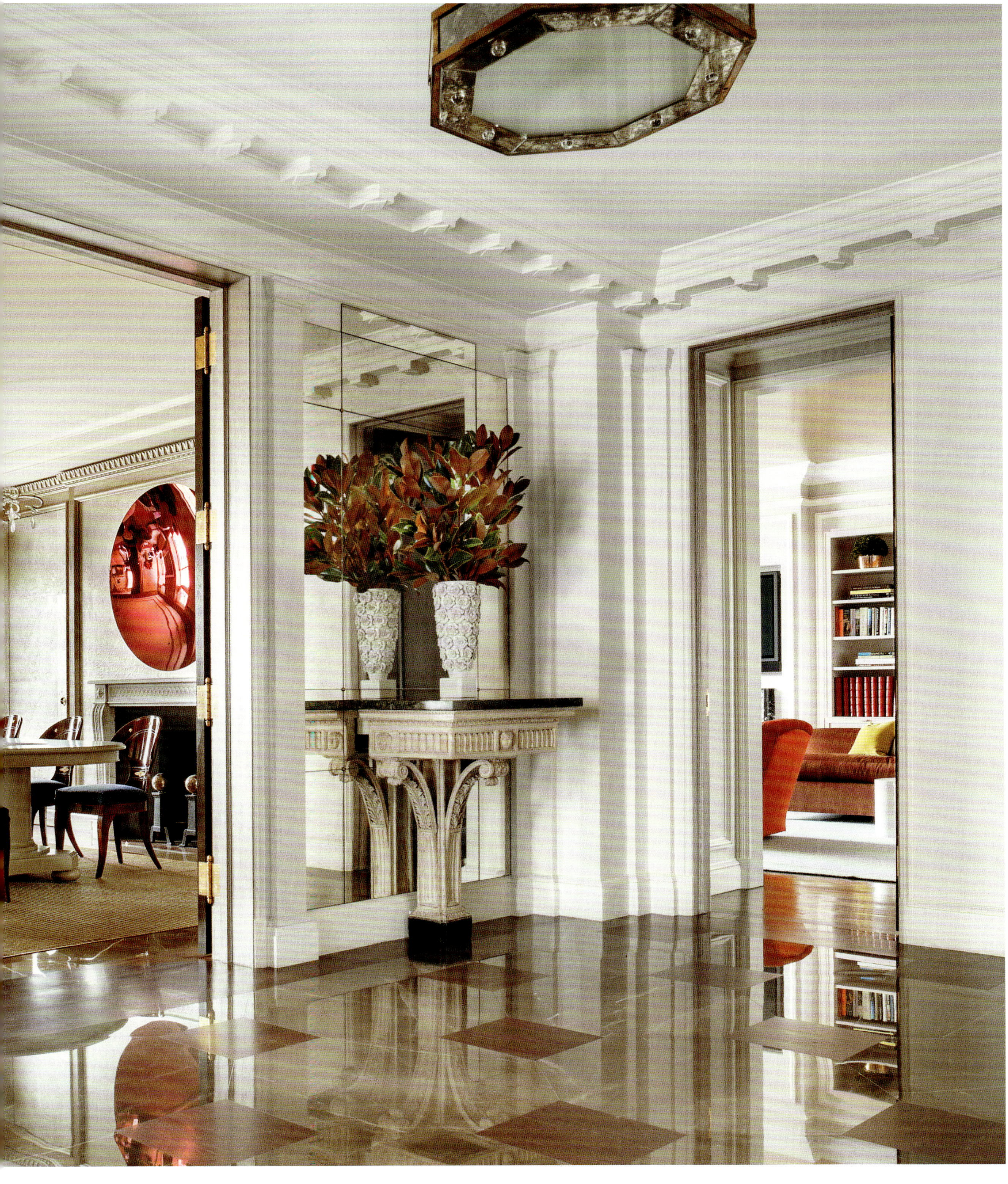

In the living room, which overlooks Fifth Avenue, all the moldings are of solid white oak cerused with silver leaf. A guilloche pattern is carved into the architrave moldings. A cove adds further definition above the plaster cornice. The floor is bleached antique walnut planks. The curtains are hung in the windows proscenium style, which creates a tailored effect.

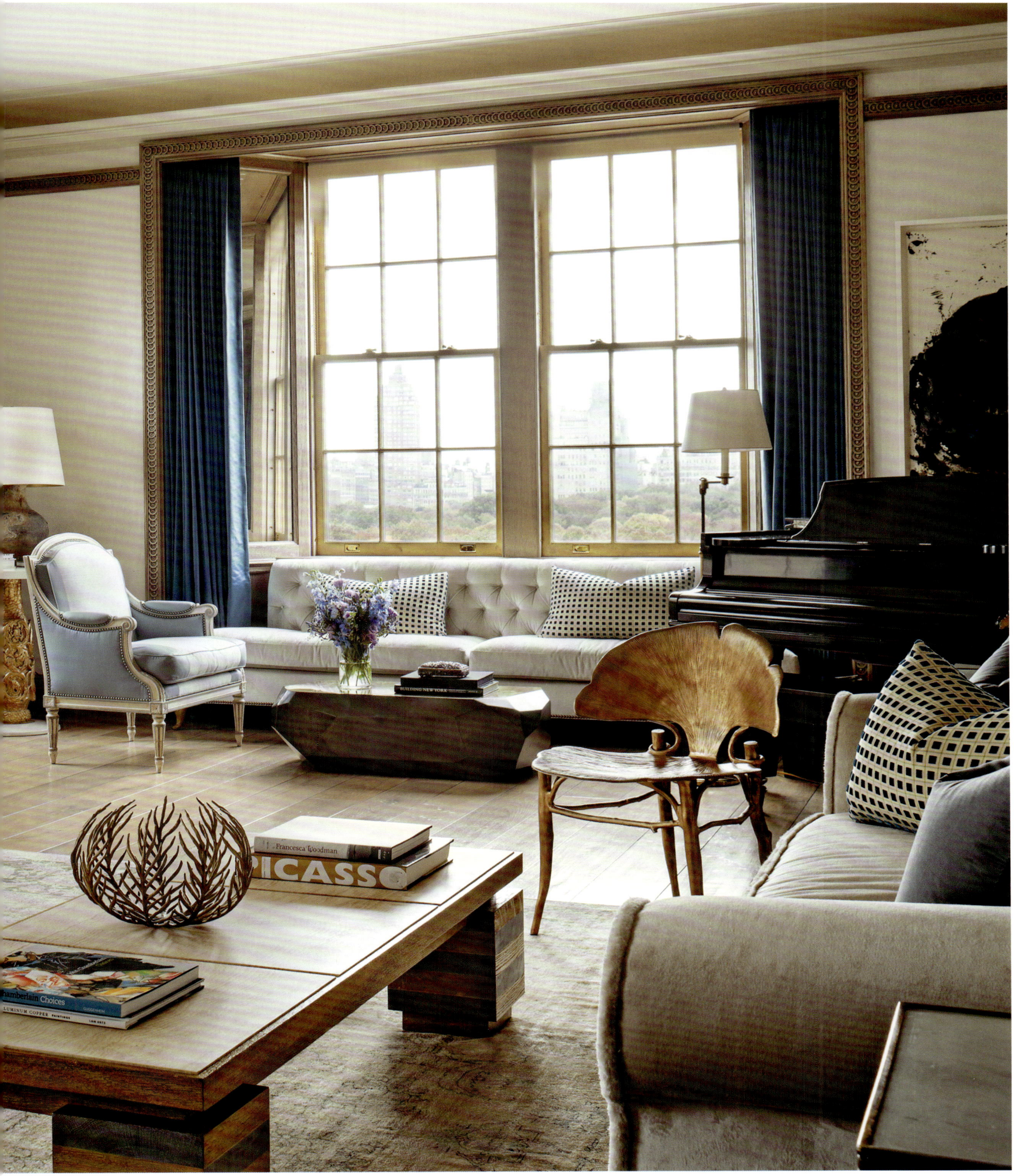
BUILDING NEW YORK
Francesca Woodman
hamberlain Choices

ABOVE: The living room walls are finished with a tinted polished plaster. At one end, a newly created opening provides an entrance to the library that can be concealed via a jib door.
LEFT: The guilloche pattern of the moldings resolves perfectly at the corners, a mathematical feat.
OPPOSITE: In the powder room, primed wood with a decorative paint finish defines corners and transitions and frames mother-of-pearl inlaid walls.

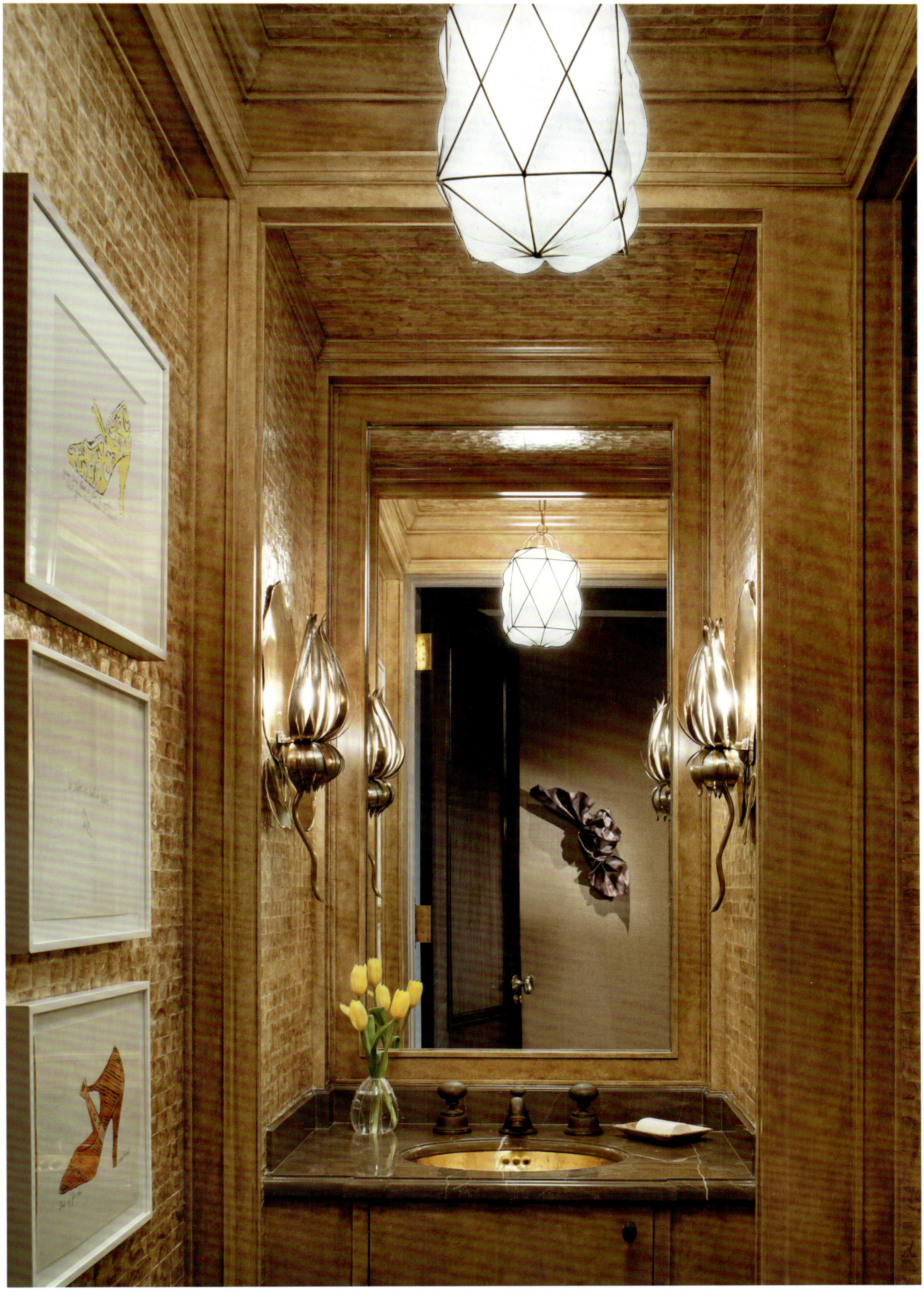

In the dining room cerused oak rubbed with silver leaf frames windows and walls inset with gauffraged leather panels. A jib door at the right leads to the family room. Below the two-step plaster beading that articulates the ceiling is a stylized acanthus molding with a bead and reel detail.

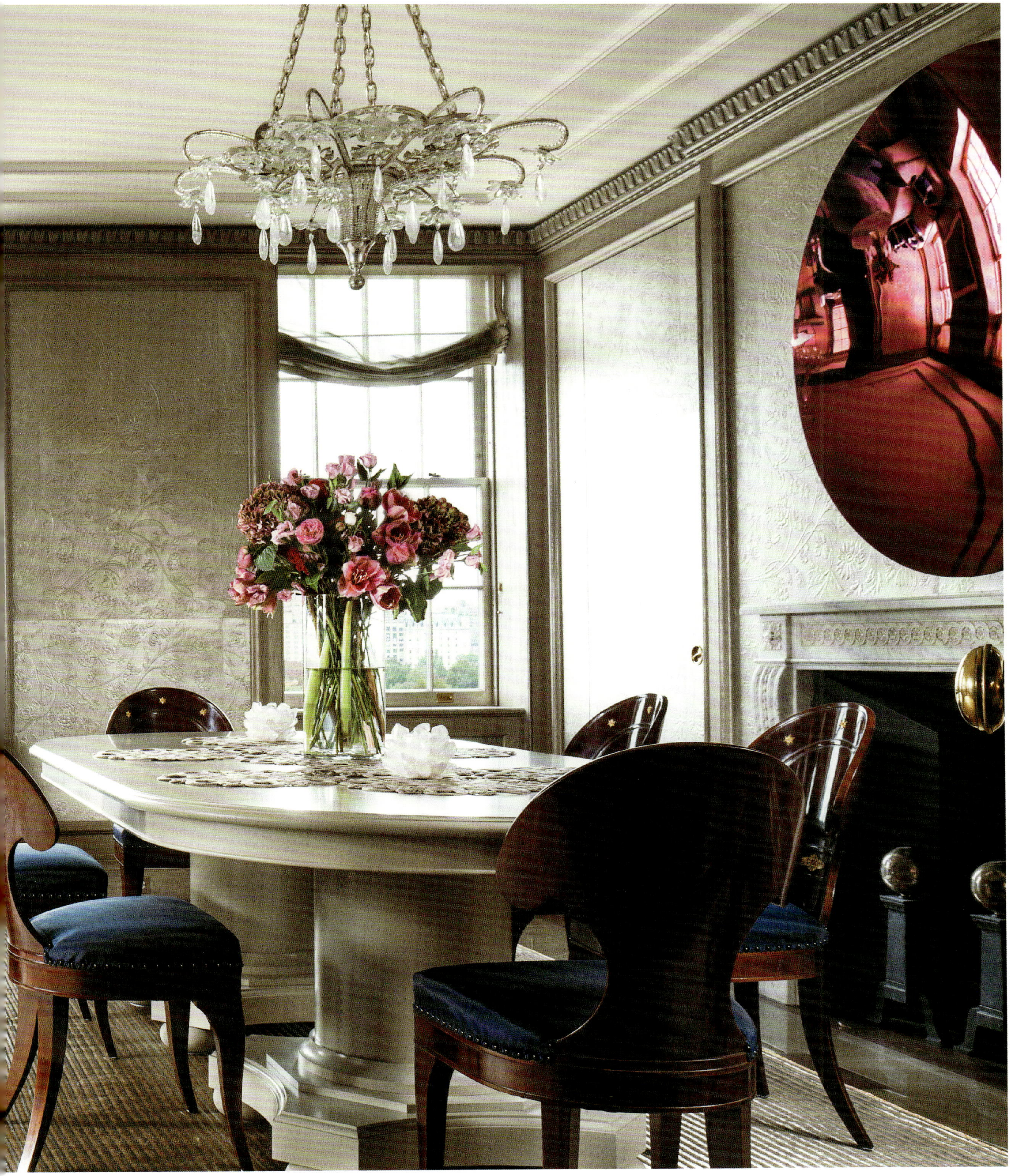

ABOVE: The library is paneled in anigre wood finished with a gray stain. The desk has a view through to the living room. LEFT: Pilasters define the divisions of the cabinetry components. OPPOSITE: For closed storage in the library, fabric is set behind wood muntins. The library opens through to a windowed alcove, which connects to a guest room and bath.

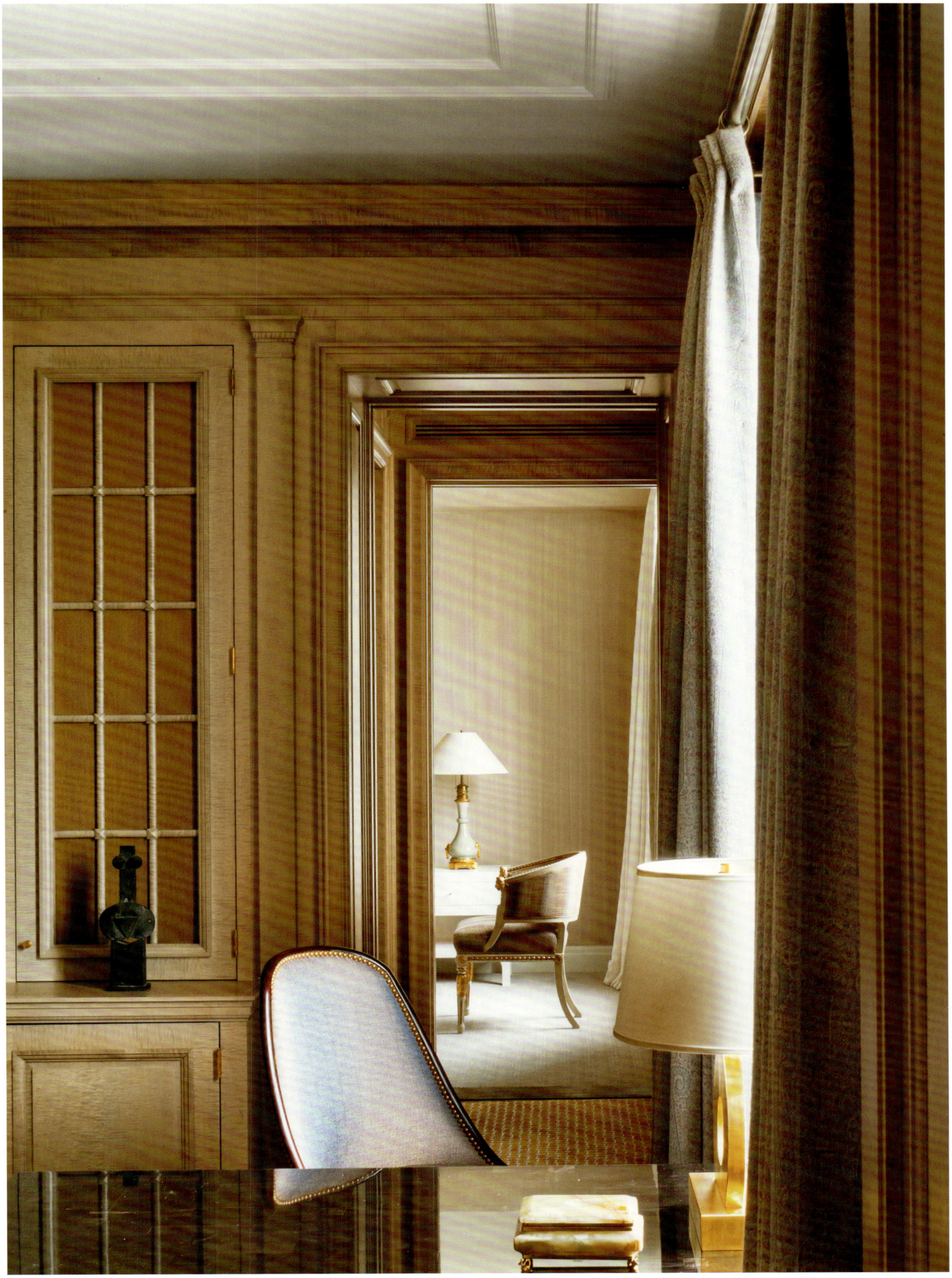

ABOVE: In the master bedroom, a plaster cornice marks the room's upper reaches. Integrated into the design is a pair of built-in cabinets flanking the cast-glass mantel. In each cabinet, the upper doors are wire mesh backed with fabric; the lower doors are articulated with wood fretwork. OPPOSITE: The master bath is lined in white marble highlighted with dark-stained anigre cabinetry and accented with patinated bronze detailing and trim.

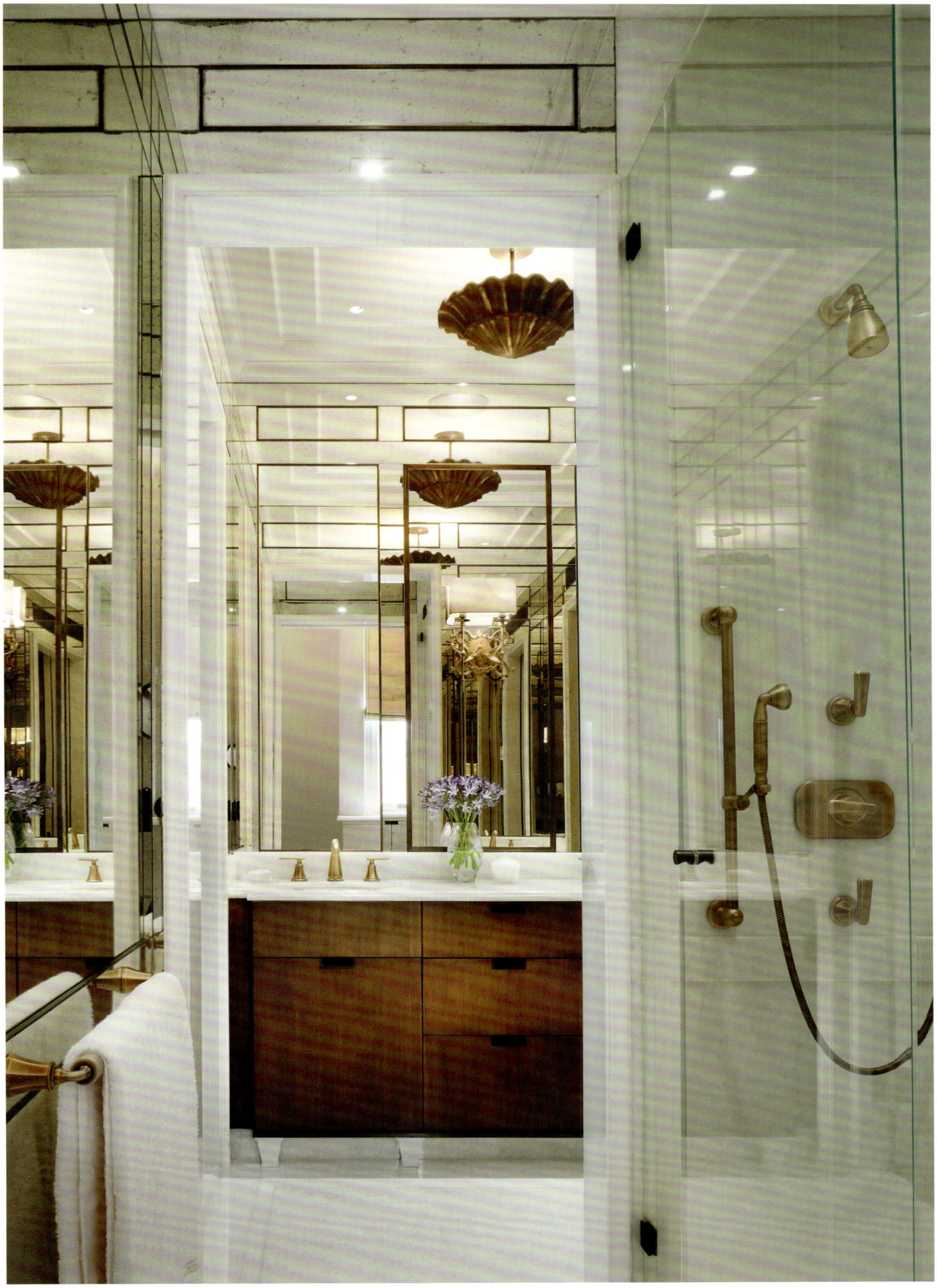

Creating a Classic

It's hard to deny the appeal of the massive, old shingle-style cottages that still dot the shore of Long Island's South Fork. For many, these weathered, cedar-shake-clad piles are archetypes of the perfect summer. That was certainly the case for these longtime clients, who found themselves deeply attracted to the exterior form of this turn-of-the-twentieth-century cottage, with its dormers, entry portico, window bays, and commanding lawns. What none of us knew until later was that the interior was devoid of original detail. No historic moldings. No artful balustrade. The sole artifact? A loose wood shake inscribed: "It's July 8th, a beautiful sunny day. 1900."

That absence of historical vestiges gave us the perfect opportunity to interpret what might have been, and to create what ought to be, in a renovation that encompassed approximately 8,900 square feet of living space. The front of the house—with a newly interpolated balustrade and completely reorganized portico columns—speaks to the style and degree of the incorporated refinements.

We began with new foundations and a fully articulated basement. Reached by a spacious areaway that runs alongside the house, it contains a light-filled playroom, an exercise room, a wine cellar, and the mechanical hub.

The radically reorganized ground floor now includes a proper entry foyer, which leads into a light-filled central stair hall detailed with a balustrade, a gracious staircase, and twin elliptical arches that frame the flanking living and dining rooms. Inserted into a bay where the main stair once nested are a powder room and a coat room. Off the entry foyer is the library, paneled in weathered cypress. Boarding effects enliven the walls and ceilings throughout, from the high wainscot paneling in the powder room to the planked ceiling over the dining porch. At the rear of the house and convenient to the pool area is the secondary entrance, with an outdoor shower, bathroom, laundry area, mudroom, kitchen, breakfast room, and secondary stair. Back-to-back fireplaces serve both the family room and a screened porch with an outdoor dining area. An open veranda faces a lily pond. Reclaimed, wide-plank oak flooring adds

183

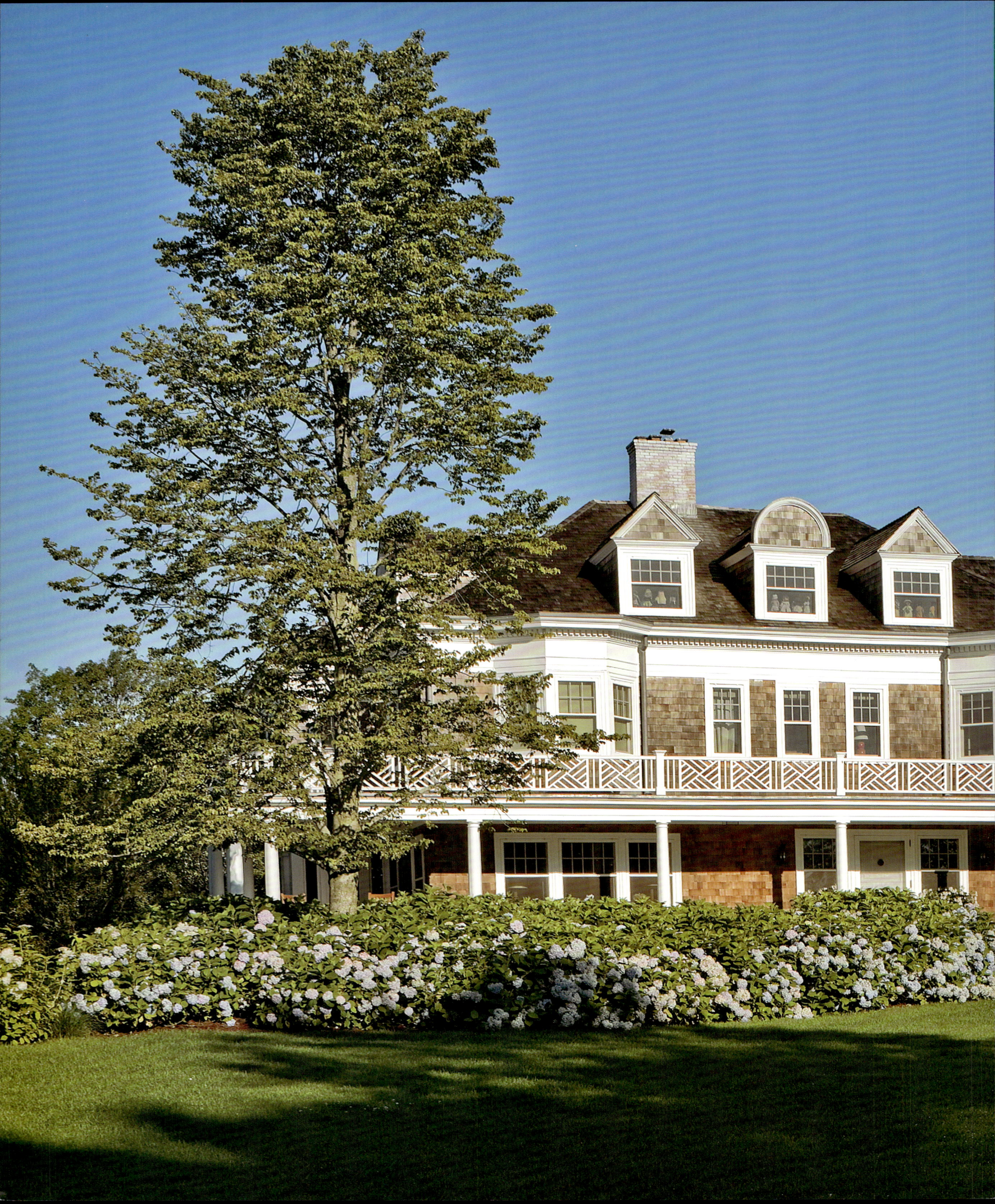

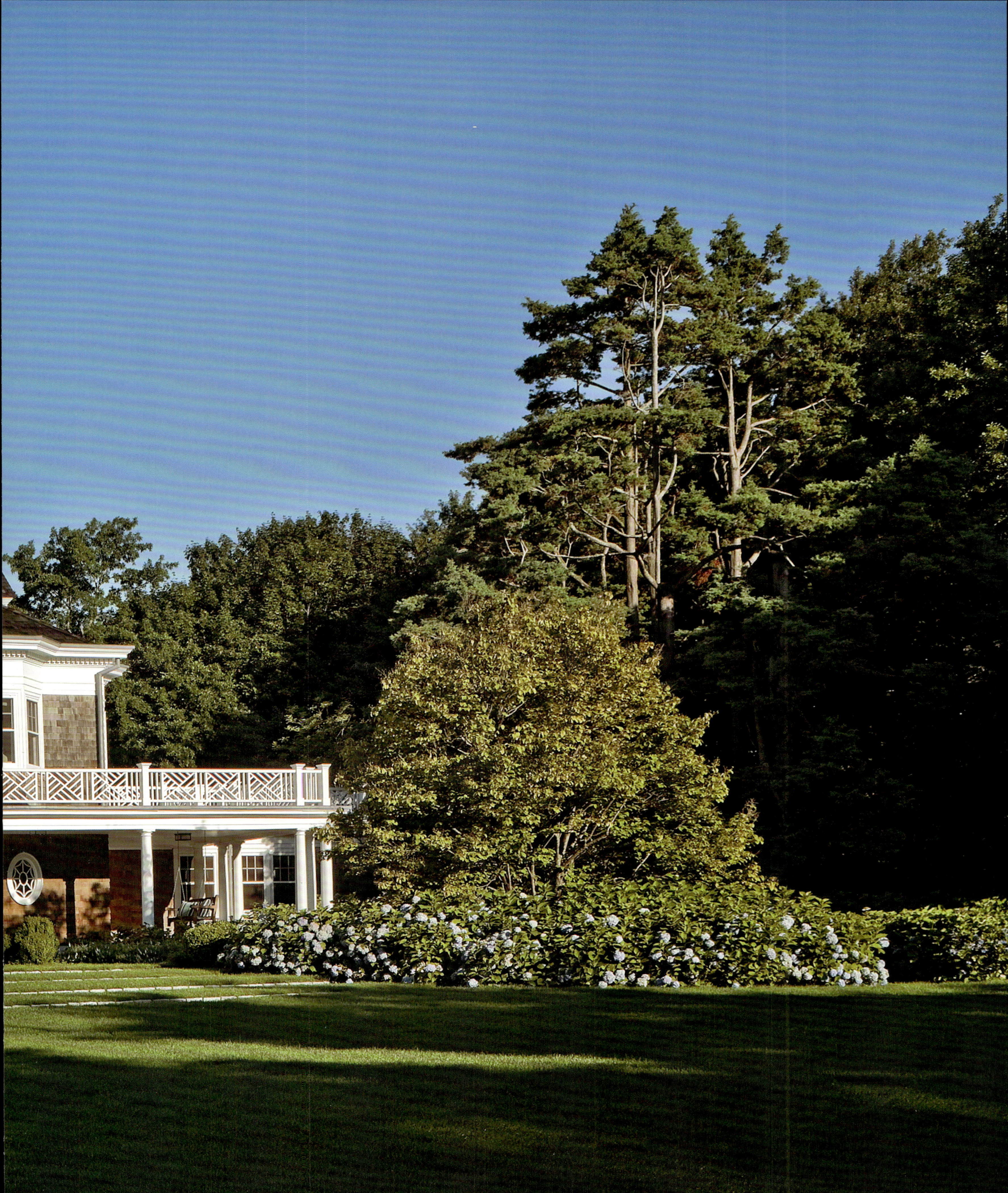

character to the rooms, as does oil-rubbed bronze hardware and polished nickel bath fittings. Interior designer Victoria Hagan was our collaborator throughout.

On the second floor are two children's rooms, two guest rooms, and the master suite—an ensemble of sitting room, passageway with his and her dressing rooms, and master bathroom. There is also an upstairs laundry and playroom. The pool pavilion, a tripartite arrangement with an outdoor kitchen, a game area with an outdoor fireplace, and a covered seating area, was the project's final component. All of these areas are constructed primarily of Ipe wood, which eventually weathers silver. The existing guesthouse, a converted garage, received minor renovations so that the family had a place to live while the main house was undergoing reconstruction. The newly constructed garage has overhead storage space for boats and an additional seven feet of clearance underneath for more storage.

Considerable thought and planning went into siting and layering the outdoor and indoor/outdoor spaces at the front and rear of the house to establish privacy and a clear processional direction. These clients felt strongly that guests should come to the front door, so we worked closely with Edmund Hollander, the landscape architect, to orient the drive and pathways toward that approach.

As much reinvention as renovation, this project leaves nothing to the imagination, and everything, too. It's now that shingle-style archetype—but for today, and with each and every component developed to the fullest.

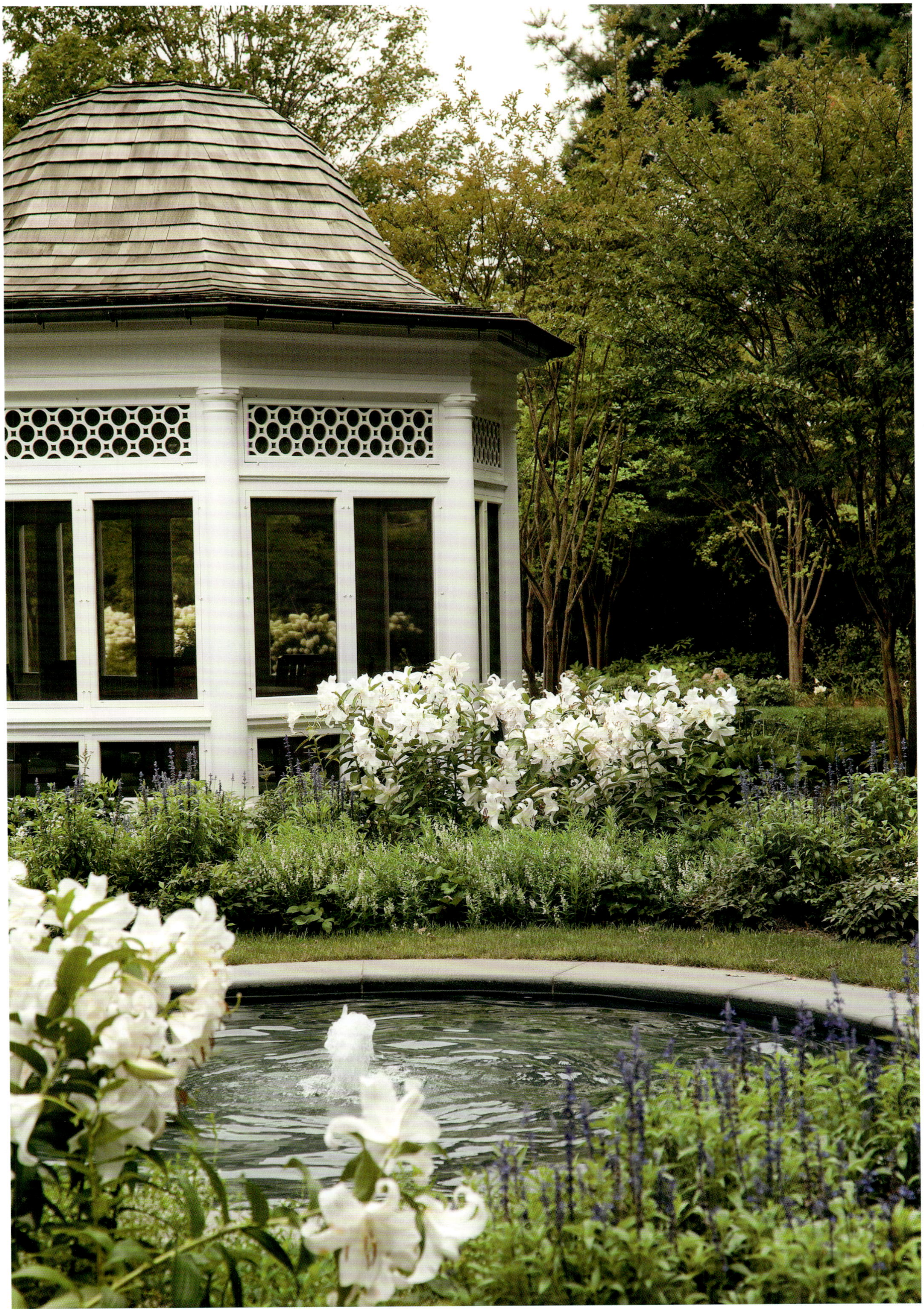

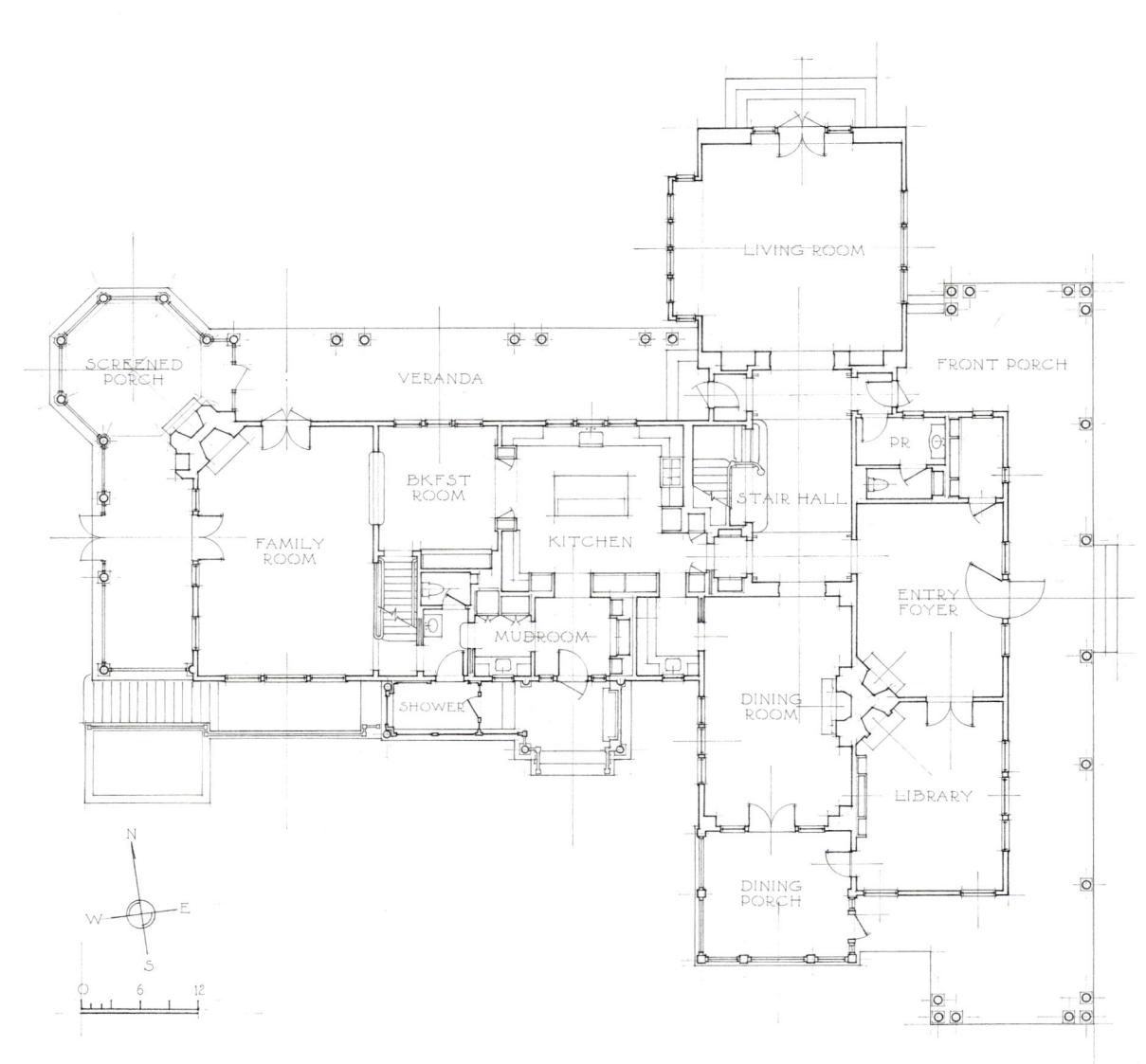

TWO SPREADS PREVIOUS: The front elevation of the house with porch and balustrade articulation. PREVIOUS SPREAD, FAR LEFT: The addition, with secondary entrance and feature windows. PREVIOUS SPREAD, LEFT: Under an octagonal paneled ceiling, the dining porch shares a fieldstone fireplace back to back with the family room and, PREVIOUS SPREAD, RIGHT, overlooks a lily pond. BELOW, LEFT: The entry has a Dutch door. BELOW, RIGHT AND OPPOSITE: The new stair hall organizes the interior circulation, with the living room to the north and dining room to the south.

188

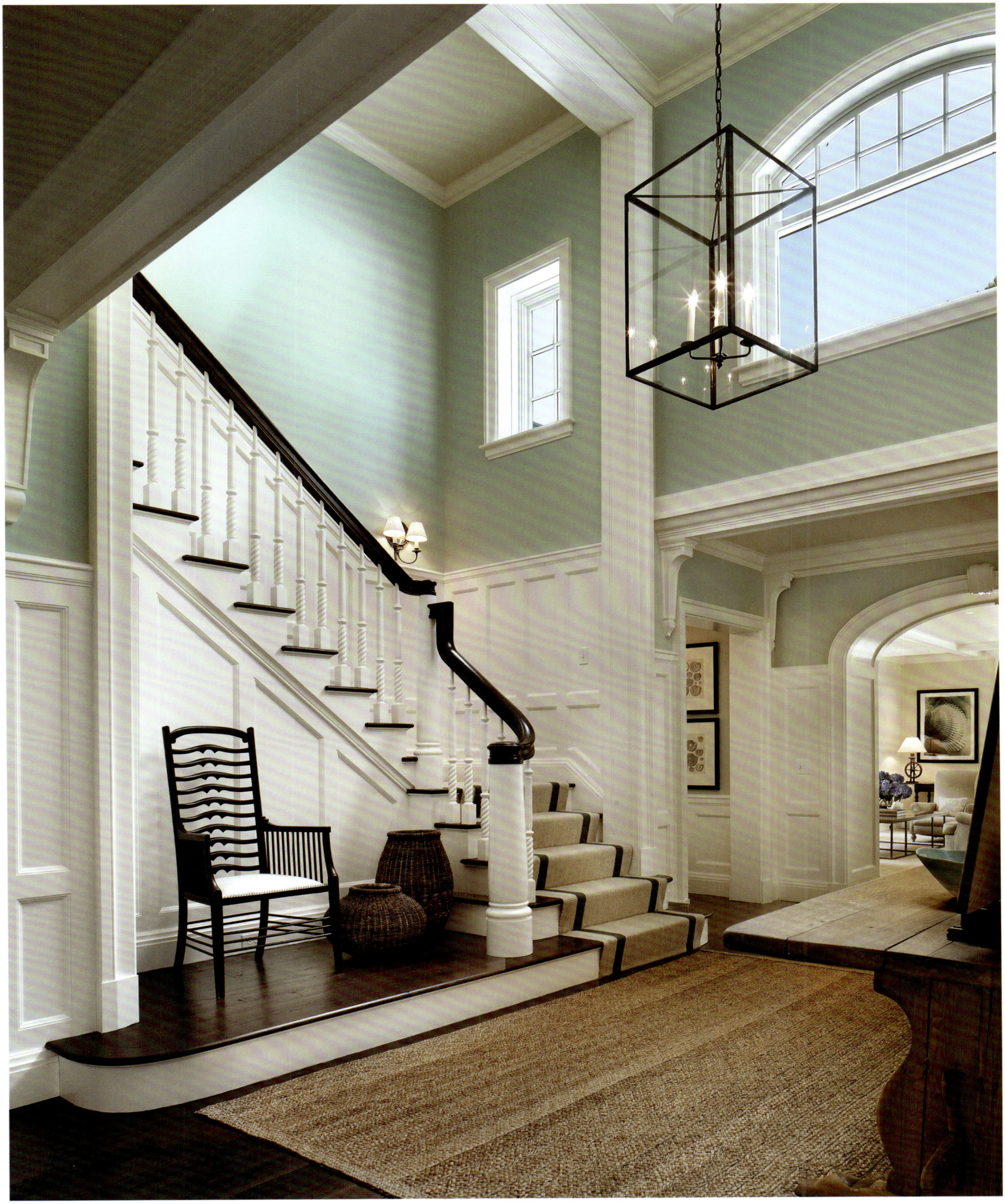

ABOVE: Under a ceiling articulated with coffers and panels, the living room encompasses convenient niches for seating groups and art placement, including an expansive bay window that overlooks the lily pond. OPPOSITE: In the dining room, French doors with sidelites open to the screened dining porch beyond. A refined molding and cornice treatment adds interest and definition to walls and the area over the fireplace mantel.

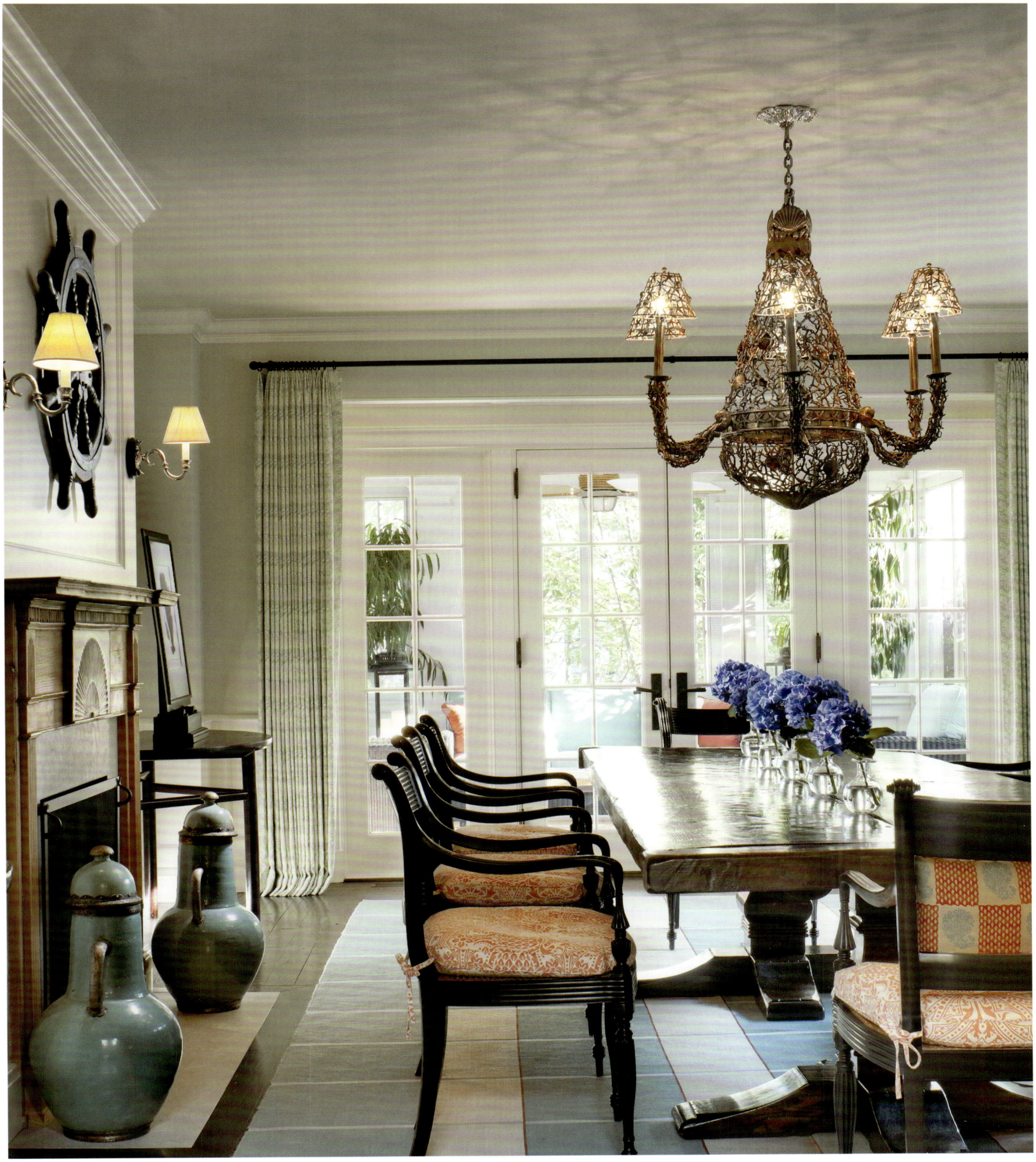

The library just off the entry foyer, paneled in weathered cypress, overlooks the front porch of the house. Cottage-style windows fill the room with light and break up the paneled expanses of the walls. Oil-rubbed bronze curtain rods fit neatly into the frieze.

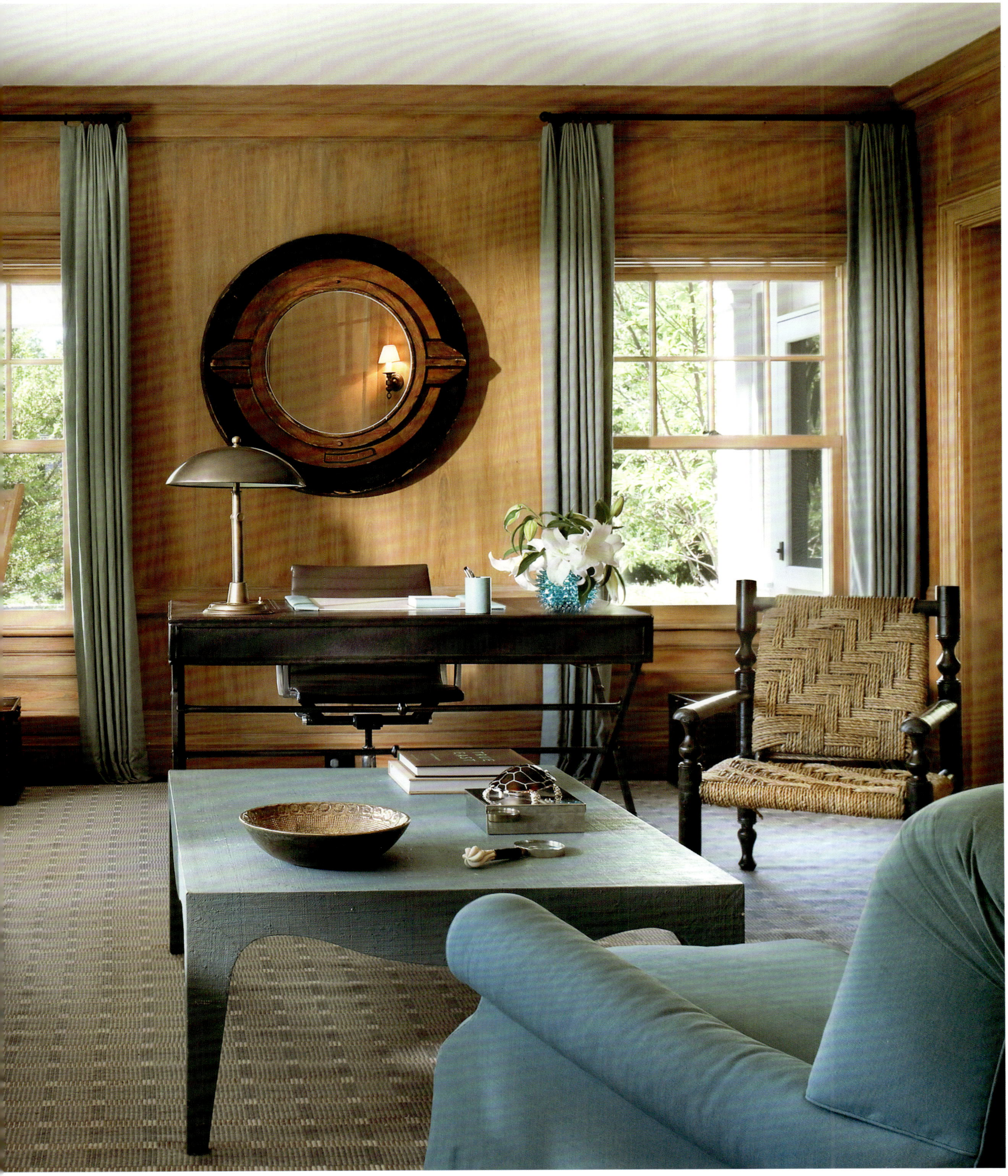

ABOVE AND LEFT: The kitchen opens conveniently to the breakfast room, left, which steps down to the family room. The antique walnut boards for the kitchen island counter contrast with the v-groove ceiling boards and the reclaimed oak floor planks. The glass-fronted cabinets contain restoration glass. OPPOSITE: The family room looks through an elliptical archway to the secondary stair, which provides primary access to the basement and second floor.

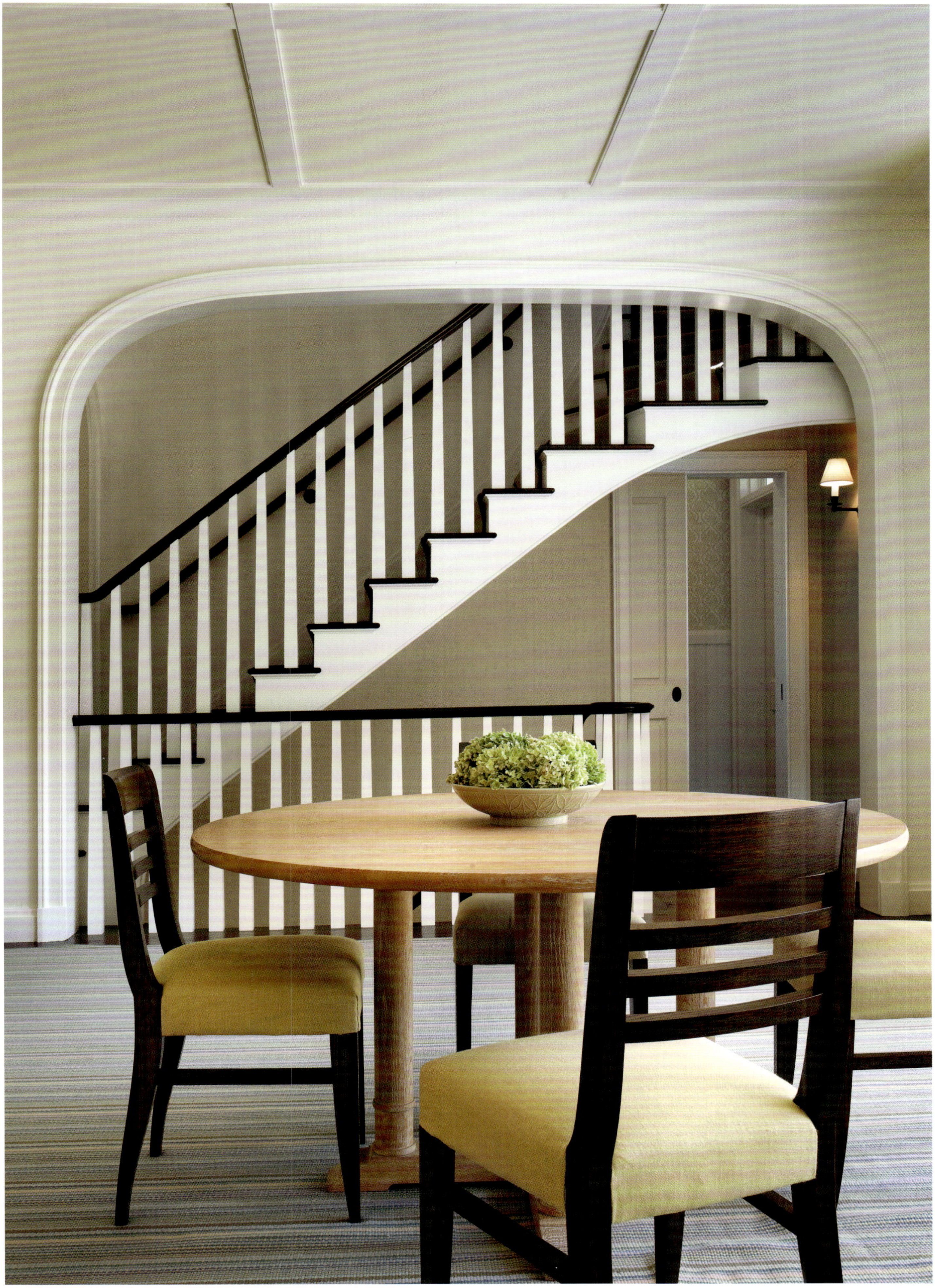

ABOVE: The master bedroom incorporates one of the bay windows on the front of the house. Set into the window is a comfortable seat and flanking cabinetry for storage. Beyond the bedroom is a sitting room with a fireplace. OPPOSITE: Reclaimed oak boards line the floor of the master bath, which is detailed with Ming green marble. The enameled cast-iron tub with nickel fittings fits neatly into the window bay. OVERLEAF: Off the back of the house is the pool area. Constructed of Ipe and cedar wood, the tripartite pavilion has a covered dining porch (LEFT), a game area with a pergola and an outdoor fireplace (CENTER), and a roofed lounging area (RIGHT).

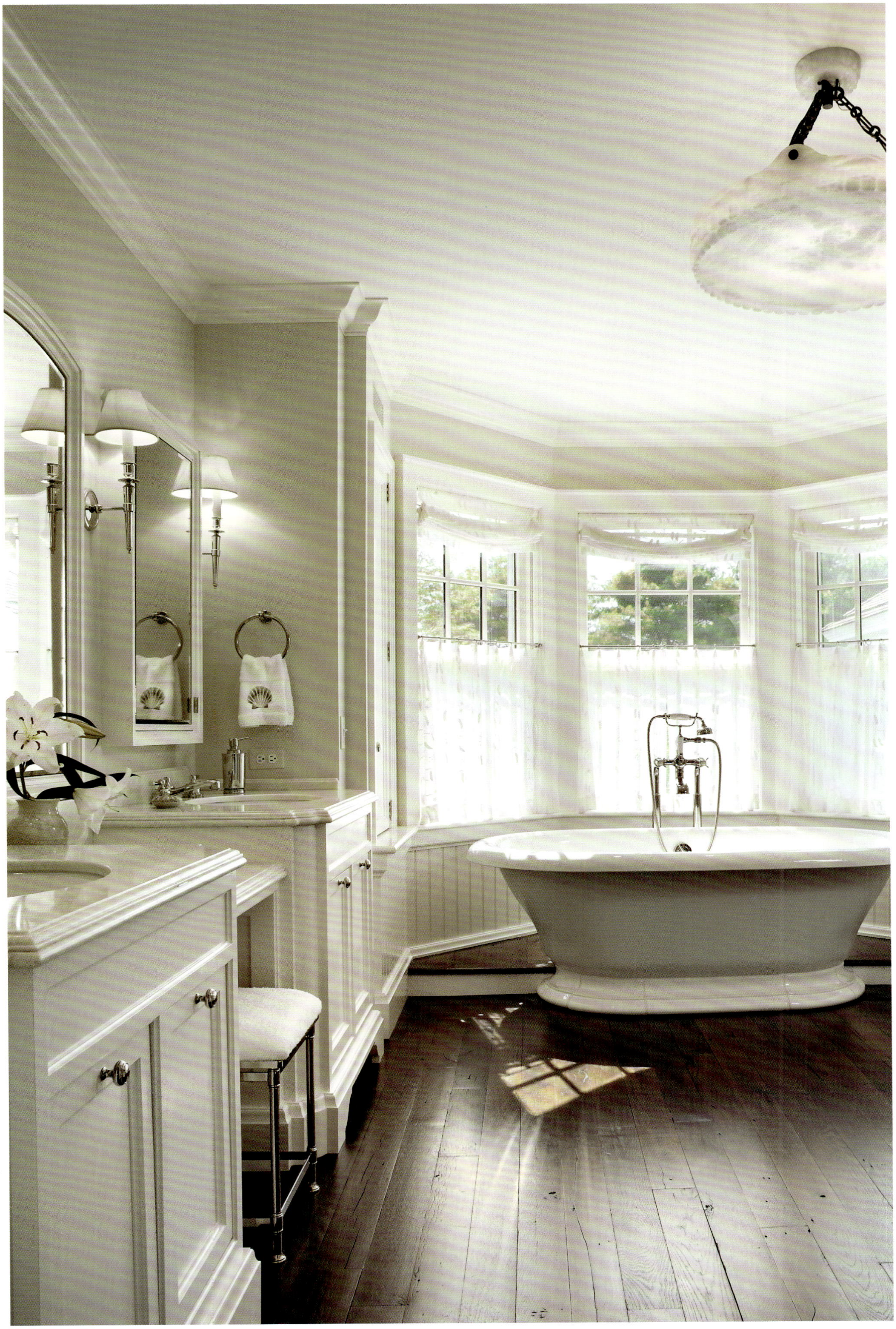

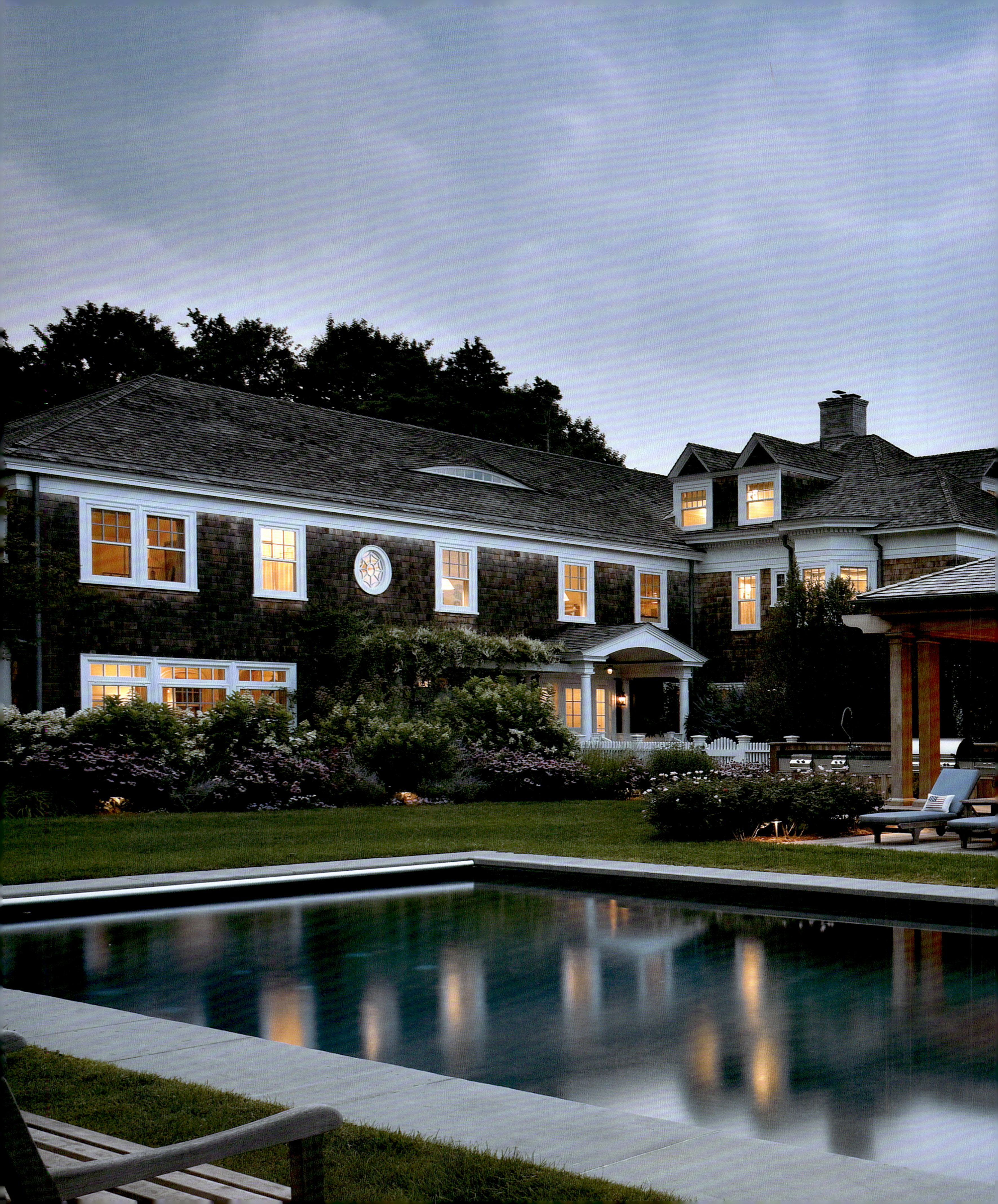

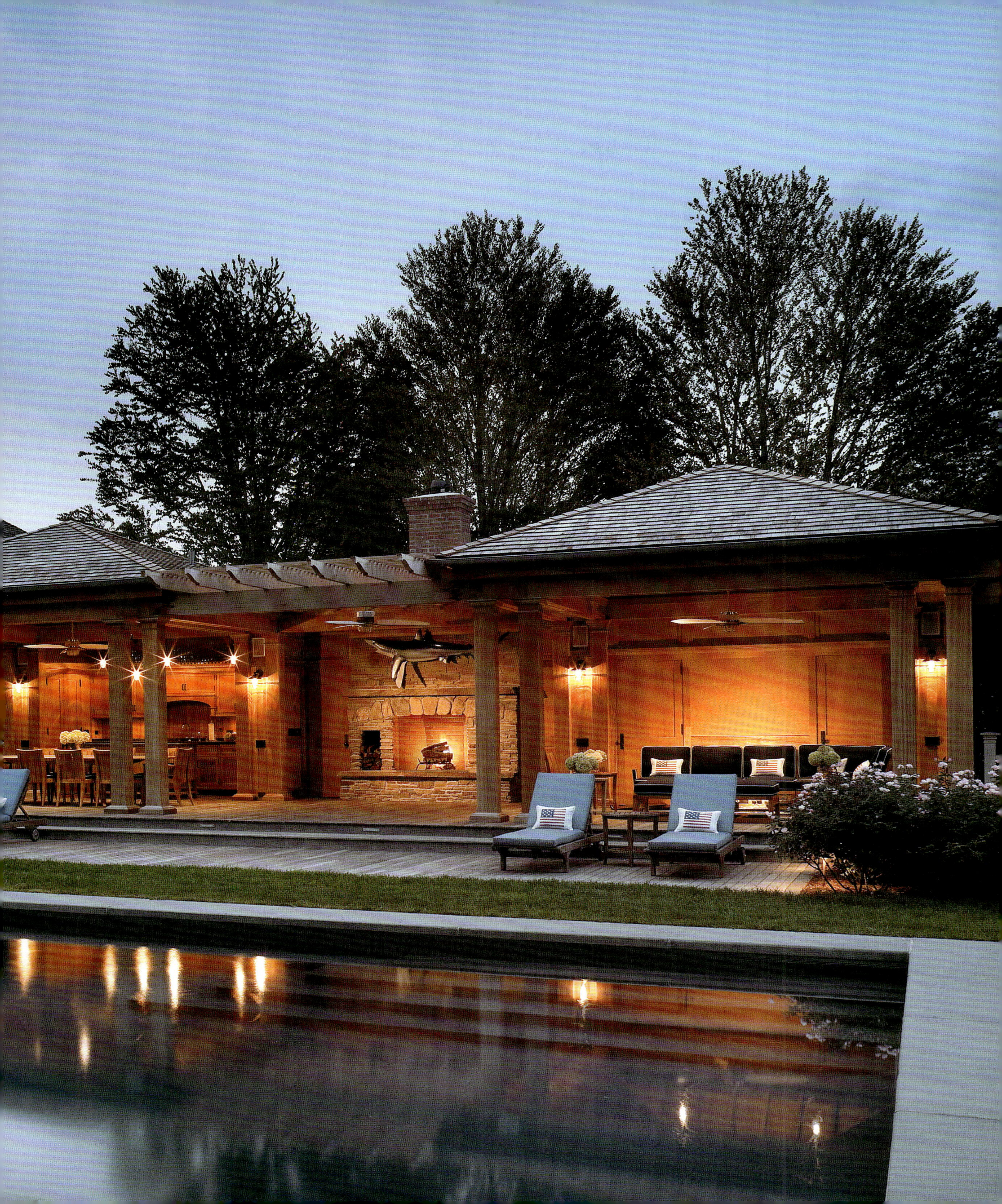

A Sweet Discovery

For an architect, large and small projects tend to be thematically similar but different in terms of complexity. In a smaller house, such as 2,000-square-foot Mason Hill Farm, the challenge is to get everything to fit. Purchased as a weekend retreat for a young family of five, the four-bedroom Greek Revival–style farmhouse sits on ninety-eight acres in upstate New York. Dating to the Civil War era, or soon thereafter, the property has breathtaking views toward both the Berkshires and the Catskills.

After years of use as a hunting cabin, the house looked in dreadful shape: a wreck with hollow-core doors, windows boarded over, floors painted battleship gray. Closer inspection, however, revealed extant traces of its original beauty. The surviving Greek Revival moldings were lovely, and elegant trim work with simple paneling under the window stool embellished each of the window openings.

The first phase of the renovation involved peeling back the veneer of time. Removal of the hollow-core doors turned up the original mortises for the cast-iron butt hinges. The builder located old doors from salvage yards in the area, plus antique hardware and hinges. When we hung the replacements, all these components fit hand-to-glove because the period mortises were still on the jambs. Rejuvenating the original floors was phase two: stripping, sanding, and repairing the original boards where necessary revealed a wonderful finish, full of character.

Opening up the living space to make the house more practical for family living proved a challenge, given the low ceilings typical of that period. Where possible, we enlarged and increased the height of doorways and passageways, then articulated those new openings with trims consistent to the originals. To expand the living room, which has exposures on two sides, we removed a summer beam and inserted structural steel as support. We also introduced a brick fireplace flanked by paired double-hung windows on the north wall, which opened the view to a lawn with an ancient white oak.

In the dining room, the massing of three windows on one wall creates a traditional but expansive opening. One curious detail: the original frame for the doorway to the basement abutted the fireplace,

201

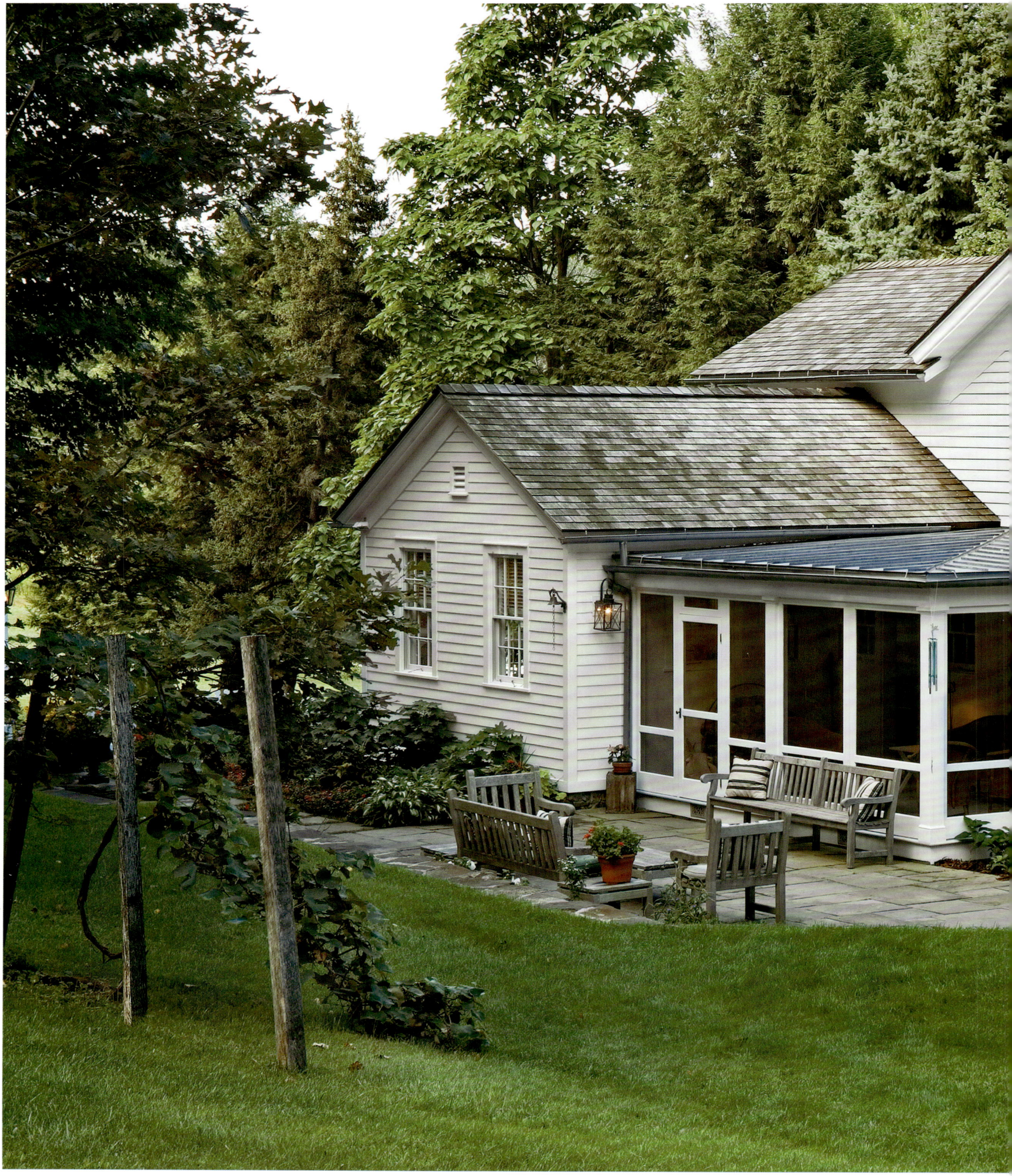

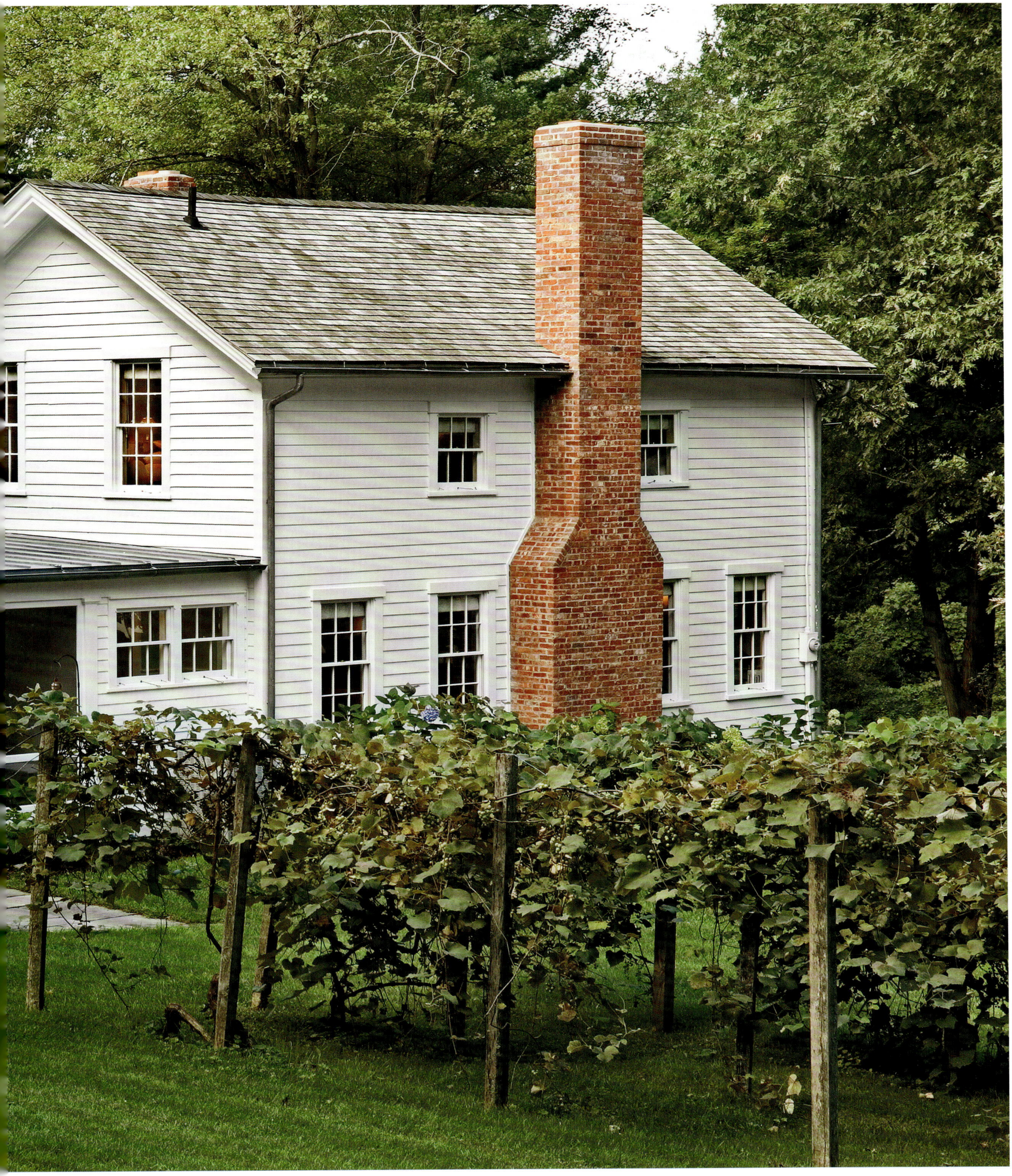

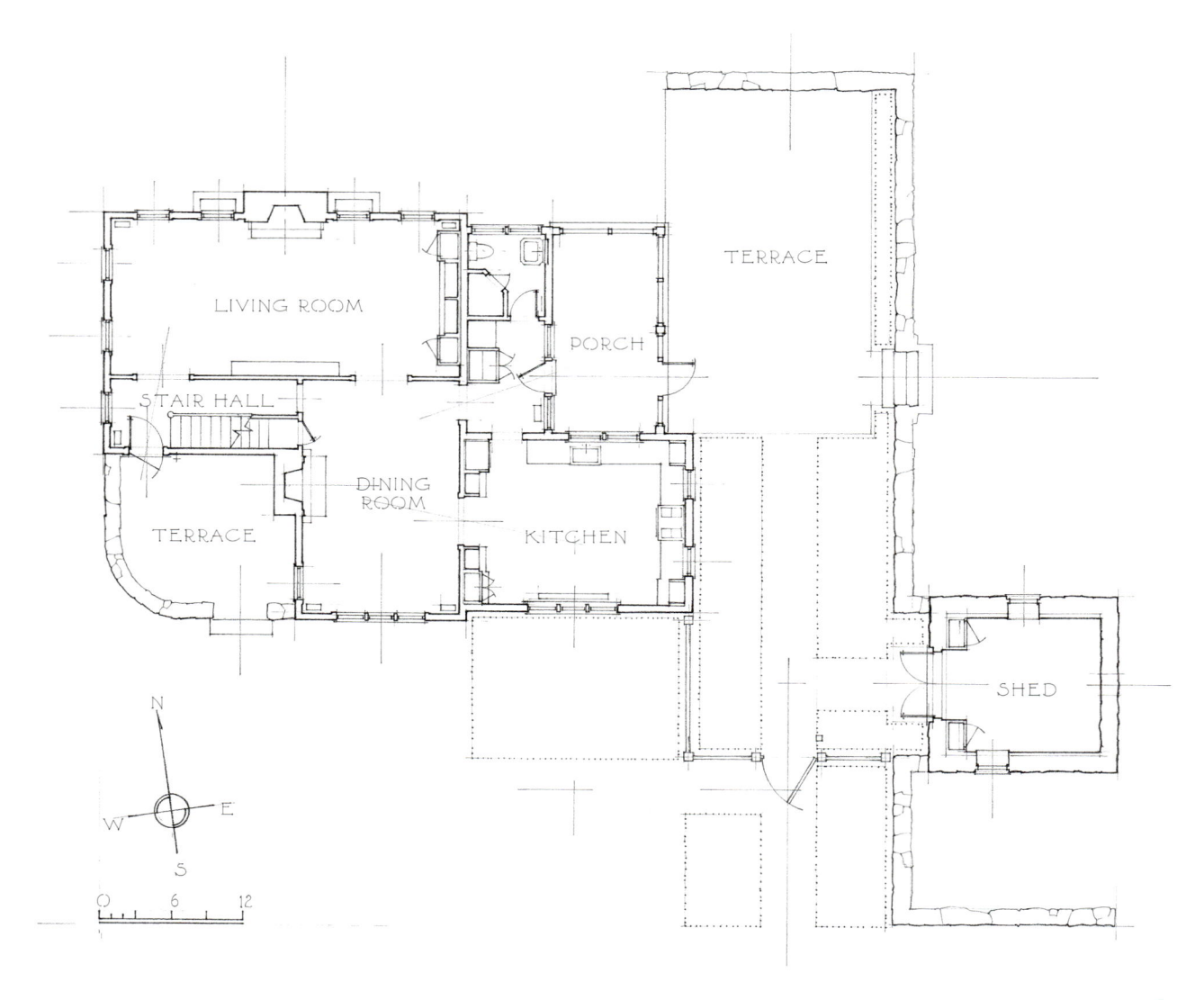

PREVIOUS SPREAD: At the back of the house, the screened porch bridges the original mid-nineteenth-century farmhouse, right, and the kitchen wing. LEFT: The front of the house, with the main entry set discreetly to the side. RIGHT: The front door was reclaimed from a salvage company. The foyer window retains its original antique glass and Greek Revival detailing.

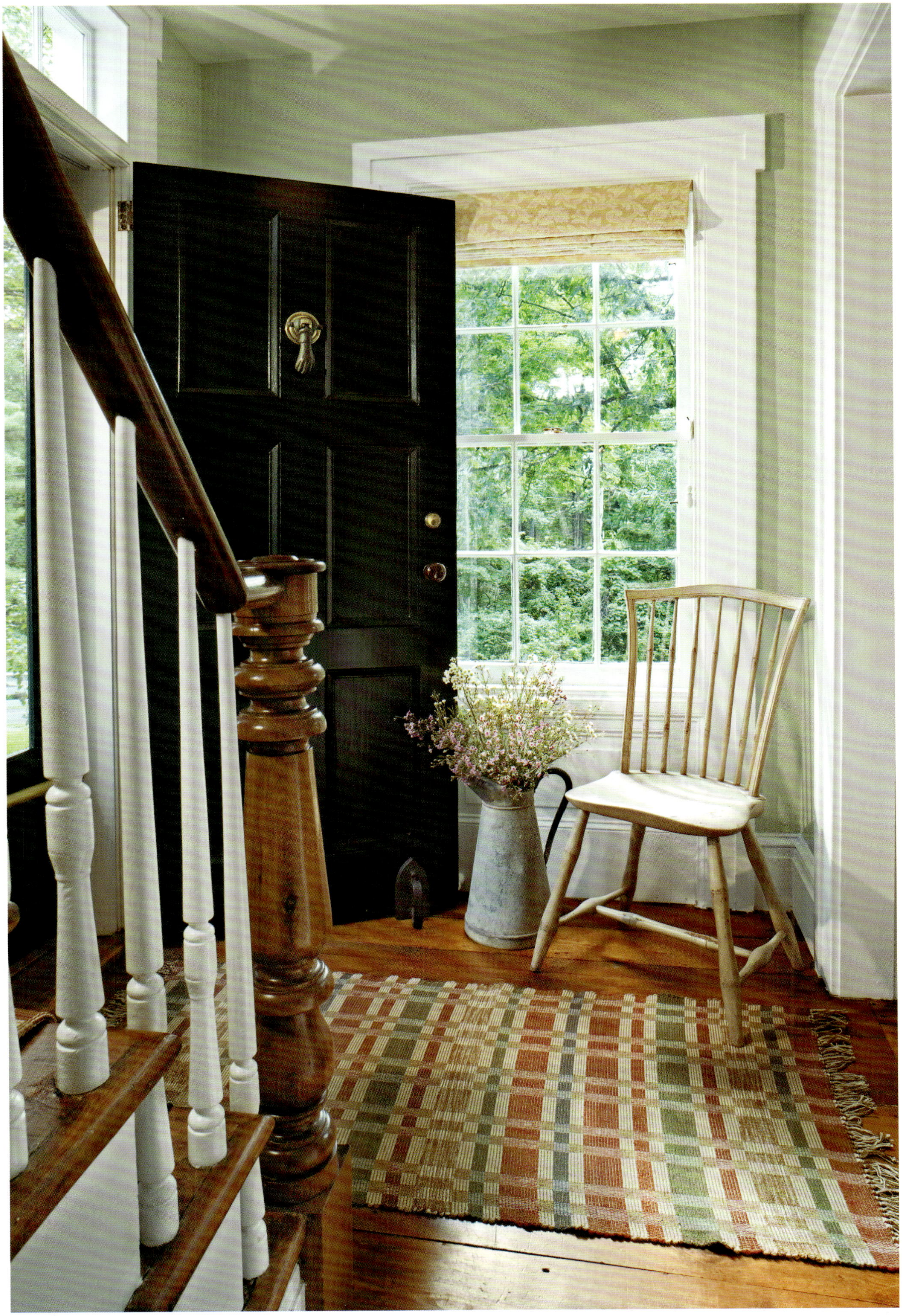

which gave us the opportunity to engage the molding of that door with the detailing of the new mantel design. The effect is quirky—and pleasantly unexpected.

The kitchen, screened porch, mudroom, and bathroom form a much-needed addition. Deceptively simple in design, the kitchen incorporates four identical upper-glass-fronted cabinets—two in the corners, and two pinched in—flanked by a pantry and refrigerator. New windows over the sink, which replicate the three-over-three double-hung style original to the house, look out to the screened porch. Taller, six-over-six windows flank the stove and align with nine-over-nine windows on the non-work wall. The family lives around the kitchen table, which overlooks the view.

The house's fourth bedroom—a cozy, six-by-five-foot space—has evolved into a study that opens off the master bedroom. A newly created internal window allows for the flow of natural light.

Like the house, the original stone shed by the garden was incredibly dilapidated, with boarded-over doors and windows. Removing the wood planks allowed us to restore the openings. The masonry was another matter: once we shored up the roof structure, we entirely rebuilt the stonework from scratch.

Working on older houses always involves surprises, some happier than others. This proved one of the happiest. Discovering that this modest farmhouse still had so many of its original elements was unexpected to say the least. But seeing it come back together? That made for some very sweet moments.

LEFT: After shoring up the roof, the stone shed was rebuilt from the ground up. RIGHT: A stone path leads to the rear terrace. FOLLOWING SPREAD, CLOCKWISE FROM UPPER LEFT: An onion-capped picket fence defines the garden entry; the dry-set stone of the terrace follows the property's natural contour; the pond to the east; the screened porch.

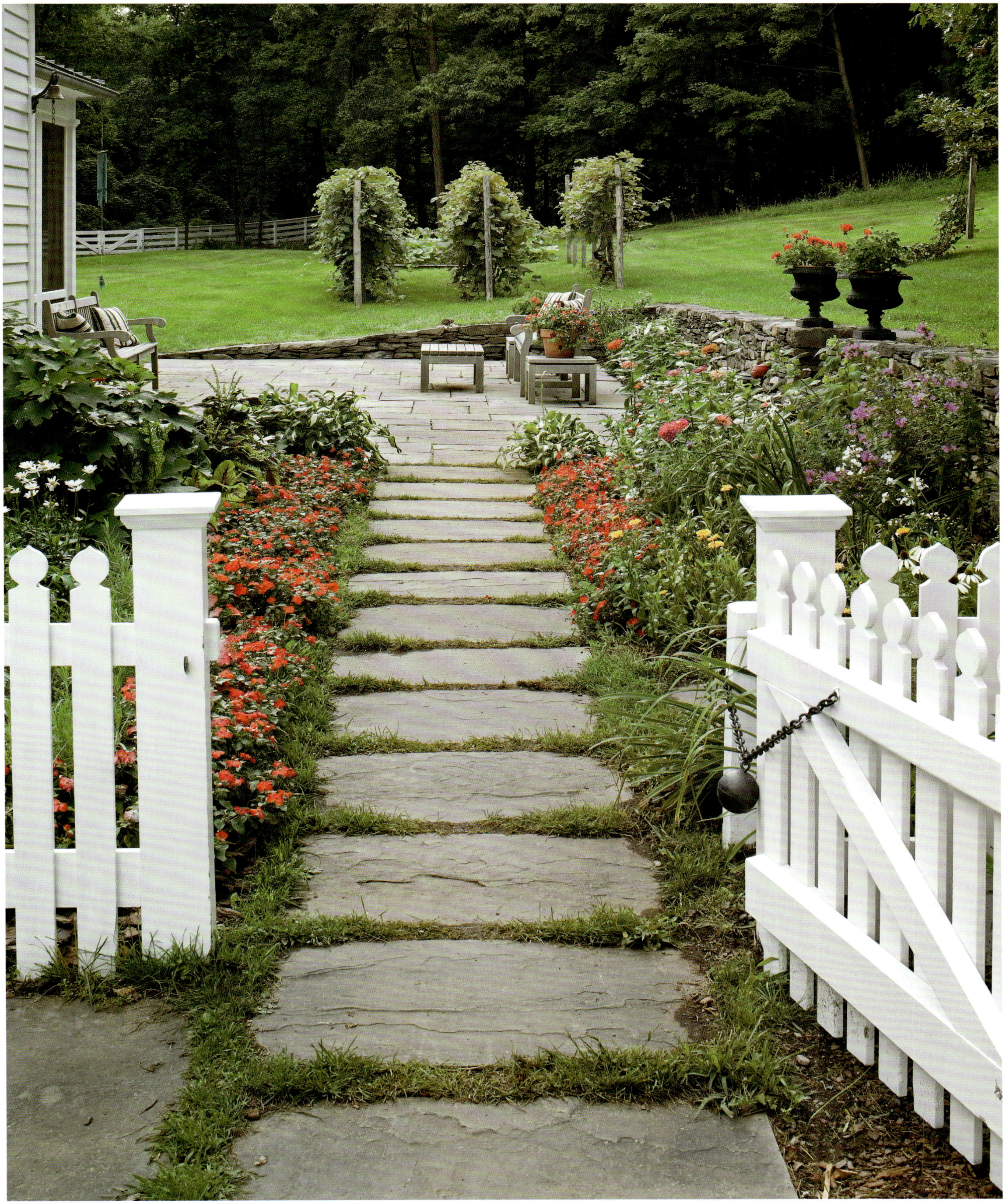

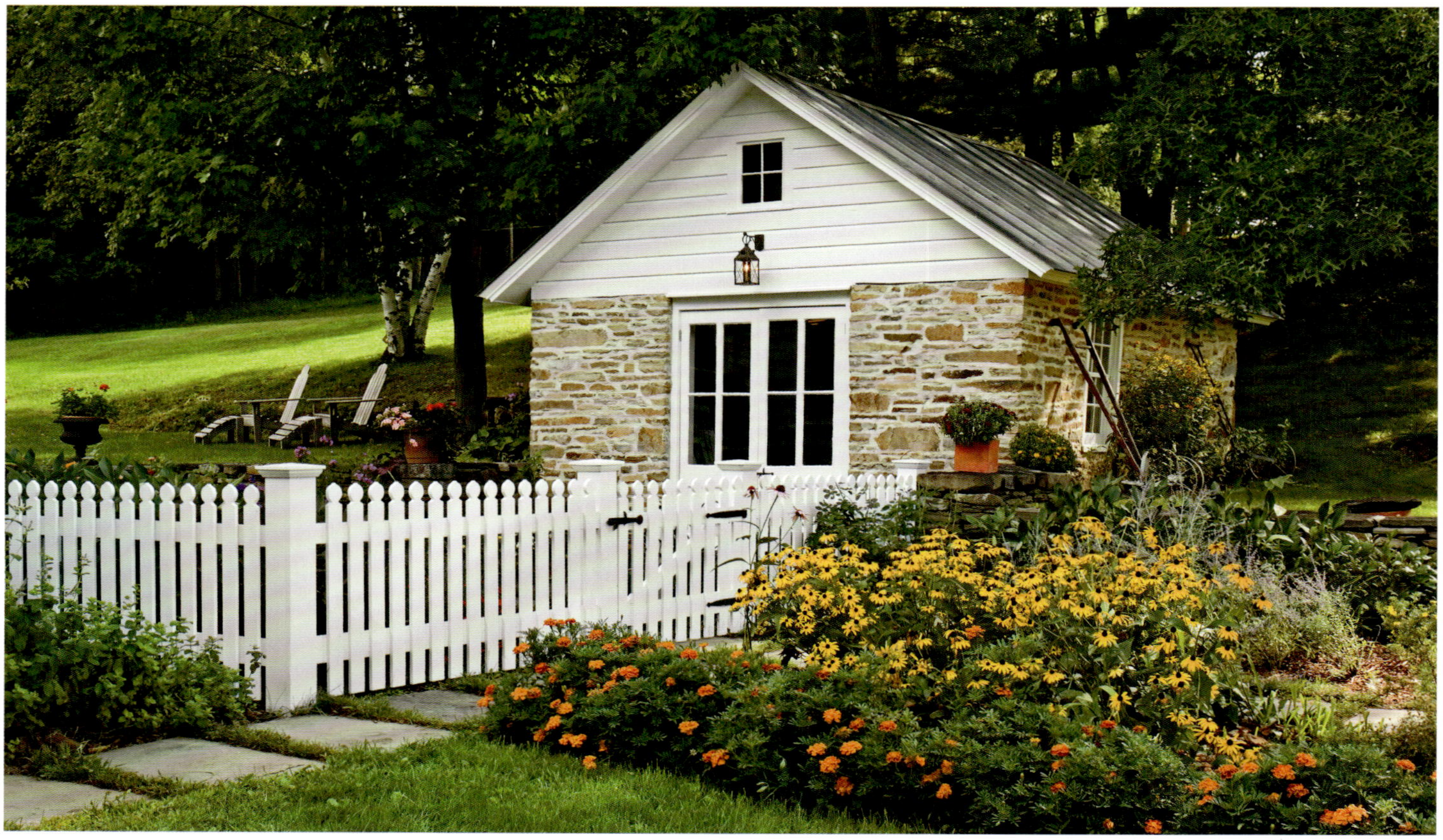

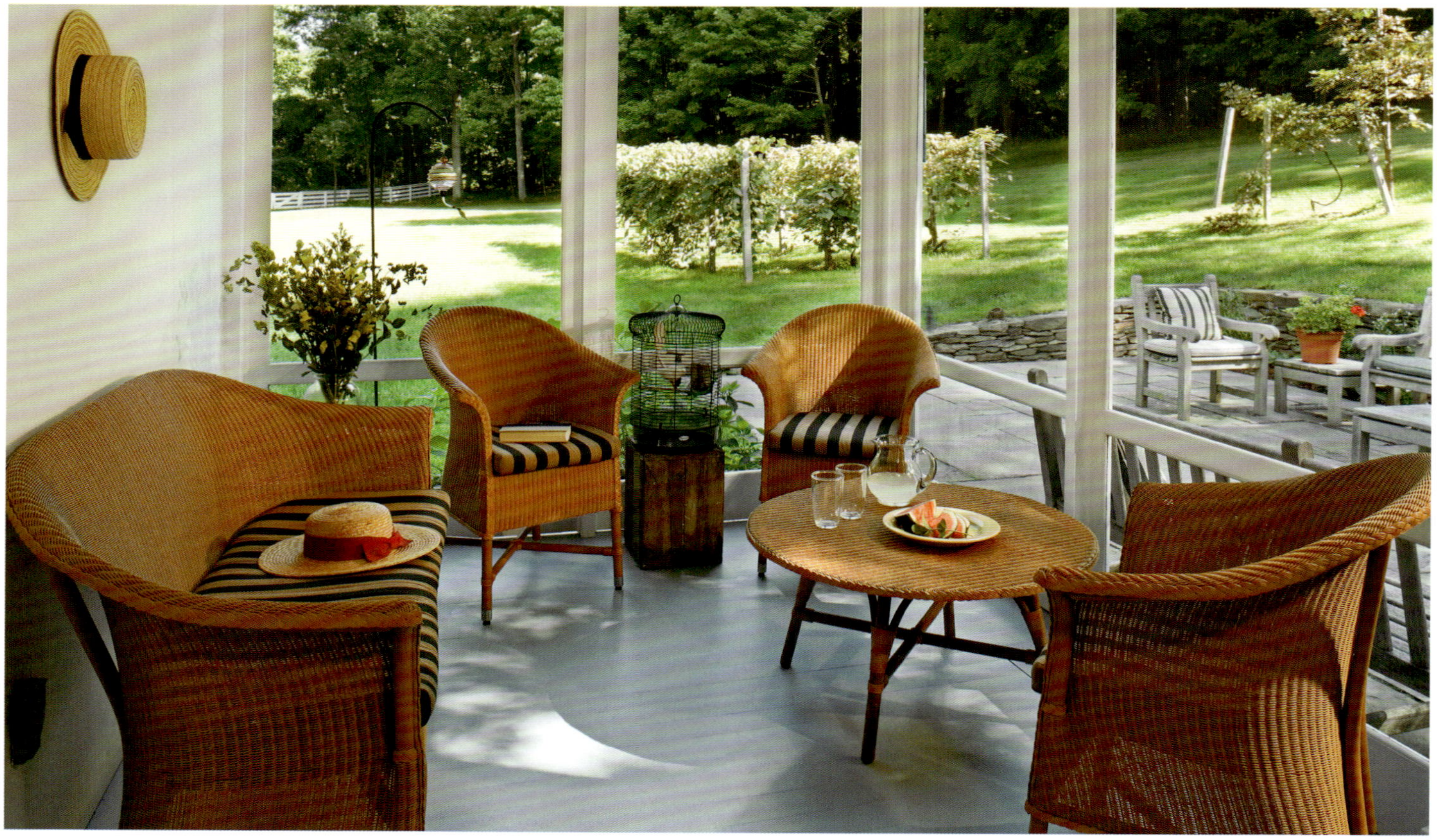

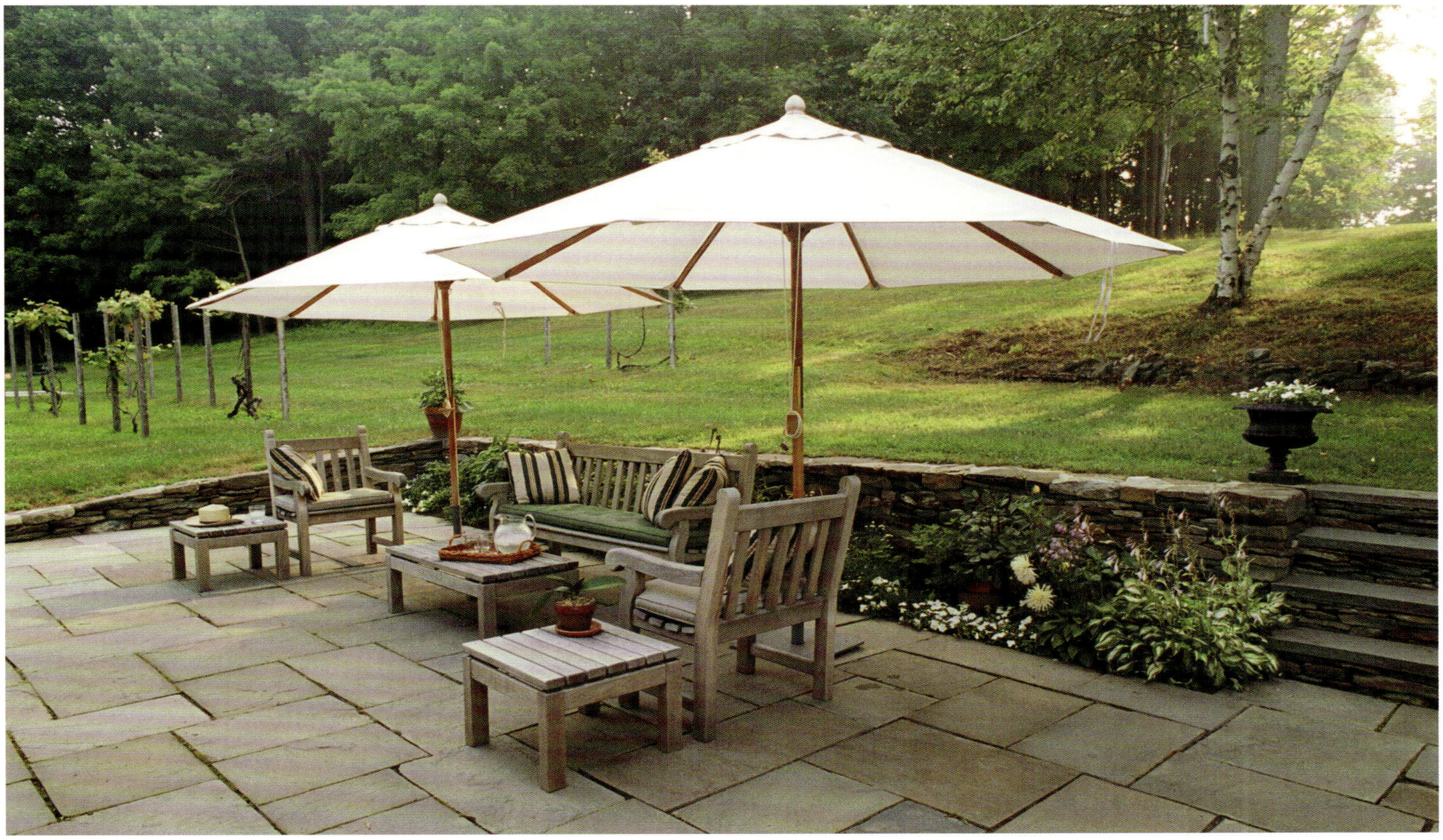

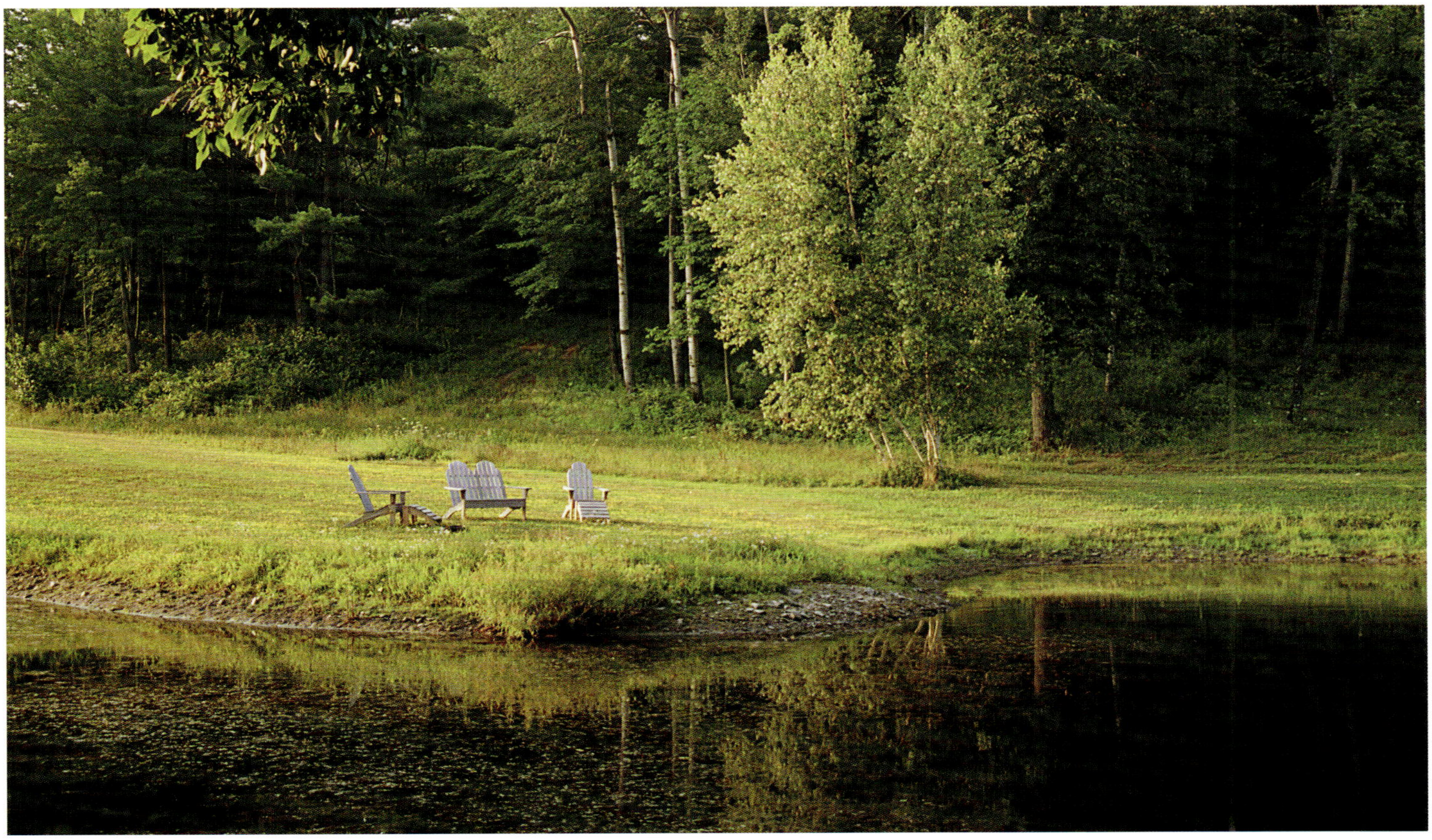

The current living room was originally two rooms with a summer beam. Joining the two required the removal of the summer beam and the insertion of steel for the necessary structural support. The firebox is made of reclaimed brick. The windows retain their original Greek Revival moldings and under aprons.

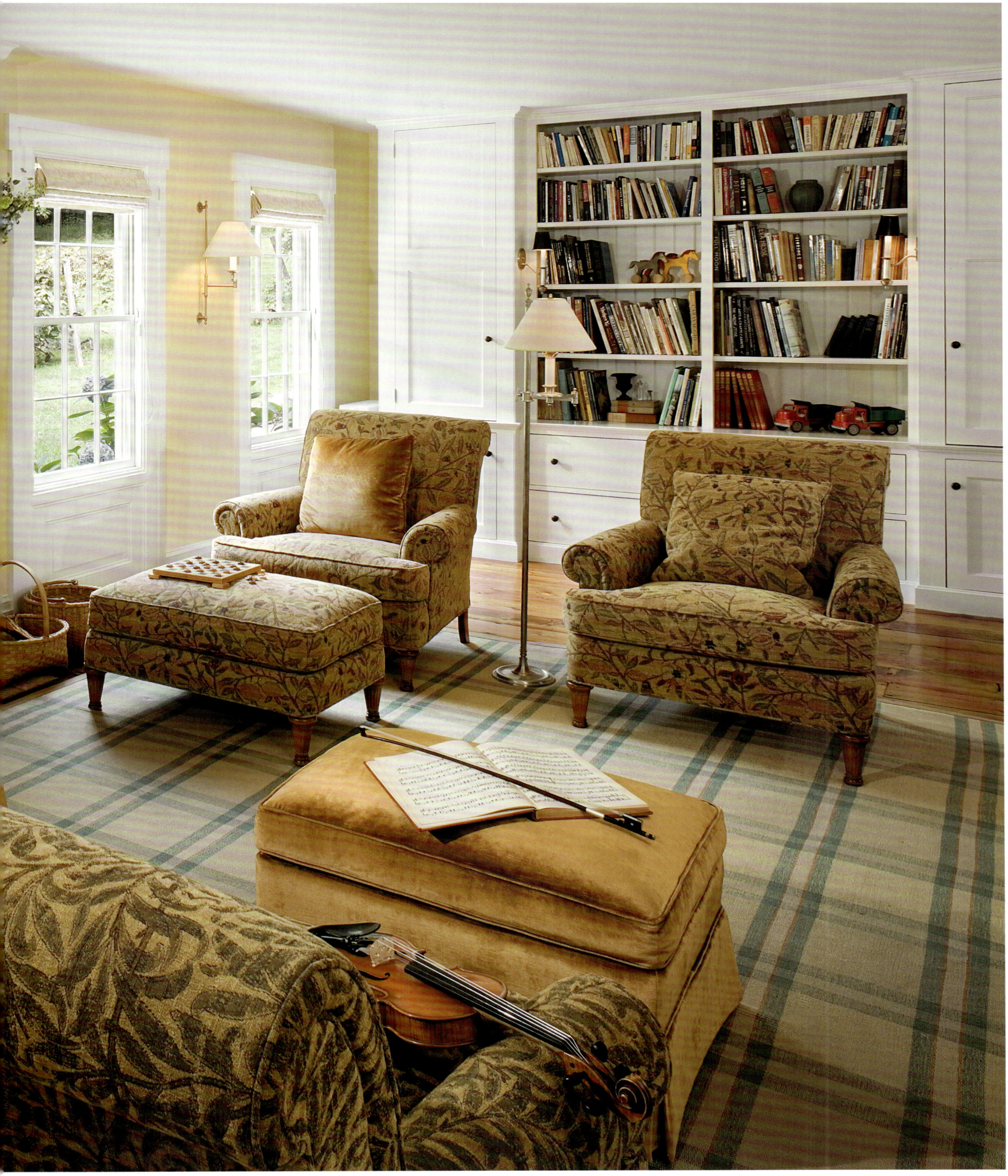

LEFT: At the classically paneled chimney breast are custom fire tools, a fireplace screen, and andirons forged by a blacksmith from Hancock Shaker Village. Wide plank floors of antique pine add texture and the resonance of history underfoot. BELOW AND OPPOSITE: The kitchen opens into the adjacent dining room.

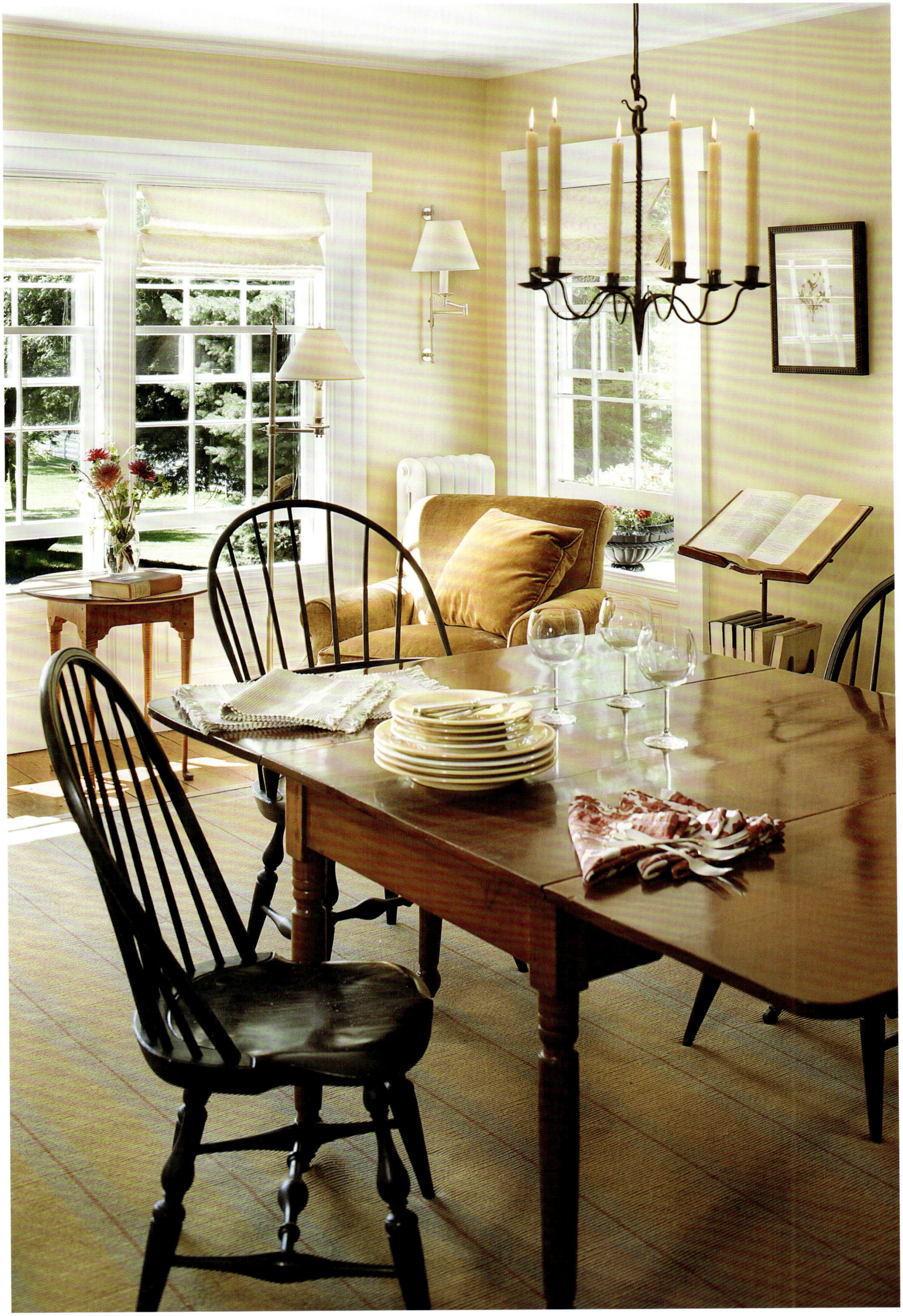

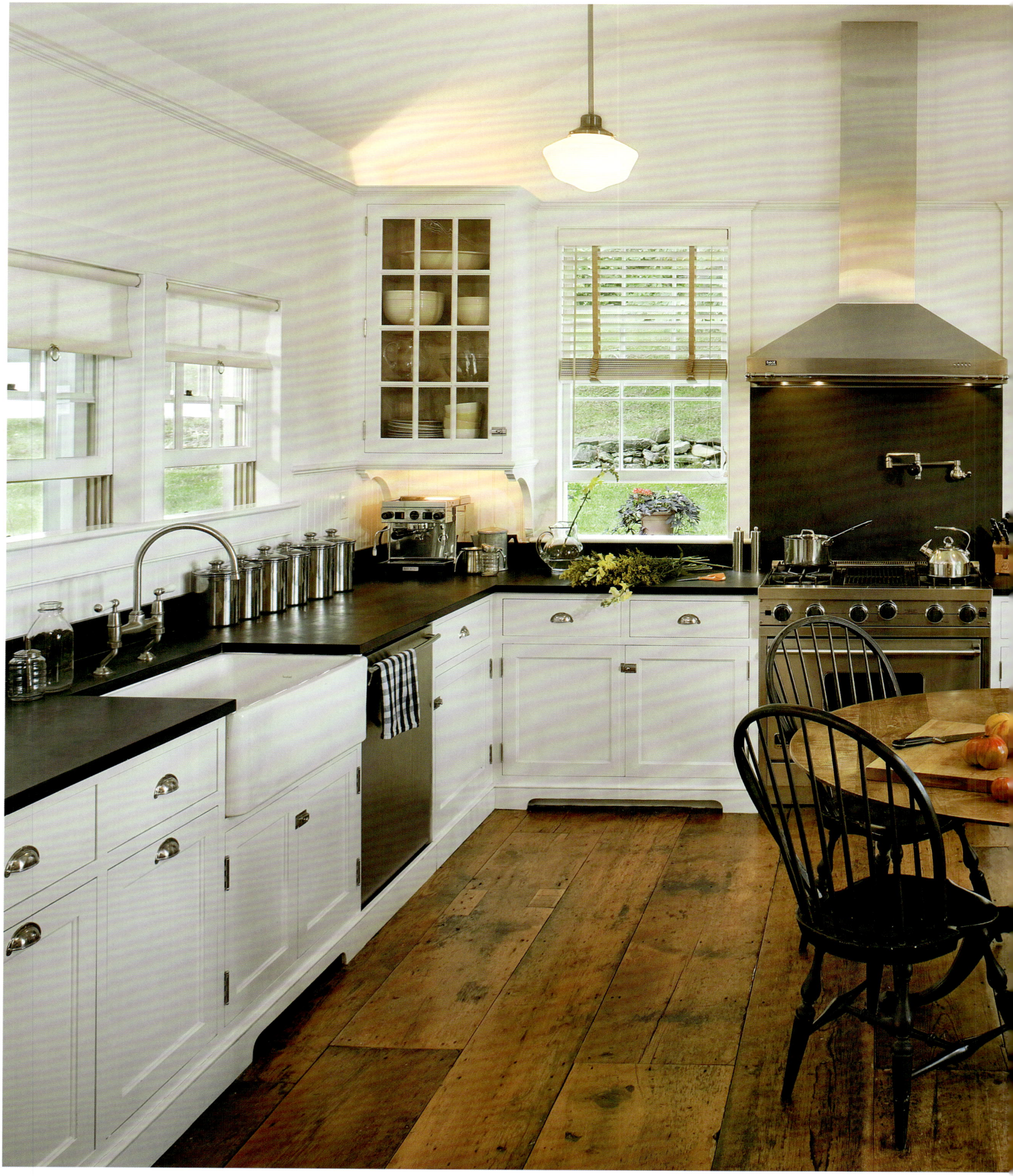

Designed for maximum light, efficient storage, and family comfort, the kitchen is the heart of the house. Exposed radiators add a period touch. OVERLEAF, LEFT: The second floor bathroom has v-groove board for the wainscot. OVERLEAF RIGHT: The master bedroom looks through to the study alcove, with an interior window that overlooks the stairwell.

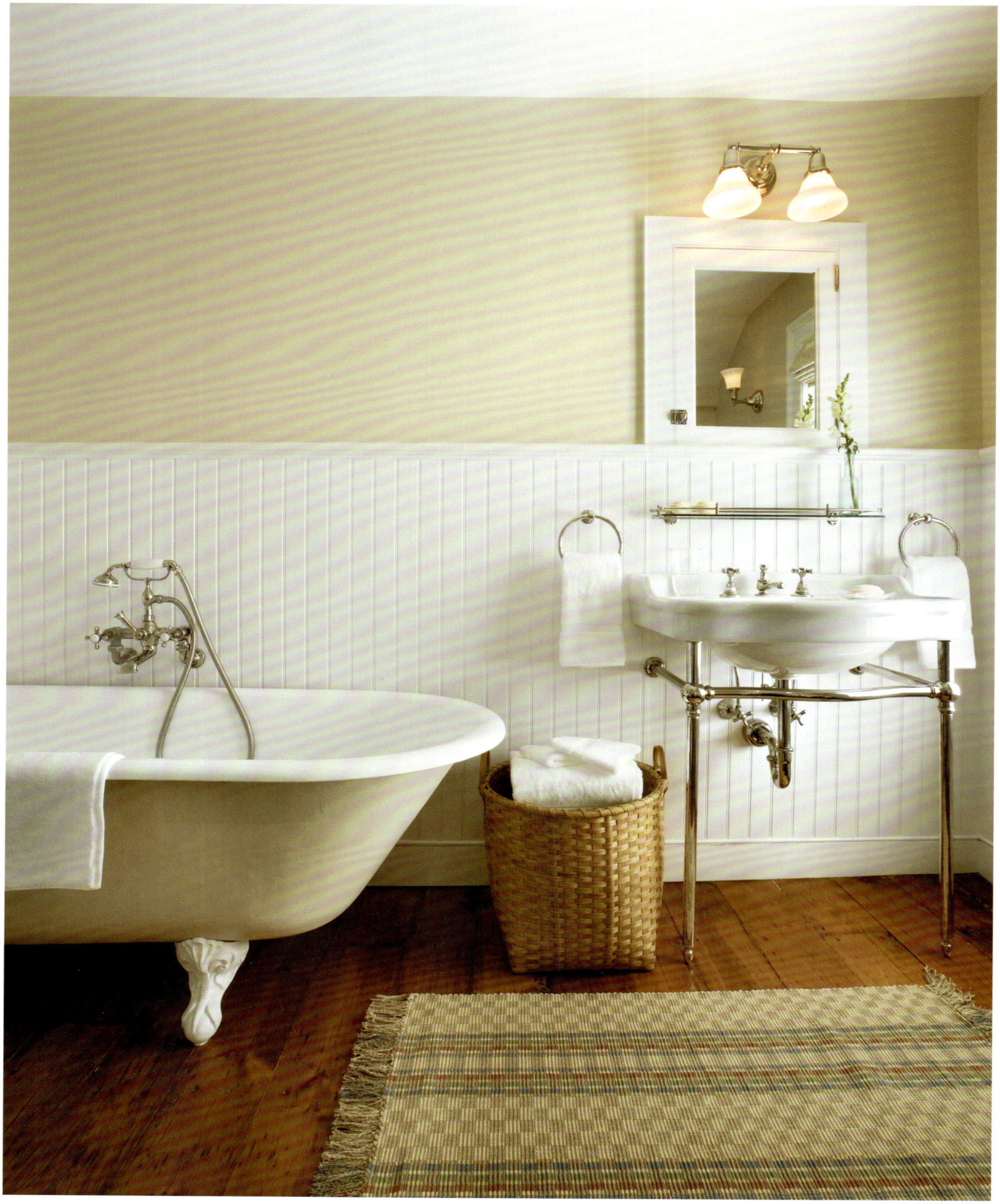

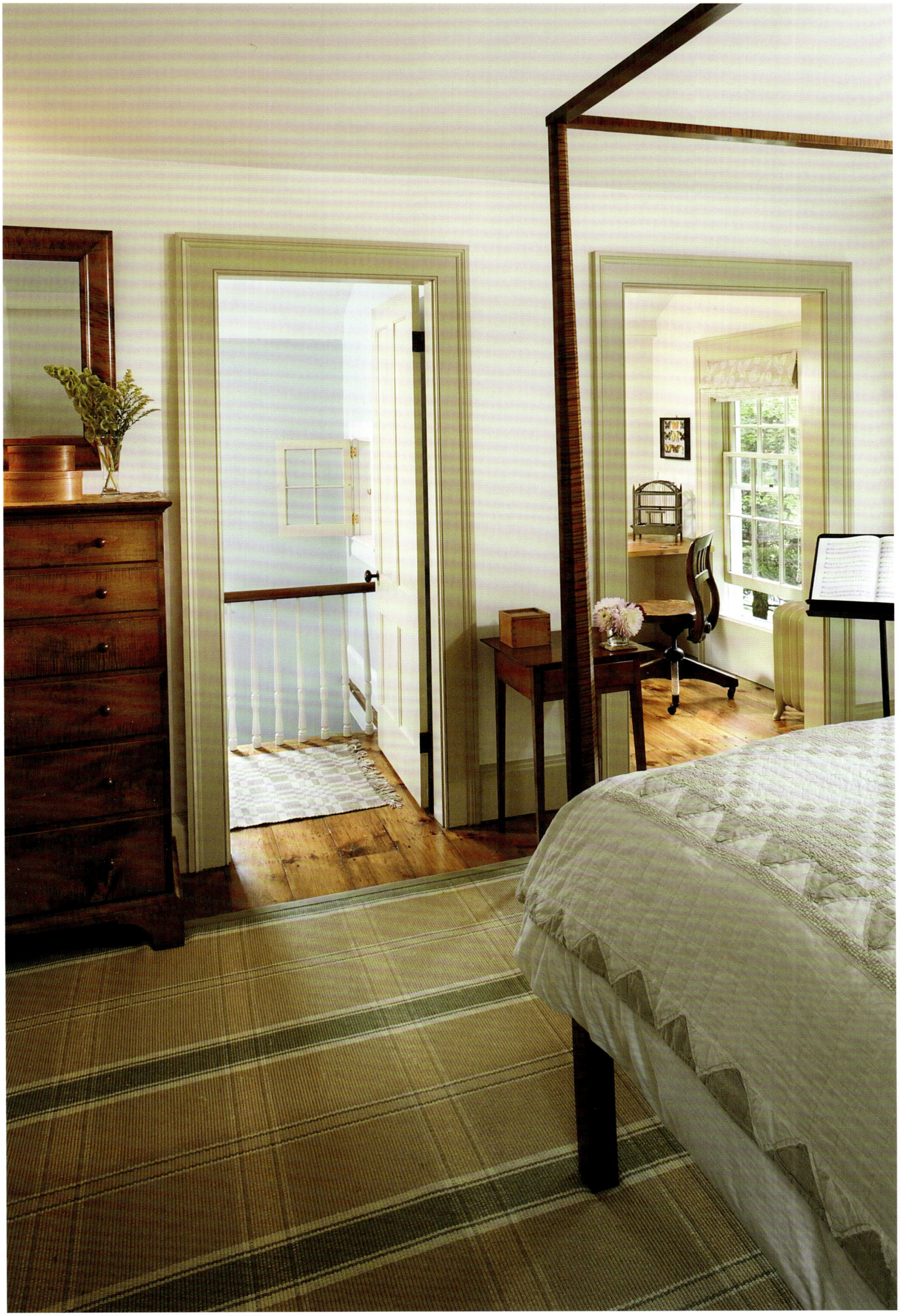

A Singular Vision

Residential renovations come in all permutations. Sometimes a client wants one component adjusted (rarely as simple as it sounds). Sometimes the desire is for a series of discrete changes (always a complex undertaking). When the latter occurs, as it did at this late-1920s Colonial Revival–style property, a redefinition of place is inevitable. In such circumstances, we invariably ask: In what way do we want to reshape what exists, and how apparent do we want our changes to be? For these clients, the answer to the first question was: significantly. To the second: not so much. The additions in question? A 650-square-foot solarium, a new swimming pool and pergola, and a 2,100-square-foot car barn for the clients' collection of antique vehicles.

Set on four and a half acres of rolling Connecticut grounds, the house overlooks a great lawn and Long Island Sound. To capture that view, we positioned the solarium—a four-season space with a fireplace—to replace an awkward enclosed porch off the existing double-height family room. Glazed doors open to an outdoor seating area covered with an awning and oriented around an exterior fireplace with a raised hearth. There we designed a stone chimney massing to contrast with the whitewashed brick chimneys of the main house. Cullman & Kravis did the decor for the solarium and the car barn and helped us convert the third-floor attic to a nautically themed bunkroom for the grandchildren.

The amount of preparatory site work was significant. Grading the area to accommodate the pool, which we positioned on axis with the solarium and flanked with a spacious pergola, was a major challenge. Since the scope of work included extensive plantings and outdoor decor, we collaborated with landscape designer Martha Baker to ensure the integrity of the surroundings.

The new pool area is adjacent to the outdoor room. Framed by bluestone coping, the rectangular pool sits between a pair of lunettes, one a rose garden, the other, a whirlpool. The abutting poolside lounge area

219

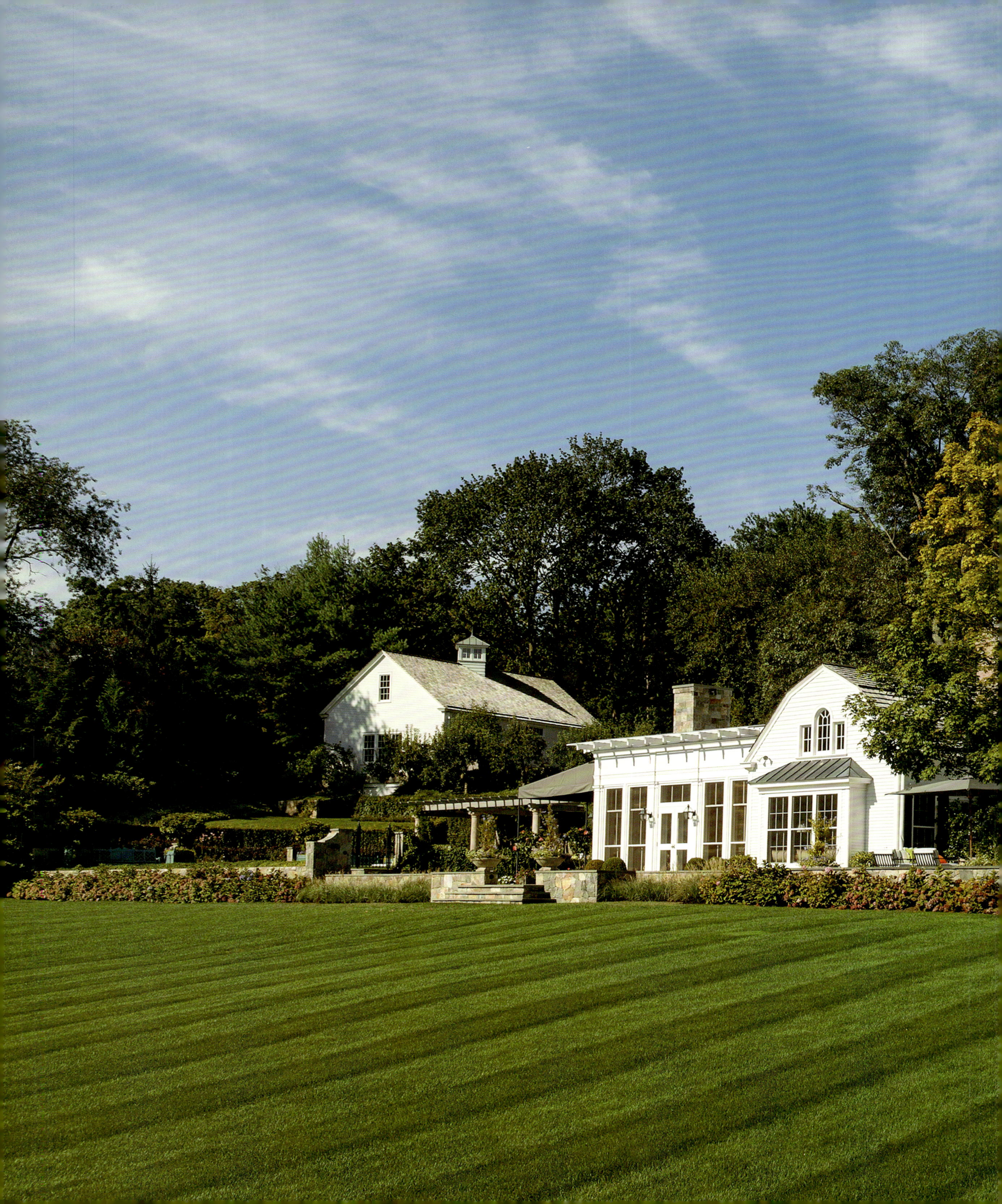

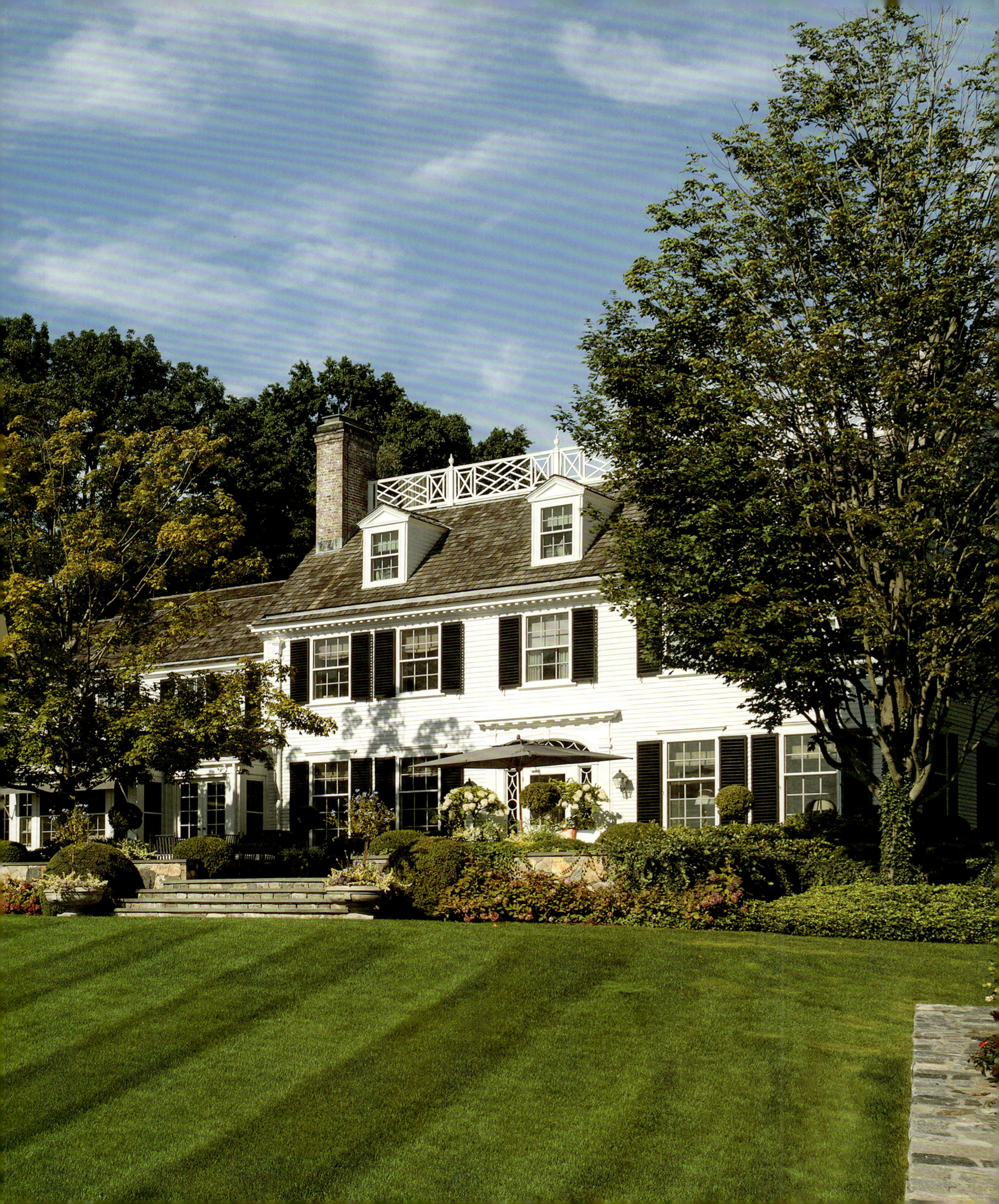

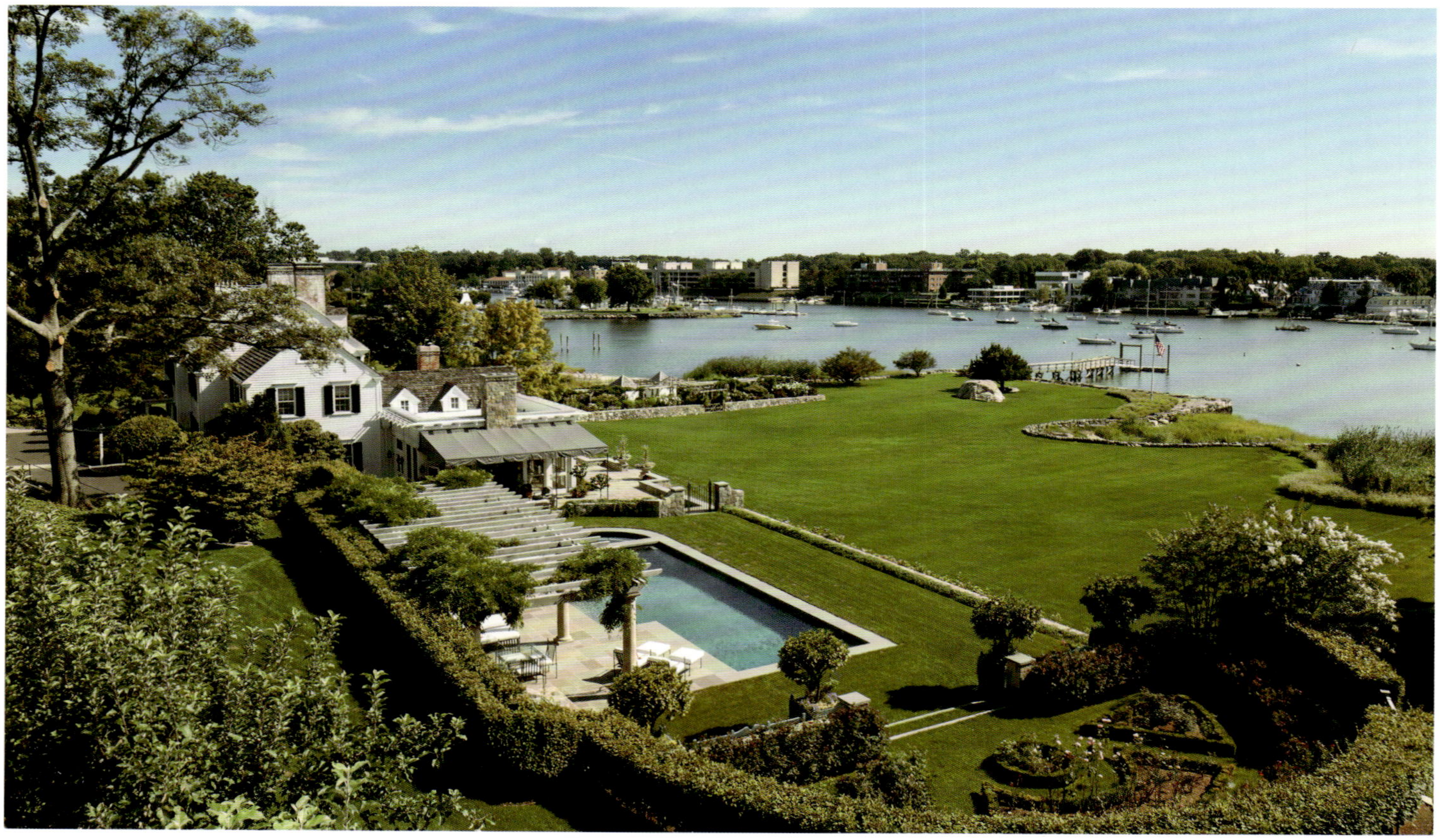

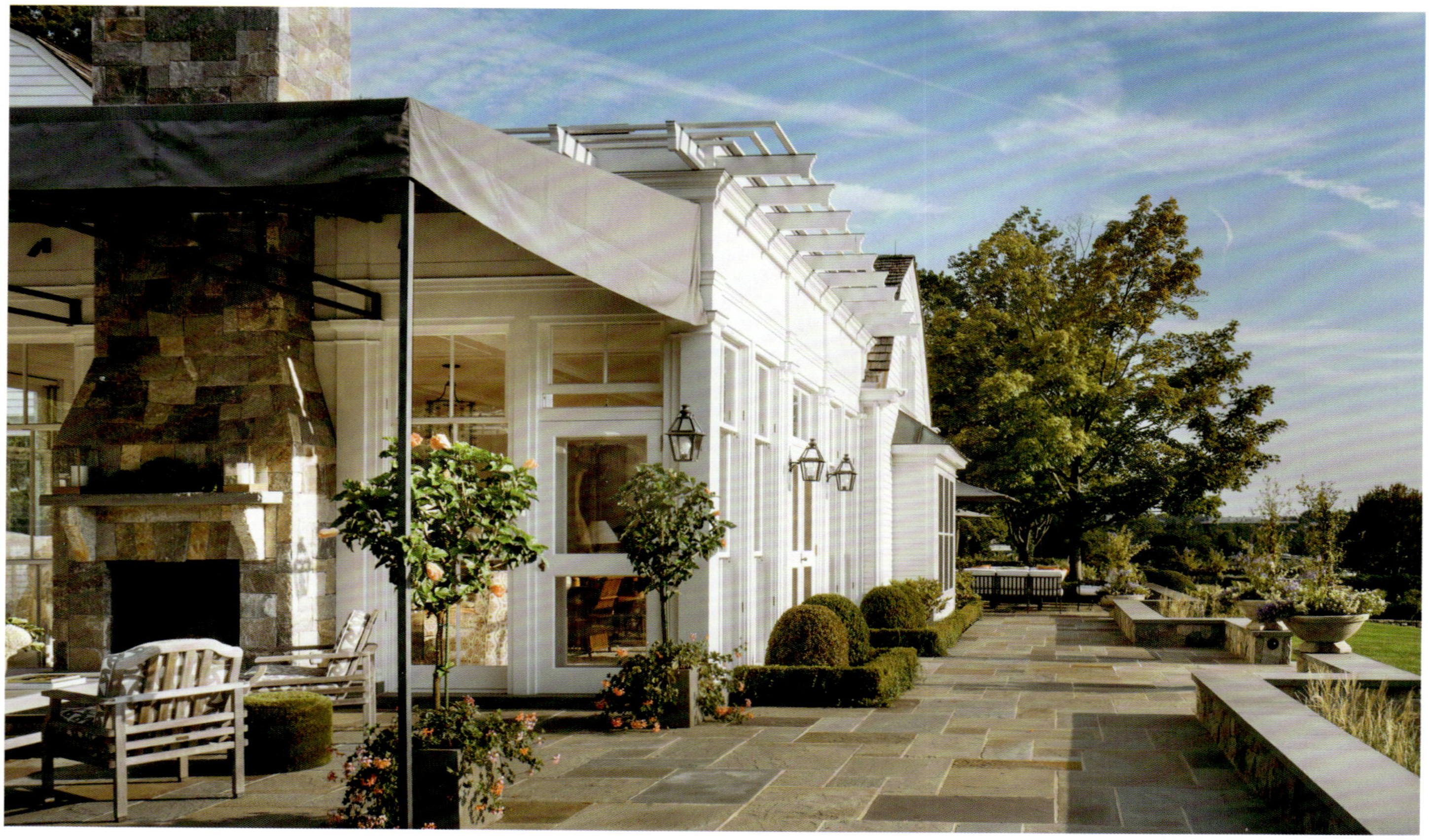

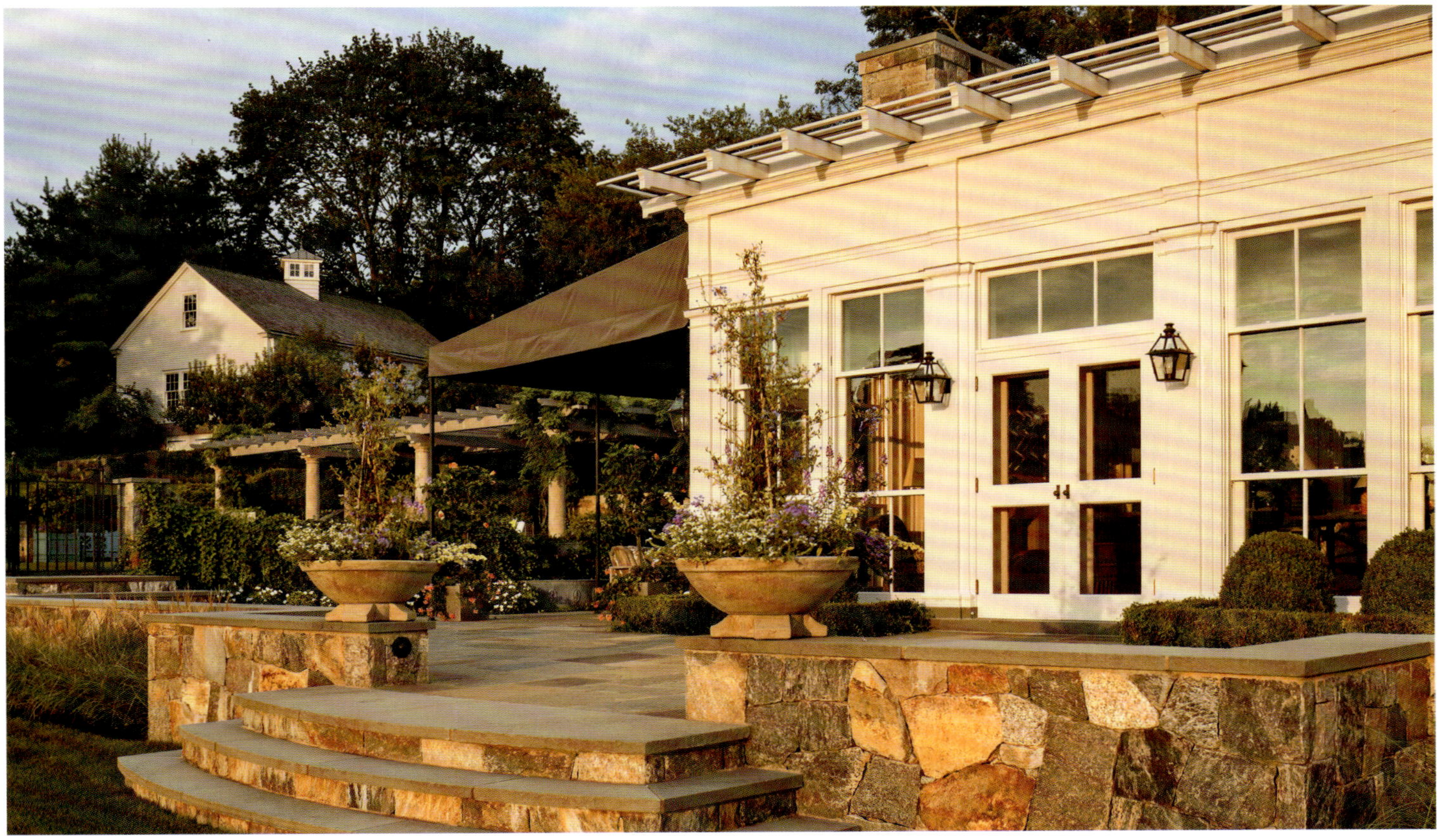

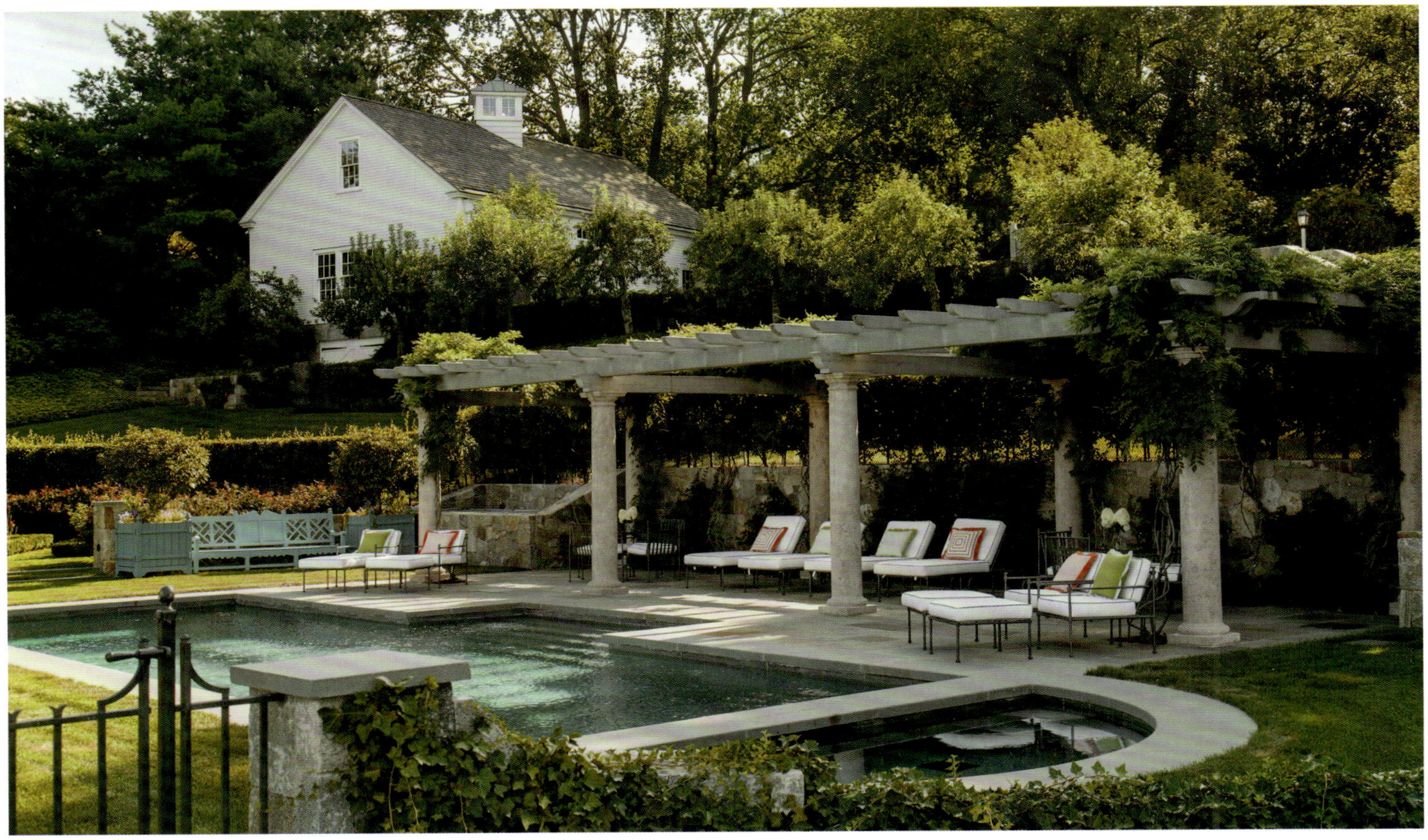

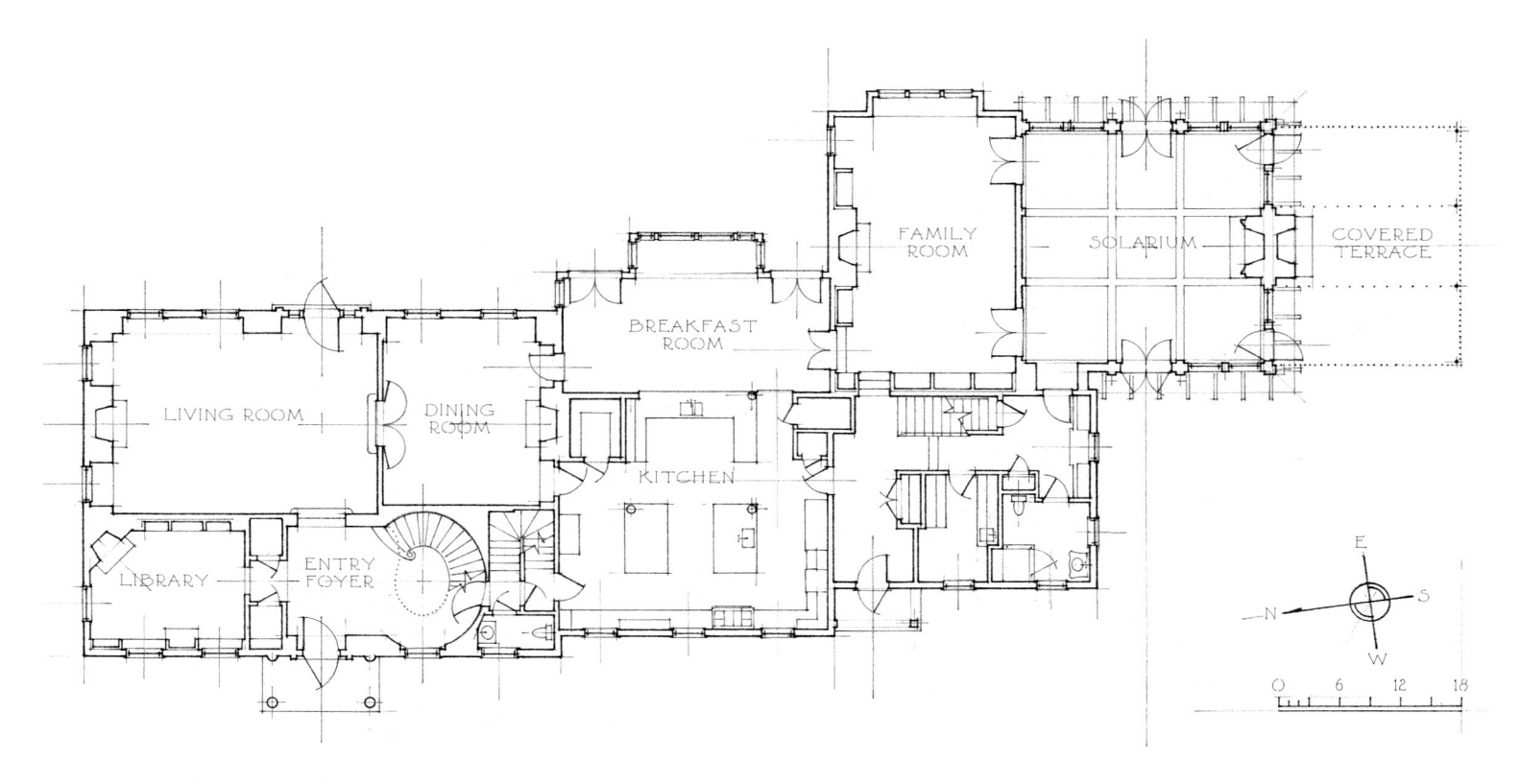

rests under a wooden pergola structure supported by stone columns. A "ha-ha" wall and twin bronze gates provide the required barrier between the great lawn and the pool without obstructing the view.

We constructed the car barn on the site of the original pool. Atop a rise and a bit of a hike from the main house, it was completely appropriate for this new purpose. To mitigate the grade differential and bring the new structure into the fold of the house, we joined the two with a stone walkway and steps, and lined the terraced slope with apple trees.

Given the Colonial Revival style of the main house and the new building's function to display classic automobiles, a barn-like structure with a work counter, a small bathroom, and a loft for storage seemed an appropriate stylistic choice. A cupola with motorized awning windows provides ventilation. V-groove boarded white oak panels with a wax finish line the walls and ceilings; with the polished concrete floor, they provide a handsome backdrop for the cars. The 1928 four-bay garage, which formerly housed the car collection, returned to its original function. Conveniently located and functional in the extreme, it brings the entire series of alterations—and the property itself—into balance.

TWO SPREADS PREVIOUS: The rear of the house opens to a great lawn and Long Island Sound. PREVIOUS SPREAD, CLOCKWISE FROM UPPER LEFT: The car barn overlooks the pool area; the addition steps down to the pool; a pergola with cast-stone columns next to the pool, with the car barn up on the rise; the outdoor room and the addition share back-to-back fireplaces. OPPOSITE, CLOCKWISE FROM UPPER LEFT: Outlookers with slats jut over the entablature housing triple-hung windows; for the pergola, Spanish cedar crossbeams top cast-stone columns; hand-carved Indiana limestone mantel in the addition; by the service entry gates, lanterns atop stone posts.

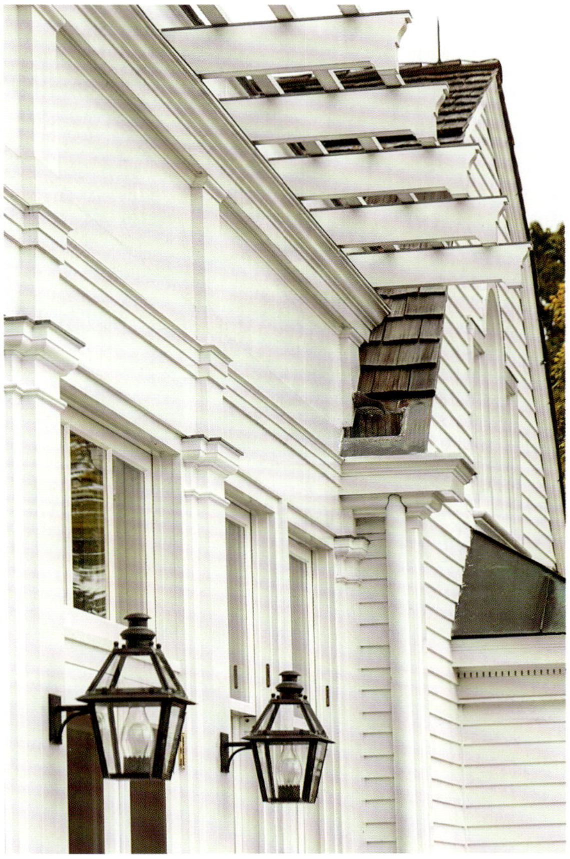

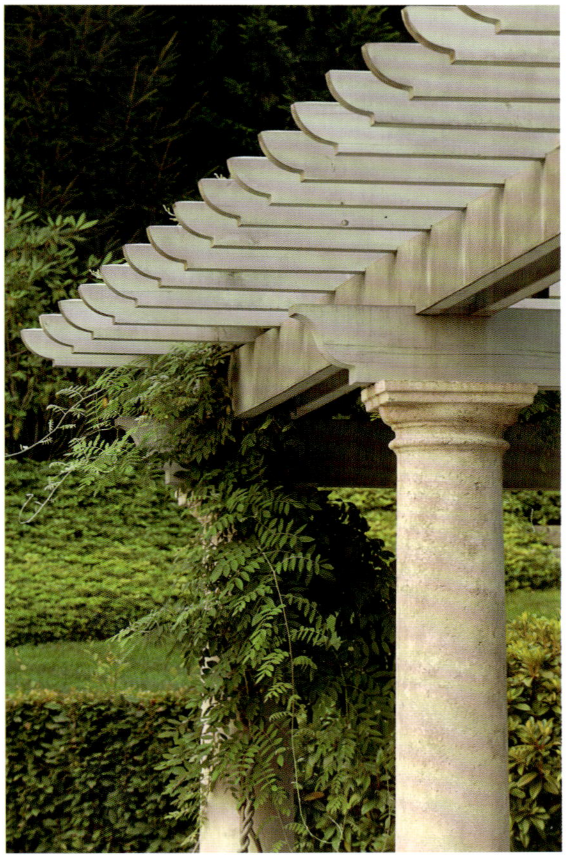

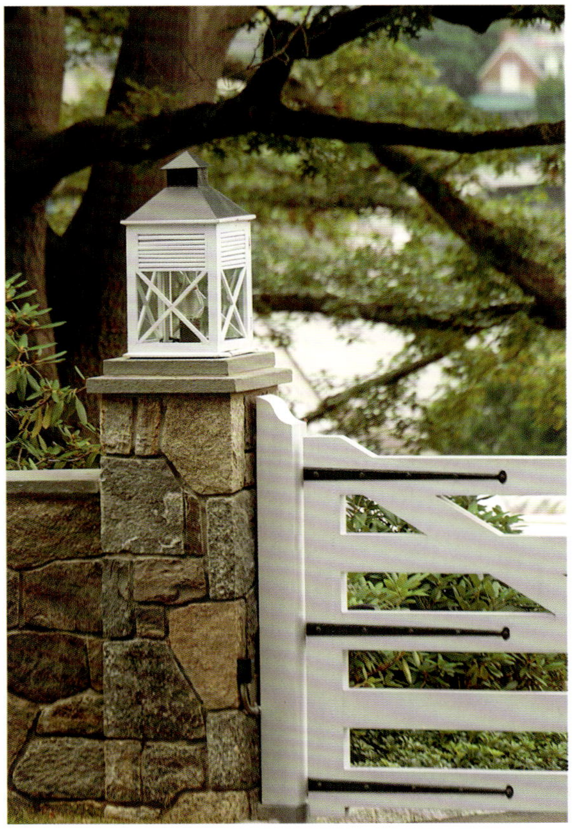

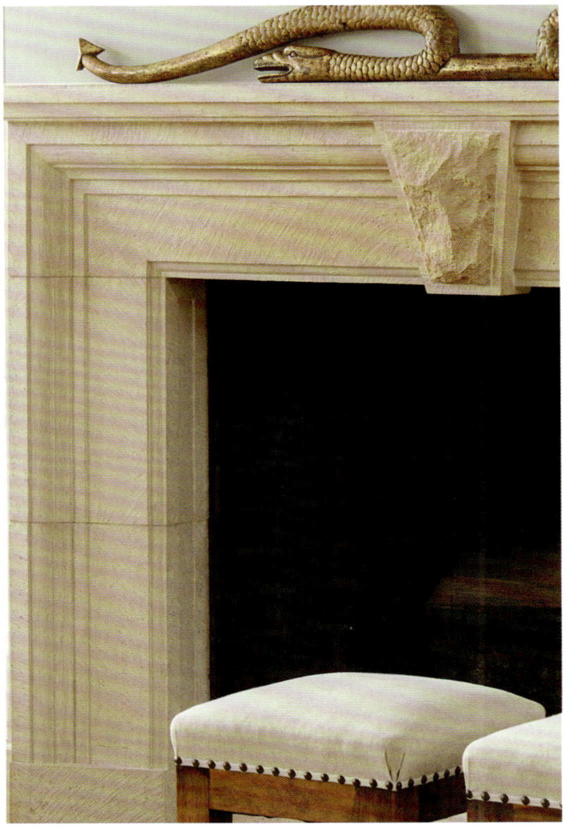

Under an awning supported by bronze posts, the outdoor room opens off the addition through symmetrical passageways. The raised hearth of the stone fireplace is at a perfect height for viewing the fire. A massive shelf creates a quasi-mantel, convenient storage for hurricane lamps and other decorative objects.

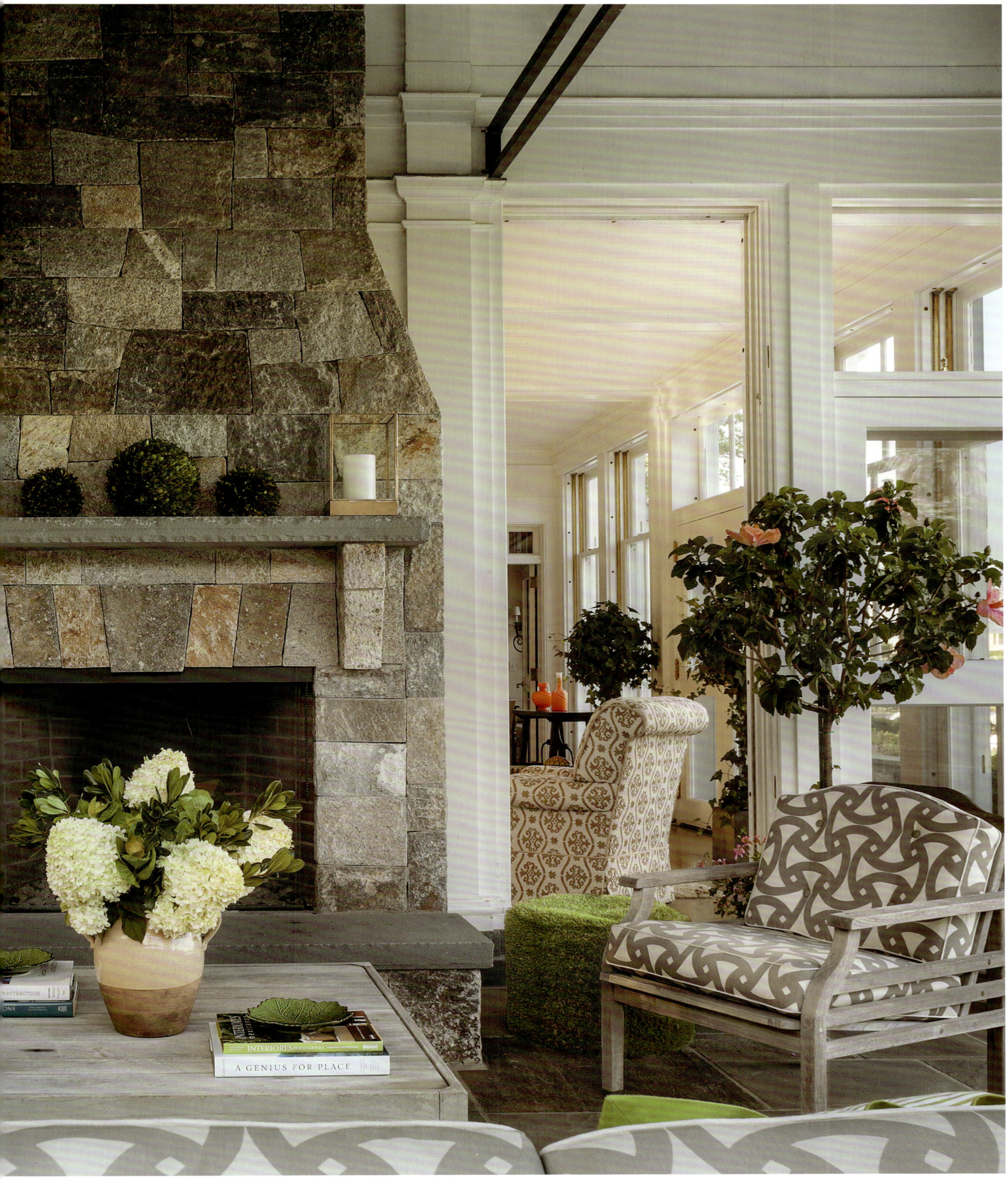
INTERIORES
A GENIUS FOR PLACE

Framing the all-season addition are triple-hung counter-weighted floor-to-ceiling windows; when the windows open, the upper components slide up into the entablature. French doors open to the adjacent exterior areas. The white-painted v-groove bead boards of the paneled ceiling add subtle textural interest overhead.

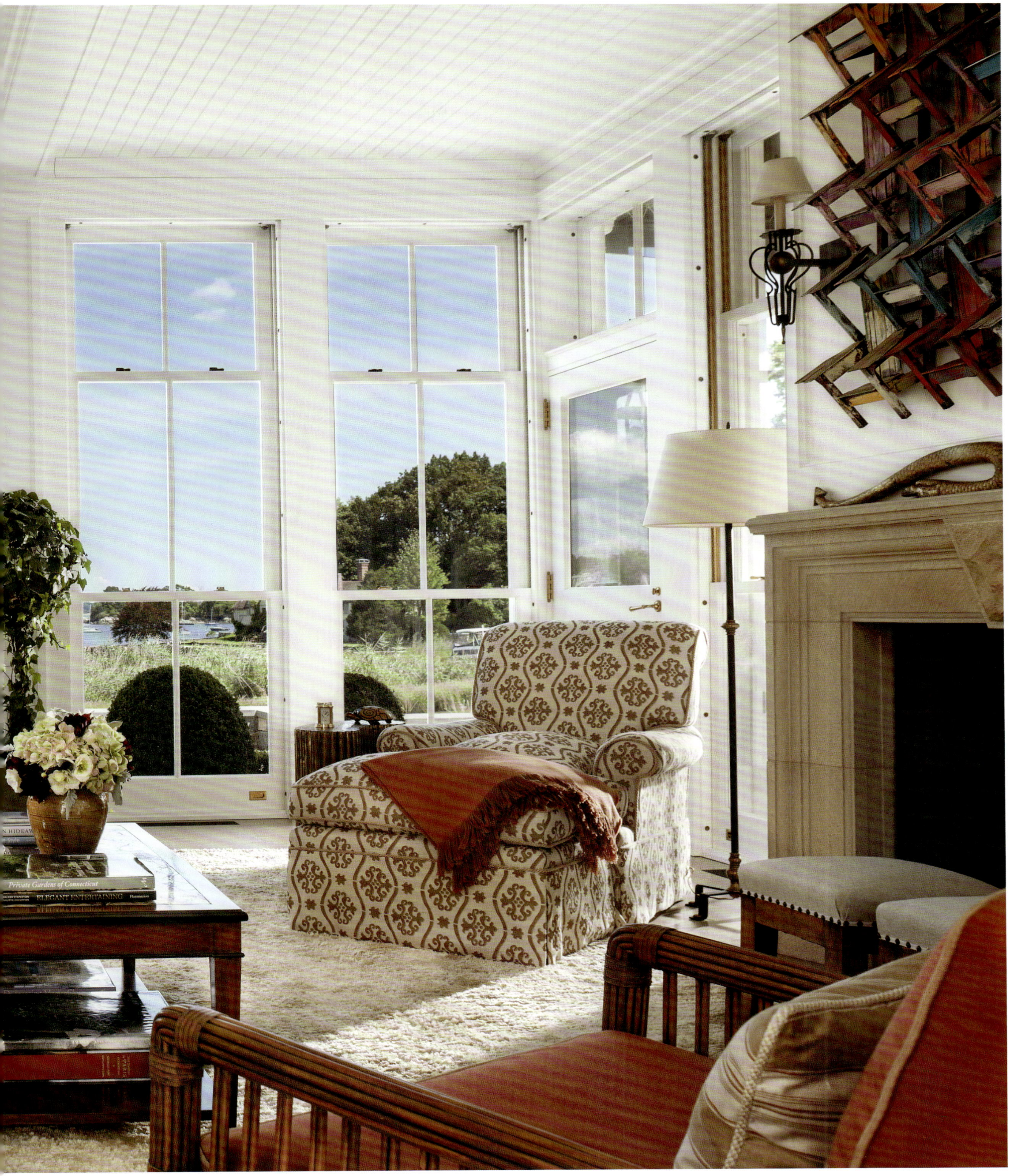
Private Gardens of Connecticut
ELEGANT ENTERTAINING

ABOVE: In the attic under the eaves is a bedroom for the grandchildren with pairs of built-in nautically themed bunk beds, integrated rolling ladders for easy access to the upper level, and "portholes" between the bunks. OPPOSITE: Across from the wall of bunks is built-in storage for books and toys, plus a scaled-down version of a window seat that overlooks the water. The light fixtures resemble a ship's running lights, with a metal safety cage over the glass diffuser.

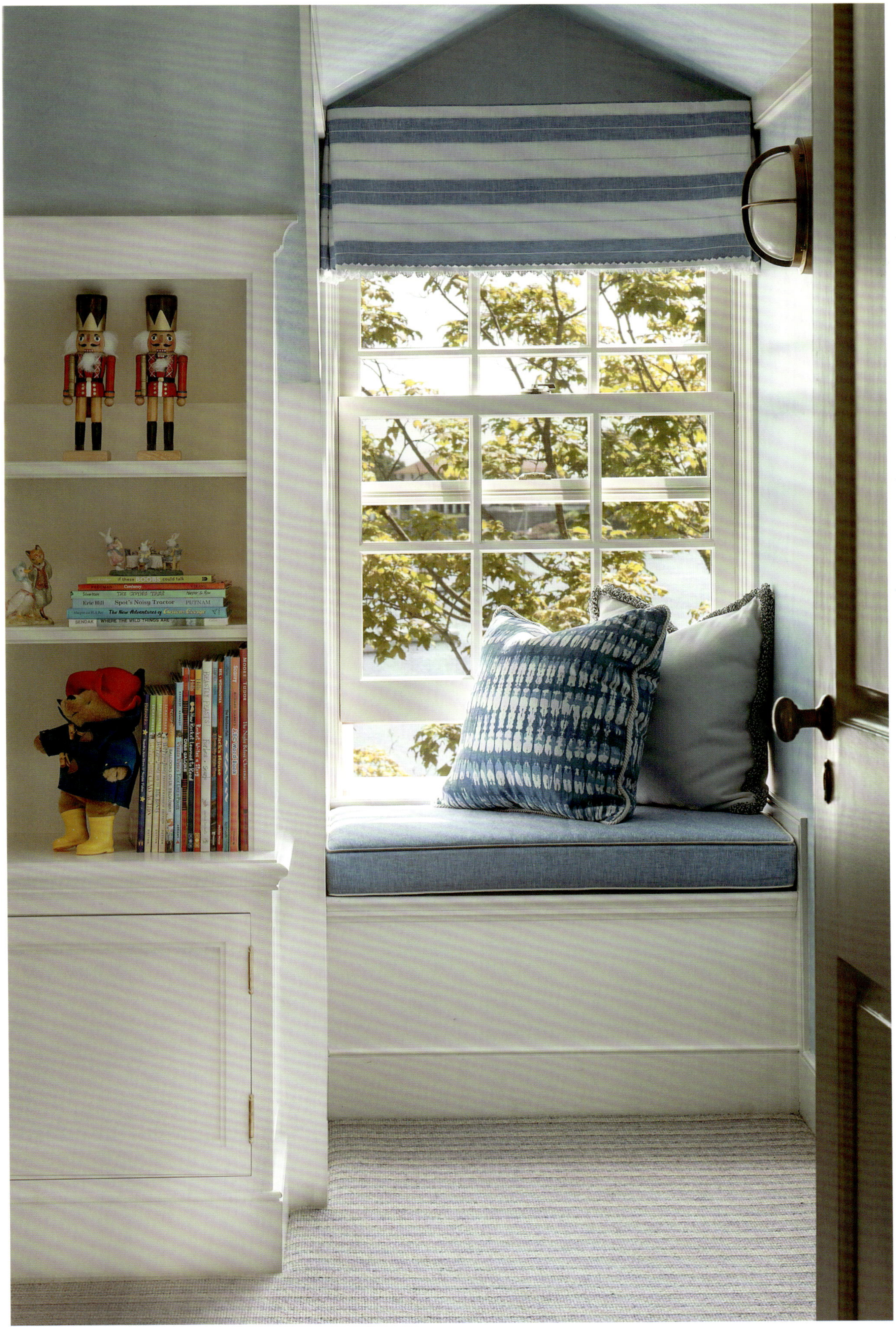

ABOVE: Atop the car barn is a cupola set at a 90-degree angle to the door transom. OPPOSITE, TOP: A glass-paned transom surmounts the car barn's pair of boarded doors, which are detailed with custom forged strap hinges and latch bars. OPPOSITE, BELOW: The interior of the car barn is paneled in waxed white oak. The counter and backsplash are Kirby stone. The radiant-heated floor is polished concrete. In addition to the central lantern, overhead lights are classic hanging fixtures of polished nickel.

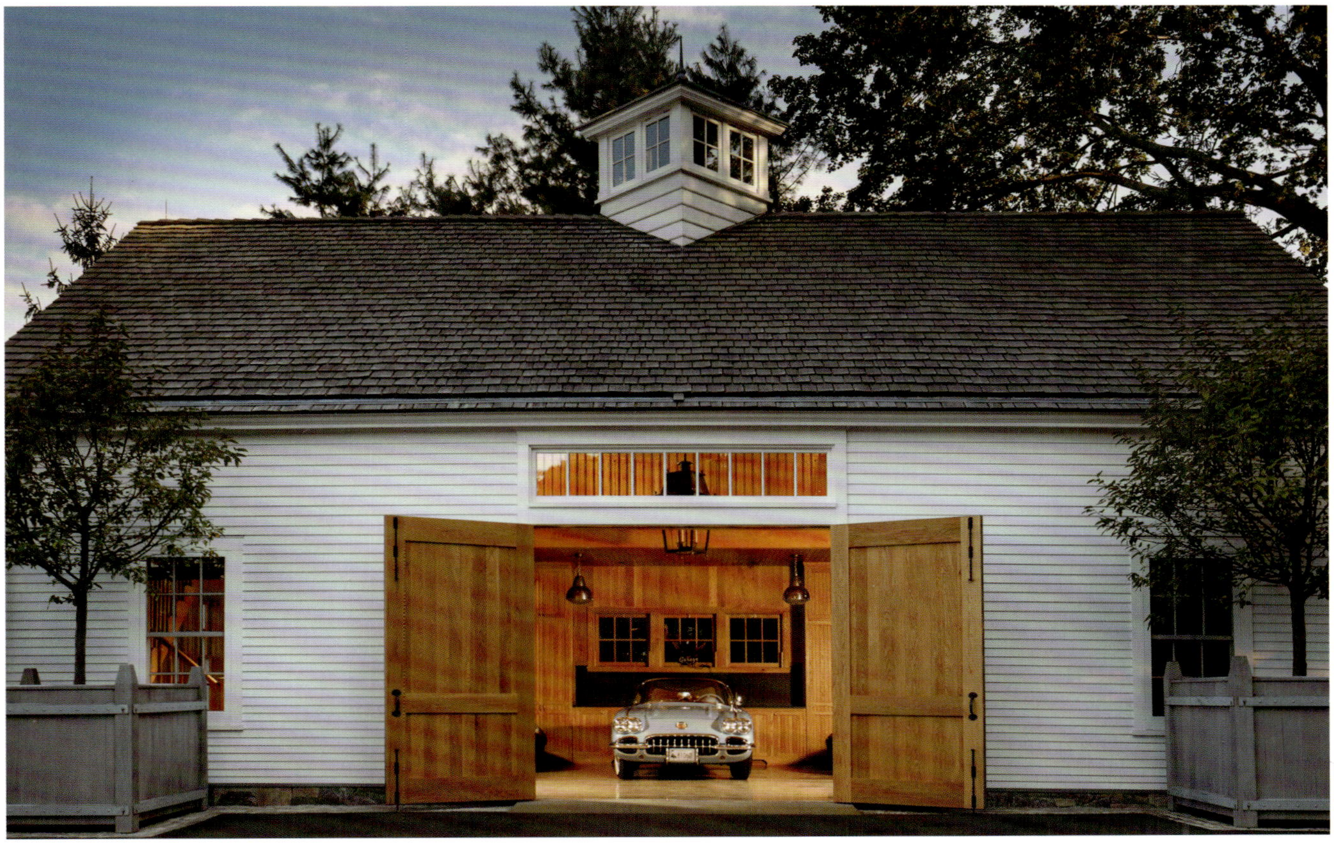

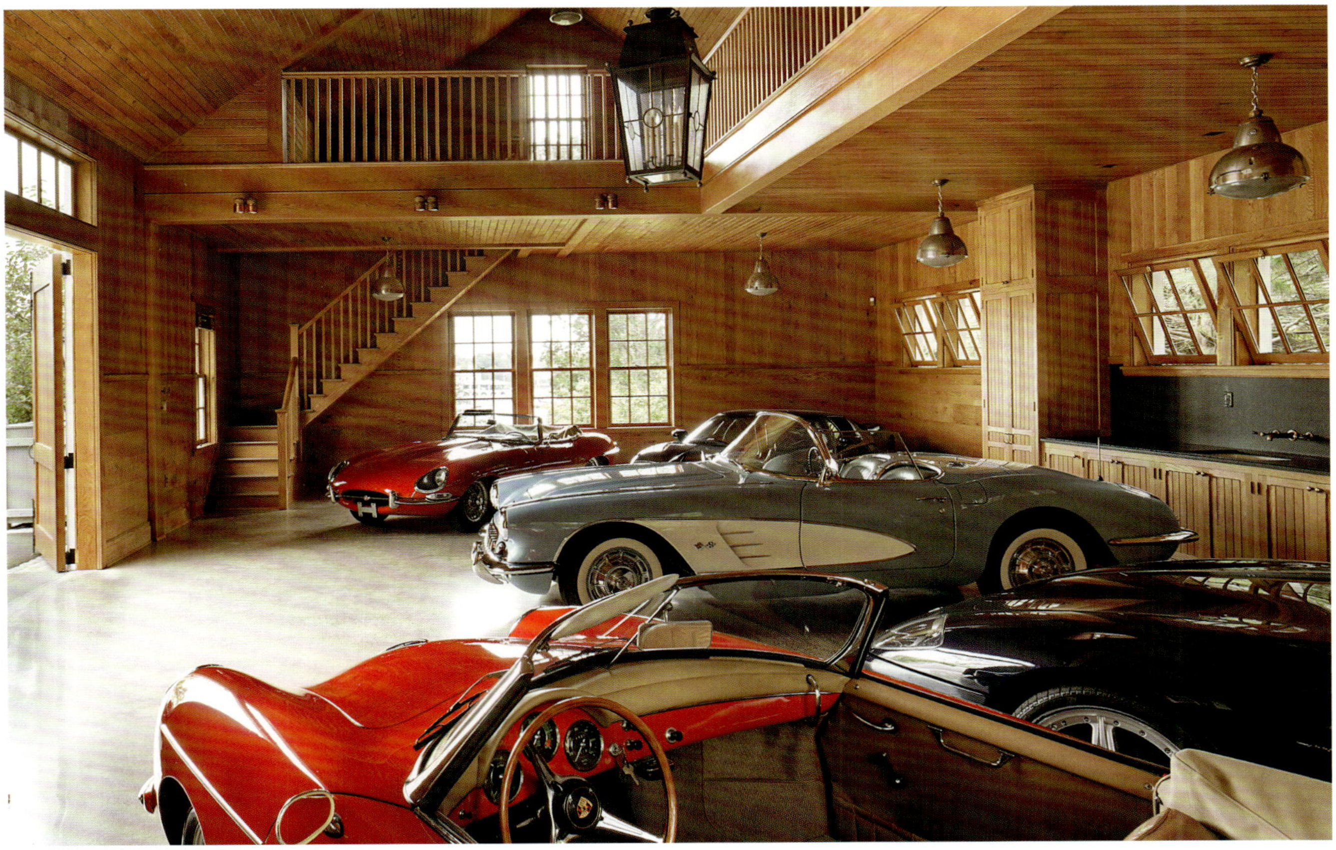

A Change of Seasons

Farmers have a particular understanding about time, technology, and living lightly on the land. So do architects. That's why when these longtime residents of suburban New Jersey commissioned us to design and build a 6,700-square-foot house on a 120-acre parcel of upstate New York farmland, we wanted to ensure that it would look completely appropriate yet live easily, functionally, and sustainably. The project grew out of a family's change of seasons: with children launched into college, the family was preparing for its next phase. Caring strongly about vernacular architectural styles, they wanted a house that felt timeless and appropriate—as if it had always been there, or at least wasn't brand new.

This property had continually been under plough, but unbuilt. In the absence of actual architectural remnants, I developed a historical narrative to drive the design. The concept began in the late-eighteenth century with a Dutch farmer (the area had been a Dutch enclave). Practical, he constructed a modest fieldstone house. As his offspring prospered, they commissioned a more stately Federal-style addition, which they connected to the original house by a hyphen of sorts. Following the model of New England connected farm buildings, the family later added a "little house" and a "back house" for the kitchen and other support rooms. During the expansion of the house, they also constructed a barn.

These historical "phases" and structural archetypes fit the clients' program perfectly. The stone structure houses the guest suite. The Federal wing consists of a classic center hall main block, with dining, living, and exercise rooms on the main floor, and a master suite with twin home offices. The little house encompasses a kitchen, mudroom, three-season porch, and two second-floor bedrooms. The back house is a family room. A nineteenth-century barn transplanted from the Buffalo area serves as the clients' workshop. To protect the machinery of today's farmer, there's a two-car garage and a covered implement shed. A pool house, swimming pool, and pergola are another nod to the modern occupants.

Period-specific building materials, finishes, and architectural elements help make the historical narrative clear. The interior of the Dutch-inspired fieldstone guest wing, for instance, is an exercise in

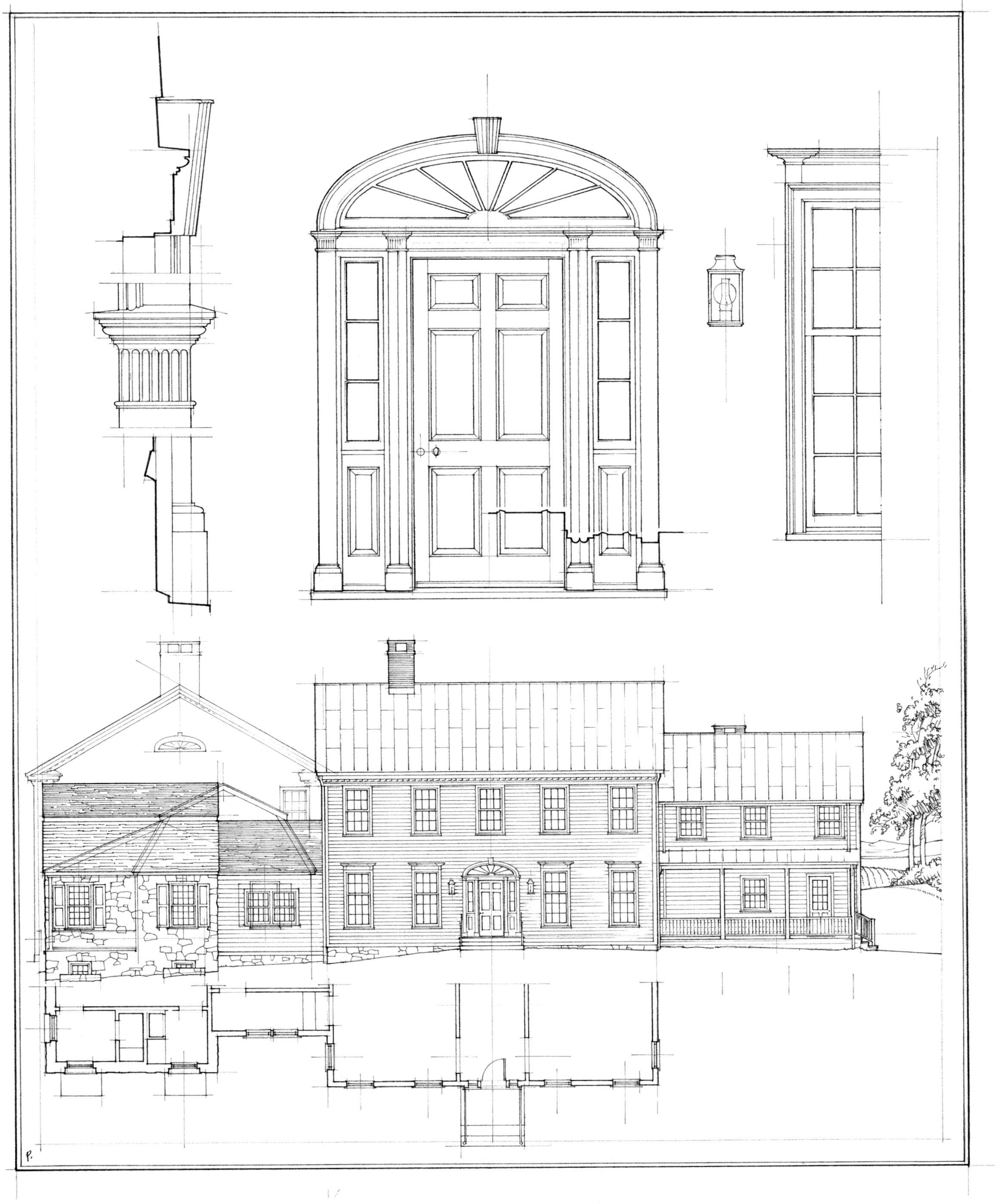
P.

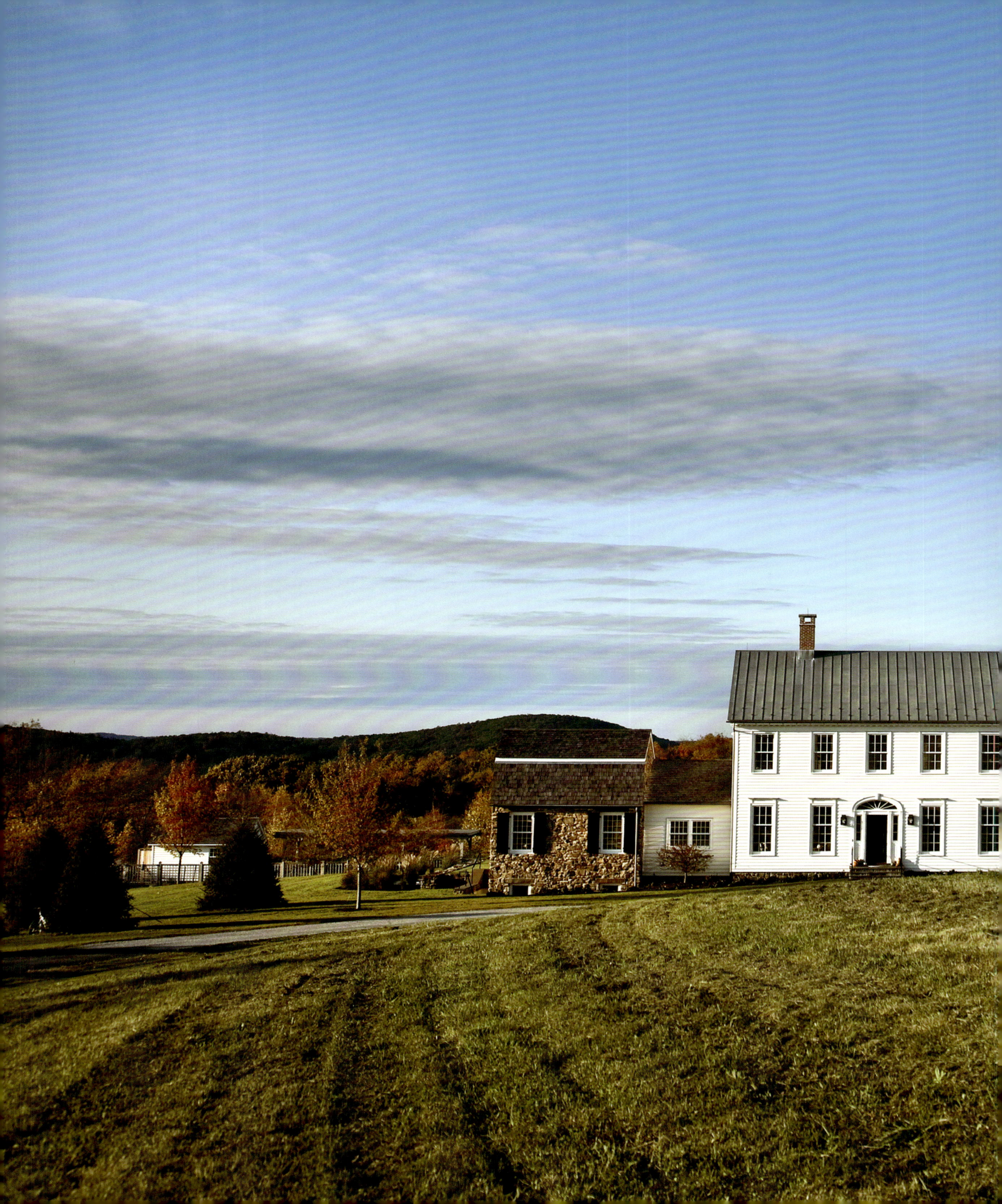

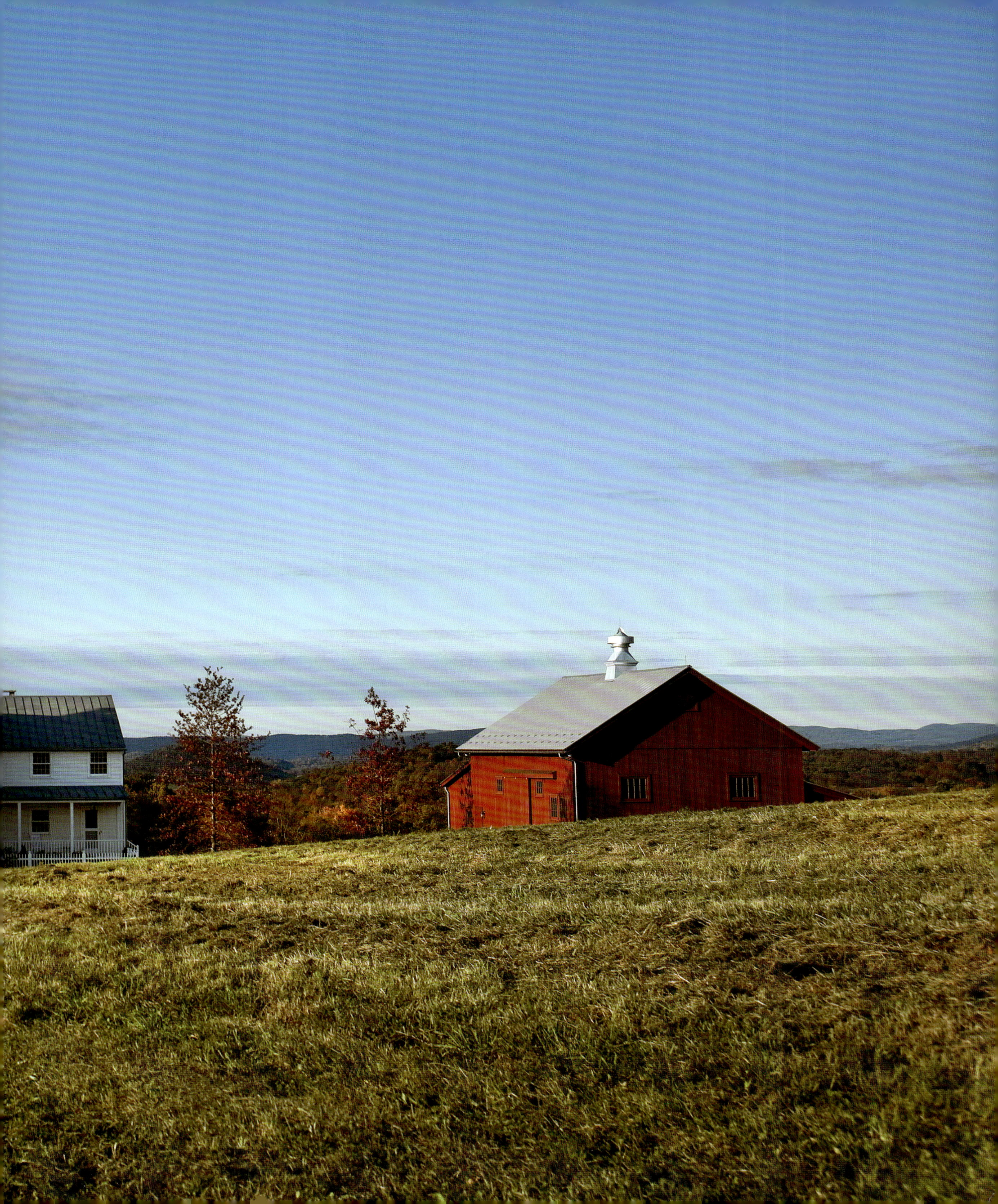

PREVIOUS SPREAD: The south elevation of the house and the transplanted barn. RIGHT: The Federal-style portion of the house, left, has a peaked roof detailed with a cornice ornamented with modillion blocks. Window lites change proportion from the Federal-style structure to the kitchen/guest wing. The clapboard also varies in height from section to section. Center is the secondary entrance to the house via the mudroom porch.

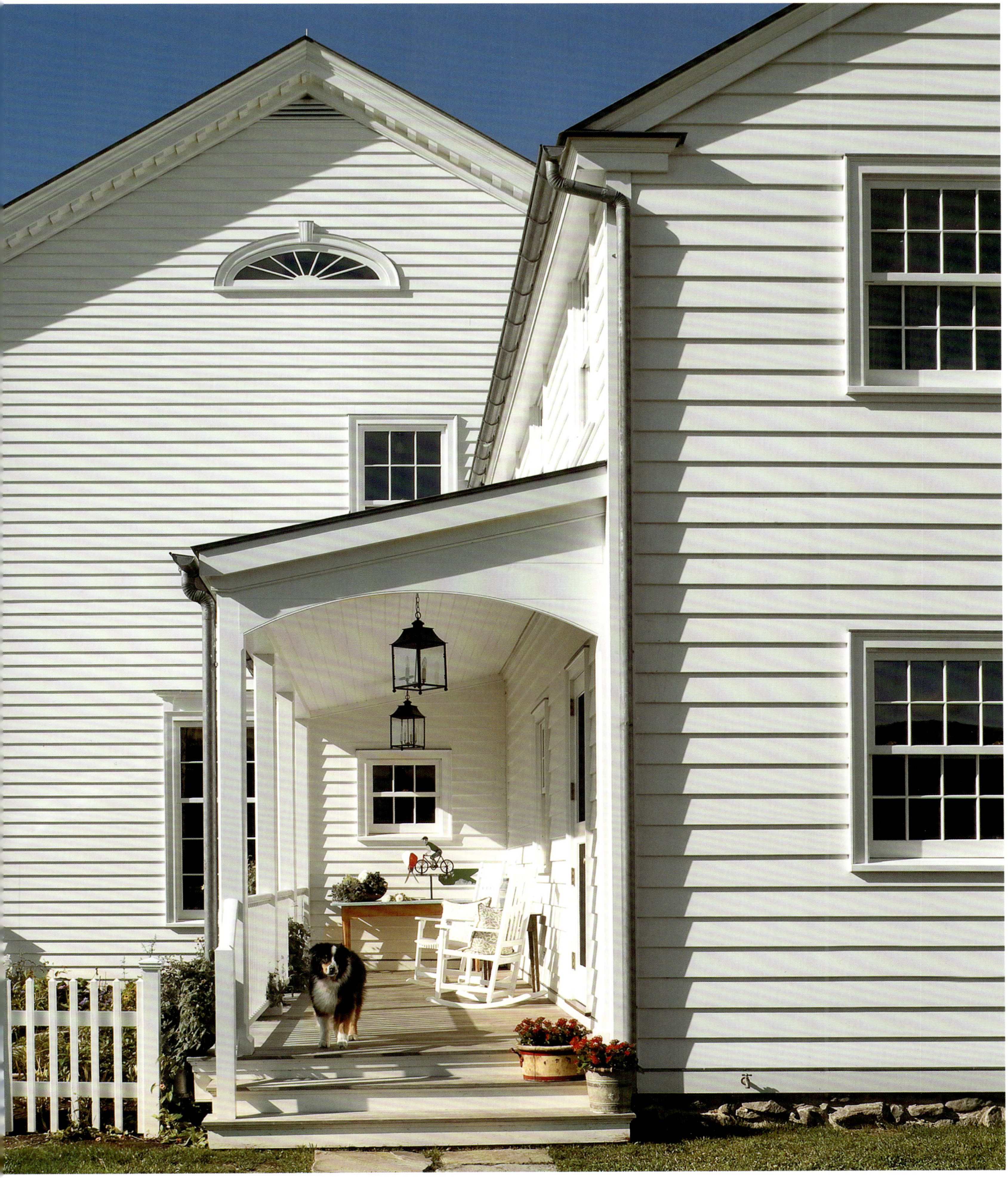

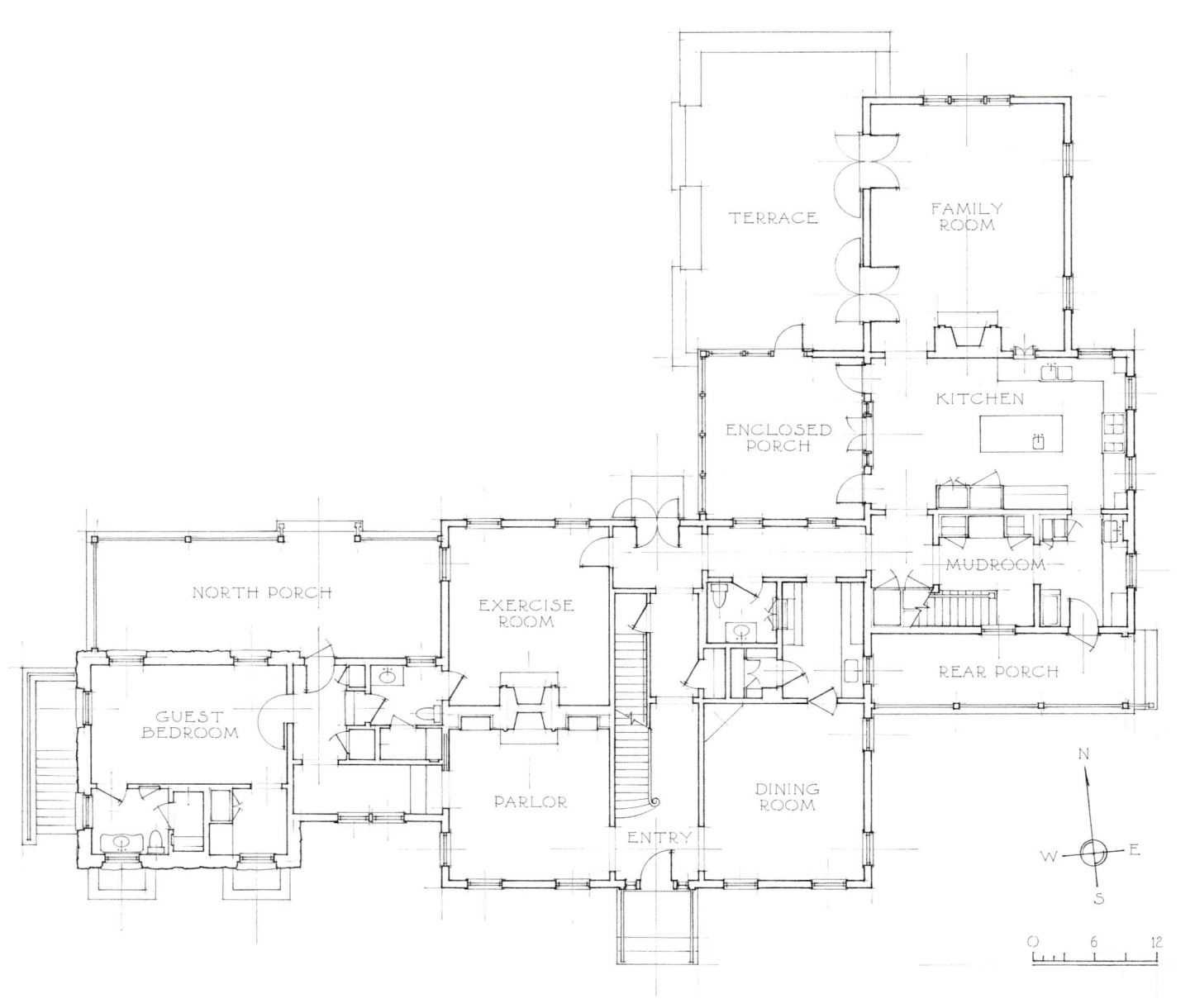

TERRACE

FAMILY ROOM

ENCLOSED PORCH

KITCHEN

NORTH PORCH

EXERCISE ROOM

MUDROOM

GUEST BEDROOM

REAR PORCH

PARLOR

DINING ROOM

ENTRY

N W E S

0 6 12

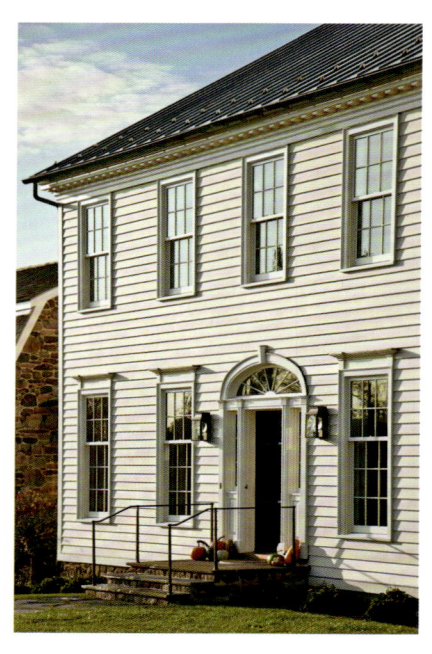

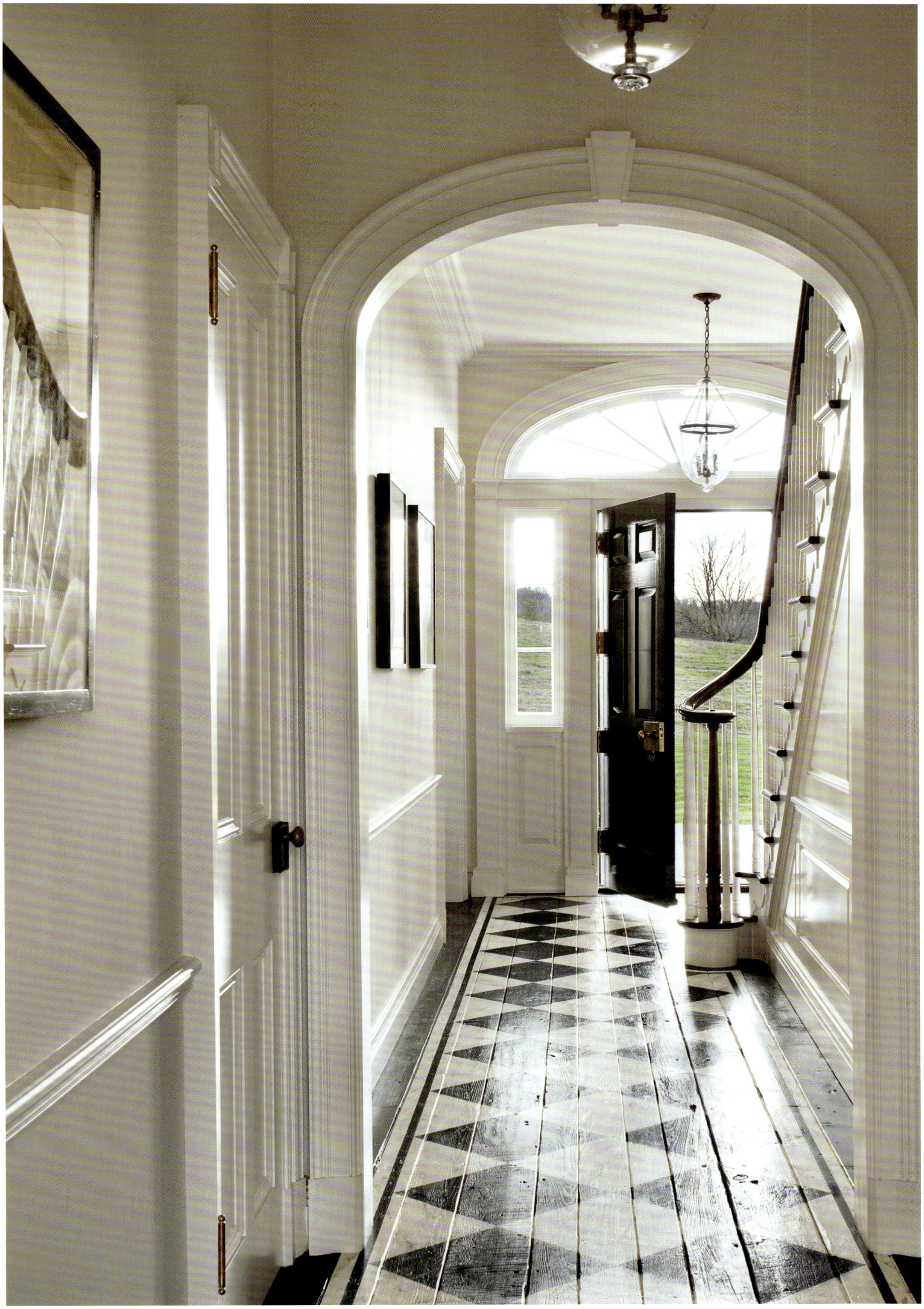

restraint. There, rustically finished parged plaster walls, natural wood windows, hewn ceiling beams, antique reclaimed wood flooring, and wooden shutters create a simple, almost monastic feel. An integrated veranda offers long, uninterrupted views to the north and west.

The main block welcomes the more refined details appropriate to its Federal style, with pulled plaster cornices, entablatures above the windows, painted paneled walls, and attenuated mantelpieces. The kitchen wing and the family room addition to the east are finished in a simpler vernacular carpentry.

The integration of antique components and the use of period-specific craft and construction techniques play a large role in creating new structures that feel rooted in the past. Most of the doors in the main wing date to the Federal period. The floors are reclaimed lumber. The parlor, exercise room, family room, and master bedroom all have antique mantelpieces. Among the contemporary elements made to resemble period pieces are the hand-carved mahogany handrail, doors built from salvaged boards that woodworkers carefully distressed, face-nailed floorboards, and rough-sawn beams in the family room. All these backgrounds proved evocative for interior designer Sam Blount, who developed the decor.

To avoid an unnatural division of the fields, the drive to the house hugs the hedgerow at the property's edge. Instead of building the house at the site's highest point, we created a little plateau about 300 yards north of that knoll and nested the complex there. Since the house faces due south and has open views in almost every direction, the world through its windows is of the rolling fields and distant mountains.

PREVIOUS SPREAD, FAR LEFT: The "old Dutch" wing has fieldstone walls, wood shutters, and a cedar shake roof. PREVIOUS SPREAD, LEFT: The Federal-style main house has a lead-coated copper roof. PREVIOUS SPREAD, RIGHT: Flanked by sidelites and with a transom fanlight overhead, the front door opens to an entry hall with random-width reclaimed pine flooring. LEFT: The front stair balustrade terminates in a scroll. OPPOSITE: A plaster cornice molding details both the parlor and the dining room.

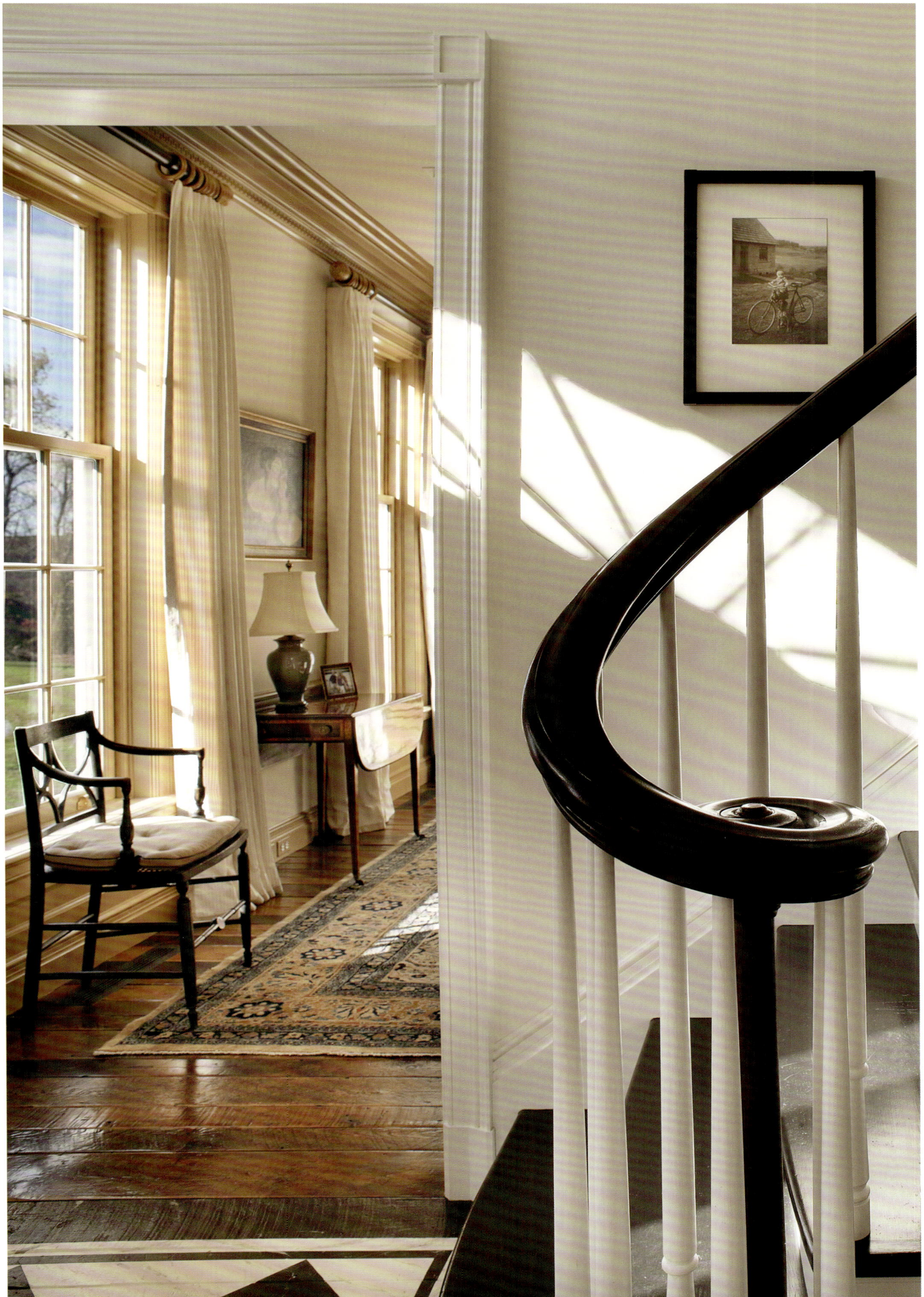

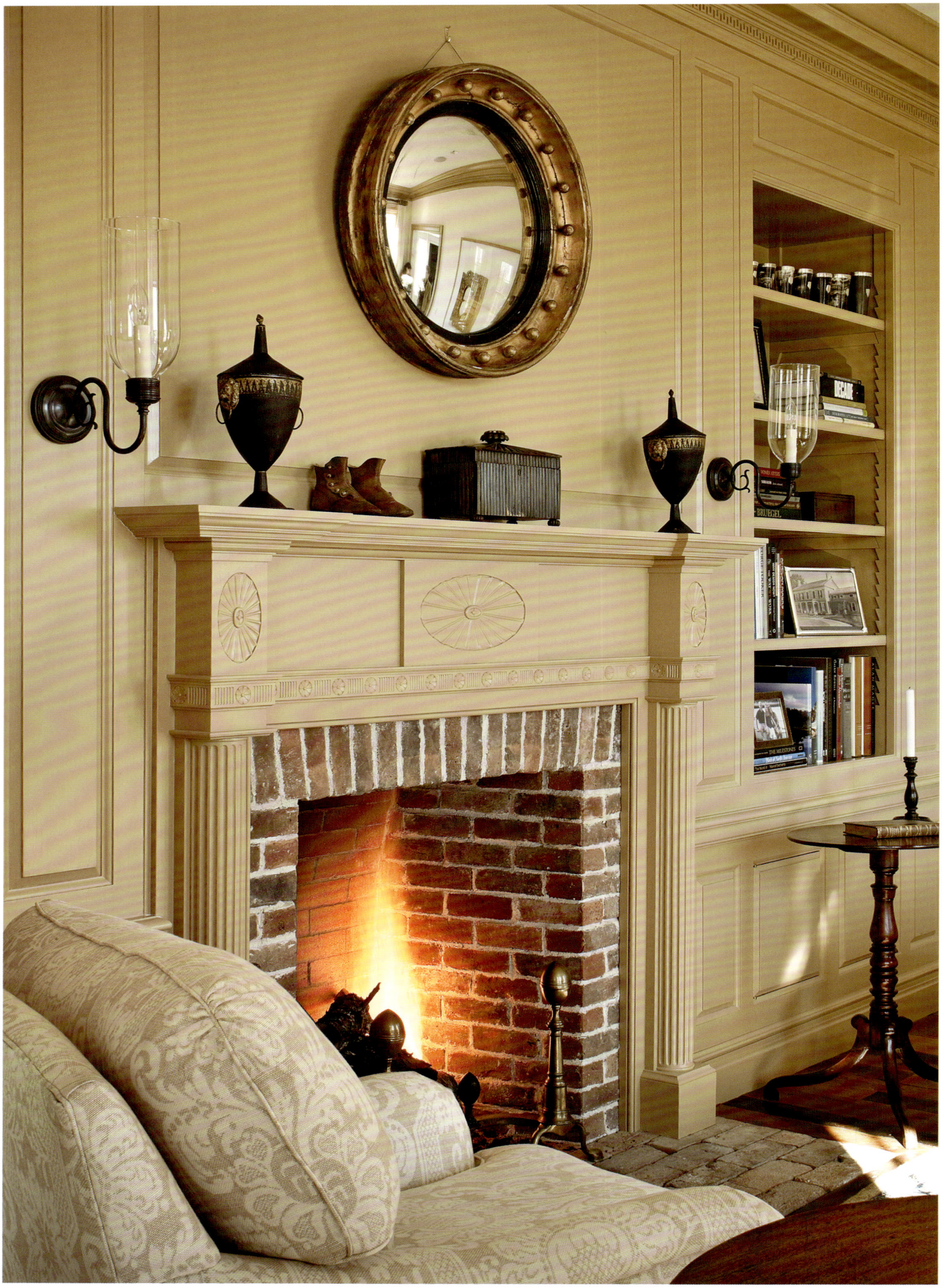
DECADE
BRUEGEL

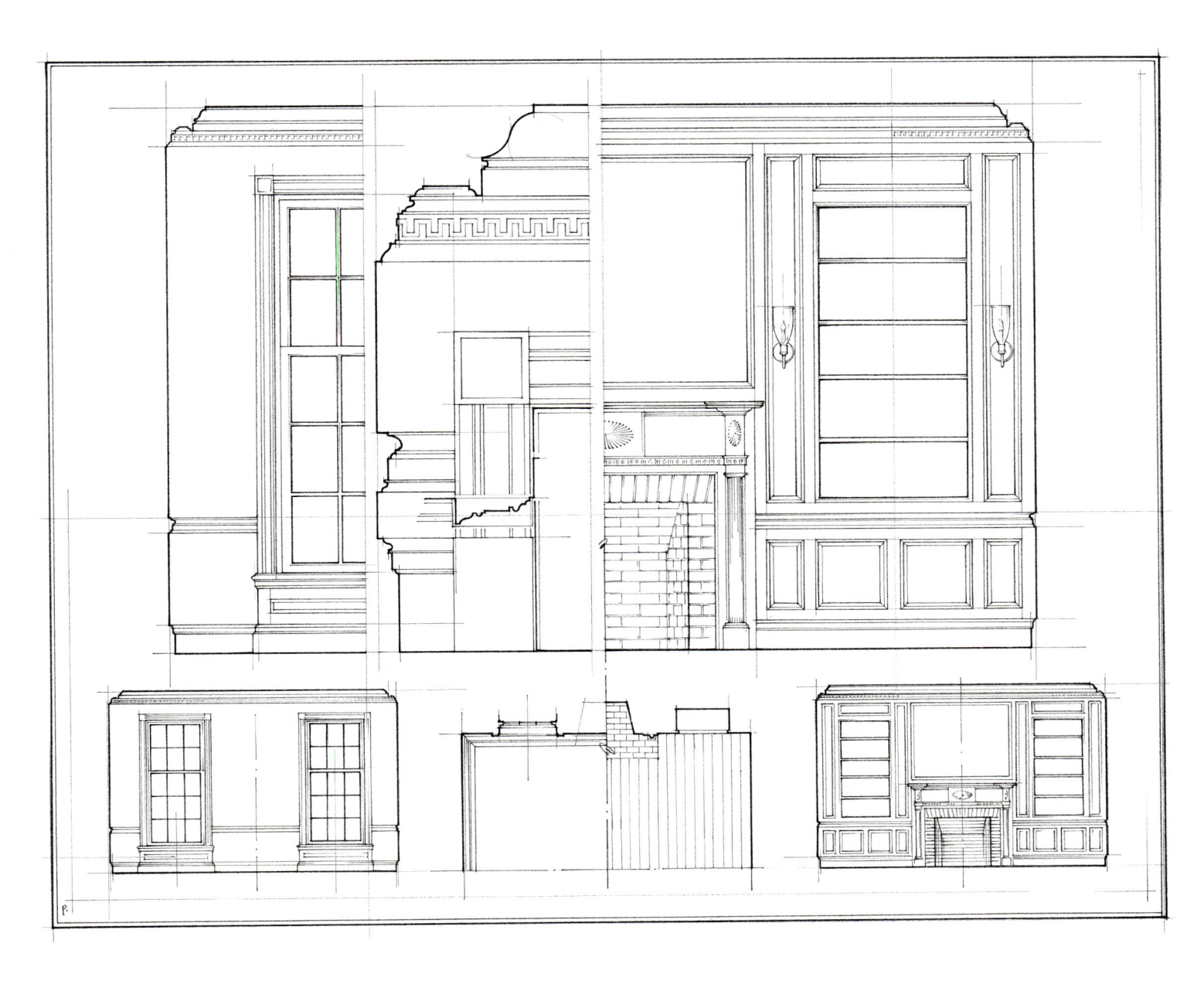

OPPOSITE, AND RIGHT: In the parlor, the firebox back and floor are in dark-red fire brick, with reclaimed used brick for the returns, jack arch, and hearth. The mantel design incorporates fluted columnettes and medallions. One wood-paneled wall has integrated adjustable shelving units with saw-tooth supports.

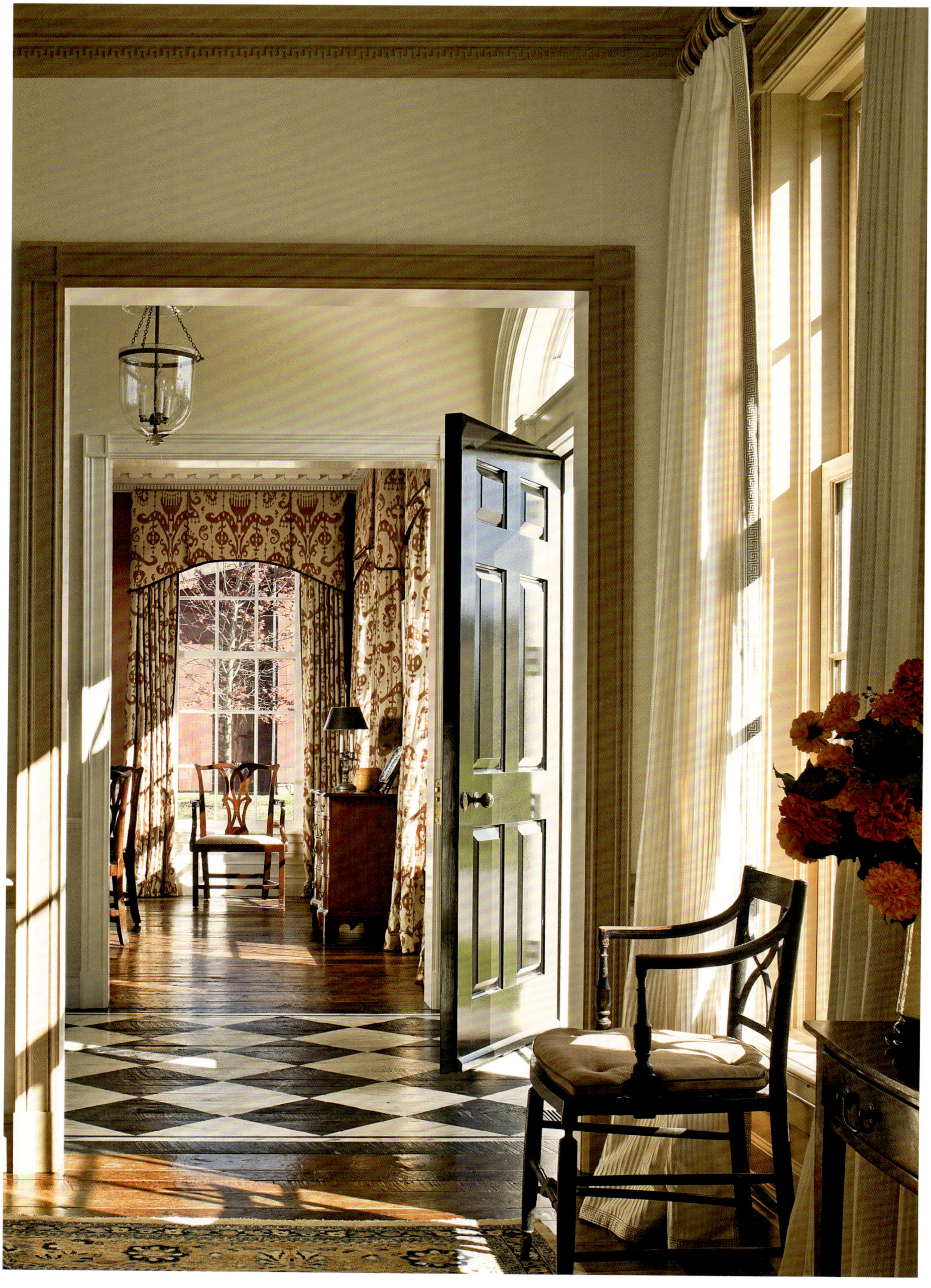

LEFT: The rooms along the front of the house—dining, entry hall, and parlor—open to each other with a view of the barn. The parlor and dining room windows are an unexpected six over nine, which brings the window stools close to the floor, adding openness to the rooms and accentuating the views. ABOVE: In the dining room, a custom plaster cornice with modillion blocks and dentils animates the upper wall surface, while paneled-wood wainscoting enlivens the lower.

The windows in the kitchen are symmetrical eight over eight, flanking the stove. The custom wood cabinetry has doors with flat panels; others have restoration glass fronts. All are set with butt hinges. The wood ceiling is flush boarded, a subtle effect. The kitchen counter is made of Bursting stone from Wales' Lake District. OPPOSITE: Weathered barn siding clads the mudroom walls. Cabinetry is a natural wood with a light stain finish. The countertop is solid oak planking.

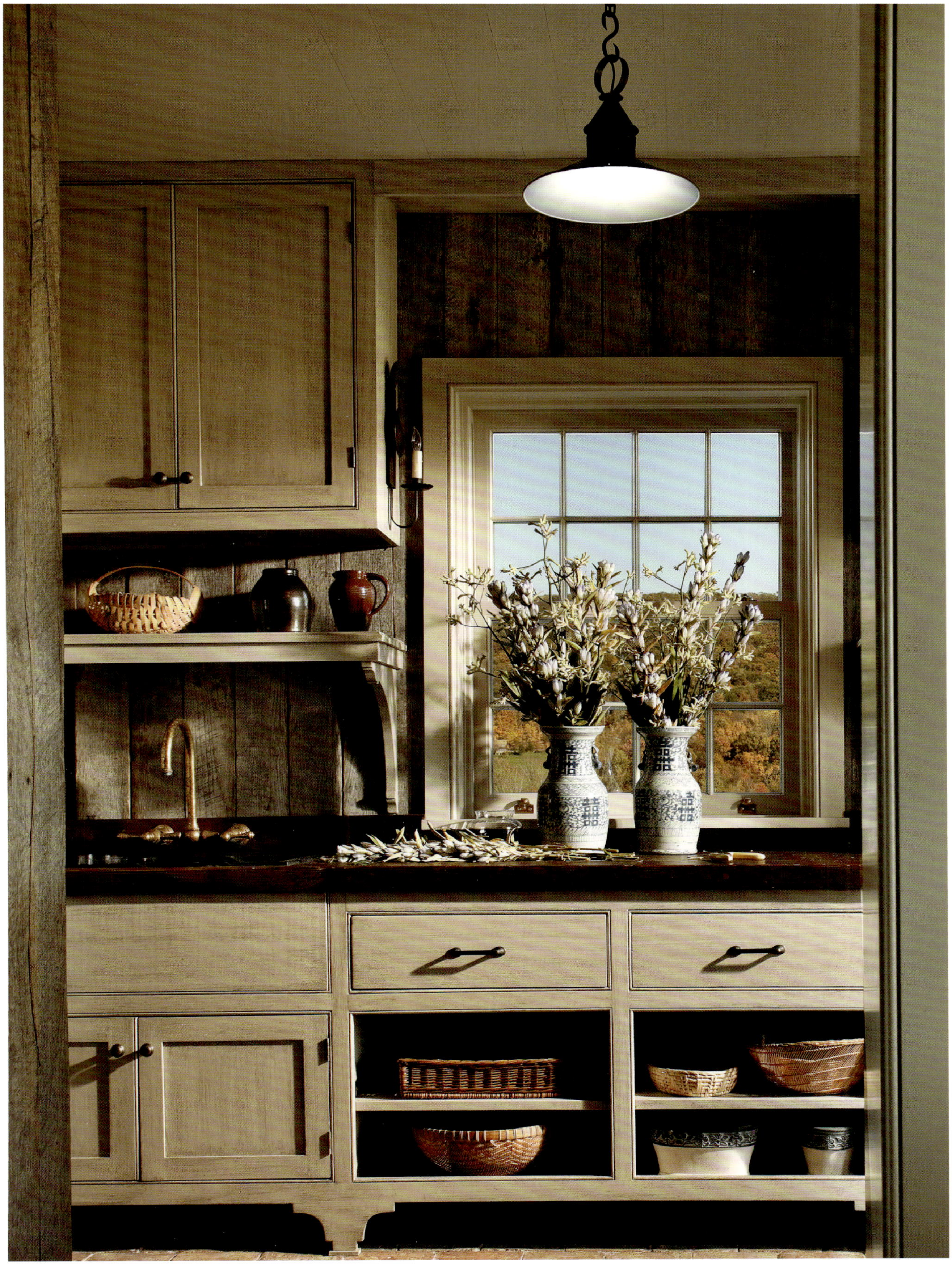

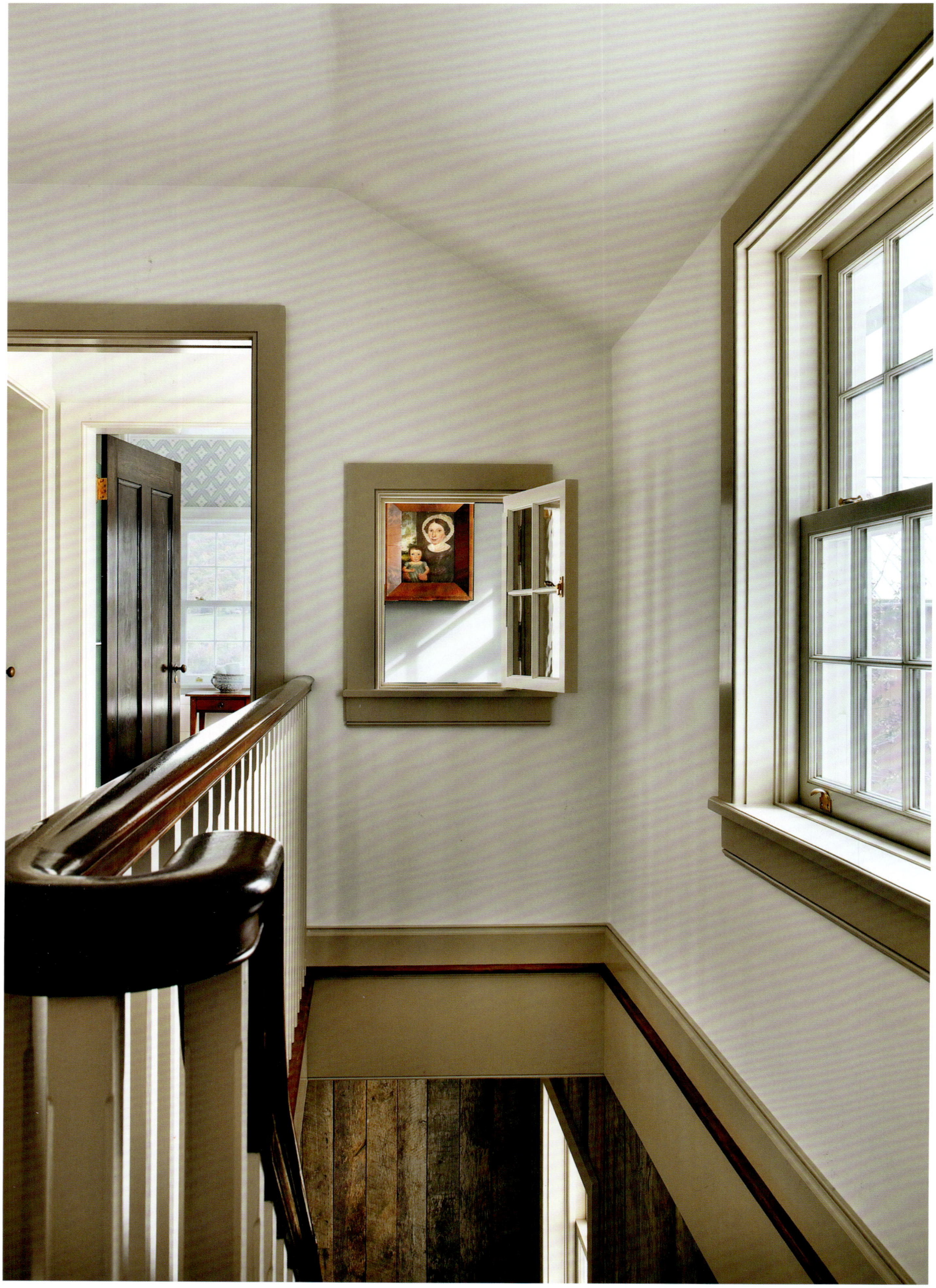

LEFT: At the top of the secondary stair, which rises from the mudroom, an internal casement window looks into a bedroom vestibule. The stair has a mahogany handrail. ABOVE: The bed alcove has two windows, shelving integrated into the wall above the headboard, and additional storage under the bed. A transom window on the adjoining wall brings light into the adjacent bath.

A guest room in the "old Dutch" wing contains many period references, including mahogany windows, reclaimed pine floors, walls with a natural plaster finish, a wood beamed ceiling, operable shutters, and parged plaster returns.

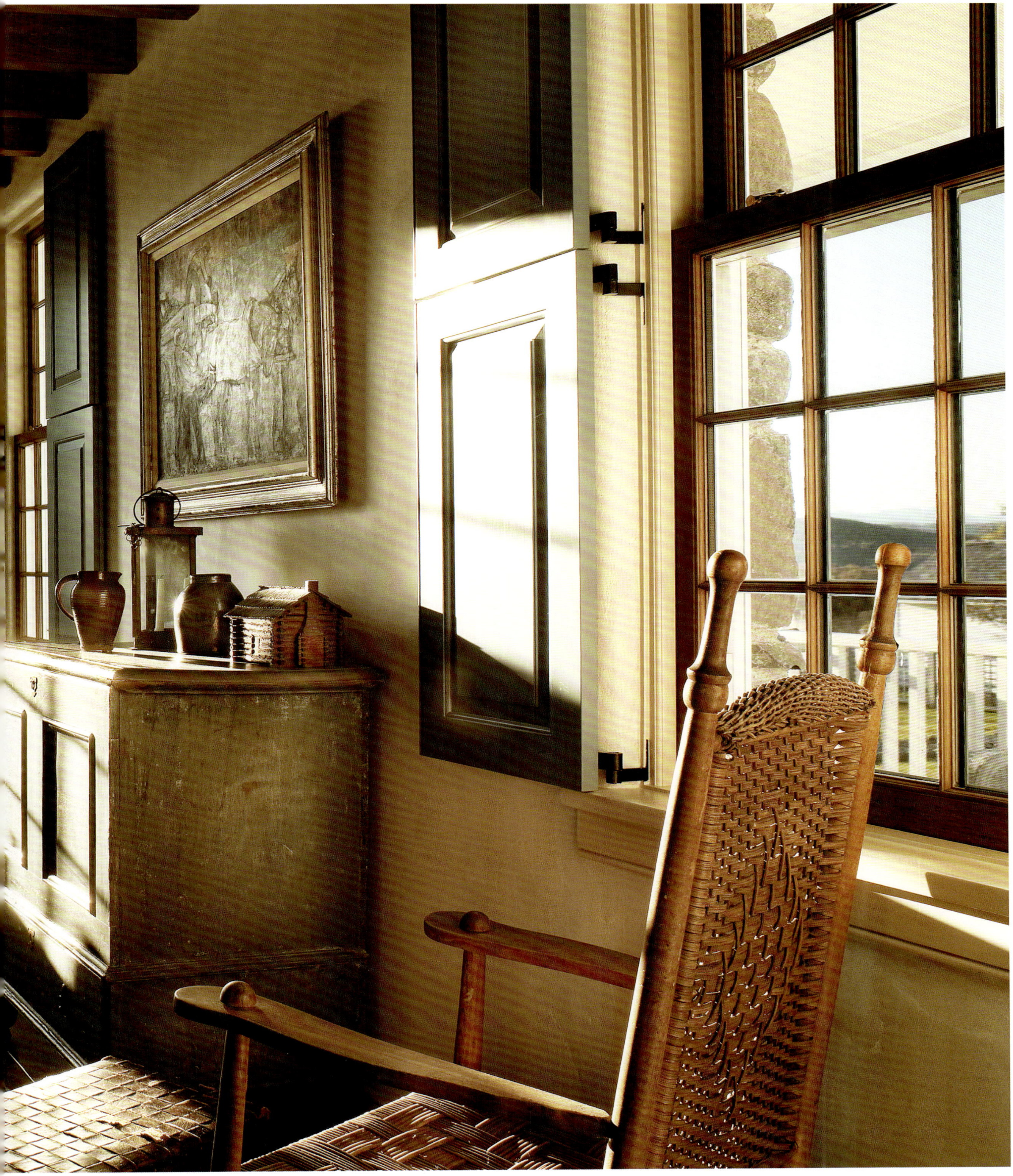

Acknowledgments

Without the initial support of the late Albert Hadley, this firm would never have come into being. I think of him often, and I remain immensely thankful for his generosity, remarkable knowledge, taste, and gentility.

To the interior designers and decorators with whom I regularly collaborate and whose work is featured in this volume, my gratitude is beyond measure. Ellie Cullman of Cullman & Kravis, I am thankful for your fresh sense of style, our close working relationship, and your continued support. David Guilmet and Patrick Bell, your love of history and constant striving for quality is inspiring. Sam Blount, Jennifer Garrigues, Victoria Hagan, Stephen Sills, Llewellyn Sinkler, and Bunny Williams, it is always a great joy to join you on a project team. The late Parkin Saunders, I am grateful that we had the opportunity to work together.

Many are the interior designers and decorators with whom I prize working, but whose projects I was unable to include here. I am particularly grateful to Eric Brown, Anthony Ingrao & Randy Kemper, Thomas Jayne, David Kleinberg, Donald MacDonald, Mimi MacDougall, Richard Mishaan, Wayne Nathan, Paula Perlini, Jennifer Post, Katie Ridder, Eve Robinson, Matthew Patrick Smyth, and Jeannine Williams for so freely sharing their talents and professionalism.

My enduring thanks go to the landscape designers Eric Groft of Oehme, van Sweden Associates; Deborah Nevins, Edmund Hollander, and Martha Baker. Francesca Bettridge of Cline Bettridge Bernstein Lighting Design, you are without peer.

I so admire the builders who contributed their labors to the projects here, because it is they who bring the work of this office to fruition. Peter Cosola, you have my ceaseless gratitude for your incomparable skill as a builder and your abiding passion for executing each and every plan to near perfection. Bill Bosley, Ed Freeman, Allan Gronningsater, Gerry Holbrook, Rick McCue, George & Jerry Pusser, Dick & James Reeve, Thomas Rogan, and Jim Romanchuk, thank you all for your amazing abilities in following the principles of "good practice."

For the skilled builders who collaborated with us on realizing projects that I could not include in this volume, I am sincerely thankful to Ken Bacco, Rob Carpenter, Pierre Crosby, Joseph and Vincent DiSalvo, Steven & Johnny Donadic, Steve Fetner, Artie Glickman, Peter Hammer, Jim Hanley, Richard Hines, Scott Hobbs, Joseph Kais, Mike Luisi, Mark Martinez, Doug Rice, John Rusk, Bernard Sobus, Joshua Wiener, Kenneth Wright, and Jim Xhema.

To my former partners, Mark Ferguson and Oscar Shamamian, you have my appreciation for those formative years.

Thanks to the consultants, vendors, and artisans Jim MacDonald, Robert Silman, Mark Hage, Robert Baird, Jean Wiart, Carl Sorenson & Steve Nanz, Paul Austi, and Jacquie Mosca, who contribute beyond measure to each project we work on together.

Over the last ten years, Durston Saylor has beautifully captured and revealed my work in two dimensions. He has taught me much about the art of architectural photography and inspired me with his tireless pursuit of the perfect shot. I cannot thank him enough. Sincerest thanks also to Bruce Buck, James Bleecker and Jonathan Wallen.

I am endlessly grateful to Paul Gunther, Henrika Taylor, and all the members of The Institute of Classical Architecture & Art who nurture and support the classical tradition in true twenty-first-century style.

My deep appreciation goes to Tom Maciag and Will Strasser, who created the firm's website and continue to navigate us elegantly through the digital universe.

The practice of architecture is the practice of teamwork, and my team is incomparable. Triveni Perera, who shepherded this book to completion along with all her other duties, has my great gratitude. Senior designers Tim Middleton, Adam Platt, and John Pelligra consistently impress me with their design, managerial, and leadership skills. Project designers Christine Song, Joel Pidel, Phil Lanzelotti, Matthew Wanner, Andrea Wang, Tomer Tal, Erin DeLosier, Izumi Shepard, and Pratik Patel make me grateful everyday for their talent, dedication, and professionalism. I could not do what I need to do everyday without Suzanne Walker-Herrera, my assistant, who effortlessly organizes my day and keeps things running smoothly and with grace.

Thanks to Janeth Diaz and Kee You Lam-The, our additional support staff. Janeth, you have my appreciation for pitching in whenever and wherever necessary.

A number of former employees were instrumental in the development of the firm, and in the work within this book. I will be forever grateful to Charlotte Worthy for her energy, commitment, and friendship. Charlotte, your design leadership and longtime loyalty to the firm is greatly appreciated. William Mincey, Roy Pertchik, Jeff Wooley, Sam Seymour, Caitriona Ryan, and Jonathan Osterman, you have my heartfelt thanks.

Without my tenacious agent Jill Cohen, this book would not exist. Thank you, Jill. You are truly one of a kind. Elizabeth White, my editor at Monacelli, has offered fresh perspective and a keen eye towards this project. To my graphic designers, Doug Turshen and Steve Turner, I marvel at your abilities. You have my deepest gratitude for showing my work to its absolute best advantage. Judith Nasatir, thank you for finding the words to express what we do here so clearly and well. Stephen Piersanti, I am appreciative for your enormous artistic gifts, and for rendering the drawings that contribute to what I believe make my practice, and this book, special.

Last but not least, thanks beyond thanks to my dear friend Elizabeth Heilman Brooke, whose encouragement and discerning eye guided me so well through this process.

Copyright © 2013 John B. Murray and The Monacelli Press LLC

All rights reserved.

Published in the United States by The Monacelli Press LLC

Library of Congress Control Number 2013930854
ISBN 978-158093-368-1

10 9 8 7 6 5 4 3 2 1

First edition

Photographs by Durston Saylor except as noted below.
James Bleecker pages 92–93, 95–101
Jonathan Wallen pages 156, 202–208, 210–217

Design: Doug Turshen with Steve Turner

Printed in China

www.monacellipress.com